LUNCHEON KINGDOM

Mount Volbono

Hammer Bro
Fire Bro
Lava Bubble
Magmato

METRO KINGDOM

New Donk City

ugby

SUPER MARIO ODYSSEY

Pack Your Bags!

2

When Mario set out to stop Bowser from forcing Princess Peach to marry him, he had no idea what it would lead to. But his attempt to save a friend quickly proved far more difficult than Mario could have ever anticipated. Much to Peach's dismay, the tuxedo-clad Bowser managed to knock Mario from his ship, sending him tumbling through the night sky.

But to where?

Thanks to a friendly flying top hat known as Cappy, Mario is roused from his slumber in a tiny area of the Cap Kingdom known as Bonneton. The local population isn't just friendly, but they've got a stake in stopping Bowser too! One of their own, Cappy's sister Tiara, was also kidnapped. And he wants to team up with Mario to get her back.

With Cappy's help, Mario soon finds himself in command of the Odyssey, an incredible airship capable of traveling to more than a dozen kingdoms scattered around the globe. From the scorching sands of Tostarena to the bustling streets of New Donk City, there's no place the Odyssey can't go.

Don your favorite hat and put your seatback in its full, upright, and locked position. The Odyssey is taking flight for Mario's biggest, boldest adventure yet!

Your 1-Up Guide

Mario's desire to stop Bowser from marrying Peach may be his ultimate goal, but the best part of any adventure is the journey, not the destination. And oh, the places you'll go, Mario!

Super Mario Odyssey takes place across numerous kingdoms bursting with their own unique customs, attractions, and wildlife. And it's up to Mario—and you!—to restore the peace after Bowser and his party of Broodals pilfer these kingdoms of their regional treasures. But the only way to reach them is by fueling the Odyssey with Power Moons.

And that's where this book comes in.

The following chapters not only guide you in Mario's quest to stop Bowser, but also reveal the tips, tricks, and tactics you need to collect every one of the more than 800 unique Power Moons.

Whether you're new to Mario or a seasoned veteran with decades of experience, you won't want to miss the "Making the Most of Your Odyssey" section of this guide, as it expertly reveals every one of Mario's abilities, both with and without Cappy. Later chapters showcase the dozens of enemies you'll meet and capture along the way, the wonderful collection of outfits Mario can purchase, and even the many souvenirs and stickers he can collect to commemorate his travels.

Super Mario Odyssey is a very special game, and it's been our honor to create what we feel is a book worthy of the title. We hope you agree!

Making the Most of Your Odyssey: A Kingdom Traveler's Guide

It's only fitting that Mario's grandest, globe-trotting adventure features Mario's biggest set of abilities! Hop right in with standard running and jumping, Mario's bread-and-butter since time immemorial, and add in more moves as you go along.

All of Mario's controls are presented here in a chart for at-a-glance reference, and elaboration on using these abilities follows.

Travel Cheat Sheet—Controls at a Glance

ORIENTATION

Action	Single Player Controls (dual Joy-Con or Pro Controller)	Two Player Controls (horizontal Joy-Con)	Notes
Camera Control	ⓡ to move, **SL**/**SR** to reset	✛ + ○ to move, ⚉ to reset	Camera sensitivity adjustable in Settings

GROUND MOVEMENT

Action	Single Player Controls (dual Joy-Con or Pro Controller)	Two Player Controls (horizontal Joy-Con)	Notes
Run	○	○	Move stick gingerly to tip-toe or walk, push stick all the way to run
Crouch	Hold ⓏⓁ or ⓏⓇ	Hold **SL** or **SR**	Causes ground pound in midair
Crouch walk	Hold ⓏⓁ or ⓏⓇ + Ⓛ	Hold **SL** or **SR** + ○	—
Roll	Hold ⓏⓁ or ⓏⓇ + tap Ⓨ or Ⓧ or flick controller	Hold **SL** or **SR** + tap ✛ or flick Joy-Con	Tap button or shake controller repeatedly to increase rolling momentum

HOPS, SKIPS, AND JUMPS

Action	Single Player Controls (dual Joy-Con or Pro Controller)	Two Player Controls (horizontal Joy-Con)	Notes
Jump	Ⓑ or Ⓐ	✛ or ✛	Hold the Jump button for max height, tap it for a shorter jump; move analog stick in midair to adjust Mario's trajectory; get a running start for a slightly longer and higher jump
Double jump	While landing from standard jump, press Ⓑ or Ⓐ	While landing from standard jump, press ✛ or ✛	Hold the Jump button for max height, tap it for a shorter jump
Triple jump	While landing from double jump, hold Ⓛ and press Ⓑ or Ⓐ	While landing from double jump, hold ○ and press ✛ or ✛	Requires precision and momentum, triple jump must be aimed in the same direction as double jump; hold the Jump button for max height, tap it for a shorter jump
Backward somersault	Hold ⓏⓁ or ⓏⓇ + press Ⓑ or Ⓐ	Hold **SL** or **SR** + press ✛ or ✛	Mario must be relatively still to produce a backward somersault instead of a running long jump; limits midair tackle direction
Side somersault	While running, move Ⓛ in opposite direction + Ⓑ or Ⓐ	While running, hold ○ in opposite direction + ✛ or ✛	Requires precision with analog stick on the 180 degree turn; limits midair tackle direction
Running long jump	While running, hold ⓏⓁ or ⓏⓇ + tap Ⓑ or Ⓐ	While running, hold **SL** or **SR** + tap ✛ or ✛	To roll upon landing, hold Crouch button
Wall slide	Jump against most vertical surfaces	Jump against most vertical surfaces	Not possible after roll, tackle, or running long jump; some slick walls prevent wall sliding
Wall jump	While Mario is sliding down a wall in midair with his hand planted, press Ⓑ or Ⓐ	While Mario is sliding down a wall in midair with his hand planted, press ✛ or ✛	Dive jump won't work after wall jump
Ground pound	In midair, tap ⓏⓁ or ⓏⓇ	In midair, tap **SL** or **SR**	Won't work during running long jump or tackle
Ground pound jump	During ground pound impact, press Ⓑ or Ⓐ	During ground pound impact, press ✛ or ✛	—
Tackle	After initiating ground pound but before impact, press Ⓨ or Ⓧ or flick controller	After initiating ground pound but before impact, press ✛ or flick Joy-Con	To roll upon landing, hold Crouch button

CAPPY

Action	Single Player Controls (dual Joy-Con or Pro Controller)	Two Player Controls (horizontal Joy-Con)	Notes
Cap throw	Ⓨ or Ⓧ or flick Joy-Con	⊕ or flick Joy-Con	Hold Cap Throw button to hold cap in place (two second max)
Spin throw	Tilt both Joy-Con pads or the Pro Controller quickly to the side, or press Ⓨ or Ⓧ during spin	Tilt horizontal Joy-Con quickly to the side, or press ⊕ during spin	—
Upward throw	Flick both Joy-Con or the Pro Controller upward	Flick Joy-Con upward	Hold Cap Throw button to hold cap in place (two second max)
Downward throw	Flick both Joy-Con downward, or press Ⓨ or Ⓧ or flick controller during ground pound impact (Pro Controller)	Press ⊕ or flick Joy-Con during ground pound impact	Hold Cap Throw button to hold cap in place (two second max)
Homing throw	Throw cap (any method), then flick controller in desired direction	Throw cap (any method), then flick controller in desired direction	Cap will home in on an available target nearby; if no targets are near, cap throw length extends in direction of controller flick

COMBOS

Action	Single Player Controls (dual Joy-Con or Pro Controller)	Two Player Controls (horizontal Joy-Con)	Notes
Cap jump	Throw and hold Cappy, then run into him	Throw and hold Cappy, then run into him	Cap jump from the ground is automatic when running into Cappy on hold
Catch jump	Any cap throw, then Ⓑ or Ⓐ just after catching Cappy	Any cap throw, then ⊕ or ⊕ just after catching Cappy	On ground, results in extra-high jump; in midair, causes Mario to spin while hovering briefly
Dive jump	In midair, throw cap, press Ⓩⓛ or Ⓩⓡ then hold Ⓨ or Ⓧ	In midair, throw cap, press ▰ⓢⓛ or ▰ⓢⓡ then hold ⊕	Can be done once per airborne period; cannot be done after wall jumping or releasing a Captured creature in midair, but CAN be done after jumping off a pole or launching off a hat trampoline

MISCELLANEOUS

Action	Single Player Controls (dual Joy-Con or Pro Controller)	Two Player Controls (horizontal Joy-Con)	Notes
Spin	Rotate Ⓛ quickly in two circles	Rotate Ⓞ quickly in two circles	Press Cap Throw button for spin throw, press Jump button for spin jump
Spin jump	During spin, press Ⓑ or Ⓐ	During spin, press ⊕ or ⊕	Descends slower than a normal jump, steer spin jump with analog stick
Quick descent	During spin jump, press Ⓩⓛ or Ⓩⓡ	During spin jump, press ▰ⓢⓛ or ▰ⓢⓡ	—
Spinning ground pound	During spin jump, hold Ⓩⓛ or Ⓩⓡ until impact	During spin jump, hold ▰ⓢⓛ or ▰ⓢⓡ until impact	Upon impact, press Cap Throw button or flick controller to start a high-speed roll
Spinning ground pound jump	During spinning ground pound impact, press Ⓑ or Ⓐ	During spinning ground pound impact, press ⊕ or ⊕	Same as ground pound jump
Hold item	Press Ⓨ or Ⓧ near grabbable object	Press ⊕ near grabbable object	—
Throw item	Press Ⓨ or Ⓧ for short throw, flick controller for long throw	Press ⊕ for short throw, flick Joy-Con for long throw	—
Swim	Ⓛ	Ⓞ	Cap can still be thrown while swimming
Descend	Ⓩⓛ or Ⓩⓡ	▰ⓢⓛ or ▰ⓢⓡ	Water-based ground pound, descend to the seafloor and Mario will begin walking on it
Ascend	Ⓑ or Ⓐ	⊕ or ⊕	The classic Super Mario Bros. swimming stroke
Water dash	Ⓩⓛ or Ⓩⓡ then Ⓨ or Ⓧ or flick controller	▰ⓢⓛ or ▰ⓢⓡ then ⊕ or flick Joy-Con	Interrupts water-based ground pound with water dash, like tackling in midair
Ledge clinging	Ⓛ left or right to shimmy along handholds, up or Ⓑ or Ⓐ to climb up, down to let go and fall	Ⓞ left or right to shimmy along handholds, up or ⊕ or ⊕ to climb up, down to let go and fall	To cling to a handhold, step off a ledge slowly or jump just short of the lip of a floor above
Pole climbing	Ⓛ up or down to ascend or descent, left or right to rotate around the pole	Ⓞ up or down to ascend or descent, left or right to rotate around the pole	Jump or tackle toward a pole to hug it; shake controller to ascend faster; press Jump button to leap away from pole toward Mario's back

Control Schemes

Like most games on Nintendo Switch, *Super Mario Odyssey* can be played in several different controller configurations.

One Player

Ideally, *Super Mario Odyssey* is intended to be played with dual controller grip, a separate Joy-Con pad in each hand. Be sure to keep a solid grip on the Joy-Con controllers, and attach the wrist straps if they make the pads more comfortable to hold securely. Of course, playing with handheld mode on the go is great too! The Pro Controller offers the most comfortable configuration for players docked to a TV.

Two Players

Two friends can play together on one console with Joy-Con pads held horizontally, Super NES-style. When using a horizontal Joy-Con, attaching the wrist strap makes the controller more comfortable to hold for most players, along with making it easier to press SL and SR.

Super Mario Odyssey changes a little bit with two players. One player pilots Mario, and the other player pilots Cappy, for a globetrotting cooperative team-up! Mario controls like single player mode as long as he's wearing Cappy, but Cappy can choose to flit away from Mario's head and act on his own at any time. Mario without Cappy still has his own full assortment of jumps, rolls, and spins, but he'll lose ready access to his cap throws and Cappy-aided jumps, the catch, cap, and dive jumps. Also, note that Mario's camera controls are handled by the horizontal Joy-Con's ⊕ button instead of the right stick and shoulder buttons.

Cappy, as a magical spinning hat, can move much more freely than Mario. Cappy can jump repeatedly in midair, mounting platforms and floors Mario either can't reach, or can't reach without some plumber acrobatics. Cappy can simply jump-jump-jump repeatedly in midair to glide up. Cappy can also mount his own offense with his own spin on Mario's ground pound attack. Cappy should move around gathering coins, demolishing foes, and scouting for Mario.

Most importantly, Cappy flying on his own still serves as a cap jump launchpad for Mario, so players can work together to get Mario wherever he needs to be. Better still, Cappy can literally lift Mario up into a bonafide double-jump by flying over Mario then jumping twice! This unique co-op jump is only possible in two player mode and can only be initiated by the Cappy player.

Motion Controls

Motion control sensitivity when aiming is adjustable at any time in Settings from the Pause menu. Don't be afraid to try all variations of this setting! If Joy-Con (or Pro Controller) motion controls don't feel natural to you at first, adjust the sensitivity until it suits you.

Motion controls also feel slightly different when using split Joy-Con, a single sideways Joy-Con, or a Pro Controller. With split Joy-con, Joy-Con (R) feels sort of like a laser pointer when aiming is possible. Pro Controller motion aim feels more like tilting and pitching a steering wheel. Both offer similar motion precision, but get there with a different feel.

Waggle Beats Mashing

Rapid waggle and button-mashing are not equals. In just about every case where you can either press a button rapidly or shake the controller repeatedly, you'll get better, quicker results from waggle. When rolling, tapping Cap Throw rapidly to pick up speed isn't nearly as fast as shaking any controller in rhythm to Mario's forward tumble. It's quicker to climb trees and poles by shaking a controller rather than just holding up on the stick.

When Capturing a Poison Piranha Plant, you can spit ink faster by shaking than by pressing a button. Paragoombas and Parabones can be made to flap their little wings much more furiously with waggling than with mashing. And so on.

Playing mostly or entirely with buttons is still fine. If you need a straightforward Cappy throw at a target Mario is facing, the Cap Throw buttons will do. Some speed challenges are going to be easier if you're rolling and climbing faster via motion controls, of course. And some moves are largely limited to motion controls. For the X or Y button to send Cappy spiraling around Mario in a protective spin throw, you must first start a grounded Mario spin by rotating the stick in a 720 motion. With motion controls, you need only tilt the controller(s) suddenly left or right. Cappy spins off in the direction you choose. Without motion controls, the move is simply not immediately at hand.

Plumber Power

The controls are built off the classic basics that trace all the way back to *Super Mario Bros.* on the NES and *Mario Bros.* in the arcade. At heart, Mario is still running, jumping, bouncing, and tossing objects in pursuit of Bowser, and his standard moves are enough to get through most of the challenges found throughout the kingdoms of the world. But there are also many variations of his classic movements, some accumulated along the way in classic games like *Super Mario 64* and *Super Mario Sunshine*, and some all-new. Mario was originally named Jumpman in his first appearances, so it's only proper that our favorite spring-legged hero travels the world with just about every kind of jump he's ever had, and some new ones too.

Run

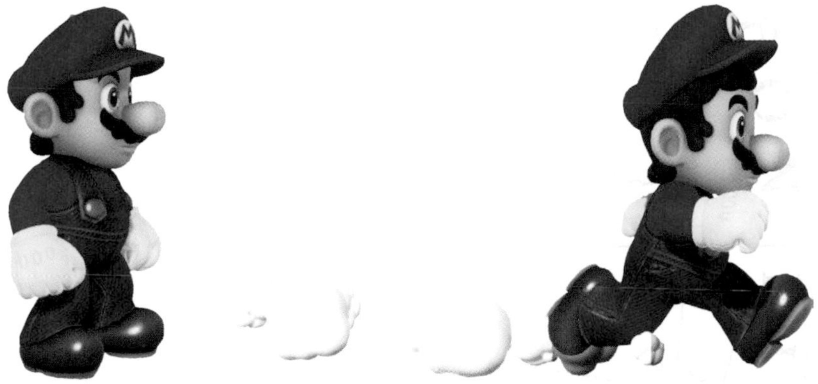

Tried and true, let Mario's potato-shaped feet carry him to the next destination. Push the stick all the way for a full-speed scamper. When it's wise to slow down, like crossing a narrow beam above a pit, push the stick slightly to walk.

Mario doesn't have a Dash button like in 2D *Mario* games. (Unless you find yourself in an 8-bit pipe...) When you want Mario to move faster than running allows, use rolling, long jumps, triple jumps, and dives.

Camera Control

If you'd like to adjust the view, tap either L or R to instantly reset the camera behind Mario. (In certain situations, this focuses the camera on something else, like a boss.) You can also manually adjust the camera's angle with the right stick. The right stick's camera sensitivity setting can be adjusted in the Settings portion of the Pause menu.

In two player mode, there are no L or R buttons, so camera control is handled by ✚ on a Joy-Con held horizontally. (Where the X button is with an upright grip in one player.)

Jump

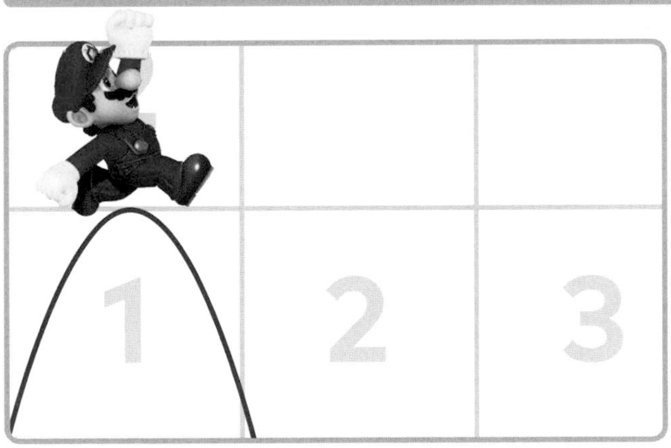

From standstill

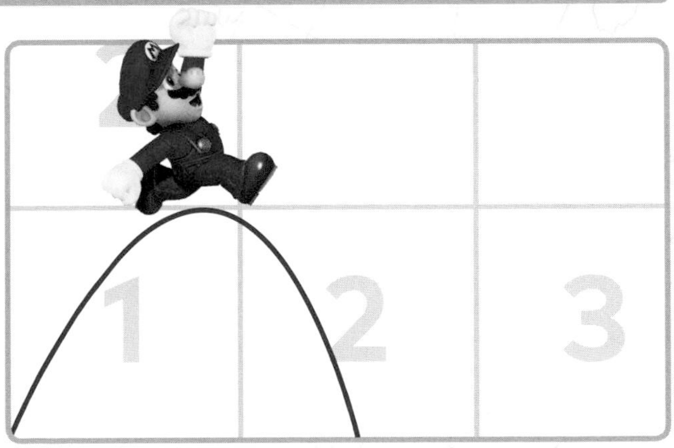

From running start

Mario wasn't originally named Jumpman for nothing! Tap the button quickly for a short hop, or hold the button down for a max-height jump. Run before jumping for a little extra distance and height, and move the stick in midair to control Mario's trajectory.

Squashing Stuff Since 1985

Damage most enemies just by jumping on top of them. If the enemy has a hat on, the hat must be knocked off first before Mario's weight will hurt them.

Some enemies and objects have a symbol on top like an impact, a clear clue that ground pounding will be effective.

Enemies with spiked helmets or shells can't be jumped upon without taking damage. Some enemies can be defeated once this spiked top is knocked off, but for enemies like Spiny, whose shell can't be removed, you just can't count on Mario's weight to crush them like with most foes.

Crouch & Crouch Walk

Hold the shoulder button and Mario shrinks down as small as possible, practically hiding under Cappy. Mario is a smaller target while crouching. Move the stick while crouching to crouch-walk. Some openings are so small that Mario can only squeeze through thanks to crouch-walking.

Roll

The fastest way for Mario to travel on his own is by rolling across open ground. Start a roll by crouching, then pressing the Cap Throw button or flicking the controller. Mario tumbles forward. To keep rolling, continue holding the Crouch button, while repeatedly pressing the Cap Throw button or shaking the controller. Shaking the controller allows for faster repeat speed boosts than mashing the Cappy button.

Drifting back toward the ground with a running long jump or tackle, hold the Crouch button to automatically roll upon landing. During ground pound touchdown (spinning or normal version), hold the Crouch button on impact and tap a hat throw button (or flick the controller) to skate right out of the ground pound's dust cloud in a high-speed roll.

Backward Somersault

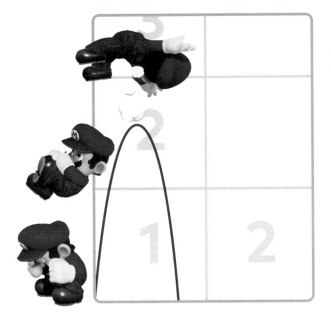

Side Somersault

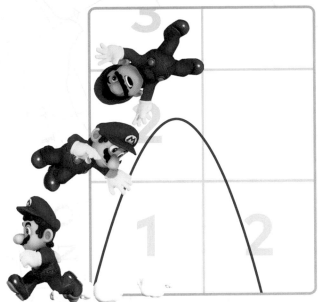

Mario vaults up out of a crouching position into one of his highest-reaching jumps. He lands facing his original crouching direction, a few steps back from where he started. When there's a ledge too high for a standard jump, it's often easy to approach the wall, face away, crouch, then backward somersault on up.

If you tackle from a backward somersault, Mario only tackles in the direction he faced when launching from the ground, even if you point the stick in another direction while he's in midair. If you want to backward somersault and then tackle in a different direction, throw Cappy at the top of the jump first. This flips Mario upright into his hat-throwing posture and frees him up to tackle in any direction.

Jump right after reversing direction suddenly for a side somersault. This reaches the same height as a backward somersault, but travels farther, and ends with Mario turned around. To vault quickly onto a ledge with a side somersault, approach a wall, move the stick directly away from it, then move the stick right back toward the wall and jump. Done correctly, Mario pinwheels up and over.

Like a backward somersault, a side somersault restricts the direction Mario can tackle. He'll only tackle in the direction he'd end up facing naturally after the somersault is done. Again, you can get around this by cap-throwing at the apex of the side somersault, which lets you tackle afterward in any direction you want. This is great for setting up a dive jump onto a high platform.

Running Long Jump

Mario's farthest-reaching basic jump is done by entering a crouch while running, then jumping right away. When performing this technique, you're not actually waiting to see Mario enter a crouching position. You just hold the stick in the desired direction, then press Crouch and Jump. Running long jumps can be performed with surprisingly little runway and have great reach, though the worst height of any jump. Perform a running long jump into a wall and Mario bounces off, stunned. Sliding along a wall and wall jumping won't work after long jumping. Hold the Crouch button while landing from a running long jump to transition into a roll. Jump while rolling and you'll also get a running long jump. On open terrain, you can bounce across the landscape rolling and long jumping!

Double Jump into Triple Jump

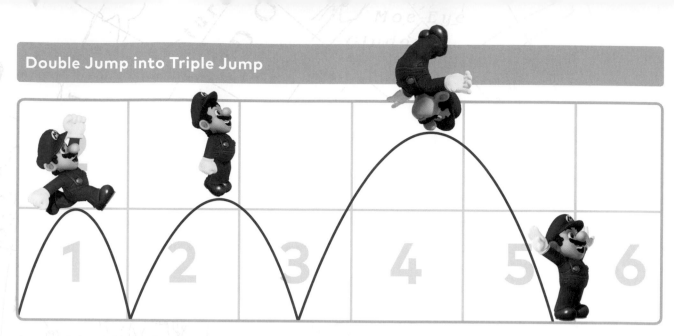

Jump again immediately after landing from a normal jump and Mario performs a slightly better jump, his arms flat down his sides from the momentum. This double jump can be performed anytime, even standing still or drifting backward.

The finishing triple jump—inch-for-inch Mario's best jump—is also done by jumping again immediately after landing from a double jump, but the requirements are stricter. The first jump can still be straight up and down, but for the second and third jumps hold the stick all the way in one direction and keep it there. You need to pick up enough speed moving forward during the second jump to give Mario momentum for the finale.

Wall Jump

When Mario slides down a vertical surface in midair, he plants one hand and foot to slow his fall just a bit. From here, jumping launches Mario up and away from the wall. Sometimes, two sheer walls will be close enough to each other that Mario can easily wall jump back and forth all the way up the shaft.

After most jumping or airborne actions, Mario can still slide along a wall and wall jump. But if he runs head-first into a wall with a running long jump or tackle, he'll clobber himself and fall all the way to the ground (or into a pit).

After a wall jump, Mario cannot bounce off Cappy in midair until after he lands again. All other airborne actions are possible after wall jumping, and you can *try* to dive jump, but if you do, Mario simply passes through Cappy.

If Mario plants a hand and starts sliding down a wall just under a platform above, deft footwork can still see him reach the next floor. Wall jump up and away from the wall, then tackle back toward the next floor from the top of the wall jump's arc. Don't tackle too early, or Mario's inertia will still carry him away from the wall no matter which way you aim. To make sure this doesn't happen, throw Cappy first, then pounce onto the landing zone.

Ground Pound

Ground Pound Jump

From midair, Mario gathers his squat form and cannonballs straight down, landing with a forceful thud that kicks up dust in all directions. This delivers more force than merely jumping on something. Bricks and boxes can be broken from above, and some enemies can only be defeated with ground pound attacks on their noggins.

Upon impact, you can initiate a downward toss with the Cap Throw button, or a high-speed roll with the Crouch and Cap Throw buttons together.

Jump immediately after slamming down with a ground pound, while surrounded by dust, for a ground pound jump. Mario turns the impact force into extra upward springing power, launching higher than a regular jump. The ground pound jump is Mario's second-highest standard jump after his triple jump, edging out somersaults and cap jumps by just about a plumber's toe.

Between the ground pound jump, back/side somersault, and cap jump, you have four short-notice high jumps that are not quite as good as a triple jump, but which don't require as much space to pull off.

Tackle

From midair, while Mario gathers himself and descends for a ground pound, press the Cap button or flick the controller for a tackle instead. Like with crouching before a running long jump, you don't have to visually confirm Mario is winding up his ground pound move, you can just fluidly press the Crouch button then the Cap Throw button in midair.

Mario flops toward the ground quickly during a tackle, but it also adds a fair bit of horizontal distance gained before landing. It's also the fastest way for Mario to suddenly change directions across a short distance, so hopping and tackling to the side can work as an evasive maneuver. Hold the Crouch button upon landing from a tackle and Mario transitions right into rolling, keeping the momentum going. Tackle into a wall, though, and Mario bounces off, like when long jumping or rolling into a vertical surface. Ouch!

With most airborne moves, you have options afterward, but a tackle means commitment. A tackling Mario is ground-bound for sure. Tackling into the top of a vulnerable creature can hurt them just the same as jumping on them can, but it's harder to aim. As an attack, it's probably better for catching rabbits than taking on Bowser's minions!

Cappy the Bonneter

The biggest addition sits atop Mario's head—his new friend Cappy replaces his trusty old red plumber's cap, helping him out in many ways. Mario's travel partner is on an adventure of his own, roused from Bonneton to track down his sister Tiara, who just happens to have been dragged into Bowser's clutches on the same misadventure as Peach. Cappy the cap can do it all. He slices and dices with throw attacks, and he can become a hovering trampoline for Mario on the ground or in midair. Most startlingly, he allows Mario to "capture" certain other creatures, temporarily inhabiting their bodies through ghostly Cap Kingdom magic, giving Mario all kinds of unique and useful abilities.

Cap Throw

Thanks to Cappy, Mario is more capable as a fighter than ever. Aim Mario with the stick and toss Cappy with either the Cap Throw button or a brief flick of the controller. Cappy can also be thrown in midair and even while swimming.

During normal throws, Cappy flies away from Mario's hand a little bit farther than the distance of a normal jump. When Cappy strikes a Capture-vulnerable creature, control transfers to the new creature. Cappy striking a non-Capturable target knocks the target back, perhaps defeating them, depending on their durability.

When Cappy returns to Mario, toss the cap again immediately for a slightly quicker toss. This can be done again after the second consecutive throw for a kind of "triple throw," the fastest Cappy attack. This is most useful against incoming enemies or projectiles that can be knocked back, since Mario can dish out hat deflections very quickly with good timing on repeat throws. Quickly knock back one sturdy foe over and over, or deftly deflect several incoming boss hats back to back.

Putting Cappy on Hold

Hold the Cap Throw button during a toss and Cappy continues spinning at max distance for up to two seconds before returning to Mario. During this time, Cappy can still block incoming projectiles and damage things near him. For example, hold Cappy after throwing him into a multi-hit coin block and he'll rapidly drain the block of all coins by spinning against it.

More importantly, holding Cappy turns the trusty living hat into a temporary platform. Jumping off Cappy from the ground is called a cap jump. Bouncing off Cappy in midair is called a dive jump, where you first toss Cappy while jumping then tackle toward him.

Toss Cappy onto certain knob-like structures and you can keep him spinning indefinitely with the same method, by holding the Cap Throw button. This works atop things like lampposts, flagpoles, and ornate bannisters.

Spin Throw

Mario throws Cappy in a protective spiral. Spin throws are immensely useful, so get used to performing them on-demand. If using dual Joy-Con, snap them both to the left or right together. If using a single horizontal Joy-Con or the Pro Controller, snap either to the side like suddenly turning a car's steering wheel. Done correctly, a spin throw is unmistakable, with Cappy circling Mario repeatedly, picking up coins and bashing baddies along the way.

Aside from using motion controls, a spin throw can also be performed by starting a grounded spin (spin the stick twice quickly) before tossing Cappy. During a spin, grounded or jumping, any cap toss will be a spin throw. (Note that this doesn't apply to Mario's spin after launching from a flower-like hat trampoline, though.)

Cappy can still capture creatures during a spin throw, but can't be held in place.

Upward Throw

Mario hurls Cappy almost straight up, slicing the air above Mario higher than his standard jump. Naturally, you can throw Cappy even higher still by jumping and performing an upward throw at the apex.

You'll need motion controls for an upward throw. Thrust the controller up evenly and suddenly, without tilting it. If using split Joy-Con, make sure to raise them both.

Upward throws are most useful for grabbing coins or hearts that are out of Mario's reach. Upward throws can also reveal invisible blocks. Cappy can be held at the end of an upward throw, though it's hard to take advantage of this with a cap jump unless you quickly side or backward somersault up into the hat.

Upward throws can also prove quite useful in games of beach volleyball...

Downward Throw

Done in midair or right next to a drop-off, a downward throw is the opposite of an upward throw, with Mario hurling Cappy almost straight down. Like with upward throws, this tends to be most useful for grabbing risky coins or fishing for invisible blocks.

Downward throws on flat ground are different. Cappy rolls away from Mario like a sawblade, striking farther along flat ground than a normal cap throw.

Doing downward throws anytime requires a split Joy-Con grip, thrusting both Joy-Con down at the same time. A downward throw cannot be done with motion controls on a Pro Controller or a horizontal Joy-Con pad. A downward throw can still be done without motion controls by ground pounding first, then tapping Cap Throw during the impact. This just requires a little premeditation. Also, be careful not to hold the Crouch button during the ground pound impact, or Mario will high-speed roll out of the dust cloud instead.

Homing Throw

During a cap throw, flicking the controller redirects Cappy's flight path. If there's a target nearby, whether an enemy or object, he homes in on it. If there's no obvious target, Cappy flies in the direction you chose with motion waggle, upward, left, right, or downward. Bending Cappy's travel path at a right angle can be helpful sometimes to pick up coins or hearts around tricky corners or over precarious drop-offs. This redirection can even trigger some hat launchers and capture out-of-sight creatures from odd angles.

Quick Return

A homing throw flick doesn't just redirect Cappy's flight. Even though he ends up traveling farther during a homing throw, Cappy returns to Mario *much* faster than during a normal throw, even a normal throw without any cap-holding. Getting Cappy back in-hand faster is its own reward, since the option of more Cappy things sooner is always appealing. But this also allows for making the most of airtime during long forward jumps, where every little action adds a little forward momentum, and where there's time for a homing throw and catch spin, with a dive jump still possible before landing.

Capture

Maybe the single biggest departure for Mario in this adventure is the ability to control dozens of creatures (and even things) by temporarily taking them over with Cappy. Capturing occurs automatically whenever Cappy strikes a capture-vulnerable target. From controlling a growing stack of Goombas, to taking over a Paragoomba and flying where Mario can't, to piloting a Lava Bubble through a molten sea, using Cappy to capture creatures opens all kinds of paths and doors.

You can check out a list of capture targets from Lists on the Travel Map, and from the Action Guide at the main Pause screen. This guide also lists which enemies can be captured in the preamble to each kingdom's walkthrough, and in the Odyssey Ecology chapter toward the back of the book.

Combos: Mario and Cappy

Cap Jump

On the ground, you can execute an extra-springy jump simply by tossing and holding Cappy, then running into him. Mario automatically bounces into an extra-high jump.

A cap jump can also be done off the ground, by jumping into Cappy on hold higher up. Using Cappy in this way by throwing him in midair then tackling toward him is called a dive jump, one of Mario's most advanced and useful maneuvers.

Catch Jump

On the ground, jump immediately after catching Cappy for a little extra lift versus a regular jump. A returning Cappy gusts up onto Mario's head in rhythm with him jumping off the ground. This isn't crucial, as ground pound jumps, somersaults, cap jumps, and triple jumps are still higher-reaching when a bigger jump is better, but it's nice when it happens.

Catch Spin

Tapping the Jump button just after a midair catch gives a little flourish twirl and slightly more hangtime, and allows Cappy to be thrown again in the same midair period.

Throwing Cappy in midair gives a little bit of forward loft, if you hold the desired direction on the stick, and so does this catch spin. In tall forward jumps where every bit of distance matters, and height isn't so important, a homing throw into a catch spin might make the difference.

A homing throw into catch spin only works to "recharge" Mario's cap toss once per airborne sequence. During long falls, if you keep trying to throw and catch spin, Mario simply whirls without tossing Cappy, and without adjusting his trajectory.

Dive Jump

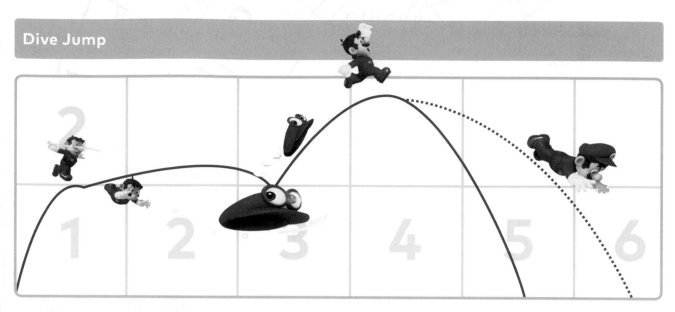

One of Mario's most advanced jumping techniques requires his plucky athletic tackle and his new friend Cappy used as a floating bouncepad.

Like with bouncing off Cappy on the ground with a cap jump, Mario can also bounce off Cappy in midair with a dive jump. During any kind of jump, first toss the cap in the desired direction, then immediately tackle toward it. Hold down the Cap Throw button used for the tackle—this holds Cappy in place, so Mario has something to bounce off!

After a bounce, direct Mario in midair as usual. You can throw Cappy again if needed, and you can tackle again for more horizontal distance gained. But a dive jump bounce can only be used once per airborne period, the time between when Mario's feet leave horizontal ground and return. Try to tackle into Cappy again after one dive jump, and Mario just passes through him. Dive jumping also won't work after a wall jump, or after releasing a captured creature in midair. Dive jumping *will* work after jumping away from pole structures like a flagpole, beanstalk, or tree trunk, though. It also works after bouncing off a hat trampoline.

Dive jumping adds lots of extra airtime, distance, and control to any jumping sequence. Compared to a standard jump with a running start, a running jump into a dive jump at the apex covers three times more ground... or soars over a gap three times wider.

Dive jumping isn't just for gap-clearing. A midair cap toss holds height briefly while adding a little momentum in the direction of the throw; tackling and bouncing also allow for midair extension or redirection. Dive jumps can save "missed" jumps, where you realize you're going to under or overshoot a landing pad.

The Jumpman Cometh

When gauging which jump to use, there's height to worry about, and there's distance. Different jump techniques are better for different things. Getting comfortable with Mario's jump potential leads to clearing wider pits, planting wall jumps farther up sheer surfaces, and mounting higher ledges than normal.

STANDARD JUMPING

When you just want to cross a gap too long for a regular jump, and the other side is about the same height as the takeoff point or lower, then a running long jump is perfect. For a combination of max height and distance with a little runway and time to line it up, the triple jump is king. To get immediate height on short notice reaching for a ledge or platform above, a ground pound jump gives the most lift, followed closely by the back and side somersaults and the cap jump. If there's not enough spring to loft cleanly up to the next floor, Mario may be high enough to cling to the ledge and climb up.

WALL JUMP AND TACKLE PARKOUR

If you can't get quite enough height with a jump to ascend to the next floor even by clinging, but there's a place to wall slide, you can maybe manage to flip up there with some deft Mario-style gymnastics. Ground pound jump or somersault next to the target wall and start sliding as high as possible. Wall jump, toss Cappy toward the desired ledge at the jump's apex, then tackle toward Cappy, like during a dive jump. After wall jumping, Mario can't actually bounce off Cappy for a dive jump bounce, but throwing Cappy in the desired direction moves Mario forward in midair ever so slightly, while helping aim the tackle afterward. With practice, this maneuver gets Mario up over many walls that can't be surmounted with his normal jumps alone.

DIVE JUMPING TO HIGHER HEIGHTS

If the next floor or ledge is even higher, above clinging reach, dive jumping can give that last little bit of height to make it up onto a high or tricky platform. Start with the highest possible jump toward the wall you can allow for, depending on the room available, then toss Cappy parallel to the wall and dive jump toward him. Take care not to tackle right into the wall, or Mario bounces off, shaken by the impact! Successfully bounce off Cappy then drift toward the wall to wall jump from much higher than jumping alone. From here, hopefully the target ledge is finally in reach! As before, aim toward the desired platform with a Cappy throw from the wall jump's apex, then tackle to a (hopefully) safe landing.

DIALING LONG DISTANCE

Dive jumping adds quite a bit of horizontal distance cleared to any airborne period. When trying to clear an exceptional chasm, get an ideal start with a triple jump or running long jump right from the edge of one side. For a terrific pit-clearing finish, toss Cappy a little past the jump's apex, then tackle toward him and hold the Cap button to bounce. Steer the midair cap jump hard forward, tackling from the apex for a little extra oomph to the forward falling arc. Getting comfortable with dive jumps adds quite a bit to Mario's airborne maneuverability, and this sequence takes him most of the way toward a plumber's mastery of Mushroom Kingdom gymnastics.

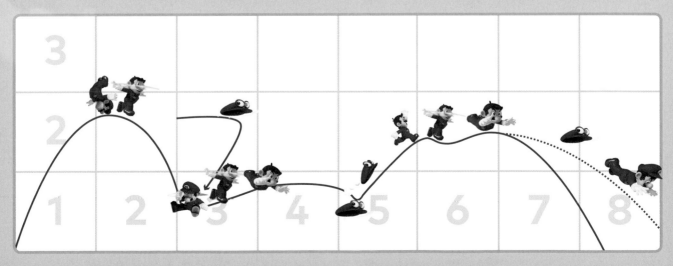

To get max distance on a long jump sequence, Mario has to eke out every bit of possible forward momentum gain, while sacrificing height potential. Launch from the edge of one ledge with a triple jump or running long jump. A bit past the jump's apex, toss Cappy in the direction of travel. Midair cap throws briefly stop Mario from falling, and they give just a bit of distance, if a direction is held. Now here's where it gets tricky. Waggle the controller as Cappy flies to change the cap throw into a homing throw, which brings Cappy back to Mario much faster. (It can help to increase the motion sensitivity setting, making it easier to aim a homing throw.) When Mario catches Cappy, press the Jump button for a midair catch spin. This also briefly holds height and gains a little distance, while restocking Mario with another midair cap throw. Immediately after the glowing catch spin flourish ends, throw Cappy forward, tackle toward him, and hold the Cap button. Steer the cap jump bounce forward hard, throwing Cappy forward again at this bounce's apex; you can't dive jump again or throw Cappy anymore after this, this throw is purely to hold height and gain a bit of momentum one last time! Fall forward after this toss, tackling anytime if it will improve Mario's flightpath.

Miscellaneous Actions

Spin & Spin Jump

Whirl the stick in two quick, full circles and Mario eases into a dizzying top-like spin. Mario's spin can be maneuvered on the ground with the stick. To keep the spin going, you'll have to keep spinning the stick in circles regularly.

A cap throw during a spin automatically becomes a spin throw, whether spinning on the ground or in midair.

Jump while spinning for a unique spin jump. While spinning, airborne Mario descends slower than in other postures, so spin jumping off a high perch gives a bit more time to observe and maneuver during a long descent. To plummet suddenly during a spin jump, hold the Crouch button. Held all the way until landing, this results in a ground pound-like impact.

Holding and Throwing Items

When holding and tossing items like rocks and seeds, Mario is surprisingly nimble, still capable of swimming, triple jumps, side somersaults, ground pounds, and ground pound jumps! Mario holding an item can't tackle, swim fast, wall slide/jump, long jump, or back somersault, though, and of course he can't throw Cappy while his hands are occupied. Toss items a short distance with the Cap Throw button, or much farther with a shake of the controller.

While kicking up dust from a spinning ground pound, tap Cap Throw for a high-speed forward roll!

Swim

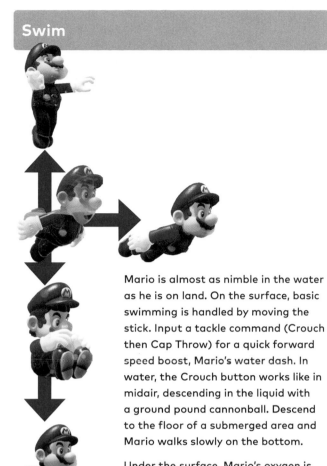

Mario is almost as nimble in the water as he is on land. On the surface, basic swimming is handled by moving the stick. Input a tackle command (Crouch then Cap Throw) for a quick forward speed boost, Mario's water dash. In water, the Crouch button works like in midair, descending in the liquid with a ground pound cannonball. Descend to the floor of a submerged area and Mario walks slowly on the bottom.

Under the surface, Mario's oxygen is limited. Return to the surface or find oxygen bubbles underwater before he runs out of air. Swimming submerged, choose direction with the stick, and adjust depth with Jump button inputs. Underwater, these strokes move Mario upward slightly. Press Jump rapidly to swim to the surface in a hurry. To descend, simply don't input Jump button swimming strokes, or plunge quickly with more water-based ground pounds.

Ledge Cling and Shimmy

Years of honest work (not to mention saving his friends) have given Mario incredible grip strength, so he can cling and climb almost as well as he can jump! Mario can cling to ledges, hanging from sheer drop-offs, the edges of platforms, and the lips of tall steps. Mario can approach a ledge cling from above or below. To grab a ledge from below, it's as easy as jumping up to the edge, where Mario grabs automatically, if he's close enough. (Jump too high and you simply clear the lip, landing on the next floor. Jump too low, and Mario slides down the wall.) To grab a ledge from above, run carefully up to the drop-off, then gingerly use the stick so Mario sort of nudges himself off the stage and begins hanging.

Once hanging, press a Jump button to make Mario climb up to the next floor. It is easier to maneuver if you move the camera behind him first. (Center it with L or R, or use the right stick; when using Mario in two-player mode, tap ✛ to center the camera, or hold ✛ and move the stick to manually reorient it). Move the stick left or right to make Mario shimmy in that direction. There are even some secrets to be found by shimmying along hand-holds that lead where jumps cannot. To drop down to the floor below, move the stick down, which is easier with the camera behind Mario. Of course, mind that you don't release your grip above a bottomless pit! Pressing up on the stick makes Mario climb up to his feet, like pressing Jump while clinging.

Pole Climb

Mario can hug pole-like structures, like flagpoles, tree trunks, beanstalks, and antennas. Hugging and climbing a pole is interesting because Mario can rotate around the structure. Tap left or right on the stick and Mario rotates his position around the pole 90 degrees in the chosen direction. Press Jump and Mario jumps away from the pole, toward his back. Climb up or slide down with up or down on the stick. Climb fast by holding the Cap Throw button repeatedly while climbing; climb even faster by shaking the controller rapidly while climbing! Climb all the way to the top of a pole and Mario does a daring handstand. From here, rotate with left or right to aim, then press Jump to somersault jump off the top of the pole toward Mario's back.

Vehicles

In some locations, Mario can commandeer vehicles and use them to travel faster. Vehicles are not only fast and fun, but also integral to solving some puzzles and uncovering some Power Moons. Besides Motor Scooters and Jaxis, you might also come to think of certain capture targets as vehicles. For example, in aquatic environments, Cheep Cheeps work like agile submarines, and Gushens like speedy hovercraft.

19

Things, Places, and People to See

There are several kinds of currencies, collectibles, and pick-ups to watch out for, along with items of interest, landmarks, hazards, and helping hands to be found throughout the globe.

Hearts

Heart pick-ups replace one heart on Mario's health gauge. They'll often be found by bashing certain blocks, or ground pounding peculiar spots.

Much more valuable than a normal heart, this power-up increases Mario's max health to six hearts! Get knocked back to three or fewer and the bonus ends. Life-Up Hearts are rarer in the environment than hearts, but can also be purchased in Crazy Cap's shop. They can also be revealed by scanning the Princess Peach bridal amiibo!

Mario's normal max health is three hearts, or health points. Taking a hit depletes one heart, and losing all hearts will K.O. Mario, while knocking some change out of his pockets where he gave up the ghost. Don't worry, he'll reappear from a nearby checkpoint or entrance, ten coins lighter. (If certain things were accomplished, like Power Moons or keys revealed, but not yet acquired, they'll have to be uncovered again.)

Mario can survive terrifying falls no problem, if he lands on solid ground. He won't even lose any hearts, but watch Mario shiver absorbing the impact! Fall into a deep pit, though, and he'll be instantly K.O.'d, permanently losing 10 coins.

Assist Mode

With Assist Mode on, Mario's max health is six hearts, by default the same as after picking up a Life-Up Heart. Pick up a Life-Up Heart during Assist Mode, and Mario has nine hearts! In a pinch, resting in one spot replenishes his hearts over time. From a plummet into the abyss, he is carried back up in a lifesaving bubble, which deposits Mario back on trustworthy ground but depletes a heart.

In addition to these health bonuses and penalty removals, designed to make the grand adventure a little easier, a guidance arrow also shows up to point the way toward the next objective. Assist Mode can be enabled or disabled as desired.

What happens when Mario falls into hot or bubbling liquid depends on the liquid. Some vats of boiling liquid are merely extremely hot, and falling into them sends Mario scrambling for higher ground, his behind smoking. You can throw Cappy to extinguish Mario, otherwise, you can't stop him running while he cools down, you can only steer his direction, so keep him away from further contact with the hot stuff while Mario cools down. If there's no safe footing nearby to flee to, it's possible to get stuck bouncing repeatedly in smoking hot soup, losing heart after heart until poor Mario succumbs to the heat. In 2-player mode, the second player can also force Mario to cap jump, extinguishing the flames. It's worth noting that in Assist Mode, Mario doesn't bounce off the lava on fire, but instead will bubble back to land.

Some especially noxious liquids are simply lethal on contact, though, and touching them instantly depletes all of Mario's hearts, leaving a ring of coins behind where he fell. Where lots of toxic sludge abounds, you may find some creature, like a Jaxi for example, that you can ride who can pass unscathed over (or even through) the poison brew.

Coins

Gold coins are plentiful across the world. They're left behind by busted blocks and defeated wildlife. They're found hovering in line formations or lying in big piles. Ground-pounding a curious molehill or crack in the floor often reveals a ring of coins around Mario, easily collected all at once with a spin throw. Clobbering a boss also usually reveals a similar ring of gold coins as a reward. The point is, there are a lot of gold coins about.

Collect as many as you can, because you'll want lots of coins to spend on Crazy Cap's item stock, on Hint Toad's Power Moon clues, and on the nickel-and-diming you'll inevitably experience through occasional clumsiness, since Mario drops 10 coins when he falls into a pit or runs out of health!

Single coins go directly into Mario's pocket. Multi-coin blocks can cough up to ten coins. Coin rolls also grant ten coins. Passing through a coin ring is worth three coins. The outlines of Regional Coins you've already retrieved are worth two coins; the outlines of retrieved Power Moons are worth five. With full health, picking up hearts grants five coins too. With coin piles, well, it all depends on the size of the pile!

Regional Coins

A fixed number of purple coins are hidden throughout each kingdom. Smaller kingdoms usually have 50 purple coins to find, while the biggest kingdoms have 100. These special coins are the local currency, legal tender toward unique local items at Crazy Cap's, the souvenir shop.

Like Power Moons, picking up Regional Coins replaces them with an outline where they once floated. Sending Mario or Cappy through the outline awards two gold coins.

Crazy Cap's Shop

Gold and purple coins can both be spent at Crazy Cap's.

Gold coins can be used in any shop, but purple Regional Coins can only be spent in the kingdom where they're discovered.

There are different stocks of items for gold and purple coins. The stock of gold coin items available grows as you travel to more regions of the world, and as you gather more and more Power Moons. Regional Coin item stocks are unique to each kingdom and unchanging. If you've discovered all the purple Regional Coins in a kingdom, you can afford to clean out the purple item stock!

Power Moons

Mario's goal is to track down Bowser, and he needs Power Moons to do it. Beating the stuffing out of the Koopa king and getting Peach back are the goals, but most of the work toward those goals involves digging up Power Moons. Power Moons are mysterious sources of energy that can be used to power up Mario and Cappy's sweet ride, the Odyssey. The more Moons you funnel into the Odyssey, the more places it can go.

Moons Over Mario

Picking up a Power Moon refills Mario's hearts. Picking up a Power Moon underwater also refills oxygen... this can be a lifesaver when diving for treasure! Once you've acquired a Power Moon, return to the area later to find the dotted outline of a Power Moon in its place, like with Regional Coins. Picking up this outline grants five coins, and still refills hearts and air.

During the first visit to each new kingdom, some Power Moons need to be collected from that region for the Odyssey to refuel and repair for the journey forward. Depending on the condition of the Odyssey and the progression of the story, you may or may not be able to travel to previous kingdoms while collecting prerequisite Power Moons in a newly-discovered kingdom. The number of required Power Moons to progress is indicated by dotted outlines found just under your coin and health tallies in the top-left corner of the display. In addition to collecting Power Moons, you usually have a local objective to complete before you can move on.

Moon Shards

Some Power Moons are broken into five smaller chunks. To assemble that Power Moon, you must gather all the shards. When picking up pieces of a shattered Power Moon, an indicator onscreen shows how many shards are left to collect. When all five Moon Shards are in hand, the Power Moon appears nearby in the environment, ready for Mario to collect.

Power Moons—Return Trips

After the initial batch of Power Moons is assembled and any imminent local threats are addressed, Mario and Cappy can return to search for more Power Moons. After the local main objectives are attended to and the Odyssey is fueled and ready to go, the locals surely still have more errands for travelers looking to extend their stays. During return trips, many things about the kingdom change, with new enemies, locals, items of interest, and Power Moons available to investigate.

Of course, you can expect that things will change again once Mario finally tracks down Bowser and Peach! There are new secrets to discover in each region for a long time.

Buried Treasures

Some items, Hearts, and Power Moons are strewn about in plain sight. Most are hidden to some degree. The usual methods—busting blocks and squashing enemies— nets you plenty. But many hidden items are tucked away in some unusual spots indeed. To help find them, you can rely on Power Moon names acquired from Talkatoo, which are usually clues, and you can look for several telltale hints that something can be found nearby:

- Conspicuous marks or cracks in the ground

- Glowing effect in an unusual spot: emanating from a rock, shining up from a spot on the ground, glowing around a Cappy perch like a bannister or spire, even trailing from a patrolling enemy

- Rumble sensation from the controller when standing above peculiar spots on the ground

- Mario's gaze: in the presence of invisible items or blocks, he sometimes gazes at the unseen object

- Mario's inquisitive foot: over seemingly unexceptional patches of ground, Mario curiously toes the turf

Rarely, there's no immediate cue or clue that something valuable is hidden. In these cases, you have to use the hint art paintings found in each kingdom to discover deeply buried Power Moons in other places!

Cat Mario and Cat Peach

Apparently fossils lasting all the way since the 2D, 8-bit era, these strange hieroglyph-like symbols can occasionally be found plastered on out-of-the-way patches of wall. Striking Cat Mario with Cappy grants 10 coins. Striking Cat Peach awards a Heart.

Brick Blocks

It wouldn't be a *Mario* game without some bricks to bust apart! Jump up from underneath or ground pound from above to test the integrity of blocks.

Most brick blocks shatter, clearing the space. Cleared blocks can open the way to platforms above or pathways below. In rare cases, you won't want to bust a block because you need it as a platform. In these cases, usually some baddie like a Bullet Bill is looking to break them for you, so watch out!

Steel Blocks

Some specially-treated bricks snap into steel instead of breaking apart. They're safe to use as platforms to stand on, cling from, or wall jump off. But nothing removes these blocks once they've hardened.

Hidden Blocks

Some blocks are invisible! They won't be revealed until something strikes them. A cap toss from the side, a jump from underneath, a ground pound from above, the usual. You can also reveal these blocks by ground pounding nearby, which causes them to appear reflective for a moment. Once uncovered, invisible blocks become unbreakable steel blocks. Invisible blocks are usually suggested by subtle hints, like a tiny shadow underneath a high-altitude Power Moon, or three blocks floating at normal jump height in a line. It's worth somersaulting up from the central block of just about every triple-block you find across the kingdoms!

? Blocks

? blocks won't break apart when struck, but you won't know what you're going to get until you hit them either. ? blocks usually become steel blocks while spitting out a coin, but sometimes spit out a Heart, Life-Up Heart, or roll of coins, too.

Multi-coin Blocks

Some brick blocks and ? blocks won't shatter or become steel blocks immediately when struck—you can hit these over and over within a brief period to pull out lots of coins before they harden. From underneath, jump up as fast as you can until all the coins are withdrawn. From the side, you can throw Cappy into the ? block and then hold him in place. His spinning quickly knocks all the coins out of the block! You can extrude a max of 10 coins from multi-coin blocks before they snap into steel.

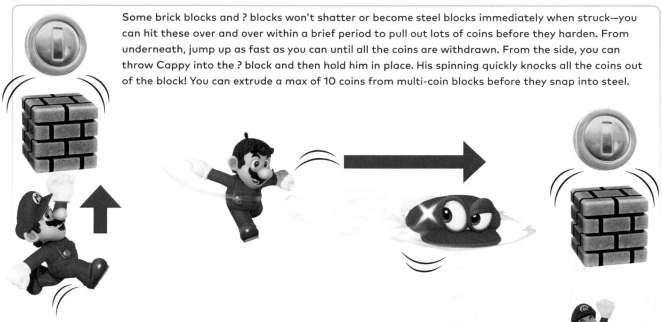

Pipe

Mario's squat form is just the right size and roundness to slip down pipes and see what's on the other side. To enter a pipe, either run into it from the side or climb atop it and crouch. You may also find pipes sprouting from the ceiling, which can be entered by jumping in from below.

8-bit Pipe

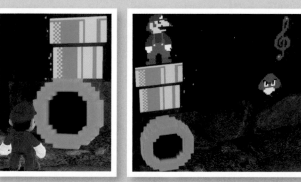

Conspicuously blocky pipes spirit Mario away into a land from the past, flat retroscapes where Mario appears and controls just like in *Super Mario Bros.*!

Run left or right with the stick, hold down to crouch (or just press the Crouch button), dash old-school-style by holding down a Cap Throw button, and jump as usual.

Environments are full of hazards from the NES era, but with *Super Mario Odyssey* twists!

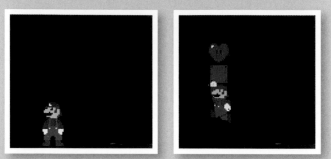

Run full-speed across small gaps and Mario won't fall!

Explore 8-bit pipes while wearing various outfits from Crazy Cap's shop to see the 8-bit spin put on each costume! To see 8-bit costumes, make sure to match your suit and hat before entering an 8-bit pipe. Mismatched costume sets result in the classic, standard overall-sporting 2D Mario.

In the flatlands found beyond 8-bit pipes, you'll find 8-bit versions of the usual collectibles: coins, Regional Coins, Power Moons, and Moon Shards.

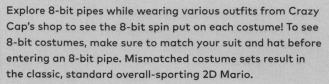

Hidden blocks and other secrets can be found in 8-bit panes, too!

Checkpoint Flag

Checkpoint flags are located throughout each kingdom. They're under Bowser's control initially, but can be replaced with Mario flags simply by visiting and touching them. Once a checkpoint flag is under Mario's control, it's a potential recovery point when defeated nearby, and instant travel to the checkpoint is possible by selecting it on the Travel Map.

Rocket Flowers

Throw Cappy at a Rocket Flower to pick it up and latch it to Mario's back on the return, instantly infusing Mario's step with fire. This puts the hotfoot effect after falling into hot liquid to shame, as Mario hurtles across the landscape, arms out for high-speed balance. Direct away from any walls or obstacles while zipping along on Rocket Flower fuel, and throw Cappy at any other Rocket Flowers along the way to keep the effect going longer.

P-Switches and Scarecrows

These devices trigger various temporary effects while they're engaged. P-Switches may cause magical vine pathways to grow over thin air, forming living, moving pathways wherever they stretch. P-Switches also may sometimes reveal hidden blocks for a limited time, among other possible effects. Scarecrows usually herald a timed platforming puzzle involving platforms that only appear while the challenge is active. On top of that, the scarecrow has to wear Cappy during the challenge, so Mario must succeed without all the tricks he gets while wearing the magical Bonneter.

Cap Clouds

These ephemeral structures aren't really anything until struck by Cappy. Then they'll spring into bright and fluffy, yet firm, cloud platforms. After a few seconds, they dissolve back into gossamer hat form. When using cap clouds as platforms, plan ahead and don't dillydally.

Hat Launcher

These strange objects are primed to catch Cappy and launch him forward, picking up coins and striking objects along the way. Some walls have hat launchers set up in dizzying arrays that propel Cappy along surprising or revealing paths.

Hat Trampoline

While these strange flowers initially clam up, they spread apart and become incredibly buoyant when struck with Cappy, or with a ground pound from above. A blooming hat trampoline can launch Mario much higher than he can ever jump under his own power, spinning gracefully along the way. Since Mario launches upward in a spin jump, his descent is slower than normal, allowing more time to drift toward desired landing sites.

There's a mild difference between a hat trampoline spin and Mario's own spinning jump in that cap tosses won't automatically be spin throws when using hat trampolines.

Slingshot

What you see is what you get—engage a slingshot with a cap throw to get Mario scooped up and launched a great distance.

Pulse Beam

Initially, these objects are inert, but if something hits them they'll emit a ring of dangerous energy. This ring expands, demolishing blocks and damaging creatures in the way.

The devious thing about the pulse beam is that there's almost never just one. Expect pulse beams floating close to each other, so that a strike against any single pulse beam causes a perpetual loop. A pulse beam's energy expands, striking other pulse beams near it, which emit their own reactions to a hit, which re-trigger the first pulse beam, and so on. The resulting wave patterns of rings expanding are tricky to dodge and jump over, and they're usually found hovering near moving or narrow platforms of some kind, to boot. No one said chasing down Bowser was going to be easy!

Mysterious Cube

What *are* these things? No one is sure. The answer will probably have to wait until after Mario and Cappy rescue Peach and Tiara!

Moon Pipe

Hmm, this is strange. Where did this come from?

Locals

Go, brave explorer! Leave nothing unexplored.

Me head into the city?! Fuggedaboutit!

Each kingdom has its own set of regional inhabitants, who come in all shapes and sizes. These locals usually cluster mainly around a main settlement in the area. Wherever locals live and work, you're sure to find a Crazy Cap's souvenir shop, and plenty of people (or robots, or dogs, or fork-like creatures, or friendly skeletons, and so on!) who could use Mario's help.

Talkatoo

This yapping feathered friend can be found somewhere in each kingdom, perched and ready to dispense indirect Power Moon clues in the form of their names. Frequently, just the name of a Power Moon is enough to point you in the right direction, so this can be a big help. Talkatoo gives you up to three names of undiscovered Power Moons at a time.

Hint Toad

When things are calm in each kingdom, you find Hint Toad hanging around near Uncle amiibo. This pathfinding entrepreneur is willing to share Power Moon location hints... for a price. Hint Toad's Travel Map markings cost 50 coins each. There are some Power Moons he can't map, but he knows most of them. Hint Toad and Talkatoo work hand-in-beak to give you a little guidance looking for more moon power.

Uncle amiibo

In each kingdom, whenever it's safe enough for Hint Toad to begin scouting, Uncle amiibo tags along. This bot can communicate with your amiibo, engaging a special function that allows Uncle amiibo to use amiibo power to locate a missing Power Moon. In effect, this means any amiibo becomes like a free Hint Toad tip! Begin a conversation with Uncle amiibo for prompts to use amiibo. This function can only be used every few minutes.

Certain other amiibo can also be engaged anywhere in the game world, even away from Uncle amiibo, by holding right on the D-pad, then scanning the amiibo. Special amiibo that grant extra features are listed here:

Super Mario Odyssey-series amiibo

New *Super Mario Odyssey*-themed amiibo of Mario, Peach, and Bowser in full wedding regalia are now available! These figures unlock special costumes and have special exclusive in-game bonuses that will be useful the whole time you enjoy the game!

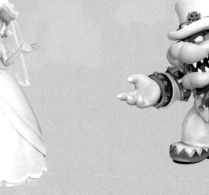

Mario (Wedding Outfit) temporarily makes Mario invincible. Naturally, there's a cooldown period before this can be reused!

Peach (Wedding Outfit) gifts a Life-Up Heart to Mario, increasing maximum health to six hearts (or nine hearts, with Assist Mode enabled). Like Mario's invulnerability, Peach won't gift another Life-Up Heart for a bit.

Bowser (Wedding Outfit) uncovers the whereabouts of missing Regional Coins, roughly in the direction Mario is facing when activating the amiibo. Once the purple coins Bowser reveals are collected, the wedding Bowser amiibo can be used again to get a new Regional Coin hint!

Cap Kingdom

Welcome to Bonneton

REGION AT A GLANCE

Population	Middling
Size	Smallish
Locals	Bonneters
Currency	Hat-shaped
Industry	Hats, Airships
Temperature	Average 71°F

INDIGENOUS FLORA & FAUNA

FROG Can Capture? Yes	**SPARK PYLON** Can Capture? Yes	**PARAGOOMBA** Can Capture? Yes	**BINOCULARS** Can Capture? Yes
MINI GOOMBA Can Capture? No	**SPINY** Can Capture? No	**BONNETER** Can Capture? No	

Posts the Stand Out

These wooden posts are used as partitions or stoppers. If they get in your way, you can pound them down, but pulling them out is recommended.

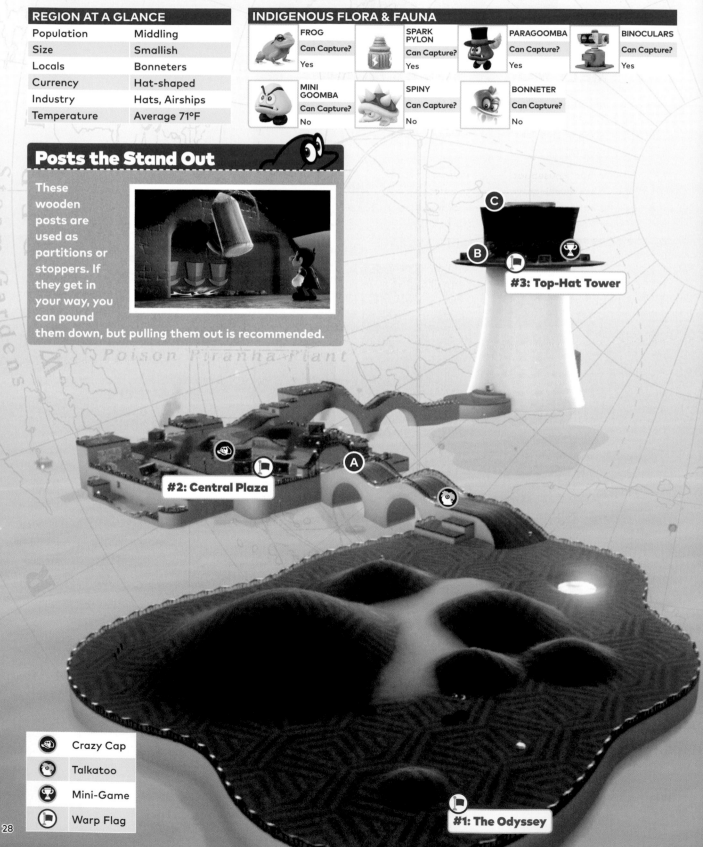

#3: Top-Hat Tower

#2: Central Plaza

#1: The Odyssey

Crazy Cap	
Talkatoo	
Mini-Game	
Warp Flag	

WORLD'S BEST HAT STAND

This eye-catching tower is famous in Bonneton, both as a landmark itself and for the spectacular view from the "brim."

Visitors are allowed inside, but many creatures call the tower home, much to the surprise of first-timers.

EXTREMELY MOBILE HOMES

In town, you will immediately notice the unique dwellings shaped like hats. These constructions double as both house and airship for the Bonneters, who take great pride in them.

Some of the larger "houseboats" even have two stories. As private dwellings, you can't just stroll inside, but the natives don't mind people climbing on top of their homes. Perhaps being atop private property comes naturally to these hat-like people.

THREE KEYS TO THE KINGDOM

1. Appreciate the distinctive architectural style based on hat silhouettes.

2. Enjoy the romantic glow of the moonlit, fog-shrouded streets.

3. Chat with the kind and ever-courteous Bonneters.

A SPECTACLE OF A BRIDGE

The bridge that connects the Central Plaza and the hills is called Glasses Bridge. It's a long, double-arched structure whose bottom is hidden in a sea of clouds. When you see it, you'll understand its affectionate nickname immediately. Many tourists enjoy the speedy thrill of rolling across the undulating structure; be sure to give it a try.

OLD-FASHIONED LIGHTING

These unique lights only appear in Bonneton. Since the area gets so dark every time the moon goes behind the clouds, the lights are designed to be switched on with a simple turn of the lantern. The elegant design of these lampposts draws many tourists. They're even lovelier when turned on, so do give each one a spin as you pass by.

THE "SOMETIMES" BRIDGE

The bridge connecting Central Plaza to Top-Hat Tower is built to retract in an emergency. If this happens during your visit, don't panic—just use the switch to restore the bridge.

The Golden Path

The "Mario's Itinerary" section of each walkthrough chapter contains straightforward, objective-based tips on completing each kingdom's main tasks. Only those collectibles needed to advance to the next kingdom are discussed in this section. Refer to the "Extend Your Stay" portion of each chapter for comprehensive assistance concerning the collectible coins, Power Moons, and numerous secrets scattered throughout the world.

Ⓐ Cappy of the Cap Kingdom

Mario is roused by a mysterious inhabitant of the Cap Kingdom known as a Bonneter—and he's got a fragment of Mario's hat! Get a feel for the movement controls as you run and jump after the escaping top hat. Crest the hills and make your way north over Glasses Bridge to the Central Plaza.

The hat's name is Cappy and he's got a bone to pick with Bowser too. Not only did Bowser take off with Peach, but he also kidnapped Cappy's sister, Tiara. Cappy proposes that he and Mario team up to go after Bowser together. Sounds like a plan!

Ⓑ To the Top of Top-Hat Tower

Bowser's henchmen destroyed the airships of Bonneton, but Cappy knows of an old airship in the adjacent kingdom. To reach it, you must make your way to Top-Hat Tower.

Ⓨ Throw Cap
You can also shake the 🎮 Pro Controller to throw.

Practice throwing the cap at the wooden posts and lamps as you cross the Central Plaza. Cappy automatically yanks any posts out of the ground, allowing Mario to collect the coins behind them.

When ready, ascend the steps near the wooden crates and toss Cappy at the switch to retract the Sometimes Bridge.

Toss the cap at the Mini Goombas that appear near the entrance to Top-Hat Tower—it's easier than jumping on them. Then hit all six plants with the cap to make the flowers blossom. Do it quickly to earn a Heart before entering the tower.

The area inside Top-Hat Tower more closely resembles a platforming level that Mario fans have come to expect. Gather up the coins from the blocks and the floats, then approach the frogs.

Of all the uses Cappy is good for, his ability to capture another creature is top on the list. Toss Cappy at the frog to take control of it.

Capture the World

There are dozens of creatures that Mario and Cappy can capture and each has its own unique special ability or move. Experiment by tossing Cappy at everything you see—both friend and foe—to see what works.

Use the frog's incredible jumping ability to leap through the rings floating off the ground. Continue up the tower, past the Mini Goombas, using the rings as your guide. As a frog, Mario can defeat Mini Goombas by just hopping into them.

Shadow Play

Always pay attention to the shadows cast on the ground, as they often indicate rings, platforms, or collectibles that you may not otherwise see. Sometimes the tiniest of shadows is your only clue that a secret collectible is floating high above.

End the capture near the door and open the chest with a toss of the cap to obtain a Life Heart. This gold and striped Life-Up Heart doubles Mario's health to six segments. Exit the inside of Top-Hat Tower through the red door.

Activate the flag for Top-Hat Tower once outside (now Mario can warp to this location) and proceed counter-clockwise around the brim of the top hat.

Numerous Bonneters warn of the damage done by Bowser's henchmen. They need you to reach the top of the tower to stop them. Follow the coins up the ramp to the top.

BOSS: TOPPER

Topper attacks with three spiked top-hats atop his head. Repeatedly toss Cappy at Topper as soon as the battle begins to knock the hats off his head one by one. Dodge his hats as they spin across the ground and make your way toward the fallen Broodal. Leap atop his head to score a hit.

The three hats spin across the arena as Topper recovers. Toss Cappy at the hats to destroy two of the three (and release a Heart) then continue to throw the cap to defend against the third hat.

Topper reappears with all three hats and the process repeats. Rapidly toss Cappy at the Broodal to knock his three top-hats from his head. Topper flees across the arena once his hats are gone, making it hard to jump onto him. Hit him with Cappy to stun him then, once again, leap onto his head to score another hit. Mario only needs to land two hits to defeat this first Broodal.

Ⓒ The Kingdom Next Door

Defeating Topper causes a Spark Pylon to appear. Toss Cappy at the pole to capture it. Spark Pylons allow Mario and Cappy to zip along an electrified wire, in this case transporting themselves all the way to Cascade Kingdom.

31

Extend Your Stay

Come Back Soon!

Mario and Cappy can return to Cap Kingdom as soon as they visit Sand Kingdom. Return to collect Power Moons, Regional Coins, and even buy some special Bonneton-themed souvenirs and outfits. Mario won't be able to collect every Power Moon from an area until after Princess Peach has been rescued, but many can be found at any time.

Souvenir Shopping

Cap Kingdom contains 50 Regional Coins in the form of purple hats. All 50 Regional Coins can be found any time after your initial visit by returning aboard the Odyssey once you've reached Sand Kingdom.

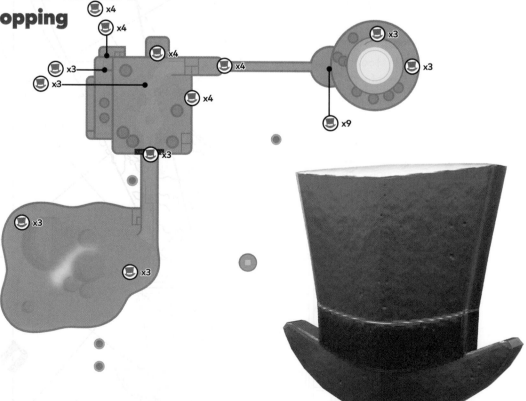

Life-Up Heart	Cap Kingdom Power Moon	Employee Cap	Employee Uniform	Boxers
ⓘ 50	ⓘ 100	ⓘ 50	ⓘ 150	ⓘ 1000

Black Top Hat	Black Tuxedo	Cap Kingdom Sticker	Plush Frog	Bonneton Tower Model
⬤ 5	⬤ 10	⬤ 5	⬤ 5	⬤ 25

Local Currency

There are four Regional Coins inside the Frog Pond area, high on a wall. Follow the instructions for Power Moon #10 to enter this area.

Enter Top-Hat Tower and capture a frog. Hop back toward the entrance and note the Regional Coins high above. Leap from the blocks on the right to activate the invisible blocks above them. Leap from there up to the four purple coins. There are five more Regional Coins in this area.

There are also three Regional Coins inside the push-block level at Top-Hat Tower (see Power Moon #08). Round the first corner to the next Spark Pylon and pause at the node atop the purple coins. Drop onto the blue block, grab the coins, then recapture the Spark Pylon.

The final three Regional Coins are inside the poison peril area of Top-Hat Tower. Follow the instructions for Power Moon #07 to find them.

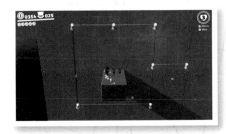

👻 Power Moons

There are 31 Power Moons in Cap Kingdom, none of which are available during Mario's initial visit. Return aboard the Odyssey any time after completing the objectives at Cascade Kingdom to gain access to some of them. Others can only be obtained after defeating Bowser.

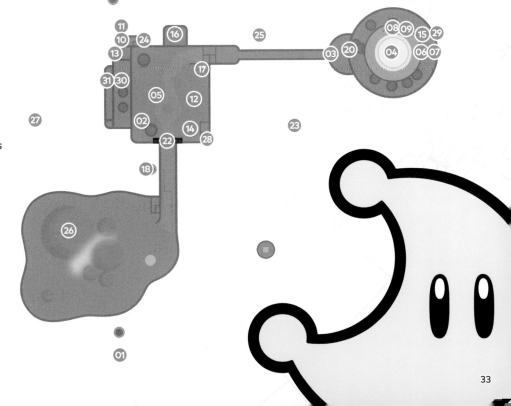

Paragoombas Take Flight

Paragoombas have made their way to Bonneton in Mario's absence. Knock their top hats off then capture them to fly through the mists surrounding Bonneton. There are several top hat islands in the mist containing coins and Regional Coins. Capture the Paragoomba nearest Glasses Bridge to explore the rest of the area. Paragoombas can only fly at an altitude slightly higher than the land they last touched down upon. If you want a Paragoomba to fly high, you need to bring them to higher ground first.

01 Frog-Jumping Above the Fog

Capture a frog and leap over the railing east of the Odyssey to the top hat in the mist. Leap to the second top hat near the three blocks. There's an invisible block above those three. Jump to the higher block and, from there, leap straight up to the Power Moon.

02 Frog-Jumping from the Top Deck

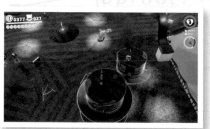

Capture a frog and hop over to Central Plaza and make your way onto the two-story top hat home. The Power Moon is hovering high above this top hat, but the frog's normal jump isn't enough to reach it. You need to shake the controller and perform the frog's high jump ability to grab it.

03 Cap Kingdom Timer Challenge 1

Throw Cappy at the scarecrow at the bottom of Sometimes Bridge to activate the first Timer Challenge. Mario won't have Cappy to assist him in his race to the Power Moon, but he's capable of plenty of useful moves to reach it before time expires. The quickest way to get back up the bridge is to perform a forward roll while shaking the controller to make Mario roll faster. Roll as fast as you can up the bridge to get the Power Moon.

04 Good Evening, Captain Toad!

Return to the top of Top-Hat Tower to find Captain Toad. Captain Toad can be found in each kingdom Mario visits and he always has a Power Moon to hand over when you find him. He's not always this easy to find, so don't get too used to it.

05 Shopping in Bonneton

Make your way to Central Plaza and talk to the yellow Crazy Cap merchant to access the inventory of items sold for standard coins. The Power Moon for Cap Kingdom costs 100 coins.

06 Skimming the Poison Tide

Leap from the top of Top-Hat Tower's north side (or capture the Paragoomba atop Sometimes Bridge) to reach the ledge halfway up the north side of Top-Hat Tower. Enter the red door and capture the Paragoomba inside. Carefully fly through the four rings above the poison tide to collect each of the Moon Fragments. The fifth Moon Fragment is up ahead, near the white platform. Collect the Power Moon that appears, but don't leave just yet!

07 Slipping Through the Poison Tide

Follow the instructions for Power Moon #06 and make your way across the poison tide to the far white landing. Continue using the Paragoomba, wait for a wave of poison to pass, then drop off the side. There's a hole in the fence below the white platform. Fly through it to reach a secret area of the level. Grab the purple coins and fly back to the white ledges. Climb the stepped platforms with the Paragoomba to reach the Power Moon.

08 Push-Block Peril

Make your way to Top-Hat Tower and enter the red door on the brim of the hat, near the sliding platforms. To find the Power Moon here, you must navigate

Pause at the node and wait for the blue steps before exiting the Spark Pylon.

a complex level of sliding blocks and tricky Spark Pylons. Numerous coins lurking off the wire may seem difficult to collect, but they're actually easy to reach. Mario can jump from the power line without falling, so long as he hasn't yet reached one of the nodes. Where this level gets tricky is when it comes to exiting the Spark Pylon.

Pause at a node to wait for the blocks to slide into position, else Mario will likely fall to his demise. Patience is critical in this level!

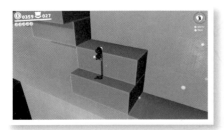

The trip back across the level from right to left on the upper blocks is even trickier, as pairs of blocks slide in and out above one another. Leap onto the lower of the pair, then leap straight up to the higher one as it slides out. Climb up and jump to the lower block in the next pair as it slides from the wall.

09 Hidden Among the Push-Blocks

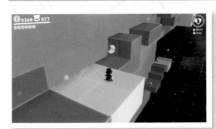

Follow the tips for Power Moon #08 until you reach the upper level of the push-blocks. Cross the push-blocks until you reach the orange platform near the L-shaped block. Turn around, wait for the block to extend, and grab the Power Moon in the alcove.

10 Searching the Frog Pond

Drop off the ledge in the northwest corner of Central Plaza and go through the door (this door was blocked by rubble during Mario's initial visit). There are five Moon Fragments inside this level to find. Collect all of them to make the Power Moon appear.

Grab the one in front of the entrance and then capture a frog and leap onto the entrance area to collect a second. Make your way around the perimeter platforms high on the wall to find the third Moon Fragment. The trickiest one to spot is inside an alcove on the platform above the square ring of coins. The final Moon Fragment is atop the tallest platform in the center of the area.

11 Secrets of the Frog Pond

Follow instructions for Power Moon #10 to enter the Frog Pond and capture a frog. Make your way to the white platform sliding back and forth beneath the narrow wall. Leap from the sliding platform onto the narrow top wall and, from there, into a recess on the wall above to find a Power Moon.

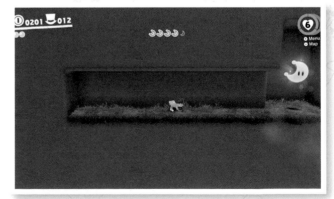

12 The Forgotten Treasure

Approach the Bonneter atop the home on the east side of Central Plaza to learn of a misplaced treasure. Cappy tries to recall where he left it by offering suggestions. First look under the pile of nearby crates by Crazy Cap. Next, drop off the western side of Central Plaza and run through the narrow strip of fog below the homes. Run across Glasses Bridge to check Cappy's next suggestion and continue south to the large hill near the Odyssey. Run to the top of the hill to help Cappy remember. From atop the hill, walk straight toward the moon and feel for the rumble in the controller. Note the two steps near Glasses Bridge and ground pound left of the upper step to find the Power Moon.

13 Taxi Flying Through Bonneton

Capture the Binoculars in the northwest corner of Central Plaza and look to the moon. Scan the fleet of airships flying past for one that looks a little different. Zoom in on it as it sails past the moon to discover it's actually a flying taxi! Spotting this anomaly earns you a Power Moon.

14 Bonneter Blockade

Return to Central Plaza once the Bonneter homes have been restored and speak to the Bonneter in the southeast house.

He says he's guarding a Power Moon and isn't afraid of anything. Test his courage by returning to him as a captured Paragoomba—the Paragoomba on the steps to the Sometimes Bridge is nearest. The Bonneter runs off and the Power Moon is yours.

15 Cap Kingdom Regular Cup

Talk to the Koopa atop the brim of Top-Hat Tower to begin the Koopa Freerunning race. To win, you need only be the first to reach the beacon atop the

hill near the Odyssey. The race begins atop Top-Hat Tower. Triple jump off the edge into a dive jump and roll across Sometimes Bridge while actively shaking the controller for speed. Triple jump and dive jump your way through Central Plaza then roll across Glasses Bridge. Sprint and jump over the smaller hill to reach the finish line before any of the other Koopas. If this race feels easy to you, don't get cocky. There are plenty more challenging Koopa Freerunning events in store!

16 Peach in the Cap Kingdom

Return to Central Plaza after defeating Bowser and continue north to the overlook where the four flowers grow. Princess Peach and Tiara are standing atop the hill there. Talk with her to receive a Power Moon from her travels. Look for Peach in each of the Kingdoms as you continue to travel.

17 Found with Cap Kingdom Art

The Hint Art appears on the side of Sometimes Bridge in Central Plaza after the town has been restored. Snap a picture of it and study the pattern. The black sky and blue circle should tip you off that it's an image from the Moon Kingdom. Take the Odyssey to the

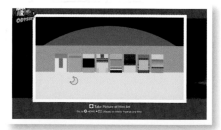

Moon Kingdom and approach the eight characters standing in a row. Stand behind them so the patterns of their outfits match those in the photo. Ground pound behind the second from the left to find the Power Moon.

Moons from the Moon Rock

Once you've defeated Bowser and return to Cap Kingdom, Cappy draws Mario's attention to the mysterious Moon Rock on an island to the east. Fly as a Paragoomba over to the mysterious cube, release the capture, and strike the Moon Rock with Cappy. This releases an additional 13 Power Moons for you to discover.

18 Next to Glasses Bridge

One of the easiest Power Moons in the entire game, this one sits atop the hat next to Glasses Bridge. Jump down (or fly over as a Paragoomba) and snatch it up! You can be sure not all the Power Moons emerging from the Moon Rock will be this obvious.

19 Danger Sign

Okay, maybe this one is just as simple. Capture a Paragoomba and fly south from the Odyssey toward the danger sign. The Power Moon is sitting atop the sign rising up out of the fog. You can't miss it!

20 Under the Big One's Brim

Warp to Top-Hat Tower and carefully climb over the railing directly above Sometimes Bridge. Position the camera so you can see the Power Moon beneath the brim and dangle Mario directly above the Power Moon, with the camera behind him. Press down on the controls to have Mario let go of the railing, falling right into the Power Moon.

21 Fly to the Edge of the Fog

Leap off the brim of Top-Hat Tower near the Koopa to land on the ledge tucked behind the north side of the tower. Capture the Paragoomba there and fly out into the fog north of the tower, toward the faint glow of a Power Moon. Use the in-game map to pinpoint the location of this well-hidden Power Moon. Other Paragoombas can be used as well, but the one specified here is closest to the target. You'll have to descend into the fog to grab it.

22 Spin the Hat, Get a Prize

Run across the metal arch atop Glasses Bridge near Central Plaza and throw Cappy at the large hat emblem in the center. Spin the hat emblem well enough to earn a Power Moon.

23 Hidden in a Sunken Hat

Capture a Paragoomba and fly due north of the hat with the Moon Rock. Note the glowing spindle atop the hat and throw Cappy at it. Perform a throw-and-hold so Cappy continues to spin atop the spindle until the Power Moon is released.

㉔ Fog-Shrouded Platform

Locate the glowing spot on the lowermost platform on the north side of Central Plaza, near Sometimes Bridge. Ground Pound the glow to unearth a Power Moon hidden in the fog.

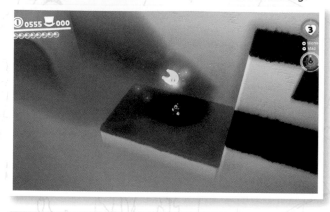

㉕ Bird Traveling in the Fog

You may notice on the in-game map that one of the Power Moon locations seems to be moving. That's a bird! The bird flies a lap around the perimeter of Cap Kingdom, skimming the surface of the fog at speed. To catch it you need to intercept it with a Paragoomba. And the easiest way to do this is by lurking along the wall near the Odyssey, not far from the two sunken hats by the three blocks. Wait for the bird to approach and fly out toward it as it nears the danger sign. Provided you follow straight behind it without dipping below it, Mario and the Paragoomba can snag the Power Moon from behind.

㉖ Caught Hopping Near the Ship!

Locate the rabbit atop the tallest hill near the Odyssey and sneak up to it and hit it with Cappy. Continue tossing Cappy at the rabbit as it flees down the hill to slow it as it runs. Chase after it while hitting it with Cappy to give Mario a chance at catching it for a Power Moon.

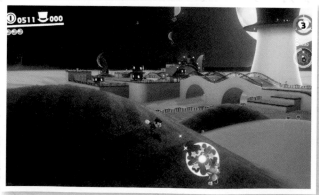

㉗ Taking Notes: In the Fog

Capture a Paragoomba and fly off the western side of Central Plaza toward the glowing treble clef above the hat. Fly through the note facing north to get a start on capturing the notes that appear. Follow the line of notes around the danger sign before time expires to earn a Power Moon.

㉘ Cap Kingdom Timer Challenge 2

Throw Cappy at the scarecrow to initiate the Timer Challenge. A key floats above one of three rising and falling blocks. Ignore the yellow blocks and dive jump onto the white block as it begins to rise. Leap to get the key then turn and dive jump back toward the scarecrow to snag the Power Moon before time expires.

29 Cap Kingdom Master Cup

Koopa Freerunning   Best 00:31.83   00:15.36

Return to Koopa atop the brim of Top-Hat Tower to take on the Master Cup race. This time a Golden Koopa has joined the field of Roving Racers and, unlike the others, this one can really jump! You're going to have to race your cleanest, fastest line to beat him. The course is the same, as is the strategy. Triple jump and dive jump off the tower and through Central Plaza, but roll as fast as you can across the bridges while shaking the controller. Don't worry, the guardrails keep you from falling off. Long jump from the first hill to the finish line!

30 Roll On and On

Descend the square warp pipe in Central Plaza to enter this challenge level. Approach the edge of the hill and begin rolling—Mario can't help but roll here. Avoid the Spiny enemies crawling about and steer Mario through the rings for extra coins. Survive the entire course without falling off (coins are optional) to reach the Power Moon at the bottom. You can earn extra coins by shaking the controller before leaping from the final jump. This helps Mario fly through all of the rings at the bottom.

31 Precision Rolling

Follow the instructions for Power Moon #30, but this time stay to the left near the beginning. The path gets very narrow after the third Spiny, but there's a Power Moon at the end of this challenging route. Keep your balance and steer Mario along the precarious edge to the reward.

Welcome to Fossil Falls

REGION AT A GLANCE

Population	Unknown
Size	Tall
Locals	Unknown
Currency	Stone Disks
Industry	Unknown
Temperature	Average 84°F

INDIGENOUS FLORA & FAUNA

CHAIN CHOMP		BIG CHAIN CHOMP		T-REX	
Can Capture?		Can Capture?		Can Capture?	
Yes		Yes		Yes	

BINOCULARS		BURRBOS	
Can Capture?		Can Capture?	
Yes		No	

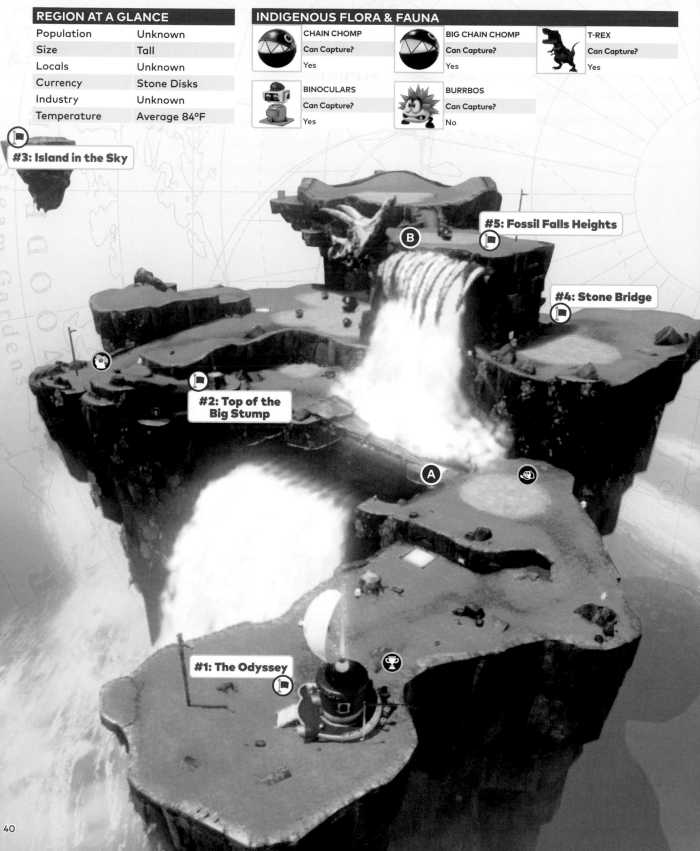

#3: Island in the Sky

#5: Fossil Falls Heights

B

#4: Stone Bridge

#2: Top of the Big Stump

A

#1: The Odyssey

A TALL DRINK OF WATER

There are many waterfalls in the Cascade Kingdom, but the area known as Fossil Falls is a special one.

There are few sights in nature as grand as the millions of gallons of water pouring every second out of this giant triceratops skeleton.

NATURE IN BALANCE

The stone spire standing near the great falls has miraculously remained balanced upright in this position, presumably for eons.

Of particular interest are the cubes of unknown material embedded in the stone. These cubes are the reason for the common theory that the spire somehow fell from the sky. While this theory is difficult to prove, it is equally hard to doubt when looking at this miraculous stone structure.

THREE KEYS TO THE KINGDOM

1. **Experience the glory of nature with eye-popping Great Falls.**

2. **See dinosaurs, prehistoric rulers of a bygone age.**

3. **Find treasures of the past, tucked away everywhere you look.**

Natural Patterns

If you look closely at the stone walls, you will notice fossils mixed in. Think of it as nature's mosaic, and remember it always.

THE ANCIENT WALL

No ordinary cliff face, this structure was carved out painstakingly over many long years by people unknown. The wall is composed mainly of fossils, and evidence suggests it has been broken many times, causing some to suggest that something is buried inside. Visitors are encouraged to explore the mysteries surrounding the Great Barrier, if they dare.

THE PREHISTORIC TYRANT

The biggest draw for tourists to this area is that dinosaurs still live here. Many people willingly put themselves at considerable risk for a glimpse of the ancient "terrible lizards."

T-Rex, most terrible of all dinosaurs, can pulverize a boulder with a single blow. On the other hand, most people don't realize how much time they spend napping.

AN OLD, ODD STRUCTURE

No one knows how a Bonneton-style structure got buried here. Bonneters travel often, so they may have lived here in the past. It is a helpful landmark if you get lost, though.

Ⓐ Our First Power Moon

Cappy was able to lead the way to Cascade Kingdom by way of a Spark Pylon, but if Mario is to get any further, he'll need an airship. And the only way to power an airship is with Power Moons. The first objective is to collect a Power Moon, the first of more than 800 that exist in *Super Mario Odyssey*.

Collect the coins and purple coins near Waterfall Basin and ascend the hill to the Chain Chomp. The first Power Moon is contained within the fossilized rock near the river and the only way to get it is

by capturing the Chain Chomp. Bait the Chain Chomp into surging toward Mario against its chain, then quickly dodge away and capture it.

Pull the Chain Chomp opposite the glowing rocks to wind up the Chain Chomp then release the controls to send it flying in the other direction. The Chain Chomp smashes through the rocks, exposing the Power Moon. After Mario releases the capture collect Power Moon #01. Collecting the Power Moon causes the stone spire to fall, providing a bridge across the river.

Ⓑ Multi Moon Atop the Falls

One of Many Moons

You may have noticed that there are four more dashed circles in the top left corner of the screen. This represents how many Power Moons are still needed to leave an area aboard the airship. Many kingdoms have at least one Multi Moon which contains three Power Moons linked together. With the three you'll earn from the next objective, you'll still need one more. Cascade Kingdom contains an initial total of 25, but the "Mario's Itinerary" section focuses on completing objectives and powering up the airship in the fastest way possible.

Continue past the ancient airship and up the slope past the slumbering T-Rex and toward the Chain Chomps. Capture the Big Chain Chomp and use it to break through the stone wall beneath the arch.

Perform a spin throw near the flowers to gain a Heart then repeat the technique to knock the Burrbos from Stone Bridge. Continue collecting the Regional Coins as you round the corner toward another Big Chain Chomp and the Ancient Wall. Capture the Big Chain Chomp and use it to smash the Ancient Wall just as you did the earlier rocks.

Ancient Wall contains the first of many 8-bit levels that replicate the style and charm of the very first *Super Mario Bros.*, released in 1985. Enter the pixelated warp pipe on the left to enter the 8-bit level. Dash and jump over the Goombas in the level as you smash the blocks and scale the cliff.

Always leave a block or two intact so you can reach higher areas!

Forever Super Mario

Fans of the older *Mario* games may expect Mario to shrink in size when hit by a Goomba, but he won't. His three (or six) health segments still apply inside the 8-bit levels.

Don't break through the top of the level just yet! First make your way left toward the tall gray rock and jump to expose an invisible block. Leap from this over the stone wall and around the corner to find Power Moon #04. Continue the ascent to Fossil Falls Heights and a return to three dimensions.

Nearly every 8-bit level has a secret like this to find.

Moon Numbering Nomenclature

Throughout this guide, we number the Power Moons in accordance with their numbered entries within the game. Access the Power Moon lists via the map screen to check the numbering.

Use either Chain Chomp to smash the fossilized rocks blocking the path across the arch. If you're having trouble getting a clear shot, pull the left-hand Chain Chomp away from the stone wall until the one nearest the wall goes idle. Ricochet one into the other to smash the blocks.

Heart in the Rocks

Mario can regain some lost life by breaking open the rocks scattered around the arena. Most rocks contain a Heart. He can usually find two Hearts during a boss battle.

BOSS: MADAME BROODE

Just when you thought you've seen the last of Chain Chomps, Madame Broode has one as a pet. Her golden Chain Chompikins is on a lengthy leash and can yank against it in an attempt to bite Mario if he's in its path. Watch for the golden arrows on the ground and run to either side to escape its chomp.

Throw Cappy at Broode's Chain Chomp twice, once to knock its pink hat off, and then again to capture it. Madame Broode tries to keep it close, so you'll have to move quickly. Try to move Broode's Chain Chomp across the arena to wind up the chain so that you can release it back into her, as you did with the stone wall earlier.

Don't be tempted to collect the coins she drops after hitting her with the Chain Chomp.

She's going to wind her pet up and send it spinning after Mario. Keep your distance and run along the edge of the grassy hills to steer clear of it. Once it settles down, capture Broode's Chain Chomp and hit her again just as before. Land three hits with her pet to defeat Madame Broode for **Power Moon #2**.

Cappy and Mario immediately make their way to the airship in the rocks. Thanks to the four additional Power Moons Mario has earned, the Odyssey can be restored. The Odyssey has enough fuel to reach the Sand Kingdom—hurry after Bowser and Peach if you want, but there's lots still to do in Cascade Kingdom...

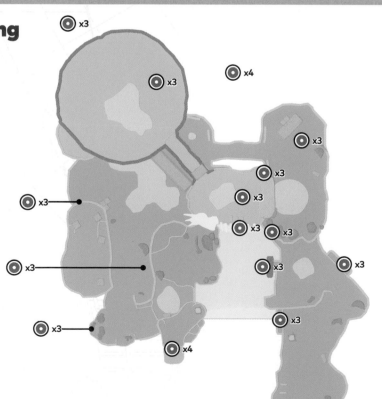

Extend Your Stay

Frequent Traveler Assistance

There is so much left to do at Cascade Kingdom—five Power Moons was only the beginning! Though you won't be able to uncover every Power Moon until Princess Peach has been rescued, there is much you can do before then. The choice is yours to either exit the Odyssey before traveling to Sand Kingdom or return after visiting other kingdoms. Either way, the "Extend Your Stay" section of each chapter is your guide to finding every coin and Power Moon in a region. The numbered entries and accompanying maps match the in-game list for easy reference.

◉ Souvenir Shopping

Cascade Kingdom contains 50 Regional Coins in the form of purple stone disks. All 50 purple coins can be found during your initial visit but Mario must depart Cascade Kingdom aboard the Odyssey and return later in order for the Crazy Cap shop to become available.

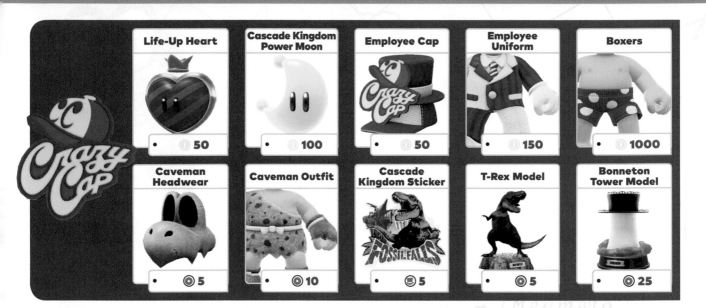

Life-Up Heart	Cascade Kingdom Power Moon	Employee Cap	Employee Uniform	Boxers
• ⓘ 50	• ⓘ 100	• ⓘ 50	• ⓘ 150	• ⓘ 1000

Caveman Headwear	Caveman Outfit	Cascade Kingdom Sticker	T-Rex Model	Bonneton Tower Model
• ◎ 5	• ◎ 10	• ☺ 5	• ◎ 5	• ◎ 25

Local Currency

The trickiest batch of Regional Coins to find in Cascade Kingdom are located high atop a cliff, behind the red door leading to Power Moons #16 and #17. Ride the second set of lifts to the very top and leap for the gray ledge. Follow this around the corner and out of the 8-bit level onto a ledge containing four more Regional Coins.

 Power Moons

There are 40 Power Moons at Cascade Kingdom. Power Moons #01, 02, and 04 were obtained while ridding Cascade Kingdom of its threat. Consult the prior pages for help.

Hints for Sale

Hint Toad is standing by in Waterfall Basin, ready to sell you a hint for 50 coins. Unlike Talkatoo, Hint Toad marks the location of a Power Moon on the in-game map. Hint Toad can provide hints for every Power Moon accessible during Mario's current visit. Some require a return trip later in his travels.

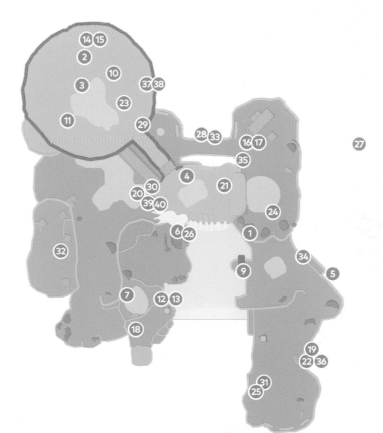

03 Chomp Through the Rocks

Make your way to the area where there are four Chain Chomps and capture the one furthest to the left when facing them. Pull back and release the Chain Chomp so that it smashes the small outcrop of fossilized rocks.

05 On Top of the Rubble

Located in Waterfall Basin, just steps across the plateau from Hint Toad, this is arguably the easiest Power Moon to find in the world. It's located on top of some rocks. Jump up and grab it.

06 Treasure of the Waterfall Basin

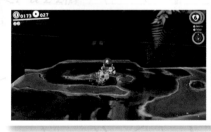

Dive beneath the water in Waterfall Basin and swim across the river to the west to find an alcove with a large treasure chest. These chests don't always contain Power Moons, but this one does.

07 Above a High Cliff

Cross the river to where the Odyssey was first powered-up and use the Chain Chomp to destroy the column of fossilized rock against the cliff. This reveals a pipe that leads straight to the top of the cliff where the Power Moon is and the Top of the Big Stump warp flag.

08 Across the Floating Isles

Return to where you fought the boss and locate the floating platforms hovering off the northwestern edge. Leap across to collect the purple coins and the Power Moon.

09 Cascade Kingdom Timer Challenge 1

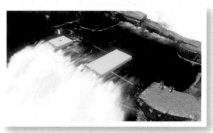

Throw Cappy onto the scarecrow near the waterfall to initiate a Timer Challenge. Make your way across the three platforms to reach the Power Moon on the other side of the river. While this may seem easy, Mario is without his trusty hat during Timer Challenges so some of his advanced jumping abilities are off-limits. There is enough time (10 seconds) to run between the platforms as they pull alongside one another, but only if you hurry. A faster, more challenging option is to perform the tackle jump.

10 Cascade Kingdom Timer Challenge 2

Return to the area where you fought the boss and throw Cappy on the scarecrow to initiate the second Timer Challenge. Triple Jump up the first three steps then turn and do it again to reach the Power Moon atop the sixth step. It's also possible to Ground Pound Jump to reach the third and sixth step.

11 Good Morning, Captain Toad!

Captain Toad is hanging out on a ledge directly below the strange silver cube. Return to the area where you fought the boss and leap over the edge toward the silver cube. Carefully fall onto the smaller ledge where Captain Toad is standing. Find Captain Toad in each kingdom to receive a Power Moon.

⑫ Dinosaur Nest: Big Cleanup!

Make your way to the Top of the Big Stump checkpoint (see Power Moon #07) and drop onto the ledge on the south with the red door. Use Cappy to enter the Dinosaur Nest. Capture the T-Rex inside the cave and use the mighty beast to eliminate the dozens of Burrbos scattered about the circular path. Dash and attack to squish them—the T-Rex can walk right over them without retribution. But be quick; Cappy can only capture the T-Rex for so long.

⑬ Dinosaur Nest: Running Wild!

Capture the T-Rex inside the Dinosaur Nest (see Power Moon #12 for location) and carefully step off the far edge of the plateau onto the ledge below. Smash the fossilized rocks on this ledge to uncover a Power Moon. Use the hat trampoline to return to the upper level and grab the Power Moon with the T-Rex.

⑭ Nice Shot with the Chain Chomp!

Make your way around the narrow cliff ledges to the left of the four Chain Chomps and enter the pipe (after powering up the Odyssey for the first time). To earn this Power Moon, you must ricochet Chain Chomps into one another so that one hits the center of a dish-shaped bullseye. One of the keys to doing this is to avoid distracting the Chain Chomp nearest the target. Stick to the foreground of the cave, capture the Chain Chomp nearest the grass, and line up your shot so that one Chain Chomp knocks into the other one like billiard balls.

Use the stone markings on the ground to help line up your shot. There are three targets to hit; a stone wall lowers after each successive shot.

1. Line up the first shot straight on with the coins and central stone marker.

2. Pull the Chain Chomp slightly left of center on the second shot so that it hits the other Chain Chomp on the right.

3. The third shot requires a double combo. Pull the Chain Chomp back so that it's lined up with the left-hand side of the fourth long stone marker.

⑮ Very Nice Shot with the Chain Chomp!

Follow the instructions for Power Moon #14, but don't use the exit pipe after grabbing the Power Moon. There's one more target to hit! Approach the foreground after hitting the third target and slip through the gap in the wall to a fourth chamber. This is the trickiest shot of all. Capture the Chain Chomp and line it up between the second and third stone markers on the ground. This hits the right-hand side of the second Chain Chomp, causing a double ricochet into the target.

⑯ Past the Chasm Lifts

Enter the red door on the cliff to the right of the Stone Bridge. Once inside, enter the pipe beyond the platforms to access the 8-bit level. Make your way across the

Here you can see both Power Moons hidden in this 8-bit level.

level to the second set of lifts. Cross the three platform lifts toward the Goomba on the lower platform. Enter the pipe to find the Power Moon.

17 Hidden Chasm Passage

Follow the instructions for Power Moon #16 and make your way across the first set of platform lifts. Carefully fall off the upper ledge and use Cappy to leap onto the ledge below. Enter the pipe to access a second small 8-bit area. Kick the Koopa Shell so that it smashes the block on the lower right. Walk through this hidden passage behind the second set of lifts, to reach the Power Moon. Exit via the upper pipe.

18 Secret Path to Fossil Falls!

The only way to reach the Power Moon hovering high above on Island in the Sky is via one of the trickiest warp paintings in the game. Provided you've been visiting the kingdoms in the order that matches this guide (choosing the upper option first at each branching path), you'll need to visit Snow Kingdom. Capture the Ty-Foo nearest the Odyssey and cross toward the northeast edge of the main cavern. Blow the wooden wall across the ice to the left then release the capture and climb up the painting on the ledge. Warp to Cascade Kingdom via the painting to get the Power Moon.

19 A Tourist in the Cascade Kingdom

Neither Hint Toad nor Talkatoo can help you with this one until you've already worked to solve it on your own (or with our help). There's a Tostarenan in the Sand Kingdom anxious to take a trip, not unlike Princess Peach's. Return to Sand Kingdom after defeating Bowser and speak to the Tostarenan near the taxi by the village. He'll comment that he's going to visit Metro Kingdom. Go to Metro Kingdom to visit him there (near the Scooter). He'll then comment that he wants to see a great waterfall. Return to Cascade Kingdom and speak to him near the Odyssey to receive this Power Moon.

20 Rolling Rock by the Falls

Return to Cascade Kingdom after sailing away on the Odyssey so that you can search the ground where the ancient airship had been. Throw Cappy at the two gray rocks on the ground there—one of them glows when hit. Continue hitting this rock as it emits colorful sparkles. It eventually crumbles, releasing a Power Moon.

21 Peach in the Cascade Kingdom

Once you've defeated Bowser, warp to Fossil Falls Heights and approach the upper edge of the falls to find Princess Peach and Tiara. Peach found a Power Moon while she was enjoying the view and gives it to Mario when he finds her.

22 Cascade Kingdom Regular Cup

Talk with the Koopa near the Odyssey to initiate the Freerunning Race. The course winds from Waterfall Basin up the slope near the Chain Chomps, across Stone Bridge, to the area near the Ancient Wall. The Regular Cup race isn't too difficult and you don't even have to take any shortcuts or make any advanced jumps. Triple jump, long jump, and roll your way toward Stone Bridge—don't fall off!—and leap over the colorful Burrbos on the bridge. Round the corner to victory! Check the section for Power Moon #36 for advanced tips.

㉓ Caveman Cave-Fan

Cross the arch at Fossil Falls Heights to where you fought Madame Broode and speak to the Bonneter near the edge. He traveled to Cascade Kingdom in hopes of spotting a caveman. Return to the Wardrobe on the Odyssey and change into the Caveman Outfit and Caveman Headwear (can be purchased from Crazy Cap after returning to Cascade Kingdom aboard the Odyssey). Return to the Bonneter dressed like a caveman to earn a Power Moon.

㉔ Shopping in Fossil Falls

The Crazy Cap store sets up shop in Waterfall Basin after Mario and Cappy depart aboard the Odyssey. Return at a later time and pay the store a visit. Purchase the Power Moon for 100 coins.

㉕ Sphynx Traveling to the Waterfall

Capture the Binoculars near the Odyssey and scan the skies above Cascade Kingdom for anything unusual. You might catch sight of a Bonneter airship or two, but there's more up there. The Sphynx from Sand Kingdom has his own balloon and can be spotted floating above this region. Zoom in with the Binoculars to earn a Power Moon.

👻 Moons from the Moon Rock

㉖ Bottom of the Waterfall Basin

Jump into the river in Waterfall Basin and swim beneath the narrow bridge that formed from the fallen spire. Hit the glowing spot beneath the rocks with a ground pound to release a hidden Power Moon.

㉗ Just a Hat, Skip, and a Jump

Cross Stone Bridge to the base of the Ancient Wall and locate the series of white top hats floating in the sky. This trail of cloud platforms leads to a Power Moon atop a small rock island. The cloud platforms aren't very large so you have to jump carefully. Use Cappy to activate the platforms and leap from one to the next with only the briefest of pauses in between. Grab the Power Moon and warp back to solid ground.

㉘ Treasure Under the Cliff

There's a Power Moon under the cliff, alongside the Stone Bridge. Activate the cloud platforms and leap from the higher of the two to pluck the Power Moon from the air. Somersault jumping or ground pound jumping into a dive is all it takes.

㉙ Next to the Stone Arch

Warp to Fossil Falls Heights and cross the arch toward where you fought the boss. There's a Power Moon just off the south side of the arch. Dangle from the rock edge and drop straight down to snag it out of the air.

30 Guarded by a Colossal Fossil

Warp to Fossil Falls Heights and climb onto the massive triceratops fossil jutting from the mountain. Carefully walk down onto the smaller, middle horn and note the glow emanating from the point. Throw and hold Cappy on the point of the horn so that it spins round and round, eventually releasing a Power Moon from the fossil's horn.

31 Under the Old Electrical Pole

As you may have discovered while playing with the Chain Chomps at Fossil Falls Heights, the electrical poles that have been erected can be knocked down. There might not be a Chain Chomp within striking range of the pole nearest the Odyssey, but the T-Rex is a plenty good substitute! Capture the T-Rex, guide him across the river toward the Odyssey and swat the electrical pole in Waterfall Basin to reveal a glowing spot containing a Power Moon.

32 Under the Ground

There's a Power Moon buried in the ground beneath the T-Rex's head. Capture the T-Rex and move it out of the way (this is a good time to use it to get Power Moon #31) then ground pound the glowing spot in the grass.

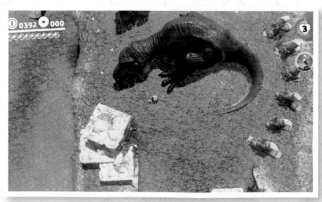

33 Inside the Busted Fossil

Warp to Fossil Falls Heights and capture the Chain Chomp nearest the warp flag. Wind the Chain Chomp up by pulling it away from the electrical pole, then adjust the aim so that it can hit the right-most fossil. Use the Chain Chomp to smash this fossil to reveal a Power Moon. It's not the easiest shot, and it may not even seem possible at first, but the Chain Chomp can reach the corner of the fossil. Aim to hit just left of the plant growing on the fossil.

34 Caught Hopping at the Waterfall!

Spot the rabbit hopping around the area between the Odyssey and Crazy Cap store. When chased, the rabbit loops around this area, but doesn't go very far. Throw Cappy at it to stun it so Mario can close on its position. Catch the rabbit to earn a Power Moon. If having trouble, try chasing it up the slope near the Burrbos so that it has to leap from the ledge. Jump down before it does and catch it as it falls.

35 Taking Notes: Hurry Upward

Make your way to the Ancient Wall and enter the 8-bit pipe. Jump through the treble clef to trigger the Taking Notes challenge. This one is straightforward with the only difficulty being added by the presence of Goombas. Dash as you move across the ledges and always dash before jumping to ensure Mario leaps with enough height and distance. Ensure you get each note before ascending to the next ledge, as there's no time to double-back.

36 Cascade Kingdom Master Cup

Long jump into a triple jump to scale the fossilized rocks near the start (watch the Golden Koopa to see where to begin the sequence) and hurry across the river via the bridge. It's possible to ground pound jump from the stone hat to reach the cliff, but you can still win if you take the long way around to the left. Roll while shaking the controller to hurry past the Chain Chomps then long jump past the Burrbos. The Golden Koopa finishes in approximately 42 seconds. Pull close to him near Stone Bridge and you'll win.

37 Across the Mysterious Clouds

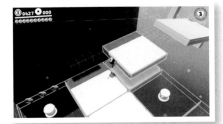

Enter the Moon Pipe near the flowers by Stone Bridge to access an area populated with dozens of cloud-like platforms that appear temporarily when hit with the cap (they can also be activated by jumping on them). The platforms begin to quiver before disappearing, providing you with a warning. Nevertheless, it's best to plan your moves from the safety of the red platforms, then cross the clouds without delay. The platforms appear instantly when the white top-hat activators are hit with Cappy, so it's possible to throw and land on a platform in a single jump. Time your jumps carefully and cross these well-spaced clouds to reach the Power Moon atop the red wall. Shake the controller as you toss Cappy to ensure it homes in on the platform activator. Cross the pendulums up ahead to the final cloud platform and the Power Moon beyond it.

38 Atop a Wall Among the Clouds

Follow instructions for Power Moon #37 and make your way across the nine-platform grid to the next pendulum. Activate the invisible block above the blocks beyond the pendulum and leap to the top of the red wall.

39 Across the Gusty Bridges

Enter the Moon Pipe located where Cappy first showed Mario the Odyssey. Pull the lever to lower the orange bridge, wait for the gusting wind to pause, then sprint across. Blue blocks are safe, only the orange ones are moved by the gusts. Wait for the orange block to move to the right, jump on, then line Mario up with the rings before the wind shifts. Use a homing throw to clear the Burrbos from the blocks ahead and carefully cross the orange bridge as it blows back and forth. Use the rings as your guide and avoid standing alongside the blue blocks when the wind changes. Time your jumps so Mario leaves his feet the moment the wind stops.

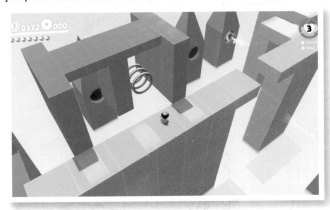

40 Flying Far Away from Gusty Bridges

Follow instructions for Power Moon #39 and make your way to the orange bridge with the gap, near the second lever. Stay clear of the wind, but throw Cappy into the gust so he can pull the out-of-reach lever on the side. This lowers a third section of bridge, leading to a side area. Cross the bridge and throw Cappy into the hat launcher just as the gusts begin. With proper timing, Cappy pulls the distant lever, releasing a Power Moon.

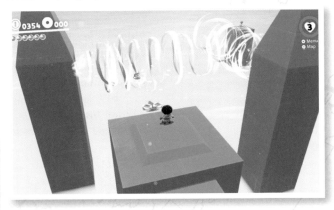

Welcome to Tostarena

REGION AT A GLANCE

Population	Middling
Size	Expansive
Locals	Tostarenans, Moe-Eyes
Currency	Pyramid-shaped
Industry	Tourism, precious stones
Temperature	Average 104°F

INDIGENOUS FLORA & FAUNA

MINI GOOMBA		BINOCULARS		GOOMBA	
Can Capture?	No	Can Capture?	Yes	Can Capture?	Yes

BULLET BILL		MOE-EYE		CHINCHO	
Can Capture?	Yes	Can Capture?	Yes	Can Capture?	No

WANDERING CACTUS		GLYDON		GOOMBETTE	
Can Capture?	Yes	Can Capture?	Yes	Can Capture?	No

JAXI		COIN COFFER	
Can Capture?	No	Can Capture?	Yes

Moe-Eyes Love Their Shades

They'll run if chased, but they're a proud people who have long inhabited these ruins. Please be polite.

#7: Ruins Round Tower

#6: Ruins Sand Pillar

#8: Jaxi Ruins

C

#10: Northwest Reaches

D A

#9: Moe-Eye Habitat

B

#3: Desert Oasis

#4: Southwestern Floating Island

E

#5: Tostarena Ruins Entr.

#2: Tostarena Town

#1: The Odyssey

TOSTARENAN TOURISM

Tostarena is a small town that serves as the hub for tourists planning to visit the Inverted Pyramid. The colorful buildings and cheerful people provide a warm welcome for visitors. They're happy to provide direction, so don't hesitate to say hello.

MYSTERIOUS ANCIENT RUINS

Head north from town and you are greeted by ancient ruins that dot the expansive desert. Though many have become conflict regions patrolled by Bullet Bills, their status as important heritage sites is undeniable.

Your eye is drawn to the large stone tower at the heart of the ruins. Due to extensive hollowing underground, quicksand has become prevalent in this area, so watch out.

THREE KEYS TO THE KINGDOM

1. Enjoy the small but lively desert village and its charming inhabitants.

2. Wonder at the Inverted Pyramid and its upside-down magic.

3. Watch for the gem iconography carved in relief on the ruins.

INVERTED PYRAMID

The true "can't miss" of this region, the Inverted Pyramid may look unstable, but rest assured it never topples and has thrilled tourists for years. It is said that the legendary artifact called the Binding Band lies within, and the upside-down pyramid symbolizes how those joined by it will never part, even if the world turns upside down.

JAXI

Just hop on the back of a curious local transport method known as the Jaxi, and as you might guess from their appearance you'll be in for a wild but completely reliable ride.

Make good use of them and you'll be exploring this unforgiving desert in comfort and style.

LIVING HEART OF THE DESERT

Here's a spot to moisten your dried and withered heart, with greenery and water to make you forget you're in the desert. The fish and birds are plentiful and well worth a visit.

Ⓐ Atop the Highest Tower

The Odyssey has touched down in the surprisingly frigid Sand Kingdom, home of the maracas-shaking Tostarenans. Talk to the shivering locals as you proceed north through Tostarena Town toward the ruins. Cappy points out Bowser's enormous footprints in the sand—he must have been here recently!

Ascend the stairs to the Tostarena Ruins Entrance, flinging Cappy at the Mini Goombas lurking about. Shake the controller to perform homing throws to not only ensure a direct hit, but also get the hat back in Mario's hands sooner. Perform a throw and hold against the ? Block to earn a quick ten coins, then continue right toward the Bullet Bill.

The safest way to deal with Bullet Bills is by capturing them. Fly the Bullet Bill through the rings to the east, release the capture, and leap onto one of the nearby platforms or blocks to avoid the Bullet

Bill approaching from the left. Ignore the Power Moons in the area for now—hit the flower to the right of the Bullet Bill launcher with your cap and bounce to the Tostarena Ruins Sand Pillar flag.

Leap across the sand geysers through the rings to the 8-bit level you see on the wall ahead. Enter the pipe and set to breaking the blocks down low. The double-stack of Bullet Bill launchers fires in both directions.

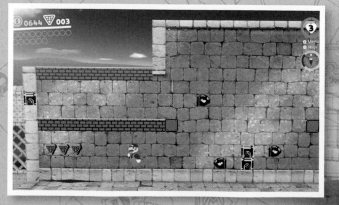

Crouch whenever a Bullet Bill is headed for Mario's head. Gather up the coins and the three Regional Coins from the far left, then break through the blocks to continue ascending the ruins.

Exit the 8-bit level and round the corner near the Bullet Bill to find three crates, one of which contains Binoculars and another that contains Power Moon #12. Smash the crate with the cap, a ground pound, or with a Bullet Bill, then capture a Bullet Bill and fly across the ruins to where the Power Moon lands.

The rainbow-colored glow is your clue that a Power Moon is nearby!

Ride the Bullet Bill back across the gap, to the stairs near the moving platforms. Ascend the stairs to the circular tower wrapped in another 8-bit level. Enter the pipe on the far side and begin zigzagging your way up the tower. This 8-bit level is a bit trickier than the last, as there are many more Bullet Bills inside the level—and unlike present-day Mario, 8-bit Mario's only recourse it to either crouch beneath them or bounce on top of them. Board the sliding platform and crouch to avoid the three Bullet Bills coming from the right.

There are two essential ingredients to a fulfilling 8-bit experience: patience and speed. Wait in a safe place before changing direction or leaping to a higher level where new threats may exist. Study their patterns, then act. Then, add speed. Make use of Mario's ability to dash to ensure he has the speed and height needed to safely jump to each new platform.

Exit the 8-bit level atop the Tostarena Ruins Round Tower and collect **Power Moon #01** to complete the objective. Mario needs sixteen Power Moons to fuel the Odyssey for his next journey, so there's much still to do.

Ⓑ Moon Shards in the Sand

Not all of Sand Kingdom is connected; bottomless canyons have split the region into a series of islands connected by floating platforms. One of these islands is home to the Moe-Eye. Board the platform atop the Round Tower and throw Cappy at the hat launchers to collect the coins. Sidestep the first pair of stone blocks then throw Cappy at the hat launcher to hit the black and yellow pulse beam beyond it. This triggers a concussive blast that radiates outward, smashing the rocks in Mario's path. Leap over the radiating rings, else Mario takes damage and is stunned.

Hit the second explosive pule beam to clear the left-hand platform, then leap onto it to get the purple coins.

Ride either of the two platforms down then leap to the northernmost one to continue. Throw Cappy at the hat launcher to trigger another explosive ring from the next pulse beam. This sets off a chain reaction with other pulse beams. Leap over each incoming blast and continue along the platform as it descends to Moe-Eye Habitat.

Moe-Eye use their special sunglasses to see things that are otherwise invisible. They move very slowly when utilizing their special sunglasses, but that changes when their shades are on their foreheads. Moe-Eye can run with surprising speed when not searching for invisible terrain.

Capture the nearby Moe-Eye before it runs away (they're very shy) and grab the first Moon Shard next to him. Notice the glow on the platform to the right—the only way to unlock its Power Moon and activate the platform is by finding five Moon Shards. Here's where they are:

1. **The first one is a freebie; it's right next to the Moe-Eye near the platform you descend upon.**

2. **Head left from the first Moon Shard toward the one floating above the poison pool. Capture the Moe-Eye and walk across the otherwise invisible platform to get it.**

3. **There's a Moon Shard sitting atop the sand dune in the northwest corner of this area.**

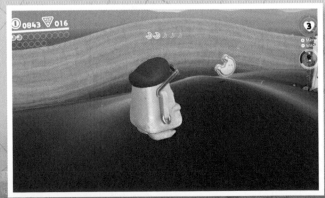

4. **As a Moe-Eye, ride the lift alongside the northwestern column to the top and use its sunglasses ability to navigate the otherwise invisible path to the fourth Moon Shard.**

5. **Release the Moe-Eye and run to the southeast corner of the area to find the final Moon Shard between two cactuses**

Grab Power Moon #02 that appears and ride the newly-activated platform north across the canyon. The Inverted Pyramid has been opened and Bowser's ship hovers above. Get there right away, Mario!

Showdown on © the Inverted Pyramid

The Tostarenans believe Bowser came to steal their Binding Band and one look with the Binoculars suggests they're right—look at the size of that ring! Roll across the desert toward the Inverted Pyramid and head inside. Capture a Bullet Bill and ride across the gap to the 8-bit level in the distance.

This particular 8-bit level has bi-directional gravity. The red and green pyramids adorning the wall indicate which way gravity is pulling. Mario will be right-side up in the green area, but upside-down, walking on the ceiling, when in the red area. Leap from the blocks near the pipe to the ledge on the left to reach the red area and cross the level to the right, upside-down.

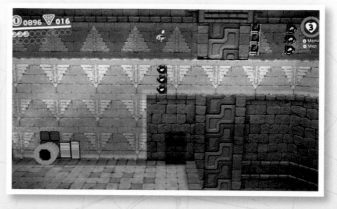

The green pit up ahead is effectively bottomless. Keep to the left until the Bullet Bills pass then leap to the ceiling, get the coins from the ? Block and crouch beneath the Bullet Bills. Leap to the inverted warp pipe on the ceiling to transition to the exterior of the Inverted Pyramid.

Make your way past the stream of upside-down Goombas outside the pyramid and note the crack in the wall beyond the warp pipe on the ceiling. Leap through this crack to find a hidden area containing numerous coins and Power Moon #10. Return the way you came and enter the upside-down warp pipe.

Leap through the crack on the right to find this hidden Power Moon outside the Inverted Pyramid.

Leap out of the 8-bit level and capture one of the Bullet Bills and steer it into the breakable blocks nearby. Pilot another Bullet Bill into the lone stone on the other side of this room to gain a Life-Up Heart. Capture a third Bullet Bill and pilot it across the gap on the far side of the room to the flowers in the distance. Bounce your way to the upper level and ascend the stairs to the very top of the Inverted Pyramid.

BOSS: HARIET

Hariet is one of the members of the Broodal Party and, like the others, she's going to use her hat to attack. But that's not the only trick up her bonnet! She begins the fight by flicking spiked cannonballs at Mario. Dodge away from them and, if possible, use Cappy to knock one back at her. The bombs ignite the ground when they explode, creating an additional hazard so steer clear.

The safest thing to do is to keep to the other side of the arena from Hariet, dodge the two bombs she hurls, then watch for her ponytail attack. Hariet twirls another bomb around by her hair, then slams it at Mario. Use Cappy to hit the bomb attached to her hair to send her spinning. The bomb explodes, knocking her hat from her. This is your chance! Leap up and bounce off her head. It needn't be a ground pound, but that works just as well!

Once hit, Hariet dons her hat and flies around the arena, dropping rows of bombs. She flies a square-shaped pattern, dropping three bombs along each stretch. Avoid the bombs—and their resulting fires—and wait for her to regroup.

Move to the far side of the arena and bait her into throwing another bomb at Mario, then jump back and hit it with Cappy. This is a great way to shortcut the fight. You needn't wait for her to unleash her ponytail bomb attack if you hit her with one of the two loose bombs she throws. Hit her with Cappy to stun her (so she doesn't run away) then bounce off her head.

Hariet again flies across the arena in her hat, dropping bombs. But this time she zigzags back and forth, making it slightly more challenging to avoid her attack. Avoid the first row of bombs then circle back and forth in semi-circle paths beyond her reach. Wait for her to settle down and begin tossing bombs again, then hit a bomb with Cappy and leap atop her head for a third and final time to collect Power Moon #03.

Ⓓ The Hole in the Desert

Defeating the Broodal didn't help the local climate. In fact, quite the opposite! The Inverted Pyramid floated into the air, revealing a massive hole leading to a frozen underground cave—that's where the cold air is coming from! Mario must descend into the frosty abyss beneath the sand and set things right.

Stop at the Crazy Cap store in Tostarena Town and purchase the Sand Kingdom Power Moon for 100 coins (Power Moon #42). Gather up the Regional Coins near town, then capture the Spark Pylon to ride the electrical lines toward the ruins. Release the capture above the arch to snag Power Moon #11.

Warp back to Tostarena Town from atop the arch and talk to Jaxi, the lion-esque taxi service in Sand Kingdom. Jaxi can be ridden anywhere you want to go in Sand Kingdom, and he's especially important for use at night when the desert is overrun by Chinchos. Not only can Jaxi run straight through enemies and cacti, but he can even cross poisonous lagoons of purple goop. Run Jaxi straight toward the beacon of light emanating from the hole beneath the Inverted Pyramid and dive right in.

Hail a Jaxi

Jaxi costs just 30 coins to ride and can be called anywhere you see one of the purple and teal signposts next to a park bench. Jaxi has but one speed: ludicrous! Fortunately, you can steer and brake to help guide him. There's no better way to get around the desert than with a Jaxi. Jaxi comes in handy later during your quest for the many Power Moons in Sand Kingdom.

The hole beneath the Inverted Pyramid leads to the Underground Temple, an icy maze filled with Goombas and Bullet Bills. Toss Cappy at the hat launcher to hit the pulse beam beyond it. This one and the one after it are needed to break the stone blocks at the base of the two towers before the first Goomba.

Goombas on Ice

Goombas have exceptional traction on ice. Even if you don't need to use a Goomba, it's worth capturing one to eliminate the risk of slipping.

Toss Cappy at the hat launcher near the Goomba to have it set off a chain reaction as Cappy collects the coins. Capture the Goomba and leap over the pulse beam's radiating burst of energy. Shake the controller to make the Goomba high jump onto the stone ledge. Release the Goomba and quickly capture the stack of ten Goombas further on. The radiating blast might knock this Goomba stack from ten to eight. If so, hurry back along the ice and capture the two Goombas you passed earlier on.

Goombas respawn after a brief period. Keep your Goomba tower at nine or ten.

Release the Goomba capture near the platform with the blocks, capture the three Goombas and leap back onto the Goomba tower to cross the ice as a tower of eleven (twelve is too many for the nearby ? Blocks). Continue along the ice to reach Power Moon #48 and the purple coins beyond it. Ride the moving platforms to the next tower, snag the Life-Up Heart from the right-hand torch and approach the edge.

Stand off to the edge to lure the Bullet Bill around the pulse beam and capture it. Don't just head for the ice right away! First fly it around the stone column on the right, to where the hat trampolines are. Bounce to the top of the pile of gold atop the column, then run along the narrow wall, hit the invisible bricks at the end, and leap atop the next tower to get Power Moon #47 from the treasure chest. Dive jump down to the platform beyond the moving columns and go through the door to the Deepest Underground.

The stone plinth up ahead once housed the Binding Ring, but it's no longer here thanks to Bowser. Capture a Bullet Bill and ride it across the gap to the platform up ahead where the guardian of the Binding Ring awaits—and he's none too happy about the missing ring!

BOSS: KNUCKLOTEC

Knucklotec enters the arena with a thud, causing icicles to crash down from the ceiling, some of which contain Hearts. Pay attention to where they are, as you may need them!

Knucklotec has two disembodied fists that fly across the arena at Mario in an effort to squash him. Watch the shadow from the flying fist, dodge out of the way when the shadow stops (try to lure it over ice patches) then capture it while the hand is stunned on the ground.

Capture Knucklotec's fist and pilot it like a large Bullet Bill back at Knucklotec in an attempt to punch it in the face with his own hand. Of course, Knucklotec isn't going to allow Mario to do this without mounting a defense. Its other hand fires a steady stream of ice blocks at Mario. Steer the fist around the ice while accelerating.

Knucklotec fires its two fists across the arena like massive snow plows. Run perpendicular to their approach and long jump to get out of the way. They then slam the ground as they did upon his entry to the arena, causing another avalanche of icicles to crash down from the ceiling. Stay clear of the shadows as you evade the falling icicles.

Now it's time to repeat the process again. Knucklotec's free hand shifts back and forth in an effort to protect its face each time you capture a fist. Aim for the face, wait for the hand to shift in front of it briefly, then shake the controller for maximum speed as the hand moves aside and punch it in the face.

After being hit a second time, Knucklotec tries to crush Mario between two open palms. Linger between the hands as they vibrate, then back somersault or long jump out of the way, before getting crushed. Remember that the only way to stun one of the hands long enough to capture it is to bait it into slamming down atop one of the ice patches. Defeat Knucklotec to gain **Power Moon #04**, another multi moon.

Ⓔ Collect More Power Moons!

Mario rid the Sand Kingdom of its winter's bite, but if you've been following along closely, you still need two additional Power Moons before the Odyssey can depart. There are several Power Moons in Tostarena Town that can be found quickly.

Use your hat to throw, and line 'em up in a row

Enter the Slots room near the fountain in Tostarena and pay the attendant 10 coins. Stand a few tiles back from the images and study the pattern. Mario must hit three moons with his hat to get the Power Moon. Throw Cappy straight ahead as soon as the normal heart appears. The timing should work that Mario hits the moon. Match three moons to earn Power Moon #44.

The next easiest Power Moon to get is atop the bell tower, near the Tostarenan dancing to the boombox atop the purple roof. Leap up to the highest point in town to earn Power Moon #05.

Fork in the Road!

Cappy alerts Mario to two locations they can visit next: Lake Kingdom and Wooded Kingdom. You're free to decide, but this guide is written to always visit the location listed first in the list. This becomes important later when you are searching for the Painting Portals that connect kingdoms. The instructions we describe in subsequent chapters may vary from your own experience if, for example, you visit Wooded Kingdom before Lake Kingdom.

Extend Your Stay

Sand Kingdom boasts the most Power Moons of any kingdom Mario visits on his journey, and it's also the first of the ones he encounters that contains 100 Regional Coins. Though you can't access every Power Moon on your first visit, there's tons to see and explore.

Souvenir Shopping

Sand Kingdom contains 100 Regional Coins. All 100 coins can be found during your initial visit.

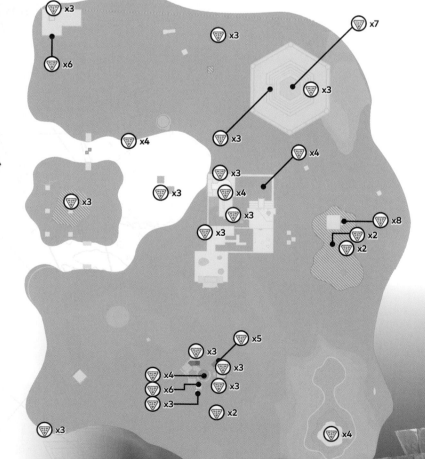

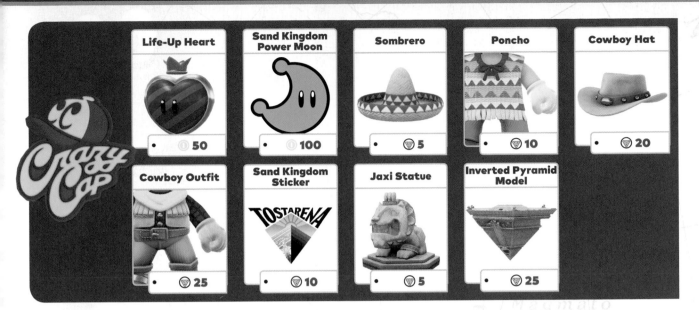

Life-Up Heart	**Sand Kingdom Power Moon**	**Sombrero**	**Poncho**	**Cowboy Hat**
50	100	5	10	20
Cowboy Outfit	**Sand Kingdom Sticker**	**Jaxi Statue**	**Inverted Pyramid Model**	
25	10	5	25	

Local Currency

Five of the purple coins reside in the Strange Neighborhood area, accessible via the rocket in Tostarena Town (see Power Moon #60 and #61). There are two purple coins to the right of the ? Block beyond the two Goombas. Use a backflip or ground pound jump to reach them. The next three are on the back side of the rotating building just after the three Goombas. Leap for the building once the yellow side is down. Mario gets Cappy back as soon as he reaches the Power Moon—you may want to collect the Regional Coins with Cappy before riding the rocket back to Tostarena.

Don't miss out on the four Regional Coins inside the circular tower's 8-bit mural at the ruins. Drop into the gap just before passing the entry pipe to uncover this hidden alcove.

Enter the Bullet Bill Maze in Tostarena Northwest Reaches and ride a Bullet Bill into the narrow right-hand room at the first split in the path. There are six Regional Coins located here.

Three purple coins exist inside the 8-bit level within the Inverted Pyramid. Reenter from the exterior mural and activate the invisible blocks above the Bullet Bill launcher on the left. Ascend to the ceiling to get these three Regional Coins.

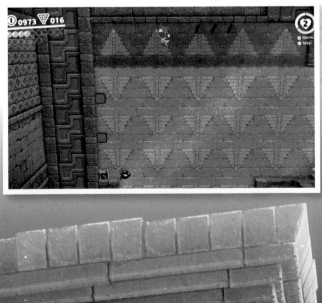

🌙 Power Moons

There is a grand total of 89 Power Moons at Sand Kingdom (69 until after Bowser is defeated). **Power Moons #01, 02, 03, 04, 05, 10, 11, 12, 42, 44, 47,** and **48** were obtained while removing the chill from Sand Kingdom and powering up the Odyssey. Consult the prior pages for help.

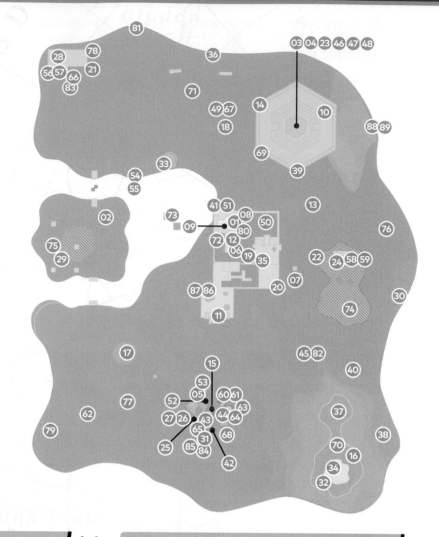

06 Alcove in the Ruins

Drop into the sand near the three sand geysers (or descend the stairs) and round the corner at the base of the ramp

of spilling sand. There's a narrow alcove in the base of the ruins, beneath the 8-bit level, with a Power Moon.

07 On the Leaning Pillar

You'll probably spot this Power Moon early in your wandering, but it can be tricky to get if you're down in the desert sands.

Instead, head up to the ruins and capture one of the Bullet Bills that are fired nearest the leaning pillar. Guide the Bullet Bill right into the Power Moon to grab it.

08 Hidden Room in the Flowing Sands

Return to the Tostarena Ruins and make your way across the flowing sand to the right of the three sand geysers. Locate the slight gap in the wall, at sand level, directly below the round tower. There is a hidden room inside there containing a Power Moon, but the only way to get it is by allowing Mario to sink into the sand. Once fully submerged, have Mario jump continuously to keep from being pulled down any further. Move under the wall to access the hidden room.

09 Secret of the Mural

Return to the Tostarena Ruins Round Tower and enter the 8-bit mural via the pipe. Ascend the tower via the 8-bit level to where the two sliding platforms are, but don't leap out of the puzzle. Instead, slip through the crack in the exterior directly below the Glydon and warp flag to uncover this secret room hidden within the tower's exterior.

13 On the Lone Pillar

Warp to the top of the round tower and capture the Glydon there. True to its name, the Glydon can glide over great distances. It can't gain altitude, but it's possible to extend its flight by following the on-screen controls and tilting up with the controls. Land Glydon on the lone pillar north of the wastes to gain a Power Moon.

14 On the Statue's Tail

Make your way to the top of the floating Inverted Pyramid and approach the Jaxi statue in the northwest corner of the six-sided structure. Throw Cappy at the glowing tail and hold the throw so Cappy continues to spin until a Power Moon is released.

15 Hang Your Hat on the Fountain

Once the fountain has thawed in Tostarena Town, leap from the middle and throw Cappy at the water spout on top. Hold the throw to make Cappy spin round and round until the Power Moon emerges.

16 Where the Birds Gather

Flocks of migrating birds can be found in many of the kingdoms Mario visits and one such flock has gathered in the Desert Oasis. The birds fly away as Mario approaches, but there's a reason for them to congregate in that spot. Do you feel that? There's a rumble. Tiptoe into position where the vibrations are strongest and ground pound to earn a Power Moon. This one is atop the small mound where the yellow birds are.

17 Top of a Dune

Climb to the top of the tallest dune southwest of Tostarena Town and feel for the rumble in the controller. Ground pound where the vibrations are strongest to unearth this Power Moon.

18 Lost in the Luggage

Ground pound the glowing area in the sand where the cardboard boxes and car tire are located. This spot is a bit easier to spot after the ice has melted and the human traveler and his car are gone.

19 Bullet Bill Breakthrough

Capture a Bullet Bill in the ruins, just below the Goombette and fly it through the hole in the stone lattice. Accelerate straight into the cage on the column behind the lattice to break the Power Moon free.

20 Inside a Block Is a Hard Place

Warp to the Tostarena Ruins Sand Pillar and drop off the ledge toward the Bullet Bills south of the flag. Note the glow emanating

from the stone block in the southeast corner of the ruins. Capture a Bullet Bill and guide it around the other obstacles toward this block.

21 Bird Traveling the Desert

There are two special birds flying throughout the Sand Kingdom, distinguishable by their golden glow and predictable, steady pattern.

This one does a lengthy loop around the southern part of the region, soaring past Tostarena Town and Desert Oasis. Hit it with Cappy to earn a Power Moon. Consider waiting atop the rooftop cactus in Tostarena Village, a palm in Desert Oasis, or even just atop a sand dune along its path. Ground pound jump and toss the hat to hit it.

22 Bird Traveling the Wastes

Locate the bird circling the wastes in the northeast part of the Sand Kingdom. Wait for it to circle past then leap up

and hit it with Cappy. Unlike the other bird, this one travels at a rather low altitude, so Mario needn't leap from any tall objects to hit it.

23 The Lurker Under the Stone

Ride the electrical wire to the top of the Inverted Pyramid (or use the slingshot) and note the moving bump in the top surface. There's

a Power Moon under the stones, and it's behaving just like one of the rabbits. Chase down the bump by cutting off its escape and stunning it with a hat toss.

Ground pound it while it's stunned to get the Power Moon. Tackle jumps can be used to close on its position, but it often dives deeper beneath the stone and resurfaces someplace else whenever Mario leaves his feet.

24 The Treasure of Jaxi Ruins

Navigate the frozen pillars of the Ice Cave (Power Moon #50) to exit a pipe atop Jaxi Ruins in the wastes. Open the left-hand

Treasure Chest with Cappy to obtain a Power Moon.

25 Desert Gardening: Plaza Seed

Locate the three pots west of the fountain in Tostarena Town and pick up the seed lying on the ground. Toss it into one of the

pots and come back periodically to check on its growth. The plant eventually sprouts a golden, glowing fruit. Hit it with Cappy to release a Power Moon.

26 Desert Gardening: Ruins Seed

This particular seed is located in an alcove on the eastern side of the ruins, near the leaning pillar (Power Moon #07). Grab the

seed and carry it back to the three pots on the south side of Tostarena Town. Toss the seed in and wait for it to sprout a golden fruit. Hit the fruit with Cappy to collect a Power Moon.

27 Desert Gardening: Seed on the Cliff

This is the trickiest of the three seeds to find. It's located on an obscure ledge on the southwest edge of the Sand

Kingdom. You need to make your way to the edge of the desert, across the canyon southwest of Moe-Eye Habitat. Drop onto the ledge, grab the seed, and round the corner to the hat trampoline.

Set the seed down, hit the flower with Cappy, then grab the seed and bounce back up. Plant the seed in a pot in Tostarena Town (west of the fountain) and check back regularly. Hit the golden fruit with Cappy to get a Power Moon.

28 Sand Kingdom Timer Challenge 1

This challenge exists atop the ruins at Tostarena Northwest Reaches. Complete the Bullet Bill Maze (Power Moon #56) to reach it or ride the electrical wires down from the Inverted Pyramid. Toss Cappy at the scarecrow then turn and leap onto the yellow block. Roll along the bottom of the obstacle then wall jump back and forth to the top. Triple jump to reach the Power Moon before time expires.

29 Sand Kingdom Timer Challenge 2

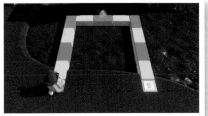

Capture a Moe-Eye and step on the P-Switch in the southwest corner of Moe-Eye Habitat. A short U-shaped path appears briefly leading to a key. Use the Moe-Eye's shades to line up with the path, then run to the key across the invisible blocks. Use the shades for safety, then sprint to the Power Moon before the timer expires. Toggle the sunglasses on and off so the Moe-Eye can move faster.

30 Sand Kingdom Timer Challenge 3

This is the first of the difficult Timer Challenges that you face and it's important to get off to a fast start. Somersault down the hill toward the platforms to build speed and run and leap across the first two gaps to reach the second yellow platform. Keep a straight line and tackle jump across the last three gaps as the platforms begin to disappear to reach the Power Moon on the other side of the poison waste.

31 Found in the Sand! Good Dog!

Approach the dog on the south side of Tostarena Town and follow it into the desert. Watch the dog begin to dig, then ground pound the area once the sand begins to glow.

Mario encounters other dogs in his travels, but they don't all home in on the Power Moon so quickly.

32 Taking Notes: Jump on the Palm

Climb the palm tree in the south end of the Desert Oasis area and grab the Treble Clef to initiate the Taking Notes challenge. Jump from palm frond to frond to collect the six notes atop the two palm trees. Aim for the widest part of each palm frond to avoid falling from the tree.

33 Herding Sheep in the Dunes

Circle around the ruins in a counter-clockwise direction to the north side. There, across the chasm, is a small circular pen with

a Tostarenan shepherd bemoaning the loss of his three sheep. The sheep haven't gone far, but he needs your help to return them. The sheep are strolling the nearby dunes (and by the lost luggage from the stranded traveler). Toss Cappy at the sheep to buck them in the desired direction and chase after them to herd them back into the corral. Return all three sheep to the pen to receive a Power Moon.

34 Fishing in the Oasis

Capture Lakitu in the Desert Oasis area to go fishing. Scan the bottom of the lake for the shadows of fish and lower the fishing line in front of them. The smaller shadows are Cheep Cheeps that yield a Heart or coins when caught, but the biggest shadow belongs to a Cheep Cheep carrying a Power Moon. Tug the rod once the fish has been caught to reel in your prize. Only the Cheep Cheep with the Power Moon puts up a fight. Feel for the vibrations, then set your hook!

Fishing Tips

Drop the bait into the sand away from the shadows then position the hook in front of the shadows by using the green bobber as a guide. This way you can sneak the hook in front of the fish without scaring them. Be patient and feel for the rumble—that's how you know they're biting!

35 Love in the Heart of the Oasis

Warp to Tostarena Ruins Sand Pillar to find the Goombette in Sand Kingdom. Goombette flees in a flash at the sight of Mario—it's a Goomba's attention she seeks. Capture one of the nearby Goombas (you'll have to hit their hat off before they can be captured) and make your way across the moving platform while dodging the Bullet Bills. Release the capture near the hat trampoline, quickly hit the flower with Cappy to open it, then re-capture the Goomba. Bounce to the higher ledge and greet the Goombette as a Goomba to earn the Power Moon.

36 Among the Five Cactuses

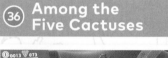

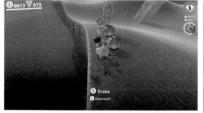

Ride a Jaxi from Tostarena Northwest Reaches east along the northern edge of Sand Kingdom until you find five cactuses in a row. Speed Jaxi through the cactuses while angling away from the canyon. The tall cactus in the middle contains a Power Moon inside it. The only way to get it is by knocking it onto the sand where it can crumble—if you knock it into the canyon, you'll have no hope of getting it. If this happens, leave the area and return so the cactus can respawn.

37 You're Quite a Catch, Captain Toad!

Capture Lakitu at Desert Oasis and float him up the hill to the north end of the oasis. They're easy to miss, but look for the shadows of several fish swimming through the sand near the cactus. The larger of them is none other than Captain Toad! Reel him in to be rewarded with a Power Moon.

38 Jaxi Reunion!

Hop aboard Jaxi and ride him across the desert to the area just northeast of Desert Oasis. There you'll find a Jaxi statue and an empty platform facing it. Ride Jaxi up onto the empty pedestal so he can see one of his family members (Jaxi used to be a statue too). He'll give Mario a Power Moon as a token of his appreciation.

39 Welcome Back, Jaxi!

Ride the electrical wire to the top of the Inverted Pyramid and locate the empty plinth, where the Jaxi Statue has gone missing. Use the nearby Jaxi Stand to call for a Jaxi and carefully ride it up the pile of sand and onto the empty pedestal. Jaxi doesn't want to go back to his life as a statue, but he appreciates the gesture.

40 Wandering Cactus

North of Desert Oasis is a tall cactus with a green button atop it. Capture this cactus and walk it several steps out of the way to uncover a glowing hole in the desert. Ground pound this small hole to unearth a Power Moon.

41 Sand Quiz: Wonderful!

Answer the Sphynx's first question (Power Moon #51) to have it slide to the right.

Now stand in front of the Sphynx and answer four more trivia questions. There's really no penalty for answering incorrectly, as you can continue guessing until you get it right. But to save you time, here are the correct answers: 30, Ice, 5, and Sphynx.

(43) Employees Only

Locate the broken grate on the west side of the gray building in Tostarena Town and crouch down to enter it. Collect the three coins and continue walking to the right, through an unseen passage, to access the area behind the counter inside the Crazy Cap store. Grab the Power Moon and leave the way you entered.

(45) Walking the Desert!

Talk to the Koopa northwest of the Desert Oasis to initiate the first Trace Walking Challenge. Study the arrows that briefly appear, noting their relation to items in the landscape, then start walking. There's no hurry, your only job is to try and walk the exact path of the arrows. You should be able to follow the arrows to the first cactus before they completely disappear. Keep the tall cactus on your left and try to maintain the same curvature of your walking path. Aim for the three small shrubs, keeping them on your right, and circle back to Koopa, aiming to pass just to the right of the lone shrub near the end. Score above 80 points to win a Power Moon.

(46) Hidden Room in the Inverted Pyramid

This Power Moon lies off the beaten path on the way through the Inverted Pyramid en route to the battle with Hariet. Complete the interior and exterior 8-bit levels, leap out of the puzzle and capture one of the Bullet Bills. Guide the Bullet Bill across the chasm toward the moving pillars atop the lattice wall.

Carefully pilot the Bullet Bill into the gap where the pillars disappear on the left. Another option is to return via the top of the Inverted Pyramid and use the hat trampoline to hover over to the pillars without a Bullet Bill. Either way, Mario slides down a ramp into a hidden treasure room containing a Power Moon and 185 coins.

(49) Under the Mummy's Curse

Return to the Deepest Underground, where you fought Knucklotec, via the small hole in the desert near the Inverted Pyramid (two Tostarenans stand nearby). Dozens of Chinchos appear from all directions, but they're not alone. There's also a Coin Coffer to the left of the slingshot. Capture it and take off running to gain thirty free coins, then turn and fire coins at the Chinchos. Be careful not to burn through your entire purse. Consider allowing the Chinchos to surround you then shake the controller to scatter coins in all directions. Defeat the Chinchos for a Power Moon.

(50) Ice Cave Treasure

Drop into the whirlpool of sinking sand in the northeast corner of the ruins to enter the ice cave. The ice is extremely slippery so move only a few steps at a time. Collect the purple coins and use the hat trampoline to reach the ledge above. Jump through the rings and continue along the upper ice walkway to the series of rising and falling pillars. Wait for the pillars to start to rise then wall jump back and forth to the top of the upper row of pillars. The upper ones are stationary. Collect the Power Moon and exit the cave via the pipe to access the top of Jaxi Ruins in the center of the wastes. This is one of the very few interior areas that only contains a single Power Moon.

A Pile of Coins

Make your way to the top of the pillars in the ice cave and look opposite the Power Moon to spot a massive pile of 125 coins. It's not easy to reach, but a well-thrown cap toss into a dive jump can get Mario to the treasure. It's important that Mario be lined up with the corner of the pillar so that he can reach the nearest edge of the distant pillar.

51 Sphynx's Treasure Vault

Circle around to the northwest corner of the ruins and stand on the stone platform in front of the Sphynx statue. The Sphynx poses a question to Mario (not necessarily a riddle). The answer is quite easy: Ring. Answer correctly to have the Sphynx move aside, granting you access to the Treasure Vault containing a Power Moon and wealth of coins.

52 A Rumble from the Sandy Floor

Descend through the warp pipe atop the roof near Talkatoo in Tostarena Town to enter a small room with a single Tostarenan. There's a Power Moon buried beneath the floor somewhere in this room and the only way to find it is by feeling for it. Ground pound the area where the vibrations are strongest—or just look at the accompanying screenshot.

53 Dancing with New Friends

Purchase the Sombrero and Poncho from Crazy Cap using the local Regional Coins and wear this new outfit to the Tostarenan guarding the door in the northwest corner of town.

He lets Mario into a private club where the crowd wants Mario to dance. Take the stage and watch as Mario unveils his guitar talents for the crowd. He earns a Power Moon at the end of the song.

54 The Invisible Maze

The entrance to this area is on a ledge in the canyon north of Moe-Eye Habitat, east of the sliding platform. Descend the chimney-like gap in the edge of the canyon to find the red door. Once inside, capture the Moe-Eye in each room and use sunglasses to navigate the invisible floor. The Moe-Eye can't jump so you'll have to make your way across the invisible floor as Mario. Use the columns on the walls as landmarks to help guide you. Similarly, you can use the Switch's built-in camera to take screenshots with the Moe-Eye's glasses on, then refer to them as you move with Mario.

55 Skull Sign in the Transparent Maze

Follow the instructions for Power Moon #54, but don't leave the first room. Instead, jump and throw Cappy at the danger sign and hold the throw so he continues to spin atop the sign until a Power Moon is released. Leap back across the invisible maze to get it.

56 The Bullet Bill Maze: Break Through!

Make your way to the ruins in the Tostarena Northwest Reaches and enter the red door. Capture a Bullet Bill and ride it from one piece of solid ground to the next. There are plenty of Bullet Bill launchers in this maze, so you needn't worry about being stranded. Accelerate on that first Bullet Bill to reach the platform near the revolving lattice wall. Swap out one Bullet Bill for a fresh one and slowly navigate through the rotating walls to the steps leading to the Power Moon and exit via the pipe to the top of the ruins.

57 The Bullet Bill Maze: Side Path

Follow instructions for Power Moon #56 and swap out the first Bullet Bill for a fresh one near the first revolving lattice wall. Return the

way you came and enter the side path on the left. Carefully navigate the spiral path to reach the Power Moon.

58 Jaxi Driver

Warp to the top of Jaxi Ruins, hop aboard the Jaxi located there and leap off the ruins. Steer Jaxi across the wastes into the doorway of

Jaxi Ruins at ground level (where the two small cacti are). This earns Mario access to a Jaxi obstacle course filled with moving platforms, eight Regional Coins, rings, and Power Moons. Anticipate the upcoming turns and use the brake to turn Jaxi accordingly. Though it might be tempting to avoid the narrower paths in favor of the moving platforms, the narrow paths are actually easier to navigate, provided Jaxi is lined up properly. Use the wider areas on the course to turn Jaxi around and align him in the direction you wish to take.

59 Jaxi Stunt Driving

Follow the instructions for Power Moon #58 and ride Jaxi to the large central area in the course. Line him up with the Treble Clef on

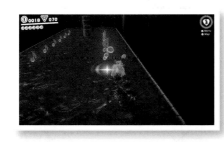

the left and sprint through it in a straight line. Ease Jaxi to the left to collect the notes on one side, then use the brakes to power-slide around the column. Sprint back through the other row of notes on the return trip without falling or missing any notes to get the Power Moon.

60 Strange Neighborhood

Capture the rocket atop the building in Tostarena Town to reach this special area. Roll down the curved hill to build speed then long jump through the rings to reach the first turn. Triple jump your way across the rotating buildings to the Goomba tower.

Wait near the block on the right for the buildings to line up then cross to the Power Moon.

61 Above a Strange Neighborhood

Follow instructions for Power Moon #60 and make your way to the part of the level with the three Goombas in a tower. Leap

onto the platform with the three blocks and climb onto them. Uncover the invisible block above the ? Block and jump and climb onto it to reach the Power Moon high above.

62 Secret Path to Tostarena!

Provided you chose to visit Lake Kingdom after Sand Kingdom, the secret path to this Power Moon originates

where Lakitu is fishing in Lake Kingdom. Head to the Courtyard area at Lake Kingdom and locate the painting in the pool where Lakitu is. Use the painting to warp to Southwestern Floating Island in Sand Kingdom, high above the desert. There you find a Power Moon.

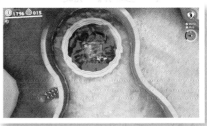

63 Found with Sand Kingdom Art

Locate the Hint Art on the side of the southeastern building in Tostarena Town. You can tell from the architecture in the diagram

that the hint lies in Bowser's Kingdom. Travel there, then warp to the Souvenir Shop location. The art hinted at something being 6 from the shop and 3 from the flag—the hint was referring to the walking stones in the garden path.

Count six steps from Crazy Cap and ground pound the stone to get a Power Moon.

64 Jammin' in the Sand Kingdom

Climb onto the roof of the southeastern building in Tostarena Town to find Toad listening to music. Toad wants to hear music that fits a certain theme. Here in Sand Kingdom he wants to hear a track that goes with "memories of a tough battle." Any of the songs with the word "Battle" in their title will suffice (look for the Battle Music description on the vinyl record in the Music List). Play the right tune, get a Power Moon.

65 Hat-and-Seek: In the Sand

One of the Bonneters has snuck off on vacation to Sand Kingdom and can be found in Tostarena Town. He's trying to

blend in by looking like a local, and he's willing to fork over a Power Moon if you promise to keep his identity secret. Look for the pair of eyes poking out from the Sombrero near the shaved ice stand to the left of Crazy Cap.

66 Sand Kingdom Regular Cup

Warp to the Tostarena Northwest Reaches and talk to the Koopa about the Freerunning Races.

This course is quite a bit different than the others in that the fastest way to the finish line isn't by running and jumping, but by taking a Jaxi! Long jump from the start and roll up the dune to Jaxi and hop aboard. Pilot Jaxi to the left of the ruins (but to the right of the three leaning pillars) and toward Tostarena Town. The finish line is on the south edge of town, near Crazy Cap. It's easiest to cut through town, but can be faster to round the southeastern corner of town, provided you don't hit the Jaxi Stand.

67 Binding Band Returned

Dive into the hole west of the Inverted Pyramid to return to the Deepest Underground and use the slingshot to reach the temple above. Numerous Tostarenans and tourists have gathered to marvel at the return of the Binding Band. Leap up and ground pound the fancy ring to pry a Power Moon from it.

68 Round-the-World Tourist

Talk to the Tostarenan near the taxi (after defeating Bowser) to initiate this somewhat lengthy quest for a Power Moon. The Tostarenan is known as the Desert Wanderer and he's very excited to finally have a taxi at his disposal. He

wants to be taken to the Metro Kingdom, but that's not all. Mario must meet the Desert Wanderer (and his taxi) in a series of kingdoms to earn a Power Moon from each location. Complete the Desert Wanderer's adventure and meet him back in Sand Kingdom to receive this Power Moon. Meet him in the following locations, in order: Metro Kingdom, Cascade Kingdom, Luncheon Kingdom, Moon Kingdom, Mushroom Kingdom, and then home to the Sand Kingdom where it all began.

69 Peach in the Sand Kingdom

Make your way to the top of the Inverted Tower via the electrical wire and look for Princess Peach and Tiara looking out over the

southwestern edge. Speak to Princess Peach to receive a Power Moon she found in her travels.

Moons from the Moon Rock

70 Mighty Leap from the Palm Tree!

Head to Desert Oasis and climb the palm tree north of the water. There's a Power Moon floating above the tree. Ground pound from the tree trunk or back somersault from one of the palm fronds to get it.

71 On the North Pillar

Use the electrical line atop the Tostarena Ruins Round Tower to reach the top of the Inverted Pyramid. Ride the electrical line down toward the ruins in the northwest corner of the desert, but leap off as you pass the lone tower with the Power Moon atop it. It's easy to leap too early given the perspective so be ready to tackle jump at the Power Moon if necessary. Better still, wait to jump off until it looks as if Mario has already passed it.

72 Into the Flowing Sands

This Power Moon is hovering just above the slope of flowing sand inside the ruins, at the base of the stairs. It's below the two moving platforms near the rings. Leap into the sand to snag it.

73 In the Skies Above the Canyon

Make your way to the top of the round tower and board the moving platform. Use Cappy to trigger the radiating explosions that burst through the stone blocks that would otherwise knock Mario off. Stay on the right-hand platform as it nears the Power Moon. Leap for the Power Moon before the platform descends then guide Mario safely onto the platform far below.

74 Island in the Poison Swamp

Hop aboard a Jaxi and ride it toward the wastes near Jaxi Ruins. There's a Power Moon on an island in the swamp, south of Jaxi Ruins. Ride the Jaxi across the poison to get it. You won't even need to release the capture.

75 An Invisible Gleam

Return to Moe-Eye Habitat and capture a Moe-Eye. Ride it up the lift to the top of the pillars as before, when collecting Moon Shards. Use the sunglasses to spot the glowing beacon on the north-central pillar. Release the capture and ground pound the pillar to uncover the Power Moon.

76 On the Eastern Pillar

This is one of the most deceptively tricky Power Moons to find in Sand Kingdom, if not the entire game. Though the stone block sitting atop a pillar east of Jaxi Ruins clearly has a Power Moon within it—and Mario can leap onto it from the dunes—there's no simple way to break it free. Of course, you may remember from Power Moon #20, that Bullet Bills can break these stones. But getting a Bullet Bill this far east takes effort, and there's very little margin for error.

Warp to the Tostarena Ruins Sand Pillar and capture a Bullet Bill. Ride it toward the right-most of the leaning pillars and leap off. Stand here to lure the next Bullet Bill around the barrier then tackle jump to the other leaning tower. Wait for the Bullet Bill to get as close as possible before you capture it.

Now the Bullet Bill's timer is reset and you have it as close as you can get it to the stone block with the Power Moon (another option is to hit it once to knock its visor off, then leap over it, let it pass under Mario, then turn and capture it while it's a little closer to the target). But the hard work isn't done yet! Now you must shake the controller to get small speed bursts the whole way there or the capture expires before you reach the Power Moon.

77 Caught Hopping in the Desert!

Unlike at Cascade Kingdom, there are three rabbits in Sand Kingdom. Don't allow yourself to be pulled in multiple directions. Pick a rabbit and keep after it. Use tackle jumps to cut it off and close off its escape, then pelt it with the hat to stun it. The rabbit will tire out, as evidenced by the sweat pouring from it. Keep after it and don't let up until it releases a Power Moon.

78 Poster Cleanup

Meet the Tostarenan on the northeast side of the ruins at Tostarena Northwest Reaches. He needs someone to clean the posters off the ruins. Mario can accomplish this with Cappy. Toss Cappy at the posters to knock them off. Back somersault from atop the cactus to reach the higher ones on the back wall. The upper ones on the side wall will be more difficult. To reach them, Mario must leap from atop the dune, dive jump, then toss the hat again before falling. It takes some practice, but all of the posters are within reach from ground level. If this proves too difficult, ride the electrical line to the roof of the ruins and drop off, ready to throw the cap.

79 Taking Notes: Running Down

Locate the Jaxi Stand in the southwest corner of the desert and ride a Jaxi to the Treble Clef where this challenge begins. Ride the Jaxi straight through the Treble Clef from the south and hold an arrow-straight line up and over the dunes to collect the many, many notes before time expires. Though it's possible to roll very quickly through the notes, the slope of the dunes makes this very difficult. It's far easier to use Jaxi.

80 Taking Notes: In the Wall Painting

Enter the 8-bit pipe on the side of the Tostarena Ruins Round Tower and ascend to the Treble Clef on the second level of the puzzle. Turn and run back to the left, avoiding the Bullet Bills as you collect the notes there. Now hurry back to the right, leaping and dashing to gather up the notes.

81 Love at the Edge of the Desert

Another Goombette has arrived in Sand Kingdom looking for love. This one is located far on the northern edge of the desert, east of the ruins at Tostarena Northwest Reaches. Return to the ruins, capture a Goomba and carefully guide him in a counter-clockwise loop around the ruins and across the desert to the Gambetta.

82 More Walking in the Desert

Return to the Koopa north of the Desert Oasis to try your skill at the trace walking challenge again. This time, you must score over 90 points in order to earn the Power Moon! Remember to keep the three smaller cactuses to your right, the small shrubs on your right, and then the lone shrub on your left.

83 Sand Kingdom Master Cup

This race is just like the Regular Cup in that you'll be riding a Jaxi to victory. The difference is that there's little margin for error or sloppy driving. The Golden Koopa typically has some trouble getting past the leaning pillars so don't follow right behind him. Keep to the right of the pillars, then cut right toward the road leading into Tostarena Town. Pass to the left of the fountain for the straightest path to the finish.

84 Where the Transparent Platforms End

Descend the Moon Pipe south of Tostarena Town and capture the Moe-Eye inside the temple. The Power Moon lies across a lengthy platform puzzle that requires you to toggle the sunglasses on and off very quickly to peek at the locations of the moving invisible platforms, then run around obstacles without the help of seeing them. Fortunately, the rings near the start ensure you never run out of coins should you struggle with this. The difficulty begins when you near the second set of rings. Keep to the front of the moving platform and walk toward the rings on an angle. Run behind the lengthy sliding obstacles and sprint through the zigzag section that follows to avoid being knocked off.

85 Jump Onto the Transparent Lift

Use the Moon Pipe south of Tostarena Town and ride a Moe-Eye to the second moving platform near the start. Drop onto the ledge further down on the right and ride it to the key. The invisible platform rises up on the other side so you can collect the Power Moon.

86 Colossal Ruins: Dash! Jump!

Warp to the Tostarena Ruins and enter the Moon Pipe near the Goombas. Note the location of the Power Moon in the distance and the locked Power Moon container in the floor (Power Moon #87). Capture the Spark Pylon on the left then capture the Rocket Flowers to send Mario speeding toward the rings. Leap the gaps, grab more flowers and head up the angled, sinking wall on the left. Steer Mario as he sprints along the tilted, sinking wall. Let the rings guide you to safety then grab another flower and leap for the Power Moon in the distance.

87 Sinking Colossal Ruins: Hurry!

Follow instructions for Power Moon #86 but dare to descend along the sinking wall after the third set of rings so that Mario can grab the key. Turn hard to the left after grabbing the key to ascend to higher—safer—ground. Reach the end

of the Colossal Ruins level and a stone bridge appears, leading Mario back to the Moon Pipe and the Power Moon he unlocked.

88 Through the Freezing Waterway

Descend the Moon Pipe east of the Inverted Pyramid to enter this frigid watery challenge level. Capture the Gushen and familiarize yourself with how it controls. Remember that the Gushen runs out of water to propel itself upward and forward so you need to land back in water to replenish its propulsion system. Much of the level is filled with poison so landing in the near-freezing water is vital. But watch out for the other Gushen, as they don't take kindly to captured Gushen! Use the blue moving platforms to reset the Gushen's takeoff point, allowing it to travel higher. This also allows the Gushen to travel without expending water. Ascend the two moving platforms then make it over the small barrier and past the poison tank. Ascend again in a burst, then propel the Gushen to the left to reach the Power Moon safely.

89 Freezing Waterway: Hidden Room

Follow the instructions for Power Moon #88 and make it to the lengthy water section with the first moving platform above it. Stay to the left, wait for the platform to approach and burst upwards. Land briefly, then propel the Gushen up even higher

and to the left. Clear the poison and drop, but don't touch the bottom. There's poison there. Stay aloft and continue left and up to continue past the poison to reach the hidden Power Moon.

Welcome to Lake Lamode

REGION AT A GLANCE

Population	Middling
Size	Limited
Locals	Lochladies
Currency	Scale-Shaped
Industry	Clothing, Design
Temperature	Average 79°F

INDIGENOUS FLORA & FAUNA

	ZIPPER		KOMBOO		CHEEP CHEEP
	Can Capture?		Can Capture?		Can Capture?
	Yes		No		Yes
	GOOMBA		DORRIE		MINI GOOMBA
	Can Capture?		Can Capture?		Can Capture?
	Yes		No		No
	FUZZIES		BINOCULARS		
	Can Capture?		Can Capture?		
	No		Yes		

The Lovely Lochladies

Lochladies are exceedingly flexible, but they also possess a deep strength. Many have become accomplished designers, and this balance may be their secret.

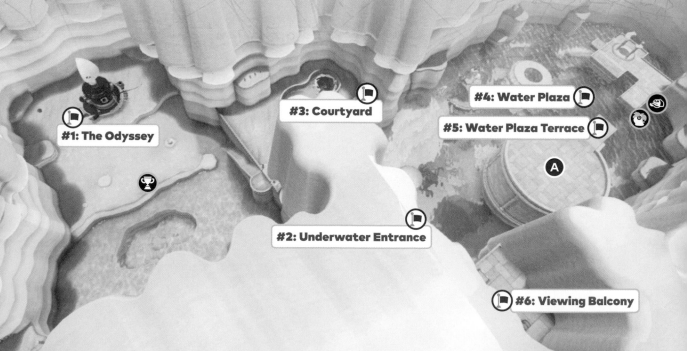

#1: The Odyssey

#3: Courtyard

#4: Water Plaza

#5: Water Plaza Terrace

A

#2: Underwater Entrance

#6: Viewing Balcony

THE DOMED WATER PLAZA

Lake Lamode, the land of fashion. The underwater Water Plaza is protected by a glass dome, but don't worry, there's air inside to breathe.

When you look up at the lake from within the plaza, you can see Dorrie swimming amid the stunning scenery.

ZIPPERS OF MYSTERY

Fitting of a kingdom famous for its fashion, you can find zipper art all over the place here. Zippers can be securely fastened as well as opened and closed freely, so perhaps they have a deeper meaning...

That said, this particular zipper is more than decoration. It actually works, so stop by and give it a try.

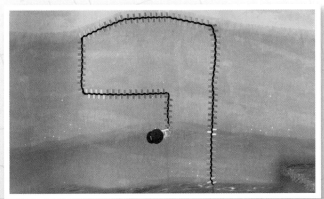

WINDOW SHOPPING

Considered the most luxurious garment this kingdom has to offer, the Lochlady Dress is displayed in the show window of the Water Plaza. Of all the garments created by the Lochladies, only the very best and most beautiful is selected for this great honor. It's a national treasure!

It's said that wearing this dress brings eternal happiness, so naturally every bride yearns for it. Sadly, this lovely, one-of-a-kind item is not for sale.

DORRIE THE AQUATIC BUDDY

This gentle creature spends its days swimming gracefully in Lake Lamode. If you're confident in your abilities, swimming alongside it might make for some wonderful memories.

Although able to live in any aquatic environment, some have heard Dorrie complain that the lake is too small. Keep an eye out for Dorrie-themed souvenirs, which tourists just love.

SOAKED IN HISTORY

Once a spot for designers to relax and even dye cloth, this soaking pool has a rich history. Since most activity centers around the lake town, this is now a well-known fishing hole.

THREE KEYS TO THE KINGDOM

1. Visit the Water Plaza, especially if you enjoy breathing air.

2. Swim with the local Dorrie for an unforgettable experience.

3. Admire the gown that qualifies as a national treasure.

🅐 Broodals Over the Lake

Mario touches down in the Lake Kingdom in time to see the Broodals circling high above Water Plaza Terrace, where they stole the Lochlady Dress. The Lochladies of Lake Kingdom are positively distraught over this development. Worse still, the Broodals broke the stairs leading to the Water Plaza. Mario has to find another way over.

No Stairs Necessary

It's possible to triple jump from the beach, toss the cap at the top of the wall on the left, dive jump, then tackle jump up to the landing. In fact, this maneuver will be useful much later, during the region's Koopa Freerunning event. For now, follow the standard route to fully explore the region.

Cross the watery area near the Odyssey to the hat trampoline on the small island in front of the columns. Bounce to the top of the flood gate, where a Lochlady mentions that the way to the Water Plaza is right behind her. At first glance, it doesn't look like anything's there, but that Zipper is special. Grab the coins from behind the crate, then capture the Zipper and tug it along the outline to create a special opening.

There are plenty of Zippers just like this that lead to hidden areas in Lake Kingdom.

Descend through the shaft up ahead, making sure to keep Mario lined up with the air bubbles rising from the bubbler at the bottom. Collect the Regional Coins near the spikes, then swim toward the fork in the path. Head to the right to collect Power Moon #08 from the treasure chest atop the ledge.

Hold Your Breath, Mario

Mario can swim underwater for quite some time without coming up for air (roughly 24 seconds),  but he does need air. Fortunately, a circular meter appears next to Mario whenever he's underwater. This indicates how much oxygen he has left. Best to swim through an air bubble, reach the surface, or capture a Cheep Cheep before the meter empties completely. Cheep Cheep never have to worry about air.

Toss Cappy at the walking Komboo to cut them in two, and continue swimming toward the Heart in the distance. The Underwater Entrance to Lake Lamode isn't much further.

Since Mario needs a total of eight Power Moons to fuel the Odyssey before leaving Lake Kingdom, it's a good idea to pick up a couple on the way to the  Broodal battle. Capture a Cheep Cheep and locate Power Moon #03 in the upper, middle recess above the Underwater Entrance warp point.

This is a good time to gather up the five Moon Shards in Lake Lamode. Find them all to gain **Power Moon #12** near the Water Plaza Entrance.

1. This one is atop a broken column right outside the Underwater Entrance warp point.

2. From Underwater Entrance, swim beneath the ledge on the right to find another Moon Shard.

3. Break through the crates in the recess on the north side of Lake Lamode. Shake the

controller to have the Cheep Cheep attack the Komboo and claim the Moon Shard in the distance.

4. This next Moon Shard is in an underwater corridor at the base of Lake Lamode.

Swim to the deepest part of the lake and look east to spot it.

5. The final Moon Shard is under the dome on the south side of the lake. Swim through the

opening in the top to get the Moon Shard from atop the small temple with the boulder blocking its door.

Continue swimming around the lake as a Cheep Cheep and pluck Power Moon #12 from the back of the massive blue creature known as Dorrie. Dorrie is terrifically peaceful so have no fear of getting close to it.

Mario can't capture a Dorrie, but he can swim alongside them.

Enter the lower level of Water Plaza, gather up the coins from the ledges and alcoves, then swim up the watery hall on the left to reach the middle level. Exit Water Plaza through the hole in the dome near the Display Window and swim to the third floor entrance.

Hit the P-Switch to unlock the shaft on the third floor of Water Plaza and swim to the roof. Hit the P-Switch near the columns on the right to lower the hat trampoline to water level—this makes it easier to reach the roof should you fall. It also makes it possible to reach the crates on the ledge, where Power Moon #05 is hidden. Use the hat trampolines on the north side to reach the Power Moon where it lands.

The flower-shaped hat trampoline makes for a quick jump to the roof—and to the crates containing a Power Moon.

Now that Mario has earned five of the eight Power Moons he needs to fuel the Odyssey, he's ready to tackle the next Broodal. Use the hat trampolines on the ledge to cross back above Lake Lamode, through the rings and past the Mini Goombas, to Water Plaza Terrace.

BOSS: RANGO

Floppy-eared Rango wastes no time in throwing his buzzsaw-like hat at Mario. Leap away from his first toss to get a feel for its range, then square up and face him in time for his next toss. Throw Cappy at his hat to flip it upside-down, revealing a hat trampoline on its reverse side. Bounce off Rango's inverted hat, follow your shadow in the air, and ground pound Rango once above him.

Once hit, Rango pulls his hat down low over his body and initiates a jumping attack of his own. Steer clear of his massive feet and the hat's blades as you run in an expanding circle, collecting Rango's coins.

Dodge his bouncing attack and be ready for him to throw his hat again. Hit Rango's hat with Cappy, bounce off the other side, and ground pound Rango just as before. For an extra challenge, jump on top of Rango's hat while he's performing his bounce attack, which also stops his attack pattern. While Rango doesn't require a ground pound, it is the easiest way to deliver a blow to his noggin. You could also jump or backflip onto his head as well.

Mario must hit Rango a third and final time to win the battle. Avoid his hopping attack after the second ground pound lands, then once again toss Cappy at his hat, bounce off the hat trampoline, and ground pound him.

Gather up the multi moon Rango Drops (Power Moon #01) and head off to Wooded Kingdom. There's plenty of time to return to Lake Kingdom later if you'd like.

Short-Range Twirls

Try to hit Rango's hat with Cappy as soon as he throws it. There's only so much distance Mario can travel from a hat trampoline bounce, and he needs to stay high enough to ground pound Rango. Don't risk running out of room!

Extend Your Stay

Lake Kingdom has a grand total of 42 Power Moons to find, most of which can be uncovered during Mario's initial visit. With at least six already discovered in pursuit of Bowser, you're off to a good start. Spend some time exploring the Zippered-hideaways within Lake Kingdom to see how many others you can uncover.

Souvenir Shopping

Lake Kingdom contains 50 Regional Coins in the form of purple Lochlady scales. All 50 purple coins can be found during your initial visit.

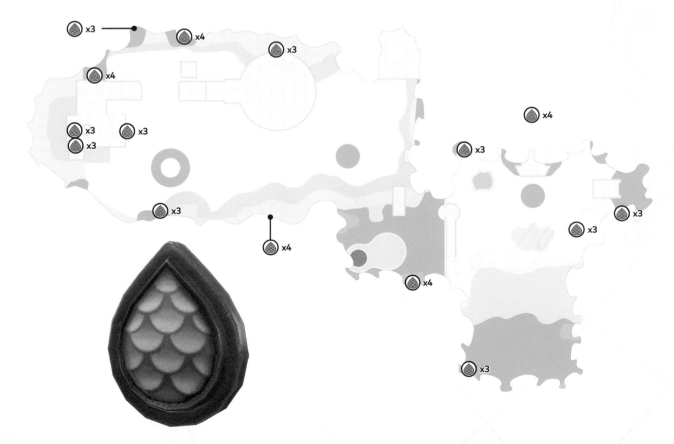

Life-Up Heart	Lake Kingdom Power Moon	Fashionable Cap	Fashionable Outfit
ⓘ 50	ⓘ 100	ⓘ 50	ⓘ 150

Swim Goggles	Swimwear	Lake Kingdom Sticker	Rubber Dorrie	Underwater Dome
💧 5	💧 10	💧 5	💧 5	ⓘ 25

Local Currency

The majority of Regional Coins in Lake Kingdom are quite easy to find, provided you look in the recesses, unzip all of the Zippers, and don't overlook some of the most obvious spots. The area near the Odyssey contains many purple coins, including three behind the 7-shaped Zipper in the wall to the left of the floodgate and three more under the water-logged Zipper nearest the Odyssey. Still, several more are even harder to find.

Follow instructions for Power Moon #14 and follow the moving platform through the crack in the rock beyond the warp pipe to find these four hidden Regional Coins.

Enter the red door high on the cliff above Water Plaza via the hat trampoline and make your way past the first group of Fuzzies. Leap for the curved ledge and clamber around the left-hand side to find three well-hidden Regional Coins.

🌙 Power Moons

There are 42 Power Moons at Lake Kingdom. **Power Moons #01, 02, 03, 05, 08, and 12 were obtained while ridding Lake Kingdom of its Broodal threat.** Consult the prior pages for help.

④ End of the Hidden Passage

Bounce from the hat trampoline in the Courtyard up to the small ledge on the wall above Lake Lamode. Capture the Zipper and unzip the lengthy rectangular panel of the wall to reveal a hidden passage. Follow the trail of coins that appears to the Power Moon at the end.

⑥ On the Lakeshore

This is both one of the easiest Power Moons to get in Lake Kingdom, and one of the most easily overlooked. Seek out the glowing spot on the ground behind the Binoculars and perform a ground pound to unearth the Power Moon hiding in the sand.

⑦ From the Broken Pillar

Exit Water Plaza on the bottom level and swim a short distance to the right, toward the broken pillar beneath the side room with the dome. Ground pound this broken, underwater pillar to uncover a hidden Power Moon.

⑨ Lake Gardening: Spiky Passage Seed

Speak with the Lochlady on the ground floor of Water Plaza to learn about the seed she lost in the spiky tunnel. Warp across the lake to the Underwater Entrance and swim back through the tunnel, past the Komboo and Cheep Cheep, toward the flood gate. Grab the seed near the air bubbler and swim up the shaft. Use the hat trampoline to exit above the flood gate. Ascend the repaired stairs and swim back across Lake Lamode with the seed. Toss it into the pot to grow. Come back periodically to check on it—it will eventually grow a golden fruit. Hit it with your hat to gain a Power Moon.

⑩ Lake Kingdom Timer Challenge 1

Find the scarecrow to start the Timer Challenge on a small island in Lake Lamode. Triple jump across the floating platforms as they bob in the water, then ground pound through the hole in the center of the third platform. Continue performing underwater ground pounds to submerge as quickly as possible to get the Power Moon before time expires.

⑪ Lake Kingdom Timer Challenge 2

Return to Water Plaza Terrace and initiate the Timer Challenge. The early jumps in this sequence are too high to reach with normal jumps so a triple jump up the stack is out of the question. Instead, use ground pound jumps or backward somersault jumps to leap from one block to the next (Mario will likely end in a hanging position on the first block). Climb up and jump again. Grab the Power Moon before the timer expires and the whole assembly disappears.

⑬ Taking Notes: Dive and Swim

Swim through the Treble Clef near the Odyssey to trigger the notes. Mario must swim along the perimeter of this large depression in the lake bottom, then ascend before the timer expires. The best way to do this, to avoid any backtracking, is to start the lap just to the left or right of the vertical notes. Mario can swim faster by pressing LZ + Y Buttons, but there's a faster way! Toss Cappy at the notes to collect several at once, making it possible to cut the lap short. Ascend through the column of notes at the finish.

⑭ Taking Notes: In the Cliffside

Use the hat trampoline to reach the 8-bit warp pipe on the ledge near Water Plaza. Leap onto the moving platform to reach the treble clef then do your best to stay on the platform as it moves to the left. Collect the upper notes as it slides across the cliffside, making sure to get the groups of three that are even higher—they can't be reached from the ground. Save the three on the bottom for last. Be sure to hold the Y Button for extra speed to boost your jump height and distance.

⑮ Lake Fishing

Head up the stairs from The Odyssey and capture Lakitu in the Courtyard. Drag the bait in front of the largest of the three fish shadows. Set the hook as soon as you feel a vibration. Reel in the Cheep Cheep carrying a Power Moon.

⑯ I Met a Lake Cheep Cheep!

There's a small ring-shaped island with an inverted dome in the lake near Water Plaza. The Lochlady there really wants to meet a Cheep Cheep, but can't get close enough. Help her out by capturing a Cheep Cheep and leaping over the ring of grass to the small pool in the center.

⑰ Our Secret Little Room

There's a Lochlady in a hard-to-spot room inside the base of Water Plaza. Return to the ground floor of the area and look for a narrow hallway in the center, behind the columns. Enter this hallway (to the right of the one with the ? Blocks) to find a door on the left. Head inside and talk to the Lochlady there to receive the Power Moon.

⑱ Let's Go Swimming, Captain Toad!

Captain Toad is at the very bottom of the circular hole in the ground floor of Water Plaza. Mario can certainly reach him without succumbing to a lack of air with the help of a Life-Up Heart. And it's even possible to reach Toad's underwater dome—and oxygen—without losing all of Mario's health without a Life-Up Heart if you are a very quick swimmer. Nevertheless, the easiest way to reach Captain Toad is with a Cheep Cheep. Capture one of the Cheep Cheeps swimming by and hop across the dry, stone floor of Water Plaza to the shaft circled by coins. Dive, dive, dive to meet Captain Toad.

⑲ Shopping in Lake Lamode

Visit Crazy Cap on the second floor of Water Plaza and purchase the Lake Kingdom Power Moon for 100 coins. While you're there, be sure to purchase the newly-available Fashionable Cap and Fashionable Outfit.

⑳ A Successful Repair Job

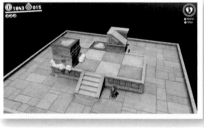

Once Rango has been defeated and the boulder blocking the red door on the south side of Lake Lamode has been removed, Mario can attempt to repair a broken statue. Capture the left-hand piece of stone and flip it around the platform until it is oriented in its original manner, but adjacent to the other piece. This is not an easy task, and takes some trial and error on your part, but it is possible. The first thing to know is that you can leave the room and reenter at any time to reset the puzzle. This can be helpful.

As for solving it, you need to use the entire board to rotate the piece so that it is upside-down, with the rough, undecorated side facing you in the lower left-hand corner. From there, move it up to the starting position, right, then into the final spot.

21 I Feel Underdressed

Return to the second floor of Water Plaza after defeating Bowser and don your Swim Goggles and Swimwear to meet the strictly-enforced dress code. Speak to the Lochlady near the locked door wearing this outfit to gain access to the display room showcasing the Lochlady Dress. Toss Cappy at the dress and hold the throw to make him spin round and round atop the bridal veil. Keep the spin going until a Power Moon is uncovered.

22 Unzip the Chasm

Unzip the small square-shaped Zipper on the rock wall just outside Water Plaza's dome, on the north side of the lake. Enter the red door and unzip the next panel to enter a larger room filled with Mini Goombas and other Zippers. Use the T-shaped Zipper to proceed to the L-shaped Zipper. Grab the stack of coins from behind the wall of the L-shaped Zipper. Grab the Key on your way across the lengthy Zipper in the floor, capture the Zipper, and unzip the chasm, dropping the dozens of Mini Goombas into the abyss. Return the way you came to the Power Moon.

23 Super-Secret Zipper

Follow the instructions for Power Moon #22 and unzip the T-shaped Zipper inside the large room. Descend the T-ramp and spot the stair-shaped ledges across the gap. Throw Cappy to uncover a series of invisible blocks. Unzip the large Zipper to drop a segment of the wall, making it possible to capture the smaller Zipper at the top. Mario—and the Zipper—will fall to a secret area containing the Power Moon. Return via the pipe.

24 Jump, Grab, Cling, and Climb

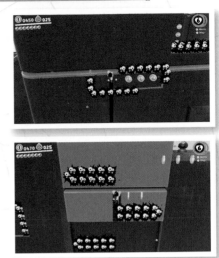

Make your way to the roof of Water Plaza and use the hat trampolines to reach the red door high on the cliff. Once inside the challenge room, use the hat trampolines to grab the narrow yellow ledges and shimmy across to the moving blocks. Stay clear of the Fuzzies as they march along the yellow paths. Get the Regional Coins from around the bend on the next yellow ledge, then continue to the right. Don't worry about the Fuzzies up ahead, as Mario can slip in behind a group of them and move between them without risk, so long as he pauses ever so slightly.

Tilt the camera after the second group of Fuzzies to spot the already open hat trampoline on the ledge below. Drop onto it, bounce to hat trampolines on the columns (use Mario's shadow as a guide) and carefully slide down the wall between the next groups of Fuzzies. Shimmy to the right where the wall begins ascending, leading Mario straight for several more groups of Fuzzies. Use the coins as a guide and snake back and forth between the Fuzzies to reach the upper area. Gather coins from the rings as you use the hat trampolines to bounce your way to the Power Moon.

25 Jump, Grab, and Climb Some More

Follow the tips for Power Moon #24 until you reach the moving wall with the ledge that ascended past the Fuzzies. Clamber off the ledge onto the red block, but ignore the hat trampoline near the ring. Wait for the yellow wall to descend then step onto its upper ledge. The wall slides upward once again, this time carrying Mario to a hidden hat trampoline. Use it to leap to the very top of the challenge level where a treasure chest containing a Power Moon awaits.

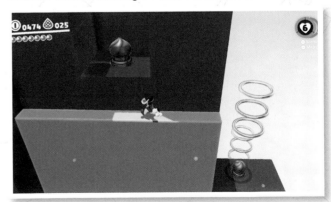

26 Secret Path to Lake Lamode!

Set sail for Seaside Kingdom, as the only way to reach this Power Moon is via a Warp Painting located in the bottom of the Bubblaine tower (accessible only after defeating Brigadier Mollusque). Swim over to any of the geysers of water aimed into

the tower and leap into the torrent. Mario is catapulted through the air to the tower. Swim to the bottom and enter the Warp Painting to return to an isolated area within Lake Kingdom known as the Viewing Balcony.

27 Found with Lake Kingdom Art

The Hint Art hangs on the staircase near The Odyssey. Snap a photo and note the difference between the two images shown: the right-hand photo shows a sixth fossil where none actually is. Sail back to Cascade Kingdom

and ground pound the area where the erroneous sixth fossil is located (near Uncle amiibo) to find a Power Moon. Note that Power Moons found with Hint Art count toward the Power Moons assigned to the kingdom where the art was, not where the Power Moon is found (this particular Power Moon is pink like those in Lake Kingdom).

28 Taxi Flying Through Lake Lamode

Return to Lake Kingdom after defeating Bowser and use the Binoculars to search the sky. With good timing and a careful eye,

you'll spot a taxi flying through the air with a sail above it. Zoom in on it for a Power Moon.

29 That Trendy "Pirate" Look

The middle Style Sister, dressed in silver, wants to see someone wearing pirate clothes. Purchase the Pirate Hat and Pirate Outfit

from the Crazy Cap store in Seaside Kingdom then return wearing those clothes.

Wardrobe Change!

The quickest way to change Mario's outfit and return to the Style Sisters atop the roof of the Water Plaza is to use the closet inside the Crazy Cap store on the second floor of Water Plaza. Jump off the balcony, exit Water Plaza through the ground floor, and swim to the hat trampoline on the small ledge. This bounces Mario right up to the rooftop. Then, when ready to change clothes, drop from the roof to the hole in the top of the dome, and leap for the Crazy Cap store.

30 Space Is "In" Right Now

The Style Sister dressed in red wants to see space clothes. Purchase the Space Suit and Space Helmet from the Crazy

Cap store in Moon Kingdom and wear the clothing in front of her to get a Power Moon.

31 That "Old West" Style

The Style Sister dressed in blue would like to see Mario dressed in his cowboy attire. Purchase the Cowboy Hat and Cowboy Outfit from the Crazy Cap store in Sand Kingdom and return looking the part of an old west cowboy.

(32) Lake Kingdom Regular Cup

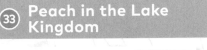

Speak with the Koopa on the beach near the Odyssey to initiate this first of two races. The Roving Racers are going to race to the top of Water Plaza Terrace and, since the stairs will be removed from the race course, they're all going to take

the underwater passage beyond the floodgate. For this first race, we recommend you take this route too. Hurry to the Zipper atop the flood gate by rolling off the beach, long jumping into a dive jump, then tackle jump onto the island with the hat trampoline.

Unzip the entrance to the underwater tunnel and swim to the other side.

Capture a Cheep Cheep at Underwater Entrance for a faster trip across Lake Lamode to the hat trampolines atop Water Plaza. It's a long route, but with a fast start, some quick swimming, and a friendly Cheep Cheep, you can beat the Koopas at their own game. In the Master Cup race we'll show you a faster route!

(33) Peach in the Lake Kingdom

Return to Water Plaza Terrace after defeating Bowser to meet up with Princess Peach and Tiara. Peach is having a wonderful

vacation and has a Power Moon to share with Mario that she found during her travels. Maybe you'll see her again in Wooded Kingdom?

👻 Moons from the Moon Rock

(34) Behind the Floodgate

Use the hat trampoline to reach the roof of the floodgate opposite the Odyssey and capture the Zipper. Unzip a

hole in the roof to enter the watery tunnel. You find a Power Moon sitting next to the hat trampoline inside the tunnel, right near the flood gate.

(35) High-Flying Leap

Swim across Lake Lamode to the ledge with the hat trampoline near the 8-bit warp pipe. Instead of leaping for the pipe, however,

guide Mario through the air along the face of the cliff to get the Power Moon floating high above the water.

(36) Deep, Deep Down

The location of this Power Moon on the map can be misleading, as it suggests it's on the roof. Quite the opposite! Capture a Cheep Cheep and hop through the opening to Water Plaza, as if descending to visit Captain Toad again. Dive to the bottom of the circular shaft and face away from Captain Toad. The Power Moon you seek is in the freshwater depths of Water Plaza, opposite Captain Toad. You can even reach it without a Cheep Cheep if you swim fast enough.

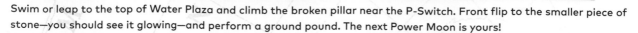

(37) Rooftop of the Water Plaza

Swim or leap to the top of Water Plaza and climb the broken pillar near the P-Switch. Front flip to the smaller piece of stone—you should see it glowing—and perform a ground pound. The next Power Moon is yours!

(38) Bird Traveling Over the Lake

There are several pink birds flying over the lake near the Odyssey, but only one contains the telltale glow of a Power Moon. Swim across the lake to the two broken columns beyond the stairs. The bird with the Power Moon often rests atop the shorter column until you scare it off. It then flies laps around the perimeter of this lake. Return to the beach near the Binoculars and wait for the bird to fly past. Leap up and hit it with your hat when it does.

(39) Love by the Lake

Capture one of the Goombas in the Courtyard and descend the stairs toward the beach where the Odyssey is parked. Carefully jump toward dry land—Goombas can't go in the water—and guide him around the back of the Odyssey to meet the Goombette waiting there.

40 Lake Kingdom Master Cup

Now that you're ready for the Master Cup, it's time to put some advanced freerunning skills to use. Ignore the Koopas as they race for the underwater tunnel. Instead, angle toward the Binoculars, triple jump across the hill to get some height, then toss Cappy at the wall near the Goombas. Dive jump to bounce from the hat, then tackle jump into the Courtyard. Hurry across Lake Lamode to the hat trampoline near the roof of Water Plaza then dive jump and tackle jump across the path of ledges and hat trampolines leading to Water Plaza Terrace. This shortcut can shave more than 35 seconds off the route the Koopas are taking.

41 Waves of Poison: Hoppin' Over

Enter the Moon Pipe near the Odyssey to take a chance at this surprisingly tricky challenge level where rolling waves of poison sweep across the area, washing over any and all solid ground. Making matters trickier is the fact that many of the platforms sink under Mario's weight. For this reason, he'll need to capture a Frog. Capture the first Frog and take your time leaping across the series of islands. The platforms get smaller and smaller, so be sure to use the Frog's shadow as a guide when you leap. Take your time and don't be afraid to remain on the same island for a few waves (leaping over them, of course) so you can get the timing down.

42 Waves of Poison: Hop to It!

Complete Power Moon #41, but don't leave via the exit pipe. Instead, carefully drop off the side of the final area toward the key in the distance. The best thing you can do to make getting this Power Moon easier is to jump in place on the island where the key is. Don't try to immediately leap back the way you came, as the odds of hitting a poison wave are high. Instead, leap over the incoming wave, turn the camera, and only return the way you came when you're not rushed.

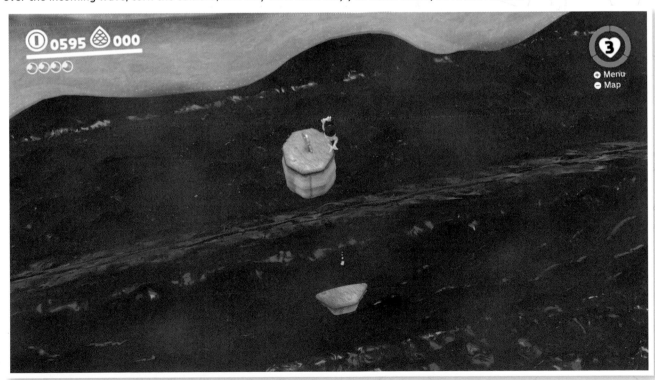

Wooded Kingdom

Welcome to Steam Gardens

REGION AT A GLANCE

Population	Automated
Size	Deep, Wide
Locals	Steam Gardeners
Currency	Nut-shaped
Industry	Flowers
Temperature	Average 82°F

INDIGENOUS FLORA & FAUNA

	UPROOT		POISON PIRANHA PLANT		BIG POISON PIRANHA PLANT
	Can Capture?		Can Capture?		Can Capture?
	Yes		Yes		Yes

	SHERM		GOOMBA		FIRE BRO
	Can Capture?		Can Capture?		Can Capture?
	Yes		Yes		Yes

	BINOCULARS		T-REX		COIN COFFER
	Can Capture?		Can Capture?		Can Capture?
	Yes		Yes		Yes

	MINI GOOMBA		YOOFOE
	Can Capture?		Can Capture?
	No		No

THREE KEYS TO THE KINGDOM

1. Smell the flowers. Not that you can miss them, but do savor the scent.

2. Admire the Steam Gardeners and their impressive devotion to their work.

3. Appreciate machines and nature living in exquisite harmony.

#9: Observation Deck

D C

#8: Secret Flower Field Entrance

#10: Iron Cage

#7: Iron Mountain Path, Station 8

#6: Summit Path

B A

#4: Sky Garden Tower

#3: Iron Road: Halfway Point

#2: Iron Road: Entrance

#5: Forest Charging Station

#1: The Odyssey

THE LIVING FACTORY

No one knows who built the giant machines dotting this land, but today the Steam Gardeners use them to maintain the greatest flower gardens in the world. The giant dome is climate-controlled and apparently self-sufficient, operating with no maintenance since ancient times.

GUARDIANS OF PARADISE

Visitors are welcomed not only by the humid air, but worker robots tending the flowers. They're known as Steam Gardeners, longtime residents of the kingdom. You'll be impressed at how long they can work without rest, maintaining themselves perfectly. But beyond being hard workers, the robots love flowers—some grow them right out of their heads! You'll feel the Steam Gardeners' warm hearts, from their flowers and also their internal steam pumps.

Birds NOT of a Feather

Local birds here seem remarkably fond of their mechanical neighbors.

FLOWERS AS A WAY OF LIFE

While you see amazing flowers on any visit, you might be lucky enough to see the famous Steam Gardens Soirée Bouquet. It features giant white flowers that charm all who lay eyes on it. As you might guess from the name, it's by far the most popular bouquet for wedding ceremonies, sought after by wedding planners the world over.

A DEEP WOOD'S SECRET

It doesn't appear on any tours, but there is an area untouched by the machines of the Steam Gardens. Here the trees grow thickly, barely allowing any light through. The Steam Gardeners do not speak of it, but rumor has it that they discourage visiting this place because of the danger posed by the giant creatures that call it home.

A GROWING WALKWAY

Be sure to try the system of paths called the Flower Road. You'll marvel at plants growing into temporary but walkable bridges. Watch your step, though—nature has no handrails.

Ⓐ Road to Sky Garden

The Odyssey lands in the southern reaches of the Wooded Kingdom, a region comprised of a complex union between rock and machinery—and a strong desire to grow flowers. Begin your stay by exploring the forested area near the Odyssey. Collect the Regional Coins hidden around the area, particularly atop the wall that rings the southern edge.

Climb onto the wall behind the Odyssey and follow it to the plateau for purple coins and more.

Follow the dirt path away from the Odyssey to the Crazy Cap store and purchase the Wooded Kingdom Power Moon (Power Moon #23) and the Mechanic Outfit. It's also a good idea to purchase the Explorer Hat and Explorer Outfit when you can (there are more than 15 Regional Coins in the vicinity of Crazy Cap).

YOU GOT A MOON!

Shopping in Steam Gardens
08/12/2017

Approach the Sphynx when you're ready to venture into the mechanical world of Steam Gardens. Answer the Sphynx's question correctly—Bowser wants flowers—to gain access to Iron Road: Entrance. Toss Cappy at the poison puddles to clean the area of purple toxin and grab the coins from the waterway.

Rusty Metal Walkways

Be careful around the orange and yellow panels, as they are sure to collapse under Mario's weight. Lucky for Mario, they'll somehow reappear after several seconds.

Beware the Deep Woods

Walk extra carefully along the edge of Iron Road, as one false step could plummet Mario into the Deep Woods, a mysterious, frightening place home to a very hostile T-Rex. We'll deal with the treasure located within the Deep Woods later. For now, know that your only escape is to plant a seed from a Steam Gardener in one of the many pots located there, and to climb the beanstalk back to safety.

The Poison Piranha Plants beyond the Warp Flag have spit purple poison throughout the area. Toss Cappy at the puddles to clean the ground of poison, then throw him at the Poison Piranha Plant. The plant catches Cappy in its mouth, giving Mario a chance to get close enough to kick it. Though it's possible to capture a Poison Piranha Plant by first throwing a rock at it (it chews on the rock), this isn't a useful tactic right here.

Eliminate the Poison Piranha Plants and begin the ascent of the Iron Road. Hop across the pistoning platforms until you reach an upper level leading to the right. Wait for the Uproot to drop from above, then capture it. Uproots can extend their root-like legs, allowing them to reach great heights. Release the stretch to fling them forward with a jump.

Make your way across the orange structure, past the other Uproots, to a narrow set of steps beyond the gray blocks. Position the Uproot beneath the platform that becomes visible (the front-facing walls go transparent so you can see) and push it out of the way.

Break the gray blocks with the Uproot and leap upward. Ascend the ledges to the right and crack open the nut on the wall to get the Power Moon hidden there (Power Moon #15) before continuing to the left. There are nuts containing Power Moons just like this all over Wooded Kingdom.

Continue moving the Uproot left to right through the red maze of platforms and walls. Flip over the Uproot on the ground, grab the coins, then raise the platform on the left by stretching the Uproot beneath it. Break through the gray blocks and exit the maze at the Iron Road: Halfway Point warp flag.

Numerous Poison Piranha Plants dot the area, including a Big Piranha Plant. Clear a path with Cappy then rush forward and kick the Poison Piranha Plant while it chews on Cappy. Try to avoid breaking the rocks apart, as they can be used against the Big Poison Piranha Plant. Toss a rock or Cappy at the Big Poison Piranha Plant then leap on its massive head as it falls to the ground. The Big Poison Piranha Plant drops Power Moon #01 when defeated.

⑧ Flower Thieves of Sky Garden

The glass container shatters, revealing a P-Switch. Don't step on it just yet! First locate the gap in the metal railing to the right of where the Big Poison Piranha Plant was and drop down to the narrow ledge below. Capture an Uproot and use it to make your way around the corner, up and over the ledges, to the nut at the end of the path. Crack it open as an Uproot to get Power Moon #16.

Step on the switch to trigger the growth of a flower road that curls its way through the air to the platform in the distance. Flower roads like this one aren't permanent so you had better keep moving. Hit the switch on the metal structure (ignore the tower to the right for now) and follow the second flower road as it winds downward into the base of Sky Garden Tower.

93

Hit the P-Switch inside the tower to run along the sloping flower road that appears to reach the Uproot on the upper platform. Capture the Uproot and use it to get the Life-Up Heart from the gray block before continuing on. Stretch the Uproot's legs to reach the

platform with the next P-Switch and step onto it. Leap from the top of the undulating flower road to the alcove in the tower and crack open the nut to get Power Moon #24 before continuing along the flower road to the very top.

The Return of Flower Road

The flower roads triggered by the P-Switches don't last forever, but they don't stay away either. Flower roads race by, lapping Sky Garden Tower continuously. If you miss one, just wait for it to pass by again.

Don't be alarmed when the flower road begins to descend. Continue following it as it rises again, then leap for the spiral stairs near the

top. Note the shadow on the floor of the tower's middle. Extend the Uproot's legs and leap to snag Power Moon #25 from the air. Release the capture and head outside.

BOSS: SPEWART

Spewart is the fourth and final member of the Broodal party to engage Mario in combat. Spewart begins the fight by spinning on one foot while coating the center of the arena in purple poison. Stick to the ring of flowers near the perimeter to avoid his gushing grossness.

Throw Cappy in a circular motion to sweep the ground clean of Spewart's poison as you close on him. Cappy knocks into him, stunning him. He recovers quickly and attempts to repaint the ground in poison, but not before Mario has time to leap into the air and ground pound him.

Once hit, Spewart tucks himself inside his hat and sets to zipping across the arena, painting streaks of purple poison in a zigzag pattern. Stay clear of the poison while you use Cappy to bounce Spewart away. Throwing the cap at Spewart doesn't harm him, but it does deflect his path.

Draw close to Spewart as he lands in the center and quickly toss Cappy at him to knock his hat off (Mario can never land upon a boss enemy still wearing its hat). Leap up and ground pound him again as he begins spewing poison once again. Spewart's pattern repeats one more time. Avoid the poison he trails through the area, then knock his hat off with Cappy, and finish the fight with a third ground pound. Once defeated, Spewart drops a multi moon (Power Moon #02).

© Path to the Secret Flower Field

Spewart's defeat didn't solve all the problems in Steam Gardens. Cappy spotted a mysterious craft above the other tower, near the secret flower

field. Warp to Iron Road: Entrance and capture one of the Uproots above the pond, along the western ledge. Follow the path over the crumbling walkway and use the Uproot to break the nut containing Power Moon #13.

Limited Access

The arrival of the strange craft atop the Secret Flower Field brought with it some unexpected changes. A number of large boulders have fallen, covering up several vital P-Switches and warp flags. Mario will have full access to the region once the visitor has been dealt with.

Return to the area previously coated in purple poison and capture one of the Sherms. Use it to blast a hole through the rocks blocking the doorway to the west, opposite the warp flag. Hit the Steam Gardener inside the maintenance room to get a seed and plant it in the pot to grow a beanstalk. Climb up to the Forest Charging Station.

The path to the Secret Flower Field is via a beanstalk in a room near Iron Road: Entrance.

Ground pound the glowing spot on the right-hand charging station to discover Power Moon #09. Round the corner to the south, where a number of Goombas are present. Climb the rocks toward the Sherms and peer out over the edge on the right to orient yourself—this area overlooks Crazy Cap and the path to the Odyssey.

Capture a Sherm and set to blasting away at the other Sherms in the area. This makes it easier to shoot the brown breakable slabs of dirt filling in the spaces on the rock wall. Be sure to clear away the dirt blocking the ledge on the upper left so that Mario can collect the Power Moon hidden there

Drop from the upper ledge if you have any trouble leaping from the side.

(Power Moon #05). Climb to the top and activate the warp flag for Summit Path.

Throw Cappy at the Rocket Flowers on the ground beneath the sloping metal ramp and steer Mario as he zooms up

the ramp. Aim for the rings, then angle left as he reaches the top. Welcome to Iron Mountain Path, Station 8. You're almost there!

Head up the ramp on the left and capture another Sherm. Blast the other two to eliminate the threat of enemy fire, then take cover behind the dirt blocks. Cannonballs soon begin rolling across the flowers from the rotating defense mechanism on the Secret Flower Field entrance. Blast the cannonballs out of your path and target each of the four circular panels bearing Bowser's logo to unlock the Secret Flower Field (Power Moon #03). Activate the warp flag beyond the door when it opens and drop down the hole to the Secret Flower Field.

ⓓ Defend the Secret Flower Field!

BOSS: TORKDRIFT

The flying object Cappy spotted earlier is known as Torkdrift, and it's stealing all of the flowers! Capture the Uproot and walk beneath the glass dome on Torkdrift's underside. Stretch those root-legs to crack it like one of the nuts you've encountered. Keep up the pressure until Torkdrift is flipped upside-down.

Torkdrift takes notice of Mario after he scores this first hit against it. Three large cubes of gray blocks appear, each providing power to Torkdrift. Mario must continue to use the Uproot to smash these cubes, all while dodging laser attacks. Stay on the move to avoid the blue targeting rings as Torkdrift readies its laser attack. We recommend

continuously moving in a counter-clockwise direction along the out edge of the dirt clearing to keep ahead of the laser. Stretch the Uproot's legs to burst the cubes, then keep moving.

Destroy the three cubes while avoiding the laser attacks to flip Torkdrift right-side up. Move under it again, stretch the Uproot's legs, and burst open the glass dome.

Torkdrift changes up its attack strategy after the second hit. Move to the edge of the dirt and stretch the Uproot nice and tall in preparation of the ripple-like energy rings that radiate outwards. Release the stretch to make the Uproot leap over the ring as it approaches. The third attempt will be a much taller stack of rings so make sure the Uproot is at its max height.

Once the radiating rings have been avoided, Torkdrift attempts to attack with its laser blast, as before. Make your way around the perimeter of the dirt clearing, bursting apart the gray cubes—use the shadows on the ground and line the Uproot up with the center—while avoiding the blue targeting rings. Shatter the three cubes then move under the center and crack the glass dome a third time. Repeat this entire routine one more time to score a fourth and final hit to collect Power Moon #04

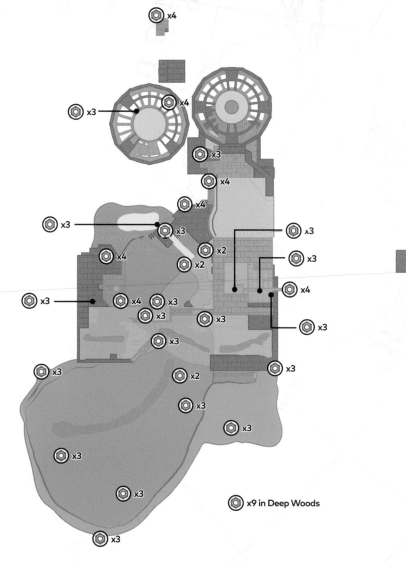

Extend Your Stay

If you've been following along with this chapter thus far, you should have at least twelve of the Power Moon entries checked off the list. This leaves dozens to discover, in addition to the rest of the 100 Regional Coins. Wooded Kingdom has many hidden ledges, tunnels, and caves that, when viewed from a top-down 2D map, can be hard to locate. Pay careful attention to the directions provided, start from the top, and work downward if you can't find the Power Moon or Regional Coins suggested by the accompanying maps.

◎ Souvenir Shopping

Wooded Kingdom contains 100 Regional Coins in the form of purple nuts. Though most of the 100 coins can be found during your initial visit, you'll need to return after defeating Bowser to get them all.

	Life-Up Heart	Wooded Kingdom Power Moon	Mechanic Cap	Mechanic Outfit	Explorer Hat
	· ⓘ 50	· ⓘ 100	· ⓘ 50	· ⓘ 150	· ◎ 5

	Explorer Outfit	Scientist Visor	Scientist Outfit	Wooded Kingdom Sticker	Flowers from Steam Gardens	Steam Gardener Watering Can
	· ◎ 10	· ◎ 20	· ◎ 25	· ◎ 10	· ◎ 5	· ◎ 25

Local Currency

The vast majority of the purple coins in Wooded Kingdom can be found while playing through the objectives and seeking out the Power Moons. Many can be found in the forest near the Odyssey, particularly along the wall that surrounds the area, or inside the trunks of a tree. Others can be found in Sky Garden Tower and in Deep Woods and other interior side areas. Here are tips for finding those most easily overlooked:

In Deep Woods, seek out the Boulder with a button on top of it and capture it. Move the Boulder out of the way to enter a tree trunk tunnel for three purple coins.

Enter the maintenance area (where the Beanstalk in Iron Road: Entrance is) as a captured Uproot and use it to reach the three Regional Coins on the shelf behind the beanstalk.

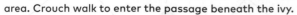

There are four Regional Coins tucked inside a tiny maintenance shaft opposite the Goombette in the Forest Charging Station area. Crouch walk to enter the passage beneath the ivy.

🌙 Power Moons

The 54 Power Moons at Wooded Kingdom expand to a total of 76 after Bowser is defeated, giving Wooded Kingdom the third most Power Moons of all. Power Moons #01, 02, 03, 04, 05, 09, 13, 15, 16, 23, 24, and 25 were obtained while taking on the Broodals and saving the Secret Flower Field from being pilfered. Consult the prior pages for help.

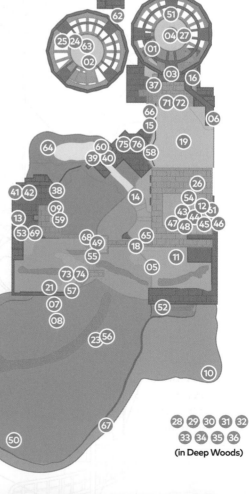

28 29 30 31 32
33 34 35 36
(in Deep Woods)

06 Back Way Up the Mountain

Warp to Iron Mountain Road, Station 8 and capture an Uproot in the pit below the ramp. Break open the gray blocks on the wall in the corner to reveal an 8-bit warp pipe and head inside. Run and jump along the side of the mountain to the platforms beyond the Goombas. Dash and jump from the upper right-hand platform to reach the Power Moon. There is no secret Power Moon area in this mural.

07 Rolling Rock in the Woods

Locate the rock under the metal fence in the woods, near the rabbit, and toss Cappy at it. There are several in the area, but only one glows in different colors when struck. Continue batting this rock around the area until it breaks.

08 Caught Hopping in the Forest!

Spot the rabbit sitting near the boulders across the dirt path from Crazy Cap. The rabbit coughes up a Power Moon if you get close enough to hit it. Mario can do this via a tackle jump or by throwing Cappy at the rabbit in hopes of stunning it. Another method is to toss a rock down the hill at the rabbit and hope it hits it. This, too, stuns the rabbit so Mario can get close enough to hit it.

10 Atop the Tall Tree

Capture an Uproot on the plateau to the east of the Odyssey and seek the tree near the southeastern edge of the area.

Stretch the Uproot to reach the wooden ledge and leap onto it. Stretch again to reach the ledge above, then use the Uproot to crack apart the nut higher up the tree.

11 Tucked Away Inside the Tunnel

Capture an Uproot on the plateau east of the Odyssey, above the waterfall, and enter the tunnel where the water is flowing from.

Use the Uproot to hop onto the Fire Bro, then stretch as tall as it will go and release the Capture so Mario can reach the upper ledge. Jump up and crack the nut with Cappy to get the Power Moon.

12 Over the Cliff's Edge

Return to the area beneath the Iron Road: Summit Path warp flag, where the Sherm is, and head around the southern ledge, to the east. Jump along the narrow ledges toward the Regional Coins in the distance and round the corner. Swing from bar to bar as you make your way through the rings near the crumbling walkway to a small alcove with a nut and a warp pipe. Crack the nut for the Power Moon and use the pipe to return.

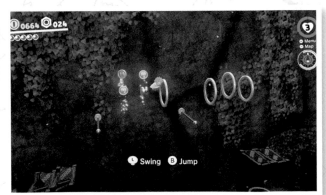

⑭ Climb the Cliff to Get the Nut

The nut containing this Power Moon is high on the cliff to the right of the entrance to the red maze at Iron Road: Entrance. To reach it, climb the wall near the Odyssey and follow it to the plateau atop the waterfall in the southeastern forest. Go through the cave with the Fire Bro and pull the lever to unlock the door. Once outside, use the Fire Bro (or nearby Uproot) to leap to the rocky ledge above the nearby purple coins. Hop along the rocks to the west, toward the red maze. Use the Fire Bro's fireballs to break open the nut.

⑰ Cracked Nut on a Crumbling Tower

Warp to Iron Road: Halfway Point and hit the P-Switch to activate the flower road leading to the tower to the north. This time, instead of using the second P-Switch to continue to Sky Garden Road, head north along the crumbling walkway. Grab the four Regional Coins around the back side of the tower before continuing to the top of this northernmost tower.

⑱ The Nut that Grew on the Tall Fence

This Power Moon resides in a nut on the fence to the west of Iron Mountain Path, Station 8. Follow instructions for Power Moon #49 to reach the Iron Cage if you haven't already done so. Drop through the crumbling walkway inside the Iron Cage to reach the top of the fence. The nut is just steps away, directly east of the tower supporting the Iron Cage.

⑲ Fire in the Cave

Return to the red maze near Iron Road: Entrance and circle around the left-hand side of the pistoning columns to find a scarecrow near a locked door. Toss Cappy at the scarecrow and enter the cave to battle a Fire Bro one-on-one, without Cappy. Dodge the fireballs while circling around the Fire Bro and leap up and bounce off the foe to earn a Power Moon.

Mario only needs to hit the Fire Bro once without Cappy to complete the challenge.

⑳ Hey Out There, Captain Toad!

Warp to the Observation Deck (see Power Moon #54 for details) and capture the Glydon. Walk out along the narrow ledge where the purple coins were and spot the isolated tower far to the east. Glide over to that platform with the Glydon to meet Captain Toad.

㉑ Love in the Forest Ruins

Warp to the Forest Charging Station and make your way to the area with the numerous Goombas. Capture the

stack of three and hop onto the towers of two Goombas to grow in height. Build your stack of Goombas until it is eight Goombas tall then approach the Goombette on the ledge.

㉒ Inside a Rock in the Forest

Capture a Sherm near the Forest Charging Station and steer it off the rock cliff overlooking the forest to the south. Pilot Sherm along the dirt path toward the Odyssey and open fire on the rocks near the tree across from the Odyssey to reveal the Power Moon.

㉖ Spinning-Platforms Treasure

Climb the gold-colored pole on the east side of Flower Field Secret Entrance and walk north along the narrow wall above the 8-bit mural. Drop to the triangular-shaped ledge below and, from there, jump south to the other, lower ledges on the cliff face. Approach the spinning platforms near the rings and leap from one to the other.

Stick close to the outer arms of the spinning platforms and carefully leap onto the orange end-caps as they rotate vertically.

This is your best chance to make the jump from one the second spinning platform to the warp pipe leading to the treasure room.

If you're having trouble, scout a path between the scarecrow and the warp pipe protruding from the cliffside at the highest point in the Deep Woods; the Power Moon is on this line.

27 Making the Secret Flower Field Bloom

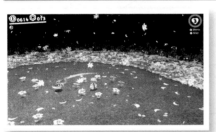

Return to the Secret Flower Field after defeating Torkdrift and leap down the hole. Note the three rings of flowers that have yet to bloom. Spin throw Cappy at each of the circles of plants to make them all bloom simultaneously. This triggers a reaction which causes the entire field to bloom, earning you a Power Moon.

28 Rolling Rock in the Deep Woods

Follow the dirt path around the edge of the Deep Woods and look for a lone rock on the edge of the path, where it comes closest to the stony ledge. Hit the rock with Cappy and look for a multi-colored glow. Continue smacking this rock with Cappy to break it and get a Power Moon.

29 Glowing in the Deep Woods

This particular Timer Challenge takes place in the Deep Woods. Locate the scarecrow near the babbling brook. The hardest part of this challenge is figuring out where the Power Moon actually is. Face the scarecrow in the uphill direction before you throw Cappy at it then immediately round the tree directly behind it and long jump into a roll straight uphill, veering off to the right of the brook. If you don't see the Power Moon after rounding that tree, you're headed in the wrong direction.

30 Past the Peculiar Pipes

Enter the warp pipe at the top of the hill in Deep Woods to trigger a maze-like sequence of pipes. Mario must enter the pipes in the correct sequence to earn the treasure, otherwise he is forced out of the area and has to try again. Each successful choice is met by additional pipes, complicating matters further. The correct sequence changes for each game, so you must find the correct combination through trial and error, and a little bit of luck!

31 By the Babbling Brook in the Deep Woods

Follow the creek upstream in the Deep Woods, past the small pool where Power Moon #33 is located and head to the left. There are a number of breakable stone blocks in this area, piled against the cliff face, and there's a Power Moon buried beneath them. The only way to break these stones is by using the T-Rex or by firing coins at them with the Coin Coffer. The latter option is much safer—and easier—though arguably not as entertaining.

32 The Hard Rock in Deep Woods

Capture the T-Rex or Coin Coffer in Deep Woods and follow the dirt path downhill toward the beanstalk near where the trail comes closest to the stony ledge. With your back to the beanstalk, spot the pile of hard rocks directly across the trail. Break through these rocks to reveal a glowing spot on the ground. Ground pound it for a Power Moon.

33 A Treasure Made from Coins

This is one of the costlier Power Moons to obtain, as you're going to have to "feed" a plant with coins from a Coin Coffer—and it costs a lot to produce fruit! Dive into the Deep Woods and capture the Coin Coffer atop the small hummock downhill from the warp pipe at the top of the area. Follow the creek downstream to the small pool where a green plant can be seen growing amidst a number of golden buttons. Fire coins at the plant to make it grow. Make sure you have an unobstructed angle on the plant (sometimes plants or the topography can be in the way) and continue shooting coins at the plant until it grows nearly as tall as the adjacent tree. Listen for the sound of it producing fruit, then climb the tree to get the Power Moon the plant produced.

It's entirely possible to run out of coins as you try to earn this Power Moon—the plant takes hundreds of coins to produce a Power Moon—but you needn't leave the Deep Woods to replenish your purse. Coin Coffers grant Mario as much as 30 coins each time a new one is captured. Also, the glowing spots throughout Deep Woods each release coins and Mini Goombas that can effectively be farmed for coins. There's plenty of gold to uncover in the Deep Woods, you just have to look for it.

34 Beneath the Roots of the Moving Tree

Drop into the Deep Woods and climb the stepped rock ledges to the lone tree with a green button atop it. Capture the tree and move it a few steps to the side. This exposes a glowing spot in the grass. Ground pound the glow to uncover a Power Moon.

35 Deep Woods Treasure Trap

Locate the warp pipe in the base of a massive tree within the Deep Woods and head inside. There are three treasure chests here that, if opened in the proper order, yield a Power Moon. Failure to unlock them in the correct sequence causes three Chinchos to appear.

Mario can defeat the Chinchos by leaping onto their heads. Nevertheless, the chests should be opened in the following sequence: middle, left, right.

36 Exploring for Treasure

Visit the closet in the Odyssey and change into the Explorer Hat and Explorer Outfit sold by Crazy Cap in Wooded Kingdom. Return to the Deep Woods area and follow the babbling brook uphill to a locked door with a Steam Gardener nearby. Show him your Explorer attire for access to a room containing this treasure.

37 Wooded Kingdom Timer Challenge 1

Head to the Iron Road: Halfway Point warp flag and note the scarecrow beside the flag. Toss Cappy at it to start the

challenge. This Timer Challenge requires Mario to swing and jump his way up a series of red bars to reach the Power Moon. Mario can release his swing in either direction so don't worry about having to make him turn around or trying to wall jump off the ivy. There's even enough time to get the Power Moon if he falls once.

38 Wooded Kingdom Timer Challenge 2

This Timer Challenge takes place in Forest Charging Station. Toss Cappy at the scarecrow from the right to start the challenge, then quickly wall jump off the center charging station to reach the yellow platform. Run and jump across the middle to the second yellow platform as it rises to the Power Moon. This is a very short challenge, but there's no time for an errant jump. You must get onto the first yellow platform in time for its second ascent, else you won't have time to reach the Power Moon.

Complete Timer Challenge 2 and ground pound jump from the top of the challenge to the upper ledge above the Power Moon. Follow this to the orange cube on the right to find a painting leading to Luncheon Kingdom. You can also reach this spot with the Glydon.

39 Flooding Pipeway

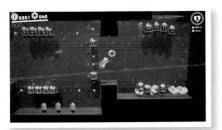

Warp to Iron Road: Entrance and leap over the railing to the pond near Talkatoo. Dive to the bottom and enter the warp pipe to access this challenge level. Floodwaters fill and empty with this Fuzzy-filled gauntlet of platforms and alcoves. To clear it, Mario needs to use the rising and falling water to swim and jump past the Fuzzies. Wait for the water to drain before moving past the first Fuzzies, then swim with the rising tide and leap out of the water at the top of the room. Swim through the gauntlet of Fuzzies up ahead while the water is high and wait on the ledge before the circling Fuzzies for it to rise again. Swim up to the Power Moon.

40 Flooding Pipeway Ceiling Secret

Follow the directions for Power Moon #39 and make your way to the upper platform in the middle of the level, above the water. Ground pound jump toward the gap in the ceiling and wall jump through the vertical shaft that becomes visible to reach the Power Moon up above.

41 Wandering in the Fog

Ride the rocket from the Forest Charging Station to this fog-shrouded challenge level. Here, Mario must find five Moon Shards while navigating with limited visibility. The first two Moon Shards are near the starting point, the second of which is just down a step from the bridge leading to the ? Block.

You should have two Moon Shards before crossing to the blocks. Collect the third Moon Shard near the Paragoombas.

Capture one of the two Paragoombas near the Moon Shard and fly up and over the third one nearby to find a solitary tower. From there, spot the coins in the air and follow them to the next Moon Shard. Descend along the coins and continue downward into the fog until beneath the platform with the rocket. Fly along the underside of the platforms to find the fifth Moon Shard near two more Paragoombas.

42 Nut Hidden in the Fog

Follow the instructions for Power Moon #41 until you reach the fifth Moon Shard. Follow the coins underneath the platform until you spot another Paragoomba. Land on the concrete platform above it to locate a nut containing a Power Moon.

43 Flower Road Run

Round the corner from the base of Summit Path to the right (alongside the ramp) and wall jump up to the ledge above the coins. Enter the red door and step on the P-Switch to trigger a flower road. Run along it, ignoring the Goombas unless trying to collect Power Moon #44, and activate the second P-Switch. Let the flower road get a bit ahead of you then run along and long jump off the sharp drop to avoid the poison. Wall jump up the section of flower road that climbs vertically, grab the three Regional Coins atop the platform, and wait for the flower road to grow again before continuing. Wait at the cascading poison for the flower road to reemerge near the coins then leap across the gap. Long jump off the edge of the flower road to reach the Power Moon.

⑭ Flower Road Reach

Follow the instructions for Power Moon #43 and capture the Goombas on the first island. Quickly assemble a Goomba Tower of at least seven Goombas and return to the flower road before it passes you by. Run along the flower road to the tower with the Power Moon atop it. Release the capture, grab the Power Moon, and leap back onto the flower road to continue.

㊺ Elevator Escalation

Warp to Iron Road Summit Path and use a Rocket Flower to reach the red door on the ledge at the upper right-hand corner of the ramp with the rings. Head inside and capture the Sherm near the caged P-Switch. Shoot the cage and press the P-Switch to ride the elevator to the lower level. Blast the Burrbos and the cage and hit the next switch. The third level contains several Fire Bros. Destroy the cage with Sherm and blast away at two of the three Fire Bros. Capture the remaining Fire Bro and hop up the ledges to get the three purple coins. Recapture Sherm, hit the P-Switch and descend to the fourth level where seven Sherms await. Use the metal pillars for cover and strafe in and out of protection as you blast the Sherms, starting with those closest. Blast through the breakable blocks to a cage containing a Power Moon.

㊻ Elevator Blind Spot

Follow the instructions for reaching the area where Power Moon #45 is. Capture the Sherm inside the entrance, but don't descend! Instead, turn around and spot the breakable brown blocks high on the rear wall of the room. Blast away at these with Sherm's cannon to reveal a hidden Power Moon.

㊼ Walking on Clouds

Warp to Summit Path and climb the ramp to where the Secret Gardeners are located. Get the seed from the one not watering the flowers and carry it to the P-Switch. Step on the switch to activate a timed series of platforms that deliver Mario to the Observation Deck (he can't warp there with the seed). Once there, plant the seed in the pot to the right of the Glydon and climb the beanstalk to the clouds.

The music for this coin-choked cloud level should bring back plenty of memories for fans of *Super Mario World*. Capture the Uproot and hop aboard the moving platform. Stretch the Uproot's legs to grab as many coins as you can—don't miss the three Regional Coins—and hop from one blue platform to the other. Land on the red block and wait for the sliding platforms to pass underneath so you can ride it to the Power Moon in the distance.

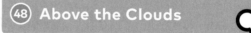

㊽ Above the Clouds

Follow the directions for Power Moon #47 and use the Uproot to make your way to the red and green blocks near the end of the cloud stage. Leap up to the upper level of this block pile and note the shadow on the ground. Stretch as high as the Uproot will go and jump straight up to get the Power Moon high above.

㊾ Secret Path to the Steam Gardens!

If you've been wondering how to reach the Iron Cage in Wooded Kingdom, you've come to the right place! The only way inside is via the warp painting leading from Metro Kingdom. Carefully leap over the railing near the Odyssey to land on the grated ledge to access it. The warp painting in Metro Kingdom leads to Lake Kingdom if you chose to visit Wooded Kingdom before Lake Kingdom.

50 Found with Wooded Kingdom Art

Locate the Hint Art on the tree directly south of the Odyssey and set sail for the Sand Kingdom. The art is a little more cryptic than prior puzzles, but those familiar with Sand Kingdom should recognize the Koopa pictured as the one who offers the Trace Walking challenge. The other hints are suggesting that you must walk north to find two small shrubs. This sounds easy enough, but the trick is understanding how far you must walk to find those two shrubs —they're clear across the Sand Kingdom, on the northern edge of the desert. Make your way around the massive hole where the Inverted Kingdom was and continue north. Ground pound the spot in front of the bushes to uncover the Power Moon.

51 Swing Around Secret Flower Field

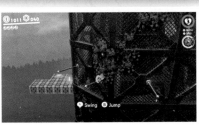

Warp to Secret Flower Field Entrance and use the golden pipe on the eastern side of the area to climb atop the wall. Note the locked panel in need of a key and make your way up and over the entrance to the wall on the other side. Descend the golden pipe to the crumbling walkway and make a tackle jump for the red bar. Swing and jump around the side of the structure to reach the key near the P-Switch. Follow the flower road to the Power Moon.

52 Jammin' in the Wooded Kingdom

Locate Toad on the ledge above the waterfall flowing into the forest after you've visited the cloud area (Power Moon #47). He's beneath the Binoculars near Summit Path. Toad wants to hear a tune that fits the theme "Sky-high coins aplenty!" Select track 75 titled "Above the Clouds" to give him what he wants in exchange for a Power Moon.

53 Wooded Kingdom Regular Cup

The Koopa hosting the race is near the Forest Charging Station warp flag. The race traverses the red maze of Iron Road: Entrance to Iron Road: Halfway Point, where you fought the Big Poison Piranha Plant. For the Regular Cup, we're going to take you through the red maze while only utilizing one of the two shortcuts possible on this course. Check the Master Cup entry (Power Moon #69) below for an advanced shortcut.

Start the race by ignoring the beanstalk and the other racers. Instead, cut past the Steam Gardeners to the left and leap over the railing to Iron Road: Entrance. Long jump into a triple jump for the fastest distance. Triple Jump across the creek to the pistoning structures and capture the first Uproot you can. Hurry through the maze with the Uproot to reach the finish first.

54 Peach in the Wooded Kingdom

Head to Summit Path and climb the ramp toward the Secret Flower Field Entrance. Step on the P-Switch to activate a timed series of platforms that can be used to reach the Observation Deck. There, you'll find Princess Peach and Tiara looking out over Wooded Kingdom. Activate the warp flag so don't need to use the timed platforms in the future.

Moons from the Moon Rock

55 High Up in the Cave

Capture an Uproot and guide it to the cave that connects the forest near Crazy Cap to Iron Road: Entrance (where the Sphynx originally was). Stretch the Uproot's legs to pluck the Power Moon out of the air from above the cave. It's also possible to use a Fire Bro. Advanced players may even get it with a tricky jump sequence.

56 Lost in the Tall Trees

Head to the Observation Deck and capture the Glydon. Look out over the forest treetops left of the Odyssey to spot a wooden crate high on a platform in the trees. Fly to it as the Glydon, release the capture, and smash the crate with Cappy to free the Power Moon. Glide back over to Summit Path to collect it.

57 Looking Down on the Goombas

Capture the Glydon at Observation Deck and soar to the uppermost section of fence near where the Goombette is— glide on a straight path toward the Odyssey. Land atop the fence and break open the nut to get this Power Moon.

58 High Up on a Rock Wall

Capture an Uproot near Iron Road: Entrance and locate the three gray blocks to the right of the red maze. Get the coins from the unbreakable center block, then leap onto it as an Uproot. Stretch tall to break the nut up above the gray blocks.

59 The Nut in the Robot Storeroom

Capture an Uproot at Iron Road: Entrance and bring it inside the robot storeroom where you planted the beanstalk leading up to Forest Charging Station. Locate the nut above the door and use the Uproot to smash it open. Or, for something different, gather up a stack of Goombas near the Forest Charging Station, drop through the hole where the beanstalk emerges and crack and use the Goomba Tower to reach the nut.

60 Above the Iron Mountain Path

Take the Glydon for a high-flying trip across the skies above the Iron Road: Entrance area. Leap from the top of the Observation Deck while facing the pond near Talkatoo—the Power Moon is high in the air above this area. Press up on the controls to descend quickly, else Glydon might soar right past it.

61 The Nut Under the Observation Deck

Capture the Uproot below the warp flag at Iron Mountain Path, Station 8 and guide it up the ramp toward P-Switch that leads up to the Observation Deck. Don't step on the switch. Instead, round the corner to the left and stretch the Uproot's legs near the railing to the left of the dirt rocks to uncover four invisible blocks high up on the wall. Leap onto the blocks and stretch again to reach the nut higher up, directly beneath the Observation Deck.

62 Bird Traveling the Forest

There's a glowing bluebird circling the Sky Garden Tower and Iron Road area, lapping an area from Talkatoo to the northern side of the Sky Garden. There are several places from which to hit this bird, but it takes patience, as it changes its altitude on alternating laps. Consider following the flower road to the platform with the P-Switch on the north side of Sky Garden Tower and wait there for the bird. Every other lap that it makes of the area, it flies low enough to be hit with Cappy.

63 Invader in the Sky Garden

Warp to Sky Garden Tower and head up the stairs to where you earlier fought Spewart. The Broodals are long gone, but there's a Yoofoe milling around and the only way to get high enough to bounce off his big purple button is to build a Goomba Tower. Capture a Goomba and quickly assemble a stack while avoiding the occasional cannonball dropped by the Yoofoe. The first hit is free, as the Yoofoe doesn't try to defend itself. After that, its arms gain blades that can damage Mario if the Goomba Tower gets hit. The Yoofoe continues to deploy cannonballs and Goombas. Build the tower with seven Goombas, move toward the Yoofoe and release the capture to propel Mario onto it. Leap up and bounce onto the purple button. Land two hits to win a Power Moon.

64 Hot, Hot, Hot from the Campfire

One of the visitors from Luncheon Kingdom needs help lighting his campfire near Talkatoo. A Fire Bro will come in handy. There are two places nearby to capture a Fire Bro. One option is to capture an Uproot and use it to climb the rock ledges above Iron Road: Entrance. Another option is to capture the Fire Bro within the cave above the waterfall in the forest area, near Toad. That one's a little farther, but easier to reach. Either way, return as a Fire Bro and hurl a fireball or two at the unlit campfire to earn the Power Moon.

65 Wooded Kingdom Timer Challenge 3

Warp to Iron Mountain Path, Station 8 and carefully leap over the railing down onto the triangular rock ledge where the scarecrow is. This is a relatively straightforward challenge, with the primary risk being that it's easy to overestimate how far the first yellow platform travels. Drop onto it without jumping then swing and jump across the bars and other platforms. Leap into a tackle jump from the final yellow platform to reach the Power Moon.

66 Moon Shards in the Forest

Five Moon Shards have been scattered throughout the red maze. Though it's easiest to get them with an Uproot, via the normal right-to-left direction, it's entirely possible to collect them in the other direction as well, provided you're up for a lot of wall jumping. While four of the Moon Shards are quite easy to spot, one is located all the way at the top of the maze, near the nut containing Power Moon #15. Break the nut then wall jump into a tackle jump to reach the Moon Shard. Or use an Uproot. The Power Moon appears on the left end of the maze.

67 Taking Notes; On Top of the Wall

Climb onto the wall that surrounds the forest where the Odyssey sets down and locate the Treble Clef on the eastern side. Face south as you walk through the note, then immediately begin rolling. You need to really watch your balance, but the only way to get all of the notes before they disappear is to roll your way to the finish line. But don't shake the controller! There's no need for the extra speed, and it only makes it more difficult!

68 Taking Notes: Stretching

Capture an Uproot from Iron Mountain Path, Station 8 and leap up and over the railing on the west side to descend down to the rock ledges to the right of Iron Road: Entrance. The treble clef is on the rock ledge above where the three purple coins were. Start the challenge and stretch the Uproot's legs to pluck the notes out of the air. Though it's possible to collect the notes using homing throws and upward throws, it's far easier with the help of an Uproot.

69 Wooded Kingdom Master Cup

Meet the Koopa at Forest Charging Station when you're ready to try the Master Cup race. As promised, this time we're going to show you how to win this race without using an Uproot. That's right, we're skipping the red maze! Long jump into a triple jump as before, bypassing the beanstalk. Dive toward the creek to land in a roll and climb the pistoning structures toward the start of the red maze, but don't capture an Uproot. Wall jump, turn and tackle jump onto the higher level—it's not easy, but it's faster than capturing an Uproot. Instead, note the gap in the fence at the left edge of the metal platform. Mario can clear this chasm with a well-timed dive jump, tackle jump combo. The Golden Koopa takes the initial shortcut, but won't bypass the red maze. Put this advanced line to use and shave over fifteen seconds off the route discussed in the Regular Cup tactics!

70 I Met an Uproot!

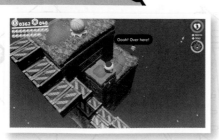

A Bonneter has made his way to the northernmost tower in Wooded Kingdom, beyond the flower roads connecting the Sky Garden with the Iron Road, and he wants to meet an Uproot.

Return to Iron Road: Entrance, capture an Uproot, and guide it through the red maze to the flower road leading to the north tower. Carefully guide the Uproot across the crumbling walkway to where the Bonneter is located to earn a Power Moon.

71 Invisible Road: Danger!

Enter the Moon Pipe at Secret Flower Field Entrance to access an area constructed of invisible platforms. There's no Moe-Eye here to help you see the floor, but there are a number of Poison Piranha Plants whose purple ink coats many of the otherwise invisible surfaces. Toss the available rocks at the plants then toss Cappy at them to capture the Poison Piranha Plant while it's chewing on the rock. Paint the ground if necessary, release the capture, and use Cappy to sweep a clear path. Watch the gap in the path after the second Poison Piranha Plant, then turn the corner to the left and leap for the revolving plus-shaped platform. Continue across the room until you reach the three Big Poison Piranha Plants. Jump across the gap just after the spinning platform and quickly toss Cappy at the larger plant on the left or right. Pick them off one by one by tossing Cappy at them then jumping atop their head.

72 Invisible Road: Hidden Room

Follow the tips for Power Moon #71 and return to the rotating platform in the center of the level. There is a hidden room on the far side, opposite the side you board the spinning platform from. It can help to capture the Poison Piranha Plant so you can paint the invisible walkway with ink and see where it's safe to walk. You can also dive jump from the edge of the rotating platform toward the doorway and trust us when we tell you that there is solid ground to land upon. Go for it!

73. Herding Sheep Above the Forest Fog

Enter the Moon Pipe near the Goombette to access this difficult sheep herding challenge. Mario must herd the sheep through a spiraling course that features several gaps, ledges, and sections without any guardrails. The key to doing this is to be patient, line Mario up behind the sheep in the direction he needs it go, and only to toss Cappy at the sheep when necessary. Much can be accomplished by walking behind the sheep. The sheep tries to avoid falling off the platforms when left to walk on its own. Don't hurry it!

The Sheep runs away from Mario so zigzag behind it to guide it through the barriers without falling. Make sure the sheep is facing straight ahead when you knock it up and over the gap in the floor.

74. Herding Sheep on the Iron Bridge

Enter the warp pipe beneath the corral in the Power Moon #73 level to access a second sheep herding challenge area. Move the sheep over to the edge before pressing the P-Switch, as iron bridge only appears temporarily once the switch is pressed. Center the sheep with the narrow walkway, hit it with Cappy, then chase after it to herd it to the far end of the bridge. Smack it with Cappy again to boot it across the gap to the corral. Stay directly behind the sheep to keep it on a straight path.

75. Down and Back Breakdown Road

Enter the Moon Pipe in the base of the pistoning columns at Iron Road: Entrance to enter this challenge level filled with Bullet Bills. Cross the stone walkway for the key as Bullet Bills shoot at Mario from all directions. Though it's possible to downthrow Cappy and capture a Bullet Bill, there's not much need. Instead, stay on foot and run and leap your way to the key. This releases a Power Moon from the locked panel back at the start, but don't head back the way you came! Instead, keep reading below for a great tip on how to earn this Power Moon and Power Moon #76 in one trip.

76. Below Breakdown Road

Follow the tips for Power Moon #75 to get the key needed for the prior Power Moon, but don't turn back the way you came.

Instead, dodge the Banzai Bill that appears near the key and drop to the stone blocks on the lower level. A second, lower altitude Banzai Bill blasts through the large wall in front of you. Capture it and guide it back across the level beneath the upper walkway. Pilot it straight into the massive stone wall below where you started to uncover this hidden Power Moon.

Cloud Kingdom

Welcome to Nimbus Arena

REGION AT A GLANCE

Population	Unknown
Size	Unknown
Locals	Unknown
Currency	Unknown
Industry	Unknown
Temperature	Average 73°F

Symbols of Peace

Perhaps signifying how peaceful this place is, many doves can be found living here. Supposedly, spotting a flock of doves grants you increased happiness.

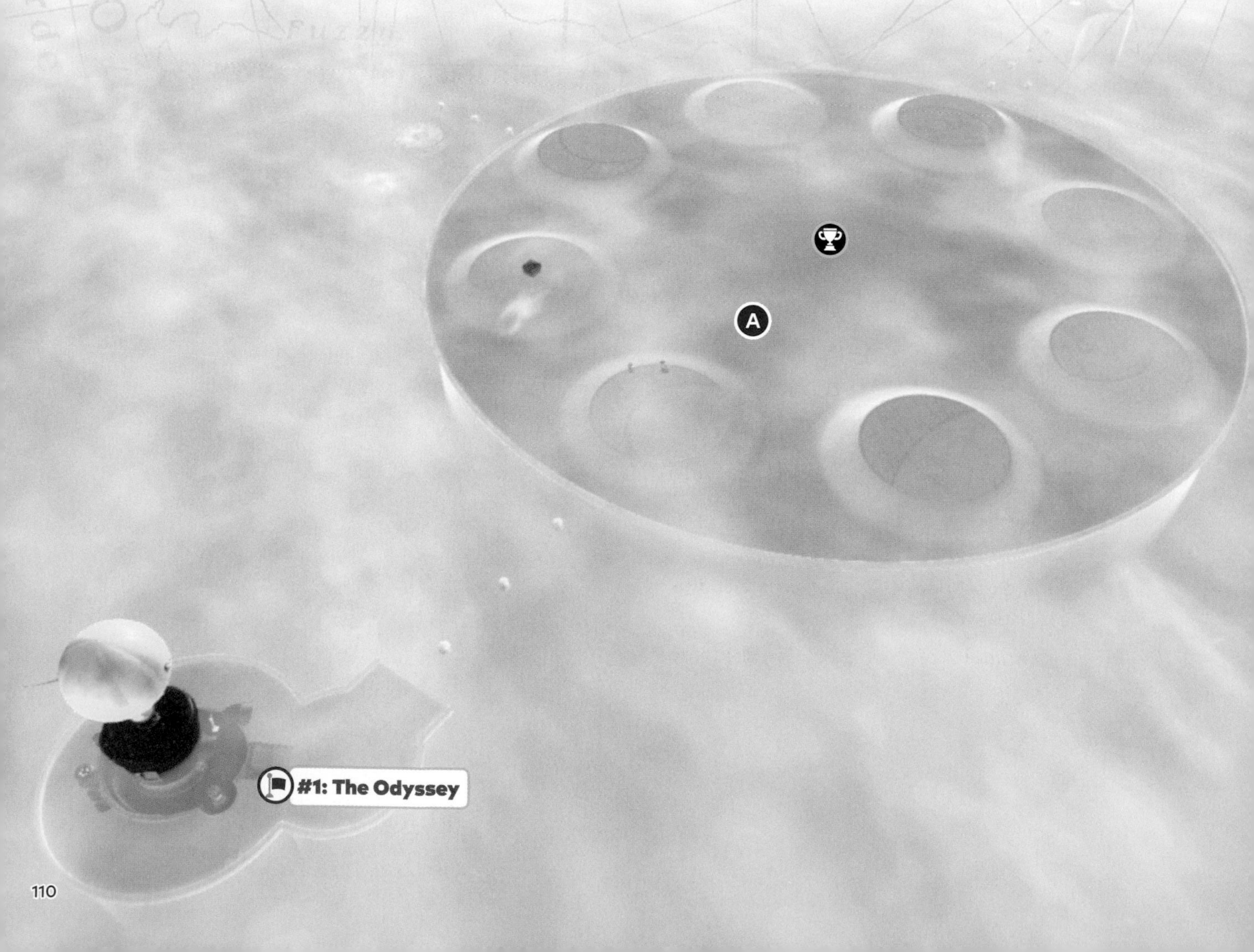

🏆

Ⓐ

🚩 #1: The Odyssey

LIFE ABOVE THE CLOUDS

Perhaps everyone has had the experience of looking up at the clouds and imagining what it would be like to live among them. As it turns out, as fantastical as it may sound, there was once such a kingdom whose citizens looked down on the world from a fluffy, puffy paradise.

STRANGELY FLOATY MATERIAL

While the particles that make up a cloud are extremely small and light, researchers have recently discovered a kind of cloud-like material that one can walk on. First discovered in Fossil Falls, this substance can change into and hold new shapes, and even support weight.

The discovery prompted certain researchers to open an investigation into whether there might have once been a "cloud kingdom" in the sky.

THREE KEYS TO THE KINGDOM

1. Navigate the vast sea of clouds that seems to go on forever.
2. Feel the unyielding cloud-floor that won't budge no matter how you stomp.
3. Explore the remnants of the civilization that once existed here.

VESTIGES OF GREATNESS

Once researchers started looking for places in the sky, they quickly found a large platform of the levitating substance, dubbed Nimbus Arena.

Mysteriously, the land had markings that accurately showed the waxing and waning phases of the moon. Now, besides the obvious "how," researchers had to question "why?"

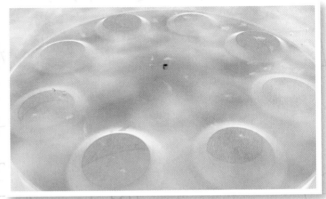

GIANT CLOUD ARCHES

Researchers are thus far baffled by the large cloud archway here. Some theorize that it's a kind of reticle that aligns with the moon. Some evidence suggests that the arch pulled this kingdom's Moon Rock to a specific location from the moon.

The only certainty is that the Cloud Kingdom will continue to interest researchers for many years.

SHOWERS OF FLOWERS

The investigation is concluded now and yielded few undisputed facts. But the bits of cloud that fall like flower petals here make it the most dreamlike place you'll ever visit.

Ⓐ Hat-to-Hat Combat

Mario's journey to Metro Kingdom takes an unexpected detour when the Odyssey catches up to Bowser in the skies near Cloud Kingdom. Not about to back away from a challenge, Bowser disembarks his airship as soon as Mario enters Nimbus Arena. Metro Kingdom will have to wait!

Don't be fooled by the tranquil setting, there's a storm brewing!

BOSS: BOWSER

Bowser leaps onto one of the raised platforms in Nimbus Arena and tosses his hat at Mario. Bowser's top hat is equipped with punching gloves and can certainly deliver Mario a beating, but we're not going to let that happen! Hit Bowser's hat with Cappy to knock Bowser's hat upside-down. Run to the hat so Mario can put it on.

Mario can run, jump and side somersault as normal while wearing Bowser's hat. Use these skills to leap over the fire rings that radiate across the ring each time Bowser leaps to a new platform. Chase after him as he jumps around the area so that you're close by when he tires.

Hurry to Bowser and unload with a flurry of punches, using his mechanical punching hat against him! Continue the flurry of punches until Bowser is knocked against the spiked fence. He falls back on the platform, stunned, then recovers and leaps to the other side of the arena. Get ready for round two!

Bowser doesn't just toss his white punching hat this time. He tries to confuse Mario by throwing two purple ones at the same time. Avoid the purple hats by running from left to right across the arena so that you're in position to hit the white hat with Cappy. Cappy can also be used to flick away the purple hats. Focus on the white hat, as striking the proper hat causes the others to disappear.

Bowser leaps to a new platform, creating another round of fire rings to jump over. More significantly, Bowser also hurls a cannonball-like sphere at Mario comprised of bricks. Punch through the brick-ball if you're unable to dodge it (it may yield a Heart if punched) and close on Bowser's position. If Mario is close enough already, he can run right under the brick sphere. Unleash another flurry of punches on Bowser to knock him into the spiked railings a second time. Two hits down, one to go!

The fight continues in much the same manner for a third sequence, only this time Bowser hurls six hats at Mario instead of three. Once again, dodge the purple hats by running across the arena, then side somersault or hit the purple hats with Cappy while angling toward the white hat.

Purple hats often drop a Heart when destroyed. Hit the white hat with Cappy and rush toward it to put it on.

Ambush Bowser with a flurry of punches, but beware, this time he's going to block them! Watch for him to briefly turn his back to Mario and stop punching. Wait a moment then leap over his tail swipe as it sweeps across the platform. Unleash another barrage of punches to knock Bowser back to his airship.

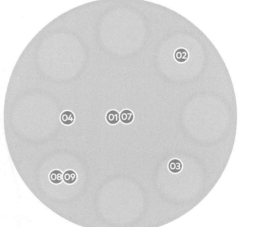

Extend Your Stay

Mario isn't given the opportunity to stay at Cloud Kingdom. Bowser's cannons made sure of that. But Mario can certainly return once the Odyssey is repaired. He won't find any Regional Coins here or a Crazy Cap store, but he will find a small number of Power Moons to collect.

Power Moons

There are nine Power Moons at Cloud Kingdom, all of which are available on subsequent visits. Mario must return after defeating Bowser for good if he's to find every Power Moon.

01 Picture Match: Basically a Goomba

Enter the warp pipe to join Toad in the first Picture Match challenge. Take a good look at the Goomba pictured in the art, because it's going to be up to you to capture his eyes, mouth, and eyebrows and reposition them back on the image, one by one. Of course, normally you'd have only your memory and this book to go by, but because you have a Nintendo Switch, you can use the system's screenshot ability to take a picture of the Goomba before you begin. Access the Switch's Album screen to reference the image (just like with Hint Art) as you place the pieces. You only need to achieve 60 points to earn a Power Moon, so Toad is pretty forgiving this time around. Each piece disappears as soon as you place it so pay close attention!

Be careful not to accidentally release a captured piece too soon, as that could ruin your score. A few details to note: Goomba's teeth point up, the glint of his pupils point upwards, and the thick part of his eyebrows extend beyond his head.

02 Peach in the Cloud Kingdom

Princess Peach and Tiara have somehow made it to Nimbus Arena. Cross the area to the north to find them admiring the view atop one of the moon phase platforms. As usual, Princess Peach rewards Mario with a Power Moon for finding her.

🌙 Moons from the Moon Rock

03 Digging in the... Cloud?

There's a Power Moon buried in the platform two platforms clockwise of where Princess Peach is located (and one counter-clockwise from Hint Toad). This is the half-moon phase platform. Move around the area of the platform closest to Peach and feel for the vibrations. Ground pound the platform to uncover the Power Moon.

04 High, High Above the Clouds

Cross the cap clouds to the western platform and ground pound the sunburst to ride it to a mass of cap clouds high above. Mario has to be quick to cross this array of cap clouds, as they don't stay active for long. Fortunately, they are positioned very close together so there's not much risk of falling. Take care to rotate the camera to ensure Mario is facing the next cap cloud head-on, else there is a greater risk of time-consuming errant throws.

⑤ Crossing the Cloud Sea

You'll likely notice the locked panel beneath the Moon Rock as soon as you break it apart. The key to unlock the Power Moon inside is directly north, beyond a sequence of cap clouds. Descend the curving stairs to the clouds and carefully hop platform by platform to the key, using Cappy to trigger the cap clouds. They don't last long, nor do they form a seamless path much jumping is required—but they do make it possible to get the key.

⑥ Taking Notes: Up and Down

Leap across the cap clouds to the circular platform to the east of Nimbus Arena and ground pound the starburst design. This sends the platform rising into the air where a treble clef is. Leap to trigger the Taking Notes even and be ready to throw Cappy. Four rows of notes are aligned off the edge of the platform at different heights, and in different directions. The only way to collect them is with Cappy, but there's not a lot of time so you need to act fast. Ground pound the platform again once it descends to the clouds to have it rise for a second trip. Don't try to collect two consecutive rows of notes in a single pass, as the platform moves too fast. Instead, aim for the top and bottom rows on the initial descent. The second and third rows are both at middle-height on the platforms path. Collect one set on the way up after the ground pound and the other set on the descent right before time expires.

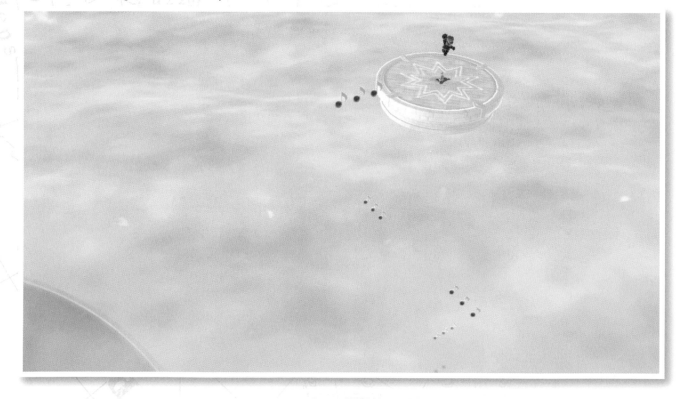

07 Picture Match: A Stellar Goomba!

This Picture Match is just like the one you completed to earn Power Moon #01, but now you have to score 80 points. That's not the only additional challenge, however. Other than the basic outline of the Goomba, the entire image is empty! Refer back to the image you captured earlier with your Nintendo Switch (and the accompanying screenshot) as you place the pieces. As a guide, the Goomba's pupils should line up with the pinched sides of his head and be roughly one pupil's with apart.

08 King of the Cube!

Enter the Moon Pipe near Hint Toad to access this magical cube comprised of a continuous multi-sided 8-bit level. There are five Moon Shards to find in the cube, one for each of the five faces of the cube that you'll visit by ordinary means. Though the cube looks complicated at first, there's only one way to proceed so don't worry about having to solve any tricky puzzles here. Just get the Moon Shards, dodge the Bullet Bills as they fly past, and squash any Goombas in your way. Also, be sure to kick the Koopa Shell in the third screen so that it eliminates the Spineys for you down below—that will make things *much* easier. The fifth and final face (for this Power Moon) takes place upside-down. Wait for the Hammer Bro to drop to the upper row of bricks then move over and bounce him off the level. Break through the blocks to get the Moon Shard.

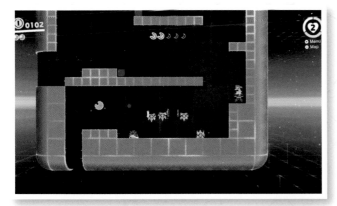

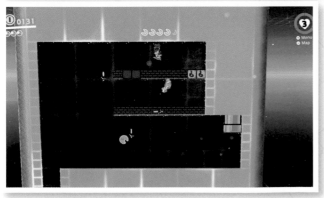

09 The Sixth Face

Follow the directions for Power Moon #08 until you reach the fourth face of the cube. There, before descending via the coin shaft on the right, trigger the invisible block above the fourth grid block on the right. Leap from the steel block that appears to the warp pipe above. This goes to a sixth face of the cube containing a Power Moon encircled by Fuzzies. Leap with care!

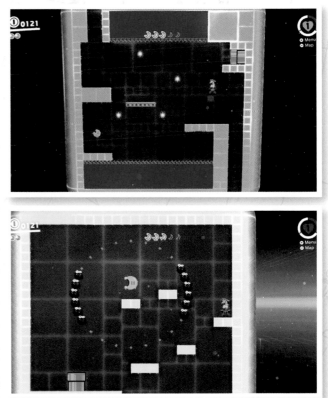

117

Lost Kingdom

Welcome to Forgotten Isle

REGION AT A GLANCE

Population	Unknown
Size	Smallish
Locals	Unknown
Currency	Leaf-shaped
Industry	Unknown
Temperature	Average 91°F

INDIGENOUS FLORA & FAUNA

TRAPEETLE		TROPICAL WIGGLER		FUZZY	
Can Capture?		Can Capture?		Can Capture?	
No		Yes		No	

KLEPTO	
Can Capture?	
No	

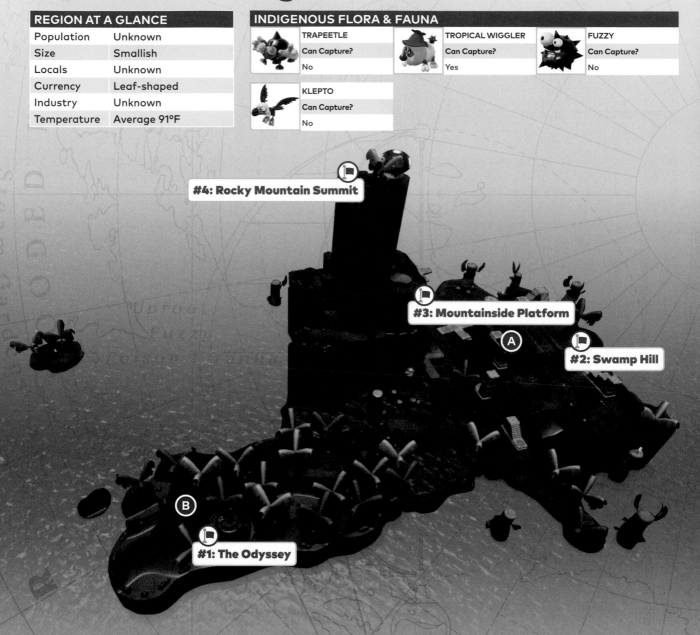

#4: Rocky Mountain Summit

#3: Mountainside Platform

Ⓐ

#2: Swamp Hill

Ⓑ

#1: The Odyssey

A Symbol from Ancient Times

Now seen all over the world, this starburst symbol is thought to have originated on these islands. But what does it communicate? The mystery may never be solved.

A DENSE, PRIMEVAL FOREST

Few visit these remote islands surrounded by poison, but they are dense with plants that have followed a unique evolutionary path. There is a strange unity between the vibrantly colored plants, the odd animals, and the sea of poison surrounding them.

NATURE'S TRAFFIC LIGHTS

The Tropical Wigglers found here are not aggressive and are mostly genial and pleasant creatures. You should, however, avoid touching them, for safety's sake. They stretch and contract their bodies constantly and have a habit of stretching across major pathways, so you may need to wait for the right moment to pass. This behavior has given them the nickname "traffic lights of the island." Be sure to look both ways before you cross.

THREE KEYS TO THE KINGDOM

1. Enjoy the breathtaking scenery, but beware the death-dealing poison.

2. Watch the Tropical Wiggler grow and shrink—it is simply mesmerizing.

3. Puzzle over the odd mechanics of these strange ruins.

THIEF OF THE SKIES

The undisputed ruler of the skies here is the Klepto. This large bird has keen eyesight that enables it to spot prey from above before swooping down to snatch it up in an instant. Once ensnared in its sharp claws, escape is quite difficult, and many smaller visitors have been carried off in this way.

RUINS STEEPED IN MYSTERY

The purpose of the distinctive ruins scattered throughout the island remains unclear. The starburst pattern that appears on them *may* indicate a spot capable of withstanding a great impact. The builders clearly mastered stonework, as these structures still operate and move perhaps centuries after their creators have disappeared.

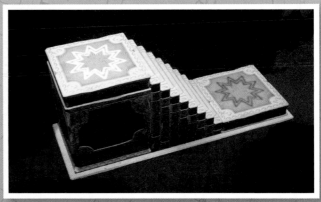

WATCH THOSE HANDS

The Trapeetle is a local hazard. Its large hands capture prey, who are held tight as the creature explodes in a tragic display seen absolutely nowhere else in nature. Best to avoid.

Mario's Itinerary

Ⓐ Rescue Cappy from Klepto!

Thanks to Bowser's cannons, Mario and Cappy are knocked out of the sky and crash land in the Lost Kingdom. Things look dire, but it could have been much worse! They could have landed in the poison sea that surrounds this region. Fortunately, Cappy's a wiz when it comes to repairing the Odyssey and it's only going to take 10 Power Moons to return the Odyssey to the sky.

Head north through the jungle toward the bridge and try not to scream when a large bird swoops down and steals Cappy from atop Mario's head. Klepto flies off to an area known as Swamp Hill, where he's content to roost until Mario forces him otherwise.

Advance to the odd-shaped ruins ahead with the starburst patterns on them. Climb the stairs to the raised side and ground pound the starburst. The ruin acts as a teeter-totter, causing one side to rise whenever Mario ground pounds the other.

You're Grounded, Mario!

While it's possible to dive jump from the ground and reach this upper ledge without using the ruins, Mario can't perform that level of acrobatics without Cappy.

Ignore the Trapeetles marching around this upper platform and approach the larger ruins to the left of the ? Block. Ground pound the starburst atop the fourth column, then climb the stairs to reach Swamp Hill.

Cappy isn't far, but you're going to have to bypass the Tropical Wigglers first. Mario can't capture them without Cappy so wait for their accordion-like bodies to retract, then hurry past them.

Klepto flies to the upper side of the ruins atop the cliff as Mario closes in on him. Run up the stairs after him to force him to descend to the lower side of the ruin. You know what that means! Ground pound the starburst on the upper side to knock Klepto in the air, freeing Cappy from its beak.

Ⓑ Collect Power Moons

Now that Cappy's safe and Mario's full assortment of moves is restored, it's time to find those 10 Power Moons needed to repair the Odyssey—and you don't have to go far to get the first one. Capture a Tropical Wiggler near the Swamp Hill warp flag and stretch it across the poison to the narrow ledge near the coins. Follow the ledge around to the left, then across to the L-shaped ruins near the tree. Release the capture, ground pound the starburst to raise the Tropical Wiggler, then use the Tropical Wiggler to reach for Power Moon #04 on the tree branch.

Note the sparkles emanating from the stone block near the poison waterfall. That can only mean one thing: there's a Power Moon inside it! Mario

Stand atop the cube with the Power Moon so the Trapeetle launches itself right into it.

can't break those blocks open himself, but the Trapeetle can! The spike on the Trapeetle's head is your cue that they can't be captured, but that doesn't mean they're not useful. The Trapeetle catches Cappy in defense anytime Mario throws the hat, but that's not all. The Trapeetle takes a bead on Mario's location, revs up, and speeds toward Mario in a self-destructive manner. Use this rocket-like attack to trick the Trapeetle into blowing up the block containing Power Moon #11.

There's another Power Moon hiding in the vicinity of the nearby ruins. Ground pound the tall column down below, on the ground near the bridge. This reveals an opening to the cave you may have seen earlier. Enter the cave beside the very first ruin you hit to get Power Moon #03.

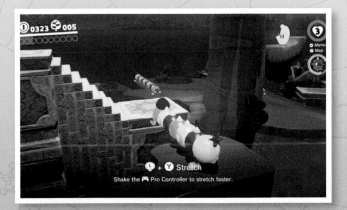
L + Y Stretch
Shake the Pro Controller to stretch faster.

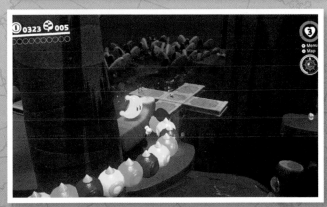
You'll need to use Tropical Wigglers to bend and twist around objects quite a lot in Lost Kingdom.

Leap off the Swamp Hill toward the four-column ruins you used earlier while making sure to leave the end nearest the cliff in its raised position. Power Moon #07 is located inside it. Don't go far, as there are more Power Moons in this area!

While you're on the lower level, capture a Tropical Wiggler and make your way west toward the many tree stumps in the northwest area. Here, you need to use the Tropical Wiggler to make your way from stump to stump while dodging Fuzzies to gather the Moon Shards needed for Power Moon #15. Three of the Moon Shards are clearly visible from the stone platform near the Tropical Wiggler you captured, but two are a bit trickier to find.

Of the five Moon Shards, the toughest to spot is tucked away inside the hole in this tree.

The fifth and final one is on the back of the tree in the northwest corner.

Continue south along the western side of the island to the Mountainside Platform warp flag. Release the Tropical Wiggler and open the red door to find an 8-bit warp pipe. Use the platforms inside the mural to reach Power Moon #06 then return the way you came, pausing to get the Regional Coins above the Fuzzies.

Back outside the red door, capture a Tropical Wiggler and use it to navigate the platforms alongside the mountain. Stretch to the stumps on the right to avoid the Fuzzies before reaching back to the second platform for Power Moon #05.

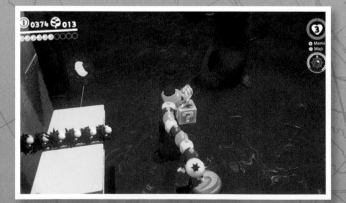

Capture a Tropical Wiggler and approach the bridge near the Odyssey. Stretch to the "knees" of the tree with the caged Power Moon atop it and gradually make your way to Power Moon #16 located under the bridge.

While you have the Tropical Wiggler, make your way to the Odyssey and drop off the cliff onto the ledge with the locked panel. Use the Tropical Wiggler to reach the key hidden in the cave near the poison. This unlocks Power Moon #17. Climb the tree and leap to the ledge to return to higher ground.

Mario should need only one more Power Moon to continue his journey to Metro Kingdom. The easiest Power Moon to get at this point sits atop the westernmost propeller. Capture a Tropical Wiggler atop Swamp Hill and use it to board the first of the two propellers. Cross to the ledge with the coins, then over to the propeller where Power Moon #01 is.

Extend Your Stay

Lost Kingdom contains a total of just 35 Power Moons and 50 Regional Coins. It's one of the smallest regions, but it contains some of the most interesting creatures Mario encounters in his journey.

Souvenir Shopping

Lost Kingdom contains 50 Regional Coins in the form of purple leaves. All 50 Coins can be found during your initial visit, though you need not search for them all until the Crazy Cap store opens during your return visit.

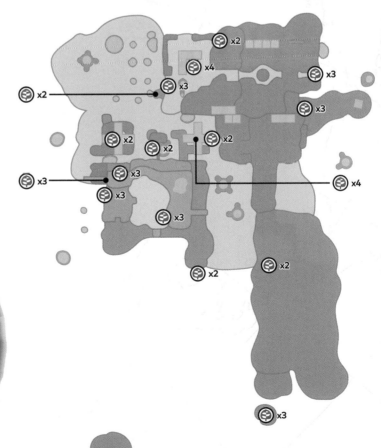

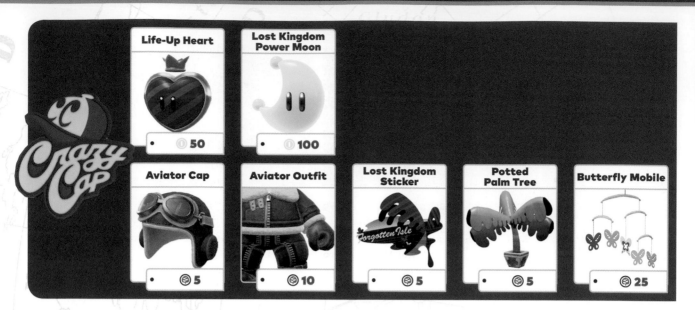

Crazy Cap

Life-Up Heart	Lost Kingdom Power Moon
• ⓘ 50	• ⓘ 100

Aviator Cap	Aviator Outfit	Lost Kingdom Sticker	Potted Palm Tree	Butterfly Mobile
• ⊚ 5	• ⊚ 10	• ⊚ 5	• ⊚ 5	• ⊚ 25

Coins In High Places

The 40 Regional Coins in Lost Kingdom are relatively easy to find, and only three are hidden behind a red door (and even they are visible in an 8-bit mural). Nevertheless, there are a few that can be overlooked in your travels. Refer to the map and the accompanying tips to find them all.

Capture the Glydon atop Rocky Mountain Summit and glide to the northwest tree stump. It's the only way to reach these four Regional Coins.

Several purple coins can be found beneath the propeller blades. Climb the shaft to the top of the propeller and let the coins rotate into you.

The easiest Regional Coins to miss are those in a small alcove near Talkatoo. Leap from Rocky Mountain Summit to Talkatoo then turn around. Toss Cappy at the 8-bit block in the wall and crouch walk through the opening.

🌙 Power Moons

There are 35 Power Moons in Lost Kingdom. Power Moons #01, 03, 04, 05, 06, 07, 11, 15, 16, and 17 were obtained while repairing the Odyssey. Consult the prior pages for help.

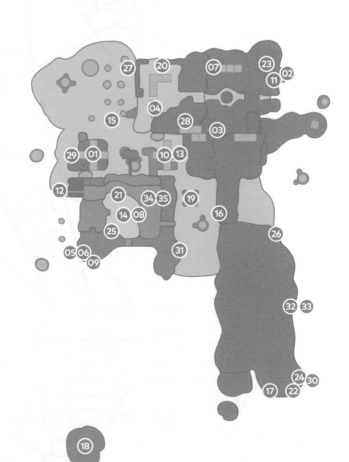

Not Again!

This won't be the only time Klepto steals Cappy. Expect to have to bounce Cappy out of Kelpto's beak on subsequent visits to Lost Kingdom as well, though not necessarily using the same set of ruins. Use a ground pound jump and tackle jump to reach the L-shaped ruins if Klepto flees there with Cappy. Thanks to the steel block on one corner, you'll have to flush Klepto to land on the starburst nearest the tree in order to hit him.

(02) Below the Cliff's Edge

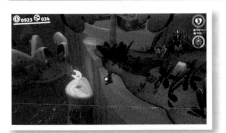

This Power Moon rests atop a tree in the northeast corner of the area, behind the four-stepped ruins that lead to Swamp Hill. Drop off the cliff near the narrow waterfall to get it. The invisible blocks above it help you return to solid ground.

(08) Enjoying the View of Forgotten Isle

Climb to the Rocky Mountain Summit (Power Moon #21) and shimmy up the tree near the Crazy Cap store. Flip upwards off the top to pluck the Power Moon out of the air.

(09) On the Mountain Road

Cross the propeller from Swamp Hill and bait the Trapeetles into blasting through the impervious blocks along the mountain road (or tackle jump around them). Continue past the second obstruction to a small group of plants with a glowing spot in the ground. Ground pound the area to find this Power Moon.

(10) A Propeller Pillar's Secret

Ground pound the flock of butterflies atop the propeller nearest the Swamp Hill warp flag. It's easy to be distracted by the rabbit jumping around, but those colorful butterflies were there for a reason. Always investigate any unusual behavior by the local fauna.

(12) A Butterfly's Treasure

Locate the butterfly on the narrow precipice extending out from the western side of the mountain (it's easiest to reach this area by dropping from Rocky Mountain Summit). The butterfly is quite timid and flies away if Mario gets too close. If this happens, walk away from the butterfly so it returns to its perch. To get the Power Moon, slowly creep toward the butterfly until Mario is above the thinnest part of the ledge (as viewed from the side) and throw Cappy to knock the Power Moon from the butterfly.

(13) Caught Hopping in the Jungle

There's a rabbit hopping around on the propeller nearest the Swamp Hill warp flag. It can be pretty tough for Mario to corner

as it leaps back and forth, but the Tropical Wiggler can hem it in with little trouble. Capture a Tropical Wiggler and stretch from one propeller blade to the one with the rabbit in an effort to flush it right back into the Tropical Wiggler's tail.

⑭ Cave Gardening

Locate the cave within the mountain near Talkatoo (easiest to reach it is by leaping from Rocky Mountain Summit) and use Cappy to make all sixteen flowers bloom simultaneously. Use a spin throw to whirl Cappy around Mario in circles while moving from one side of the cave to the other. The flowers close their blooms after a few seconds; you need to work fast to get them to all bloom at once.

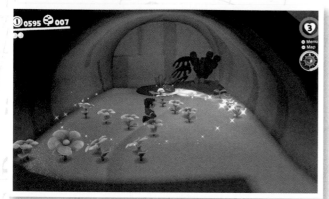

⑱ Soaring Over Forgotten Isle!

Make your way to Rocky Mountain Summit (Power Moon #21) and capture the Glydon. Spot the Power Moon on the lone island way out in the distance and fly to it. There's a slingshot to deliver Mario back to safety.

⑲ The Caged Gold

The Power Moon inside the cage is easy to spot as you cross the bridge the very first time, but opening it can be quite tricky.

Neither a ground pound nor a dive-bomb with the Glydon will do it, but fortunately Forgotten Isle is home to a critter with a bit more pop. Cross the bridge to the Trapeetles below the Big Swamp warp flag and bait one toward the edge nearest the cage. Line Mario up between the cage and the Trapeetle then throw Cappy at the Trapeetle. Leap out of the way as it takes flight and watch it soar across the gap, smashing through the cage's bars. Leap from the mountain road to get the Power Moon.

⑳ Get Some Rest, Captain Toad

Capture a Tropical Wiggler beneath the propellers and make your way across the tree stumps where the Moon Shards for Power Moon #15 were located. This time, head to the northwestern corner of this swamp area, just past the Fuzzies and look for the cave opening. Stretch the Tropical Wiggler into the cave to find Captain Toad and a whole bunch of coins.

㉑ Shopping on Forgotten Isle

Ground pound the large red button on the mountain road to make it possible to wall jump your way to Rocky Mountain Summit, where

Toad decided to place his Crazy Cap store. Head inside and buy a Power Moon for 100 coins and know that you need only warp here in the future.

㉒ Taxi Flying Through Forgotten Isle

Capture the Binoculars and scan the sky for a flying taxi, beneath a balloon. It will likely be out beyond the Odyssey, to the northeast, but it's on the move so look around. Zoom in on it once you spot it.

(23) I Met a Tropical Wiggler!

A Bonneter has traveled all the way to Forgotten Isle in hopes of meeting a Tropical Wiggler. He's on the narrow rock fin near the Trapeetles below Swamp Hill. Ground pound the nearby four-column ruins so that the end nearest Swamp Hill is raised. Capture a Tropical Wiggler near the warp flag and guide it down the stair-like columns to the lower end. Ground pound the upper starburst to raise the end with the Tropical Wiggler and stretch across to the Bonneter for the Power Moon.

(24) Lost Kingdom Regular Cup

The freerunning races at Lost Kingdom are among the harder ones Mario can enter, as they wind their way across the entire region, finishing at the Rocky Mountain Summit, near the Crazy Cap store. As with other recent kingdoms, we're going to save the most advanced shortcut for the Master Cup. Here, we'll focus on providing tips to help you win the Regular Cup.

The first thing you need to do to win the Regular Cup is to master using a dive jump to climb your way to Swamp Hill without using the starburst ruins. Consider practicing this before starting the race, as the other Koopas use wall jumps and tackle jumps to scale the same cliffs without using the ruins.

Dive jump past the Tropical Wigglers and make your way over the propeller to the Trapeetles on the mountain road. Don't worry about using the Trapeetles to break the blocks! Instead, just leap off the cliff and tackle jump around the obstruction to safety. Leap around both obstacles, hit the big red button and wall jump up the rock chimney to the finish line. Begin the wall jump on the right-hand face so as to end it nearest the finish line.

(25) Peach in the Lost Kingdom

Princess Peach and Tiara have once again made their way to the highest lookout in the kingdom Mario is visiting. This time they're atop Rocky Mountain Summit. Warp to the peak and chat with Peach for a Power Moon.

🌙 Moons From the Moon Rock

(26) The Shining Fruit

This one's a freebie. Look for the Power Moon hovering below the tree branches to the right of the path, just north of Hint Toad. Climb the tree to pick it.

(27) Jump Down to the Top of a Tree

This Power Moon sits atop a tree below the cliff edge in Swamp Hill, above the stumps. It's easy to reach by jumping down from the narrow cliff ledge, as the name implies. But it's more fun, and just as straightforward, to get it by flying a Glydon to it from atop Rocky Mountain Summit.

㉘ Line It Up, Blow It Up

Two new blocks have landed near the Tropical Wigglers nearest the propeller in Swamp Hill, and the upper one contains a Power Moon. You probably know by now that the only way to break them open is with a Trapeetle, and that's what you're going to do. And you're going to do it with the Trapeetle beyond the propeller, near the mountain road. Frst you need to ground pound the ruins near the block with the Power Moon to get it out of the way. Toss Cappy at the Trapeetle and retreat to the propeller and line it up with the blocks. Stand a little east of center on the propeller so the Trapeetle flies over Mario's head at an angle and hits the block.

㉙ Taking Notes: Stretch and Shrink

Capture a Tropical Wiggler and guide it across the tops of the propellers to the treble clef beyond the second propeller to the west. The notes appear in sweeping arcs that extend beyond the reach of the propeller, and they don't stay around for long. To collect them, use the Tropical Wiggler, but limit how many times you move him. Keep his rear legs planted where they were when you trigger the treble clef, and sweep through the first set of notes, then release it. Gather up the next notes as you stretch to the rock ledge between the propellers and release the stretch. Finally, curl through the last group of notes as they blink, warning you that time is about to expire.

㉚ Lost Kingdom Master Cup

If you've won the Regular Cup using the tips outlined above, then you're ready for our advanced Master Cup trickery. Get started by rolling as fast as you can across the jungle floor, toward the bridge. Once on the raised platform beyond the two posts, turn and dive jump to the left-hand tree. From there, dive jump onto the cage, then on an angle toward the right-most edge of the cliff near the propeller. You won't be able to spot the ledge you're leaping for until you're airborne (without taking time to pan the camera), but you can make it.

You've just cut nearly 20 seconds off the course. Leap around the Trapeetle obstacles as before and wall jump your way to victory!

㉛ Lost Kingdom Timer Challenge

The Timer Challenge begins on mountain road, near the triangular bed of flowers is, below Talkatoo. This is a rather straightforward puzzle—the Power Moon appears atop a tree near the Odyssey. Run and leap across the platform that appears then make your way across the top of the trees to get the Power Moon. Dive jump off the edge of the platform toward the red tree, then leap across the other trees to the Power Moon. If you're fast enough, there's even time to fall from the last tree and climb up to the Power Moon before it disappears.

㉜ Stretch and Traverse the Jungle

Descend the Moon Pipe north of the Odyssey and capture the Tropical Wiggler. To navigate this challenge area, you must use the Tropical Wiggler's ability to effectively be in two places at once to depress pairs of P-Switches. Begin by standing on the right-hand P-Switch, stretch to the one on the left, and then hurry across the exposed tree stumps before the poison geysers reappear. Repeat this technique at the next pair of poison geysers.

Give the Fire Breathing Piranha Plant a wide berth unless trying to unlock Power Moon #33. Break through the bricks and stretch past the two Tropical Wigglers up ahead. The last section before the Power Moon contains a sequence of tree stumps leading across a massive poison geyser. Move from stump to stump as fast as you can to get out of the way of the geyser before it erupts again.

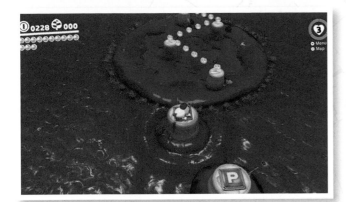

Approach the center, where the caged Power Moon is, and watch as Klepto swoops in and steals Cappy yet again. Mario must get Cappy back if he's to get either of the Power Moons in this challenge room.

Ground pound past the purple blocks and close in on Klepto's position in the far right-hand corner of the area. Mario can't knock Cappy from his beak here, but he can flush Klepto to the purple starburst blocks on the left. And that's what you need to do! Leap to the upper starburst block where Klepto has gone to chase him off. Ground pound the block he was on, then chase him to the blue blocks on the lower left corner of the room. Use the purple starburst blocks to close in on his position. He flies away again, this time back to the same spot where he was, only the block is in a lower position. Ground pound the raised purple block near Klepto to knock Cappy free! Toss Cappy at the lever to unlock the Power Moon.

(33) Aglow in the Jungle

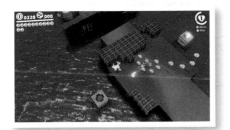

Follow the instructions for Power Moon #32 until you reach the section with the Fire Breathing Piranha Plant. Clear away the blocks on the sides so that the plant's fire can reach the torches on either side of the area. Position the Tropical Wiggler either on or in front of the torches to get the Fire Breathing Piranha Plant to spit flame at the torch. Move away without being hit so the flame ignites the torch. Light both torches to earn the Power Moon.

(34) Chasing Klepto

Leap from Rocky Mountain Summit to the ledge below, on the east side of the mountain, and enter the Moon Pipe.

(35) Extremely Hot Bath

Follow the strategy for Power Moon #34 but don't leave after getting the Power Moon. Instead, capture one of the Lava Bubbles in the area and swim around the tall tower beyond the cage. Leap high into the air as the Lava Bubble to pluck the hidden Power Moon out of the sky.

Welcome to New Donk City

REGION AT A GLANCE

Population	Crowded
Size	Ridonkulous
Locals	New Donkers
Currency	Portrait-stamped
Industry	Information, Ads
Temperature	Average 81°F

INDIGENOUS FLORA & FAUNA

	SPARK PYLON		URBAN STINGBY LARVA		URBAN STINGBY
	Can Capture?		Can Capture?		Can Capture?
	Yes		No		No
	SHERM		GOOMBA		MINI GOOMBA
	Can Capture?		Can Capture?		Can Capture?
	Yes		Yes		No
	POISON PIRANHA PLANT		BIG POISON PIRANHA PLANT		FUZZY
	Can Capture?		Can Capture?		Can Capture?
	Yes		No		No

Fun Tidbit: RC Cars

Many New Donkers are getting into the noble sport of RC Car racing. Find a local enthusiast, and you'll open up a whole new world.

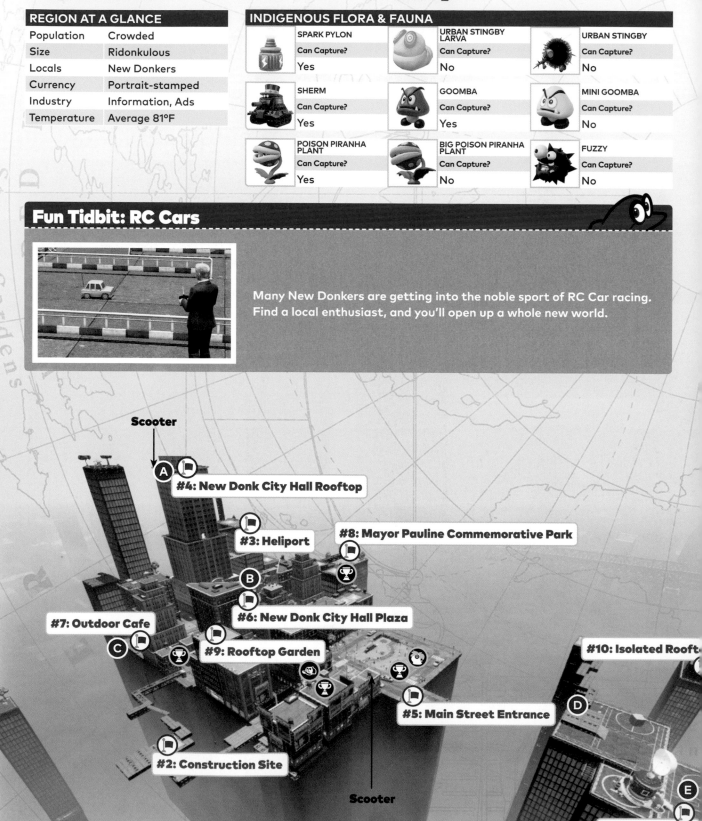

Scooter

A

#4: New Donk City Hall Rooftop

#3: Heliport

#8: Mayor Pauline Commemorative Park

B

#6: New Donk City Hall Plaza

#7: Outdoor Cafe

C

#9: Rooftop Garden

#10: Isolated Roof[t]

#5: Main Street Entrance

D

#2: Construction Site

Scooter

E

#1: The Odyssey

SCRAPING THE SKY

The skyscrapers of New Donk City are most people's first association with the city. But even among those, New Donk City Hall stands out as the very symbol of this great city, so don't miss it. Who knows, you might even run into world-renowned Mayor Pauline!

A MILLION-COIN VIEW

If you've come to New Donk City, you owe it to yourself to see it at night. The best viewing spot is the landmark New Donk City Hall, but sadly the interior is closed for construction, so you'll have to aim for one of the neighboring buildings.

If it's festival season, you'll have a chance at a once-in-a-lifetime experience, but the timing is a bit irregular, so be sure to check the schedule beforehand.

THREE KEYS TO THE KINGDOM

1. Appreciate the constant Power Moon-based progress and development.

2. Visit those welcoming souls who just leave their doors wide open.

3. Participate in the citywide festival if you can (schedule subject to change).

CRAZY CAP FLAGSHIP STORE

There's probably only one brand that the entire world knows, and that's Crazy Cap. Their original flagship store is right here in New Donk City.

The unique storefront is converted from an old theater. Theater space is no longer much in demand, with so many street performers in the city.

ALWAYS BE CONSTRUCTING

New Donkers are used to construction and new developments. There's always work being done below ground, on rooftops, and inside buildings, so power lines never get taken down—they run throughout town.

Unaccustomed travelers should watch out for the cranes, girders, and manholes scattered everywhere.

SCOOTING ACROSS TOWN

These motor scooters may look old-fashioned, but they pack a punch and are perfect for tooling around the city. Be sure to try one out!

Ⓐ The Scourge on the Skyscraper

Mario's unexpected pit stop in Lost Kingdom cost him valuable time, but Cappy's intuition was right. Bowser had been to Metro Kingdom, and he's even advertised his wedding all over town. But that's the least of the city's troubles. Mayor Pauline has to find a way to restore the city's power. And the only way that can happen is if Mario deals with whatever has caused the city's residents to flee to the rooftop south of New Donk City.

Scamper across the girders to the right and ride the Spark Pylon down to the City Outskirts. Numerous Urban Stingby Larvae have apparently swum in on the rain and some are hatching into Urban Stingby. Swat the larvae with Cappy before they hatch to rid the area of this pestilence. Cappy can dispatch the Urban Stingby bugs as well, but it's a bit riskier. Urban Stingby behave much like a Trapeetle—sidestep their path as they attempt to divebomb Mario with self-destructive aggression.

Bowser erected a massive roadblock beyond the park, cutting off the direct path to New Donk City Hall. Take the road on the left, where the Sherms are, and either ride the Scooter past them or capture a Sherm and use it to blast the Urban Stingby bugs and other Sherms.

Follow the coins through the Construction Site, past the Goombas, to the Sherm atop the girder beyond the warp flag. Capture the Sherm and drive to the nearest suspended iron beam. That's a good spot from which to blast the crumpled piece of scrap metal below the taller beam. This causes the beam to fall, giving Mario a way to throw-and-hold Cappy at the ? Blocks.

Exit the Construction Site onto the street ahead then turn around and run the length of the girder where the coins are to find Power Moon #08. With 80 other Power Moons to find, you can be sure they won't all be this obvious.

Mayor Pauline

And he has the nerve to be advertising this wedding of his all over New Donk City?! A bit tasteless, if you ask me.

Ⓐ

With the Odyssey in need of 20 Power Moons, Mario has plenty of time to help Mayor Pauline.

Nice Wheels, Mario!

Hop aboard the Scooter in the corner of the City Outskirts area nearest the Odyssey. Not only stylish, the Scooter can be used to run down Urban Stingby Larvae, avoid Urban Stingby bugs, and even jump and bounce off the Sherms guarding Mario's advance.

This massive advertisement blocks the path north in the tackiest of ways.

Ⓚ Aim Ⓨ Shoot

You can also aim with the 🎮 Pro Controller. Ⓡ Reset

No reason to bring a hat to a tank fight when you can bring an actual tank!

Continue past the broken-down taxis and around the corner to the plaza in front of New Donk City Hall. Five Sherms stand guard in front of City Hall, but it's not clear what they're protecting. Capture the Sherm atop the girder where the Heart was and use it to blast the other Sherms to pieces. Strafe side to side as you fire to constantly stay ahead of the incoming volleys.

Blast away at the Urban Stingby and their larvae in the area then release the Sherm capture and follow the trail of coins up the stairs near the Construction Access warp flag. Continue to the first rooftop, where the Goombas are, and either use the Spark Pylon or a series of wall jumps on the rear of the building to reach the Heliport. Take a moment to pluck Power Moon #09 from above the swaying beam before entering the New Donk City Hall Interior via the open door on the adjacent building.

Cross the crumbling walkway and ride the lifts to the right of the Mini Goombas up. Leap and dash across to the left, use Cappy to get the Regional Coins from the descending lift before continuing the ascent. Use homing throws to clear the Urban Stingby and Mini Goombas out of the way before venturing anywhere near the crumbling walkways.

Climb the yellow and black striped poles to continue your ascent of the skyscraper's interior, but skip the next landing.

Continue to the top of the left-hand tower, wall jump off the wall on the left, and continue climbing the tower above to the blue fencing. Leap from pole to pole to reach the treasure chest in the upper left corner for Power Moon #34.

Fight your way past the Urban Stingby on the main path wrapping around the interior of the building. The ? Blocks in the corner contain a Life-Up Heart which comes in handy. Grab it before heading back out into the rain.

From New Donk City Hall Rooftop, use the Spark Pylon to access the top of the skyscraper where a mechanical beast known as the Mechawiggler is attempting to suck up the city's electricity. Mechawiggler knocks Mario to the plaza below and descends the building to attack.

133

BOSS: MECHAWIGGLER

Don't waste a single second when the battle starts: Capture one of the Sherms off to the side and open fire on Mechawiggler's glowing orbs. Strafe left and right across the area to dodge the incoming projectiles while continuing to pepper Mechawiggler with Sherm's cannon attacks. Aim for those sections of Mechawiggler that appear curled back on itself so a single attack can destroy multiple orbs.

Cappy provides great advice once the initial set of orbs has been destroyed, and that's to keep firing! Continue blasting away at the orbs as they turn purple. But be quick about it! You need to fire Sherm's cannon as rapidly as you can to inflict critical damage. So keep blasting until you see Mechawiggler go dark.

Mechawiggler doesn't stay dark for long. It turns gold—your cue that it's temporarily invincible—and disappears into a portal. Watch for the golden ray of light to emerge from the portal and steer Sherm out of its path. Mechawiggler emerges from the portal and speeds across the arena in an attempt to collide with Sherm. Keep clear of it as it disappears into another portal. The portal shifts to another location, the golden ray appears again, and Mechawiggler emerges in another attempt to stampede Sherm. Continue to avoid Mechawiggler during this phase to stay safe.

Mechawiggler zips across the arena three times before returning to the side of the building. It emerges from its portal alongside a barrage of energy projectiles. Steer clear of the inbound projectiles while firing on Mechawiggler once the orbs turn purple. Continue firing on Mechawiggler until the last purple orb is destroyed and a chain-reaction ripples through its lengthy body. Pepper it with attacks until it explodes, releasing Power Moon #01.

Hearts from Above

Mechawiggler launches its attacks from the orbs that haven't been damaged. Consider leaving one or two in-tact so it can launch a pair of projectiles at Sherm. Shoot the energy volleys out of the air to gain a Heart.

134

Ⓑ A Fresh Start for the City

All New Warp Flags

Many of the warp flag locations have shifted since Mechawiggler's destruction. The map accompanying this chapter uses the location names and warp flag locations as they appear during daylight, after the brief period spent exploring Metro Kingdom in the rain.

The destruction of the Mechawiggler cleared the skies of rain. Come morning, the city was back to its old self, free of Bowser's ugly posters and roadblocks. But there's still lots to be done to restore the city's electricity. Mayor Pauline is waiting for Mario outside City Hall, but don't head straight there. The Odyssey still needs 14 Power Moons, and one isn't very far. Enter the girder beyond the platform with the Spark Pylon nearest the Odyssey to find Power Moon #13.

With daylight comes a host of new Power Moons to find, starting with this one near the Odyssey.

Ride the Spark Pylon down to Main Street Entrance and head north to New Donk City Hall Plaza where Mayor Pauline is waiting. Mayor Pauline wants to stage a festival, but she needs four musicians to play backup. Mario is going to receive a Power Moon for each of the musicians he finds, so this is a great chance to help Pauline *and* power-up the Odyssey in the process!

1. The very first musician is just outside city hall. Talk to the drummer to the right of Mayor Pauline to get Power Moon #02.

Country Names in the City

If the street names sound familiar to you, it's because they're named after many of the side characters from the Super NES game, *Donkey Kong Country*. Cranky, Rambi, Expressom and more are all names from the big gorilla's first ever solo adventure.

2. Head to the east end of the street near City Hall and ride the Spark Pylon to Mayor Pauline Commemorative Park in the northeast corner of the city. Talk to the bassist in the park for Power Moon #04.

3. Use the Poles on the side of the building across the street from the Outdoor Café to flick Mario up to the roof, one level at a time. From there, use the Pole to flick Mario to the roof of the triangular building. Aim for the skylight so there's plenty of room to land. Talk to the trumpeter for Power Moon #05. It's also possible (and easier) to reach the trumpeter by riding the Spark Pylon lines to the roof of the building to the east and hit the red button to gain a temporary walkway between the buildings.

4. The final musician is the guitarist. Head down the street toward Main Street Entrance to find him jamming in the northeast corner of the park. Talk to him for Power Moon #03.

ⓒ Powering Up the Station

The band's together playing a familiar song—a jazzy rendition of the original *Super Mario Bros.* theme song—but Mayor Pauline needs some more help. Exit the auditorium and head west toward the beam of light emanating from the sewer near Outdoor Café. Capture the Manhole Cover to slide it out of the way and dive on in to the Underground Power Plant.

Follow the walkway around the corner to the second pipe and enter it. The next room contains several large platforms that Mario needs to get spinning if he's to make his way across the poison-filled room. Use the hat launcher to knock Cappy into the green platform to get it spinning then leap across. Continue to use Cappy to clear the path of poison and to distract the Poison Piranha Plants while you kick them out of the way. Use a homing throw to clear away any Urban Stingby you encounter.

Turn the camera so you're facing where you were, leap to the top edge and then to the platform on the right where Power Moon #35 is hidden. Continue to the pipe in the corner of the room.

Mayor Pauline has somehow made it to the power plant room before you—and so have two Big Poison Piranha Plants! Clear away a little of the poison then throw Cappy at the Big Poison Piranha Plant before it spits any more poison. The plant briefly collapses—perhaps out of exhaustion but probably because Cappy doesn't taste good—giving Mario a chance to bounce on top of it. Defeat both Big Poison Piranha Plants to earn Power Moon #06.

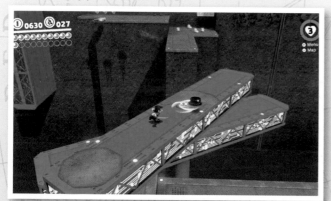

Use Cappy to hit these two rotating platforms in the same direction.

Use the hat launcher to get the vertical platform spinning then carefully leap onto it as it becomes horizontal.

Ground pound the red button atop the pump to get the power flowing once again to New Donk City. With this accomplished, it's time to celebrate! Mayor Pauline invites Mario to participate in the festival. And you absolutely should say yes!

Festival On-Demand

You're not going to want to miss the festival, but sometimes life gets in the way of gaming. If you absolutely must skip the festival right now, don't fret. Talk to the man nearest the stage anytime inside the New Donk City Hall Auditorium for another shot at it.

ⓓ A Traditional Festival

Mayor Pauline and the band take the stage for a wonderful rendition of their hit song, "1-Up Girl". As special as it will be to take the stage, as the guest-of-honor, Mario gets to participate in a city-wide 8-bit mural erected on the sides of the city's largest buildings.

This is an extremely special moment, both for Mario and us gamers getting to experience this game. So, take your time making your way through the various sections of the 8-bit level. Avoid the barrels and fire pits, hit the blocks for coins, and enjoy this time-warp back to classic gaming.

Jump up; don't be scared. Just jump up and your cares will soar away.

Things get a little trickier as Mario makes his way to New Donk City Hall. Spring along the curved wall to get inverted. You've played as an upside-down Mario in Sand Kingdom, here's your chance to do it again! Carefully avoid the barrels as you traverse the area upside-down. Guide Mario as he freefalls through the columns of coins before finally getting returned to his normal right-side-up path.

The final climb to the finish takes place along what should be, for those old enough to have played many videogames in the 1980s, a very familiar assembly of ramps. Use the additional blocks to take cover from the barrels as you collect the "DK" coins. Slip under the final platform where an old nemesis is standing and hit each of the ? Blocks beneath him to clear a path for the warp pipe. The warp pipe delivers Mario to the stage so head on up and dance a little with Mayor Pauline before talking to her to get Power Moon #07.

Ⓔ Collect More Power Moons

At this point, if you've been following along closely, you should only need four more Power Moons in order to fuel the Odyssey. And we're going to show you how to grow three of them right now!

Ride the Spark Pylon down into town and locate the three seeds in the corner of the park near Talkatoo. Pick one of them up and carry it to the northeast of that same park, near where the guitarist was earlier. Toss it into the flower pot so it can start growing. Return later to harvest Power Moon #22 from the fruit.

Garden Variety Surveillance

Having trouble spotting the flower pots or want to check to see how your fruit is ripening? Capture the Binoculars near the Main Street Entrance warp flag and scan the city rooftops. It's best to know exactly where they are before grabbing the seeds.

Grab another seed from the plaza and carry it toward the taxi parked behind he Scooter. Bounce from the taxi onto the fire escape and use the wooden crate to jump onto the roof.

Cross the three rooftops to find the flower pot. Return later when the fruit ripens to earn Power Moon #21.

The third flower pot is a bit trickier to spot, but it's not far. Grab the third seed from the plaza and head northwest toward the corner of Expresso and Main. The flower pot is on the roof of the corner building next to the one where the Slots room is. To get to the roof, head around to the alley behind the Slots house and wall jump up the sides of the alley to reach the roof. If you didn't think you could wall jump while carrying a seed, think again! Mario retains a surprising number of non-Cappy abilities while carrying items. Plant the seed in the flower pot and return later to collect Power Moon #23.

Now that you have some time to kill while waiting for the Power Moons to bloom, how about a little RC Car action? Capture the New Donker playing with the yellow RC Car near the Scooter and guide the RC Car to the finish line. This particular RC Car doesn't control as well as some advanced models you'll get a chance to use later—this one turns best while in reverse. Pilot the RC Car around the barriers and into the cage to get Power Moon #31.

Once you've proven yourself here, you can enter the nearby building for high-speed RC Car action!

Extend Your Stay

Metro Kingdom contains the second most Power Moons in the world, with some of the most difficult to find not becoming accessible until after Bowser has been defeated. There is much to do at Metro Kingdom, from driving RC Cars to outrunning a T-Rex while driving a Scooter. Best of all, the streets of New Donk City are completely free of enemies once the festival takes place.

◎ Souvenir Shopping

Metro Kingdom contains 100 Regional Coins in the form of purple coins stamped with Mayor Pauline's portrait. They can all be collected during Mario's first visit.

Local Currency

There are a lot of Regional Coins to find in Metro Kingdom, and a lot of nooks and crannies for them to hide in, but the majority are quite easy to spot. Though there are a number of them tucked inside challenge levels, the bulk are out in the open, atop rooftops and balconies, and in the many fire escapes that decorate the city. Get up high, be thorough, and sweep across the city in a methodical manner to find them. A few of the trickier ones are detailed on the next page.

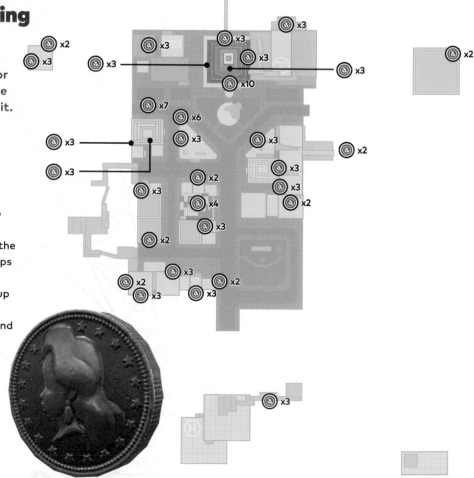

Crazy Cap	Life-Up Heart	Metro Kingdom Power Moon	Black Fedora	Black Suit	Builder Helmet
	ⓘ 50	ⓘ 100	ⓘ 50	ⓘ 150	◎ 5

Builder Outfit	Golf Cap	Golf Outfit	Metro Kingdom Sticker	New Donk City Hall Model	Pauline Statue
◎ 10	◎ 20	◎ 25	◎ 10	◎ 5	◎ 25

Enter the triangular building southwest of New Donk City Hall and hop aboard the Scooter for a shot at six Regional Coins.

Stay aligned with the yellow markings on the street as there are three purple coins on the first right-hand strip of yellow, then three more in the center of the alley immediately after that. Leap over the crates to maintain speed.

The other hard-to-spot Regional Coins are near the top of New Donk City Hall. Warp to New Donk City Hall Rooftop and approach the door, but don't head inside. Instead, wall jump back and forth between the walls rising up above the doorway. There are three coins at the very top of this shaft.

Power Moons

There are 81 total Power Moons at Metro Kingdom. Power Moons #01, 02, 03, 04, 05, 06, 07, 08, 09, 13, 21, 22, 23, 31, 34, and 35 were obtained while helping Mayor Pauline restore New Donk City to its pre-Mechawiggler glory. Consult the prior pages for help.

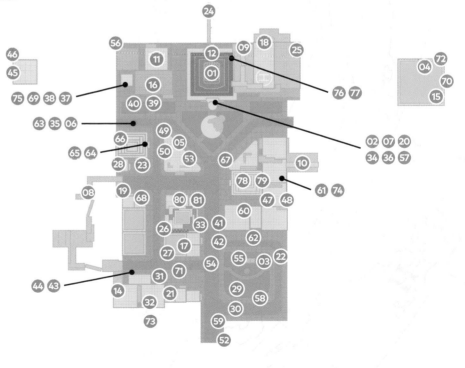

⑩ Girder Sandwich

Locate the vertical maze of girders on the eastern side of the city and wall jump your way up to the top of the smaller 7-shaped  girder (viewed from the south). Wall jump off the office building to reach the top of the girder where the Power Moon is located.

⑪ Glittering Above the Pool

There's a Power Moon hovering above the rooftop swimming pool in the northwest corner of the city. Mario can reach it by bouncing off the patio umbrella. As for reaching the rooftop itself, try leaping from the roof of New Donk City Hall. Better yet, dive from the top of the antenna into the pool—you might even be able to grab the Power Moon on the way in (see Power Moon #12 for details).

⑫ Dizzying Heights

Of course, there'd be a Power Moon atop the highest point in the city! Ride the Spark Pylons to the uppermost level of New Donk City Hall (see Power Moon #20 for more details) and start climbing. Mario can hop onto the gold-capped ledges and climb the vertical columns. Leap for the golden antenna and climb all the way to the Power Moon. Now that you're up here, why not dive into the swimming pool on the neighboring building?

⑭ Who Piled Garbage on This?

Bounce off the taxi behind the Scooter to reach the fire-escape leading to the rooftop where the flower planter was.

Continue westward across the neighboring rooftops to find a pile of garbage bags in the corner, behind billboards. Knock aside the garbage bags and ground pound the glow to uncover a Power Moon.

⑮ Hidden in the Scrap

Warp to Mayor Pauline Commemorative Park and investigate the chunk of scrap metal from the former  Mechawiggler. It must have landed in the park after exploding. Climb on top of it and ground pound it to uncover a hidden Power Moon.

⑯ Left at the Café?

Head to the northwest corner of the city and use the Spark Pylon on the rear of the building with the rooftop café to reach the café. Stand off to the side and wait for the birds to congregate. There's a Power Moon buried in the tile where those birds gather. Walk closely toward that spot and feel for the vibrations in the controller. Ground pound the spot where the vibrations rumble the strongest.

⑰ Caught Hopping on a Building!

There's a rabbit hopping around on the building across from the Rooftop Garden warp flag, overlooking the south plaza.

Mario can't just go after the rabbit head-on, as it will quickly leap to one of the other grass-covered rooftops. Instead, warp to the Rooftop Garden and use the Pole there to flick Mario across to the roof where the couple is sitting on a bench. The rabbit should be there. If not, chase him to that position. Mario lands in a sprint after using the Pole. Sprint toward the rabbit and hit it with Cappy as Mario barrels into it.

(18) How Do They Take Out the Trash?

There's a garbage dumpster high atop the girder that rises above the heliport in the northeast section of the city. And there's a Power Moon inside that dumpster free to anyone who can reach it. But how? The answer is as easy as it is shocking. Warp to New Donk City Hall Rooftop and drop to the level below it on the east side. Use the Spark Pylon to ascend all the way to uppermost level of the skyscraper. Approach the northeast corner overlooking the dumpster, and jump for it! Tackle jump partway through the freefall and steer Mario through the air toward the dumpster as if he could fly. It's a terrifying leap, but one that is well within his reach.

(19) Metro Kingdom Timer Challenge 1

The three white and black panels seesaw under Mario's weight, tipping downwards the longer he spends on either end. To reach the Power Moon floating above the third platform, Mario must use his weight to angle the platforms so that he can leap from their raised end to the next higher platform. A quick way to reach the Power Moon is to run across the first platform, leap from the upward end and tackle jump to the far end of the second platform. Run to the right, to ensure it tips upward to the left, then run left and leap for the third platform. Immediately ground pound the right-hand end of the third platform to ensure the angle is steep enough for Mario to reach the Power Moon.

(20) Metro Kingdom Timer Challenge 2

Ride the Spark Pylons to the very top of New Donk City Hall and hop aboard the Scooter (it's best to not wonder how it got up here). Drive over the P-Switch to make a checkerboard platform appear. Drive a clockwise lap around the platform, aiming for the key up ahead. Accelerate through the key and around the turn to get the unlocked Power Moon before it disappears. If you fall off, just warp to New Donk City Hall Rooftop, drop a level on the east side of the building, and take the Spark Pylon there all the way to the top.

(24) How You Doin', Captain Toad?

Captain Toad is hanging out on a metal beam extending far to the north behind New Donk City Hall. Walk around the building and tiptoe out onto the beam to greet him. Ever-cheery Captain Toad found a Power Moon inside one of the buildings and wants Mario to have it. Isn't he the best?

(25) Free Parking: Rooftop Hop

Hop aboard a Scooter and ride it to the northeast corner of the city. Slowly and carefully drive it up the switchbacking stairs near the blue fence (in front of the building east of New Donk City Hall). Tap the throttle ever so lightly as you make the turns to avoid falling off the stairs. Leap with the Scooter up the ledges to the rooftop where a man stands near a parking meter and a small ramp. Drive the Scooter up onto the ramp (the tires lock into place when successful). But instead of paying the meter, the man gives Mario a Power Moon.

26 Bench Friends

There's a man sitting on a bench around the corner from the Crazy Cap store and he could really use some company. Take a seat on the bench next to him—it won't take long, just a momentary gesture to show you care. Travelers are often the recipients of random acts of kindness. Take this opportunity to pass it forward.

27 Shopping in New Donk City

Enter the Crazy Cap store and proceed to the counter in the yellow portion of the shop. Purchase the Metro Kingdom Power Moon for 100 coins to add another Power Moon to your collection.

28 Metro Kingdom Slots

The Slots at Metro Kingdom play just as the ones at Sand Kingdom—there's even a friendly Tostarenan serving as host! The one difference is that there are four rotating icons instead of just three. Once again, stand directly in front of each icon, wait for the heart to appear, then toss Cappy from two tiles away to hit the Power Moon that appears next in the rotation. Do this for all four to win the game.

29 Jump-Rope Hero

The two ladies in the plaza near Talkatoo are just waiting for someone to jump in and join them in a game of jump rope. Stand back and wait for them to get the rope swinging then jump in and start hopping over the rope as it swings past. This isn't quite as easy as it sounds, since the speed of the rope increases after every five jumps. Consider rotating the camera so that it's on an angle (or aligned with the rope) so you can best see it pass over. Lightly jump as the rope begins its downward trajectory. Clear the rope 30 times without a miss to earn a Power Moon.

30 Jump-Rope Genius

If you're looking for a challenge, then you've come to the right spot. This is arguably the most difficult Power Moon to earn in the entire game. The task is clear: jump the rope 100 times without a miss. The speed of the rope increases every five jumps, but only until 50. Once you've cleared the rope 50 times, the speed is set. Continue tapping in that same rhythm—not too hard—to keep pace with the ladies swinging the rope. It can be very tough to not inadvertently jump too high so be sure to tap lightly and avoid moving Mario around.

32 RC Car Pro!

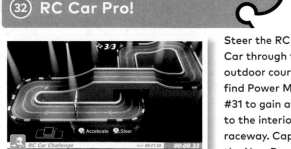

Steer the RC Car through the outdoor course to find Power Moon #31 to gain access to the interior raceway. Capture the New Donker on the podium to take control of his car in an attempt to earn a Power Moon. To do so, you need to complete a three-lap time trial in under 30 seconds.

The key to getting a fast time is to hold the Left Stick in the up position the entire race, from start to finish. Steer smoothly with the Right Stick, especially while going around the first hairpin turn leading into the bridge. Herky-jerky steering going into the bridge will cost speed and the car won't make it up the ramp. If this happens, back up and try again from before the hill.

The other critical aspect of this event is driving a clean line. Swing the car through turns without hitting the walls to maintain maximum speed. Similarly, aim for the inside corner as you enter the turn and swing wide on the exit. Continue practicing until you get the hang of it. With a touch of practice, you should be able to get your lap times below nine seconds each. Sub-eight second lap times aren't impossible!

33 Taking Notes: In the Private Room

Enter the building on the west side of Main Street, a block south of New Donk City Hall, to find a treble clef in a small room with two 8-bit warp pipes. The first set of notes appears inside the 8-bit wall. Enter a warp pipe and gather up the notes as quickly as you can to trigger phase two. Exit the pipe on the other side and circle the room to gather the notes that appear atop the perimeter ledge. This activates the third phase of the challenge. Use Cappy to help collect the notes in the center of the room then return to the warp pipe to gather the final batch.

36 Celebrating in the Streets!

Return to the New Donk City Hall Auditorium and speak with the man to the left of the stage— he'll let you experience the joy of the festival anytime you want! Make your way through the 8-bit level to the sequence in which Mario is upside-down. Dodge the barrels falling upwards and leap to the top (bottom?) of the ? Blocks. Reveal the invisible block above (below?) the ? Blocks and leap onto it. Then leap into the warp pipe. This drops Mario into a separate area, filled with coins, ? Blocks, and a Power Moon. Return the way you came.

37 Pushing Through the Crowd

Enter the building in the northwest corner of the city, near the Outdoor Café warp flag. Here, you arrive in a crowded alley filled with hundreds of pedestrians. Use Cappy to pull the lever on the wall to reveal a Power Moon on the far side. Quickly run, jump, and bounce your way through the crowd. Don't worry about being rude, just bounce off their heads and crowd-surf your way to the far end of the alley before the timer expires.

38 High Over the Crowd

Follow the instructions for Power Moon #37, but don't bother with pulling the lever. Make your way through the crowd to the green awning nearest the warp pipe in the distance and bounce from the awning to the metal platform high above the crowd. Leap from the second awning to the red poles and swing and jump your way to the Power Moon in the distance.

39 Rewiring the Neighborhood

Head to Crazy Cap and purchase the Builder Outfit. Wear it across town and show it to the man standing outside the building west of New Donk City Hall. He has a hardhat on and won't let anyone inside who isn't wearing a Builder Outfit.

Once inside, Mario must navigate a series of electrical wires connected by Spark Pylons, all while dodging a gauntlet of Fuzzies and Burrbos. Make your way to the first platform then take the wire on the left to reach a dumpster containing 50 coins. Cross to the taller building with the water tank in the distance and ride the Spark Pylon up and over the building (see Power Moon #40) to the far side.

Now you must navigate the maze of electrical lines to pick up five Moon Shards, all while dodging a number of Fuzzies. Fortunately, Mario automatically comes to a rest at each intersection if you allow it. Be patient and move between the Fuzzies to collect the Moon Shards.

The trickiest one to get is in the left corner, as there is no intersection along the left-hand edge. Wait until the Fuzzies

coming from the right are just about to touch Mario before heading toward the Moon Shard—this ensures Mario doesn't catch up to the Fuzzies patrolling in front of him. Fuzzies never enter the center of the maze so use the central Spark Pylon to wait for the Fuzzies to pass.

Hat Launching Detour

Once past the Spark Pylon that led up and over the roof, take the lone Spark Pylon on the left out to the distance where a series of hat launchers and rings awaits. Toss Cappy at the hat launcher on the right to pick up 50 coins.

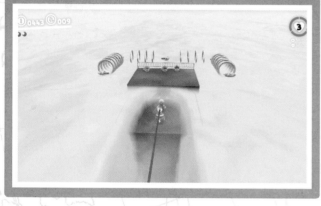

⑳ Off the Beaten Wire

Follow instructions for Power Moon #39 until you reach the Spark Pylon that leads up and over the high-rise building. Release the capture atop the roof and drop to the lower roof beside it. Smash open the middle crates to reveal a hidden Power Moon.

㊶ Moon Shards Under Siege

Capture the lone Taxi that has a button on its top. It's parked on Main Street just north of the plaza. Mario can't necessarily drive the Taxi, but attempting to makes the Taxi drive Mario to a special part of the city where Sherms do battle over Moon Shards.

Immediately capture the nearest Sherm and set to blowing up the scrap metal cubes and burned-out taxis in the way.

And yes, shoot the other Sherms too. Destroy the scrap metal cube beneath the girder to create a bridge to the first Moon Shard.

Drop off the girder and shoot the taxis cluttering up the street. The one in the back right-hand corner was parked atop a Moon Shard. Shoot the taxi to reveal it.

Pilot the Sherm up the stairs and shoot the scrap metal cube to the right of the next set of stairs. This drops a girder, creating a ramp. Destroy the Sherm atop the blue wall and locate the Moon Shard to the left of it, under the scrap metal cube. Take a moment to reveal the invisible blocks leading to the rooftop directly behind this third Moon Shard.

Ascend the ramp to the upper level of the area and fight your way across the narrow bridge, past the three Sherms defending the path. Blow up the scrap metal cube on the left to drop another, narrower, girder in place and drive across. The fourth Moon Shard is behind the scrap metal cubes up ahead.

The fifth Moon Shard is floating above the ground, under the girders that you just crossed to find the fourth Moon Shard. Return the

way you came and cross the previously-invisible blocks to the rooftop in the corner. Look across to the fifth Moon Shard.

42 Sharpshooting Under Siege

Follow the instructions for entering the Sherm shooting range at Power Moon #41 and capture a Sherm. Continue through the course, clearing out Sherms along your path until you reach the long blue staircase. It's hard to see through the driving rain, but there's a small metal ledge high above the stairs (and above the Sherm atop the blue wall). There is a scrap metal cube above that metal ledge that is glowing. You know what that means! Blast it with a Sherm to uncover a Power Moon. To get it, drive a Sherm along the path to where the fourth Moon Shard was, release the capture, and toss Cappy across the gap to uncover a path of invisible blocks.

43 Inside the Rotating Maze

Capture the Manhole Cover near the construction site nearest Crazy Cap and drop down the hole to enter the rotating maze challenge room. There are five Moon Shards scattered throughout the rotating maze, along with Fire Breathing Piranha Plants. The maze is quite simple to solve and thanks to the top-down view, the Moon Shards are all visible. Just use Cappy to rotate the yellow pieces of the maze—the blue walls are immovable.

The one tricky Moon Shard to get is the one in the lower left corner, which actually rests on the yellow platform. Mario has to stand on the wood floor and throw Cappy from afar in order to rotate the Moon Shard to him instead of the other way around. Dispatch the Piranha Plants by kicking them aside while they chew on Cappy. Don't worry, he'll come right back. There's a Heart in the lower right-hand corner if you need it.

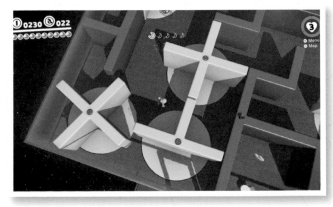

44 Outside the Rotating Maze

You may have noticed the canned vegetables atop the roof of the rotating maze while getting Power Moon #43. That's your cue that there is a ceiling to the maze. Exit the maze after collecting the Moon Shards and ground pound jump onto the glass roof. Cross above the maze and drop onto the ledge below, where a hidden Power Moon is. Use the hat trampoline to return the way you came.

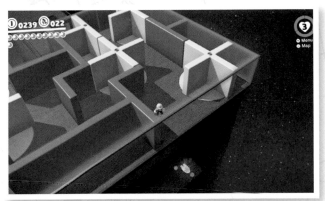

45 Hanging from a High-Rise

Make your way through the alley at Power Moon #37 and enter the warp pipe to reach the lone building in the northwest corner of Metro Kingdom. Capture the Rocket for a ride to this challenge level that wraps around a skyscraper.

Here, Mario must swing and jump across a series of moving red bars. Patience is key, as it's important to make sure the bars have slid into position before jumping for them. Also, remember that Mario can jump backwards off a bar; he doesn't have to be facing the correct direction. Leap for the man encouraging Mario and round the corner to the back half of the challenge. Here's where things get tricky.

Grab hold of a bar on the rotating contraptions and wait for it to spin into the right-hand position and leap. To get the purple coins from the second one, ride the bar to the upper position, then release the grip so Mario falls straight through the coins to the other bar. Dismount the final rotating set of bars from its upper position.

46 Vaulting Up a High-Rise

Follow the instructions for Power Moon #45 and make your way across the first sequence of poles, but don't leap to solid ground when you see the New Donker calling out, "What an athlete!" Instead, stay on the pole and ride it up, then wall jump to the blue wall on the left and upward to the next red pole. Continue wall jumping from one pole to the next to scale the side of the high-rise. The Power Moon is on a ledge high above.

47 Bullet Billding

Enter the open doors in the alley north of the plaza where you met the guitarist and grab hold of the yellow and black striped post. Climb up from either side into a handstand and wait for the post to slide in the direction Mario is facing to flip forward onto the next post. Climb up to the girders and avoid the Bullet Bills while making your way to the next sequence of striped posts. Keep Mario on the side of the beam opposite the Bullet Bills for safety and collect the coins. Scamper around the right side of the beam and leap to the next one as they draw close. Grab the Regional Coins and continue in this manner to the third beam and then onward to the Power Moon.

48 One Man's Trash...

Follow the instructions for Power Moon #47 until you reach the area with the Bullet Bills. Capture one of them and fly it in the direction you started. There's a platform floating high above the starting point that only be reached with a Bullet Bill. Steer the Bullet Bill right into the dumpster atop the platform to find a hidden Power Moon.

49 Motor Scooter: Escape!

Enter the triangular building to the southwest of New Donk City Hall via the open door on the north. Hop aboard the Scooter awaiting Mario in the alley and give the throttle a hefty twist! Follow the yellow painted lines on the street to line up with the rings and coins (and Regional Coins) as you race to escape a rampaging T-Rex. Leap over the wooden crates blocking your path to avoid being slowed down, but also make sure to swerve whenever the T-Rex is directly behind Mario—the T-Rex bites Mario whenever he stays directly in front of it for too long. Continue outmaneuvering the T-Rex while jumping over the crates (or riding on top of them) as you make your way to the end of the alley. Pick either left or right side at the end, cruise atop the crates, and take a leap of faith. Collect the Power Moon on the lower level before exiting the area.

50 Big Jump: Escape!

While outpacing the T-Rex for Power Moon #49, swerve back to the left side of the screen when the really wide yellow markings appear on the ground. Leap onto the wooden crates and quickly align yourself with the third row of crates from the right. A double-stacked crate quickly appears. Leap onto it to pluck a Power Moon out of the air before the T-Rex destroys your chances at getting it.

51 Secret Path to New Donk City!

You likely spotted a warp painting on a pillar during your travels in Sand Kingdom. But if you hadn't gone through it to get the Power Moon atop the Isolated Rooftop, then this is how. Warp to Jaxi Ruins and leap down to safety, beyond the poison. Head to the pillar near the Jaxi Stand northwest of the ruins and look for the painting on the north side. Go through the painting to access an otherwise unreachable Power Moon in Metro Kingdom.

52 A Tourist in the Metro Kingdom!

This Power Moon is linked to a multi-kingdom quest that begins back in Sand Kingdom and travels to numerous destinations. After defeating Bowser, return to Sand Kingdom and speak with the Tostarenan near the taxi by Tostarena Town. The taxi driver is going to take the Tostarenan to Metro Kingdom as the first stop on his tour. Sail to Metro Kingdom on the Odyssey and, if you hadn't already done so, complete all of the objectives available (if you've experienced the festival, then you've done so). Warp to Main Street Entrance to find the Tostarenan and his taxi parked nearby. Speak with the Tostarenan to get this Power Moon.

53 Found with Metro Kingdom Art

The hint art in Metro Kingdom is located on the side of the triangular building across from New Donk City Hall, nearest the Outdoor Café. It's near the top so drop from the roof onto the ledge to reach it. It can be tough to figure out the region it's referring to, but the art is actually from on the third floor of Water Plaza in Lake Kingdom, near the water-filled shaft that leads to the roof. Face the water shaft to the left of the Lochlady and ground pound the very same stone tile that Poochy is looking at in the photo.

54 Bird Traveling in the City

There are two birds flying around the city that, when hit with Cappy, yield a Power Moon. The one responsible for this Power Moon circles the eastern portion of the city, usually flying laps around the plaza but it sometimes heads farther north. Buy hints from Hint Toad and refer to the marker on the in-game map to see where the bird is currently located—the "x" on the map moves with the bird's position.

The bird often flies at different altitudes, which can make it difficult to hit. Sometimes it flies directly over the Roving Racers atop the nearby roof, but you may need to wait a while for it to head that way. Instead, watch for it to circle the plaza near Talkatoo and stand in the road on the eastern side. The next taxi to pass will stop so as to not run Mario over. Bounce off the taxi and toss Cappy at the bird when it passes by.

55 Mario Signs His Name

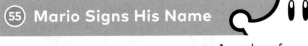

A number of brightly-colored letters have been delivered to the plaza park after Mario defeated Bowser. Capture these letters one at a time and move them into the plinths to spell out Mario's name—the statue is a token of Mayor Pauline's appreciation. The sign automatically lights up so the colored sides face the Odyssey.

56 Surprise Clown!

There's a man standing in the very northwest corner of New Donk City that can use a good laugh. He wants to see someone in a clown outfit. The Clown Hat and Clown Suit are sold at the Crazy Cap in Luncheon Kingdom. Return to Metro Kingdom wearing that outfit and give the man the laugh he craves in exchange for a Power Moon.

57 A Request from the Mayor

Mayor Pauline has lost her handbag, but you needn't go far to find it. It's on the metal platform high above the city, to the east of New Donk City Hall. Warp to the Heliport and drop off the side to the west to find it. Return the bag to Mayor Pauline outside city hall, but that's not all!

She wants to know if you'd like to learn more about her in the form of a quiz. Though you're not likely to know all the answers to the questions, guessing is perfectly acceptable. Just continue answering questions until you get four right in a row. Here are some of the correct answers to questions you may be asked.

What do I plan to eat for dinner tonight? Fried mushrooms.

What do I just adore? Cake.

What is my most treasured possession? A hat.

What do you think my hobby is? Going on walks.

What am I bad with? Fixing machines.

Which of these things did I actually do a long time ago? Captured by ape.

Mayor Pauline's story about losing her purse when captured by the ape (Donkey Kong) segues nicely into Mario handing her the item he found. Mayor Pauline appreciates the gesture and rewards Mario with a Power Moon.

58 Jammin' in the Metro Kingdom

Speak with Toad near Talkatoo to see what song he'd like you to play for him. His hint this time is "Revving a tiny engine!" If you've spent any time racing the RC Car around the indoor track, then you'll no doubt have the song "RC Car" in your music list (entry #80). Select that song to earn a Power Moon from Toad.

59 Sphinx in the City

Capture the Binoculars and scan the skies for the Sphinx floating high above the city. You'll see plenty of taxis

floating overhead, especially to the northeast, so look to the northwest if you don't spot the Sphinx right away. You might even spot the Sphinx directly above a close friend of Mario's.

60 Free Parking: Leap of Faith

A second rooftop scooter parking service has opened up and this time, the route to it isn't quite as obvious. The parking service is offered on the rooftop just north of the plaza—too high to reach by bouncing off a taxi and with no staircases or ramps anywhere nearby. To reach it, you're going to have to go big!

Warp to Heliport and ride the Spark Pylon to the top of New Donk City Hall where you find a Scooter and P-Switch. Drive the Scooter across the P-Switch to activate the checkerboard platform and race in a clockwise lap around the top of city hall until you're pointed south, toward the Odyssey. Race toward the edge of the path and leap from the edge. Aim for the rooftop just north of the big red button and bounce off it and onto the roof where the parking station is (the one with the two air conditioners). Don't act surprised when the man says Mario is the first to park his Scooter here.

(61) Metro Kingdom Regular Cup

The Roving Racers are staging their race on the rooftop of the eastern edge of the city, overlooking the plaza. The race takes place in the rain and runs northwest across the city, to the rooftop swimming pool high above the Outdoor Café, west of New Donk City Hall. There are a number of Volbonans stuck into the side of the high-rise from which Mario and the Koopas can flick themselves.

As with previous races, there are a number of ways to reach the finish, some faster—and more difficult—than others. For the Regular Cup, jump onto the second girder and head left toward the big red button. Ground pound the button, dive jump across the gap in the checkerboard path and roll toward the Pole on the corner of the next building. Flick Mario across the street to the rooftop café (aim for the metal balcony and dive jump to clear the gap) then bounce from the umbrella up to the Volbonans. Outpace the blue Koopa to the finish. Refer to the Power Moon #74 entry for an even faster route!

(62) Hat-and-Seek: In the City

Fancy yourself a perceptive traveler? If so, then this is the Power Moon challenge for you. There's a Bonneter in Metro Kingdom, riding aboard the head of one of the New Donkers. You're going to have to search the sidewalk strollers along Main Street for a man in a suit wearing a hat... with a pair of giant Bonneter eyes on the back! Speak to the Bonneter to get the Power Moon.

(63) Powering Up the Power Plant

Capture the Manhole near the Outdoor Café and return to the Underground Power Plant. Make your way past the Poison Piranha Plants and Urban Stingby bugs as you did when first powering up the city before the festival. Enter the warp pipe at the rear of the area to encounter a puzzle involving a large power plug. To power up the plant, you need to complete the circuit by fitting that cube into the slot behind it.

Like the similar puzzle in Lake Kingdom, the plug can only fit one way. Fortunately, there is a clear solution to this puzzle. Rotate the plug in the following order: Down, Left, Up, Right, Right, Up, Left, and Up.

(64) Up on the Big Screen

Go through the doors on the east side of the building that Peach and Tiara are on to enter a theater with the original *Super Mario Bros.* playing on the big screen. Actually, *you're* going to be playing on the big screen! Enter the warp pipe on the left to return to 1986 and relive World 1-1 of one of the most classic of all classic games. Most of what you (might) remember is the same as it always was, with just a few small exceptions. Namely, there are five Moon Shards in the area. Don't worry, they're hidden in plain sight and easy to find. Just avoid the Goombas, kick that Koopa Shell out of your way, and grab as many coins as you can while picking up those five Moon Shards. You won't find any 1-Up Mushrooms or Fire Flowers, but it's a small price to pay to have a live audience cheering your every move!

(65) Down Inside the Big Screen

Follow the instructions for accessing Power Moon #64 and enter the fourth warp pipe you encounter in the game—the one after the pair of Goombas. Just like in the original, this particular warp pipe leads to a bonus room filled with coins. Only now, there's also a Power Moon tucked inside too. Dash and jump to reach it!

(66) Peach in the Metro Kingdom

Ride the electrical line north from the Rooftop Garden to the taller building behind the Slots. Use the Pole to flick and ground pound your way to the roof to find Peach and Tiara. Chat with Peach to get the Power Moon she found in New Donk City.

 Moons From the Moon Rock

67 Hanging Between Buildings

Ride the Spark Pylon to the rooftop of the building directly southeast from New Donk City Hall and ground pound the large red button. A checkerboard pathway appears connecting the building with the triangular one across the street. Follow the path to the Power Moon over the narrow part of the path and ground pound jump to get it. The button and its corresponding pathway are always available, but the Power Moon doesn't appear until after the Moon Rock has been opened.

68 Crossing Lines

Warp to the Rooftop Garden and capture the Spark Pylon for a ride across to the building to the north. Leap off the wire (without releasing the capture) as Mario passes under the coins. This makes him leap from the electrical wire straight into the air to get the coins and Power Moon floating above it.

69 Out of a Crate in the City

This Power Moon is hidden inside a wooden crate on the short building in the northwest corner of the city. It's on the roof of the building where Mario entered the crowded alley for Power Moon #37. Wall jump between the two buildings in the alley to reach the crate. You'll have to dive jump from the water tower to reach the Power Moon once it flies off to the top of the bagel sign.

70 Bird Traveling in the Park

Warp to Mayor Pauline Commemorative Park and scan the area for the bird circling the park. Stand atop the railing and bench between the trees and Mechawiggler scrap so Mario has some extra height. Wait for the bird to approach, then leap up and smack it with Cappy.

A Clue!

The woman near the wrecked Mechawiggler in the park may mention that Mayor Pauline lost her handbag. Keep a look out for it!

71 Metro Kingdom Timer Challenge 3

This Timer Challenge takes place between the Crazy Cap store and the construction site. It's quite straightforward in that Mario need only hurry down the street, across the swinging girder, and onto the raised platform to the right. The tricky part is remembering that you don't have Cappy to help you. So that means, no dive jump! Roll down the street for speed, and up the ramp toward the swinging girder. Triple jump across the beam and around the corner toward the Power Moon.

72 Found in the Park! Good Dog!

Make your way to Mayor Pauline Commemorative Park and approach the dog in the corner. Take him on a walk around the park but watch closely as he sniffs and begins digging. Ground pound each of the spots in which he starts digging. Though most spots simply yield eight coins, he'll sniff out a Power Moon if you bring him toward the trees on the south side of the park.

73 RC Car Champ!

You'll have had to have already earned Power Moon #32 in order to get a shot at this one. Now, instead of simply completing three laps in under 30 seconds, you need to finish in under 26 seconds. It's imperative that you get off to a good start, with no flaws rounding the first turn into the hill. Since you're starting from a standstill, the first lap will naturally be the slowest, all else being equal. Aim for a first lap of 9.00 seconds. Your second and third laps then need to be 8.50 seconds or better. Of course, much faster times are possible...

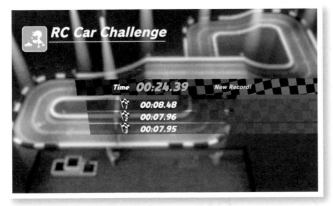

74 Metro Kingdom Master Cup

This route can shave up to 10 seconds from the one outlined for the Regular Cup, but it's a bit trickier. Start by leaping out ahead of the Koopas and tackle jump down onto the street below. Aim for the southeast corner of New Donk City Hall and capture the Spark Pylon there. Ride it to the roof and roll across the southern walkway on New Donk City Hall Rooftop. Dive jump into a tackle jump, aiming for the Volbonans on the side of the high rise leading to the finish. You won't likely reach the Volbonans, but Mario can tackle jump straight onto the umbrella. Zigzag up the side of the building using the Volbonans to reach the finish. Finishing times below 32-seconds are possible!

75 Hat-and-Seek: In the Crowd

Return to the mob of pedestrians pushing their way through the alley where you found Power Moon #37. There's another Power Moon in the crowd, but this time it's in the possession of a Bonneter riding atop the head of one of the many New Donkers. The Bonneter has the hat on backwards so his eyes are only visible from behind. Consider making your way through the crowd, to the far end of the alley, to watch for him as he appears. Or, similarly, stand near the doors that the crowd exits through and watch for a pair of eyes. Talk to him before he gets away to get the Power Moon.

76 Scaling Pitchblack Mountain

Leap down from the Heliport onto the mesh platform connecting the two buildings and enter the Moon Pipe. This challenge level takes place in near-darkness and features a mountain in the form of a pyramid. Explore the path around (and through) the base of the mountain to gather up the coins then begin your ascent. Bait the Stairface Ogre into slamming its stair-like blocks down on the floor. Leap up to its head and, from there, leap to the next higher level on the mountain.

Mario won't be able to leap directly to the third level of the mountain so look for a ledge halfway up the wall, in the corner, and leap for that. Wall jump up the shaft to reach the next level. The Power Moon is hovering atop a column in the center of a pit of spikes. Ground pound jump off the button atop the Stairface Ogre on the upper level then toss Cappy at the Power Moon and dive jump to reach the column.

77 Reaching Pitchblack Island

Follow the steps for earning Power Moon #76 and head around to the back of the mountain, on the side opposite where you entered. Ground pound jump from atop a Stairface Ogre for height then dive jump out into the distance, tackle jump out of the dive for further distance to land on a small island in the poison. Ground pound the floor of the island for a Power Moon. Return via the invisible block path leading back—toss Cappy to reveal the blocks.

78 Swinging Scaffolding: Jump!

Enter the Moon Pipe atop the building adjacent the large red button to access this next challenge level. Run across the three swinging beams and capture one of the two Hammer Bros in the distance. Toss the hammers at the breakable blocks and the other Hammer Bro to create some temporary safety, then continue across the next series of beams as Mario—it's easier to walk as Mario across the swinging beams than to hop as a Hammer Bro. Capture either of the Hammer Bros up ahead and continue up the side of the building to the third set of swinging beams. Continue using the Hammer Bro to beat back the other blocking Mario's path across the beams. Jump to safety and collect the Power Moon.

⑦⑨ Swinging Scaffolding: Break!

Follow the tips for Power Moon #78 until you reach the second pair of Hammer Bros. Capture either of them and carefully hop along the beam toward the massive block off to the left. Break apart the block with your hammers until the Power Moon is revealed. Use the Hammer Bro's jump ability to leap directly from the solid beam to the one with the Power Moon—there's no need to try and land on the small vertical beam.

⑧⓪ Moto Scooter: Daredevil!

This Scooter-based challenge is accessed via the Moon Pipe atop the roof northeast of Rooftop Garden, south of the triangular building. Hop aboard the Scooter and accelerate across the P-Switch to activate the first section of the course. Unless you're very secure in your Scooter driving, we recommend ignoring the rings and instead stay on the lower ground. Watch for the incoming rocket from the distant Sherm and leap over it as you cross the crumbling walkway.

The second section is a twisting staircase of ledges. Hit the P-Switch and angle left so that you can swing back to the right while ascending the stairs. Perform rapid jumps up the stairs and do your turning while in the air to avoid oversteer. Drive through the rings and leap for the central red girders to hit the next P-Switch.

The third and final section contains myriad Sherms guarding a wider left-hand path. Those with the driving skill should take the right-hand path, grab Power Moon #81, and shortcut past the Sherms.

There are two Sherms nearest the fork in the path. Cut the inside corner, passing them on the right, then aim for the third Sherm and jump onto it. The Scooter crushes the Sherm, though it won't bounce off it like a taxi. Skirt the fourth Sherm then drive a straight path through the half-dozen Sherms up ahead. Leap from the end of the red girders to get the Power Moon down below.

⑧① Full-Throttle Scooting!

Follow the instructions for Power Moon #80 until you begin the third segment, then turn hard to the right and follow the path of crumbling metal panels leading up and away from the Sherms to this next Power Moon. Jump up the stepped platforms while aiming for the second panel from the left so as to not cut the corner too sharp. Round the turn for the Power Moon then leap down and continue past the Sherms to the exit Moon Pipe.

Snow Kingdom

Welcome to Shiveria

REGION AT A GLANCE

Population	Middling
Size	Deep, Wide
Locals	Shiverians
Currency	Snowflake-shaped
Industry	Cakes, Racing
Temperature	Average 14°F

INDIGENOUS FLORA & FAUNA

BINOCULARS Can Capture? Yes		**CHEEP CHEEP** Can Capture? Yes		**GOOMBA** Can Capture? Yes	
TY-FOO Can Capture? Yes		**LAKITU** Can Capture? Yes		**SPINY** Can Capture? No	
SHIVERIAN RACER Can Capture? Yes					

Some Animals Brave the Cold

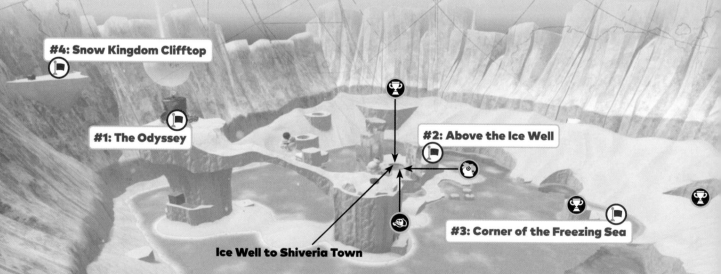

When the weather is clear, you might spot a few animals making the best of the cold. Be sure to keep an eye out!

#4: Snow Kingdom Clifftop

#1: The Odyssey

#2: Above the Ice Well

#3: Corner of the Freezing Sea

Ice Well to Shiveria Town

A FROZEN LAND

The Snow Kingdom is a world of ice and snow that freezes the body but dazzles the eyes. Stay alert though—one bad step can drop you into the dangerously frigid sea. Despite the cold, the town of Shiveria is famous for its warm hospitality, and on clear days, the view can't be matched.

BOUND BOWL GRAND PRIX

THE sporting event here is the Bound Bowl Grand Prix. Only Shiverians are allowed to participate, but when you watch a race, you'll understand why no one else COULD participate. Only Shiverian sturdiness could survive a race based on bounding violently through the course and crashing into one another. Be sure to see it if you get a chance!

A WARM COMMUNITY

Shiveria is a huge excavated settlement beneath the ice. It's warmer here than up above, but you'll want to bundle up all the same.

Despite the cold, the cheerful Shiverians will thaw any traveler's frozen heart. And if you visit the center square, you'll see the fiery passion the Shiverians have for their traditional races. Take one look at the screens showing the action, and you'll be caught up in the excitement too!

ICING AND RACING

Beyond racing, Shiverians are known for elaborate baked goods. Especially renowned is the Frost-Frosted Cake, which is very popular at weddings. By tradition, only the Shiverian Elder is allowed to make this extraordinary confection. What's more, they are specifically created as the grand prize for the Bound Bowl Grand Prix, so the only way to get one is to convince the winner to let you have it.

THREE KEYS TO THE KINGDOM

1. Swim only in short bursts if you like being warm enough to stay alive.

2. Dig for the gate to the town, which is frequently buried in the snow.

3. Bound your way through a race (build and species permitting).

CREVASSE MENACE

Lurking in the local crevasses you may find a Bitefrost. These creatures move through the ice under their prey, then thrust upward, chomping. Caution (and jumping ability) is advised.

155

Mario's Itinerary

The Snow Kingdom lives up to its name on arrival, buffeting the Odyssey and Mario with a blizzard on touchdown. Mario visibly shivers in the cold. Visibility is terrible in the storm, and there are drop-offs leading to narrow paths and frigid water in most directions, so take care. A clue points down a narrow walkway toward a small, frozen plateau.

Wooden Plugs and Updrafts

The Odyssey is perched high above ground level on a ledge. Fall below, and there seems to be no way back up. Look for wooden pegs plugged into the ground, as seen in other places like Cap Kingdom. Here, the pegs are keeping geysers of warm air stopped up. Throw Cappy at a peg to uncork it, and you can ride the resulting updraft to higher ground.

Extreme Temperatures

Despite the chilly conditions in Snow Kingdom, Mario can get by with normal activity and a healthy amount of shivering. Once the Snow Hood and Suit are purchased from the shop

here, at least the shivering can be alleviated, and Mario can jump around in comfort. However, Snow Suit or not, it's never safe to stay in frigid water for long. When swimming in icy water, the edges of the screen begin to frost over, indicating that it's unsafe for Mario to stick around. Stay in the cold water too long and Mario begins taking damage! Swim only for short periods, balancing time spent underwater with time spent drying off, or capture a Cheep Cheep.

Atop the small snowy plateau, you find the first checkpoint, Above the Ice Well. Near this checkpoint, a thick mat of snow covers up the entrance to the underground dwelling of Shiveria. Throw Cappy to knock aside enough snow to expose the well, then dive in.

Let's see what's under the snow!

Ⓐ The Cake Thief's Parting Gift

As if that weren't bad enough, he blocked the entrance to our race course! We need 🌙 Power Moons to get back in! Ⓐ

Falling down the well spits Mario out into the town. Explore the wide subterranean halls and visit the souvenir shop while progressing toward the main gathering space. A downcast vibe can be detected among the Shiverians, and it turns out this is for good reason: Bowser has stolen their famous, exquisite Frost-Frosted Cake, and set up barriers between the locals and their treasured race course! Dealing with stolen cake might have to wait a bit, but more immediately, race circuit access can be restored by retrieving Power Moons in four spoke rooms off the main chamber of Shiveria Town. Explore these starting with the right-most one, near the pole leading up to the main chamber's second floor, then proceed counter-clockwise through them all.

Icicle Cavern

An icy surface in here leads to slippery footing. Momentum in any direction needs to be compensated for by running in the other direction, or by jumping and then redirecting suddenly in midair with a tackle. *Or*, you can capture a Goomba, who has much surer footing here than Mario. There are lots of Goombas about, and a respectable stack of them is useful throughout this cavern.

Watch out for the circular shadows. These indicate a shaky stalactite above. Step under the shadow and keep moving so the icicle plunges down and sticks, without hitting Mario. Knocking down an icicle safely like this means you don't have to worry about it anymore, and it can also create a small platform.

Coax down the icicle at the foot of the small platform holding a Goomba button, then use the top of the fallen ice as a step. A stack of at least four Goombas can trip this button and expose a Power Moon behind nearby ice.

Collect Power Moon #18, the Ice-Dodging Goomba Stack Power Moon, then cross to the other side and climb up to the main shelf there. On the Goomba hike up there, you find small gaps to jump, icicles to dodge, and fallen ice to use as steps.

At the top are more Goombas to recruit, some high Regional Coins that are easy to nab with a tall stack, and some even higher Regional Coins between columns that are easy to pocket thanks to back and forth wall jumping. Note the big circular platform suspended here. At points along its edge, fractured-looking ground can be seen right underneath an icicle shadow. Step under all the shadows here to knock down stalactites into weak flooring, shaking loose a huge chunk of the shelf up here. The way is open to Power Moon #01, and the exit pipe.

Hollow Crevasse

The top-right spoke (relative to the center of Shiveria Town) leads to a room with square water pools in between a grid path on the ground. Five Power Moon shards are spread in sight at ground level. Is there a catch? No, just ice monsters that burst up from the snow. Watch out for Bitefrost shadows on the paths here, and jump off them quickly if they surge upward, carrying Mario into the air for a bite. The Bitefrosts can also be avoided by using the pools, but then there's obviously the hypothermia problem. Also, the moon shards aren't in the water. Collect all five shards to create a Power Moon up above, near the room's exit. Climb the big steps toward the exit, improvising Bitefrosts as raised platforms as needed.

At the top, collect Power Moon #02. Before exiting through the pipe, look above the path that led here to see a slit in the rock just big enough to allow a handhold. Jump up and press against it for Mario to cling to the tiny ledge. Now shimmy to the right, until the hand-sized channel opens up into a little room. Hop up and crack open the treasure chest for Power Moon #12, the Treasure in the Ice Wall. With two Power Moons in hand, this room is clear.

Snowy Mountain

Next up, the top-left spoke contains Snowy Mountain. This chamber involves an ice climb upward, with hat trampolines and updrafts giving much-needed vaults upward. Use Cappy to brush aside piles of snow and knock open closed hat trampolines.

Before ascending all the way, at an updraft spigot, notice a curious gap in the wall beyond. Cappy can clear the snow clogging the small gap, then Mario can pass through to discover a path farther around the edge. At the end of this wraparound passage, find Power Moon #07 and some hidden Regional Coins down the deep shaft below!

Head back to the last updraft spigot and launch upward for a surprise encounter with another dastardly hare henchman.

BOSS: RANGO

Bowser's flagship was seen with the Frost-Frosted Cake on the Shiverian's gigantic projection screen, but the Broodals' ship is here at Snowy Mountain. Rango jumps down to stop Mario and Cappy with his blazed buzz saw hats. Beware the slick surface up here, which makes Mario scamper furiously against his slides to correct inertia on the ice. If health is needed during the battle, break the rocks embedded in the ice floor, since they sometimes turn up Hearts.

Meanwhile, Rango throws dangerous hats in wide arcs at Mario, but while he's throwing hats he's not wearing them. Be ready to strike one of his hats with a cap toss of your own, and Rango's hat flips upside down and becomes a temporary hat trampoline. Launch off Rango's flipped hat then glide gracefully down onto his head while he cluelessly wonders what happened. To speed things up, you don't have to use Rango's own hats against him. With skillful jumping, you can also bypass this step. Time a jump aimed at Rango's head to launch just as he throws his hats.

After hitting Rango, he goes mad for a bit, bouncing toward Mario relentlessly with blades bristling on a big hat. Run away quickly and hit Rango with cap tosses to redirect him and slow him down. When he returns to his hat throw attacks, stomp on his head again.

When Rango's finally worn down with Mario stomps, the way back out is clear, and Mario receives Power Moon #04.

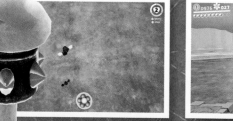

158

Wind-Chill Cavern

The bottom-left spoke is the last blockade to clear before reinstating racing season in Shiveria, if you proceeded counter-clockwise through them. The violet muck around solid ground here is poison, so falling is doom as surely as if it were an empty pit. Cloud-like Ty-Foo creatures blow gusts of forceful air on platforms here, which push Mario and stray Spinies alike into the poison. Observe Ty-Foo patterns, then move around them in between gusts. Spinies cannot be directly defeated, so dodge them, or knock them off and into the muck with rapid cap throws. Guide Spinies past a Ty-Foo and the Ty-Foo will probably inadvertently take care of the Spinies for you.

When crossing on the far end, ride the platform being passed between two Ty-Foo clouds, then capture the farthest Ty-Foo and use it to block the next loose platform out of its slot, opening the path forward. Run through as Mario. Before continuing, climb up onto the platform you just blew through the opening, then look atop the arch it popped out of. There's a subtle X mark on the arch! From the top of the platform, jump toward the arch, toss Cappy at it, then tackle and hold down the Cap Throw button to dive jump. Control Mario after the bounce to land on top of the arch, in position to ground pound the X and gain the Atop a Blustery Arch, Power Moon #09.

The next platform leading to a Ty-Foo is covered in tempting coins, but the Ty-Foo here covers the entire length of the platform with its gusts. Run up to it quickly when it's pointed sideways and capture it. This Ty-Foo isn't confined by platforms like the others in this room, so float around freely and collect the Regional Coins floating over the poison liquid. Float over to the platform crawling with Spinies and blow them all off into the poison to reveal Power Moon #03 on the back of that platform!

Snowline Circuit

The ⓑ Frost-Frosted Cake got stolen, so for now the racing prize is a ⓜ Multi Moon! Ⓐ

With Power Moons collected from all four spoke hallways, and all four barriers removed, the slalom route to Snowline Circuit is open. To go, just hop down the hole in the center of town. A pipe at the bottom leads right back up here if an immediate return is needed.

The chamber below overlooks the gorgeous wintry racetrack. Organizers down here are trying to get the next race set up, but they're one racer short. Unfortunately, Mario is too small to race with the Shiverians.

Head into the waiting room next door.

Before heading upstairs, curve around to the right to find three hidden Regional Coins. Head upstairs to discover a shivering Shiverian racer, scared to come out and compete.

Capture the racer and bound up the path, tapping the Jump button or shaking the controller whenever the round racer touches down to get a boost of speed and bounce distance. Bounding with good timing is the most important thing to learn when it comes to Shiveria races. Bound up to collect the four Regional Coins and the coin rings along the way, then tumble back down to the Snowline Circuit entry queue. With a Shiverian body, there's nothing stopping Mario from entering now! You get a chance to run a training lap before the real deal, so take the time to get comfy bounding.

That's what you think.

The Bound Bowl Grand Prix

When you're ready to race for real, you run a three-lap race against seven other bounding Shiverians. The track runs around four wide, banked, 90-degree turns, but in between there are various curves and quirks to the track to keep it from being a series of turns and straightaways.

When bounding off a banked surface, a Shiverian racer can change directions laterally very suddenly, with a speed boost to boot. This is great on wide corners, where you can instantly go from max speed in one direction to max speed in a new direction. But it can be bad on straightaway stretches with sharply angled slopes. Bounding off a sharp angle when you really want to keep going forward might jet the Shiverian racer off the side, into the rough. When coming down at weird angles, avoid bounding if you're not sure of the trajectory. Otherwise, always bound! You have to bound almost every bounce and aim them all well, never going off track, to get truly good bounding race times.

Win the race to take the prize: Power Moon #05. You could've taken the cake, but that's been stolen. This Multi-Moon

plus the two Mario picked up in each spoke room, equals 11 total, not counting any others you may have picked up along the way. This is enough to get the Odyssey going to the next kingdom.

Extend Your Stay

Racing Season

After the Shiverian races are back on, the sun's finally out, so there's plenty more to explore here now, too. The blizzard has subsided, visibility is up, and Ty-Foos are out on the surface.

❄ Souvenir Shopping

Snow Kingdom contains 50 Regional Coins in the form of purple Snowflakes.

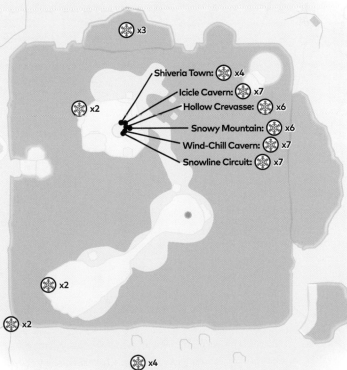

❄ x3

Shiveria Town: ❄ x4
Icicle Cavern: ❄ x7
Hollow Crevasse: ❄ x6
Snowy Mountain: ❄ x6
Wind-Chill Cavern: ❄ x7
Snowline Circuit: ❄ x7

❄ x2

❄ x2

❄ x2

❄ x4

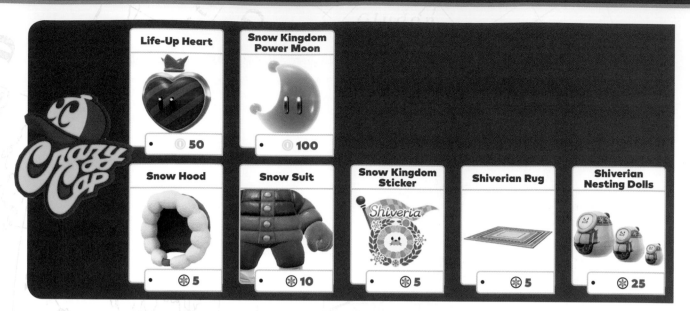

Life-Up Heart	Snow Kingdom Power Moon
⊙ 50	⊙ 100

Snow Hood	Snow Suit	Snow Kingdom Sticker	Shiverian Rug	Shiverian Nesting Dolls
❀ 5	❀ 10	❀ 5	❀ 5	❀ 25

Coins in High Places

In Icicle Cavern, the sub-room off the main chamber filled with Goombas, don't miss the purple coins hovering high up between two facing pillars.

In Snowy Mountain, a bonus Power Moon is tucked away around a corner toward the top. The gap under this Power Moon that looks like a bottomless pit hides purple coins.

Find some spare purple coins by curling around and to the right inside the waiting room off to the side in Snowline Circuit.

Power Moons

There are 55 Power Moons in Snow Kingdom. Power Moons #01, 02, 03, 04, 05, 07, 09, 12, & 18 were obtained while reinstating the races. Consult the prior pages for help.

01 02 03 04 05 06 07 08 09 11 12 18 20
21 23 29 30 34 36 37 41 42 45 46 48

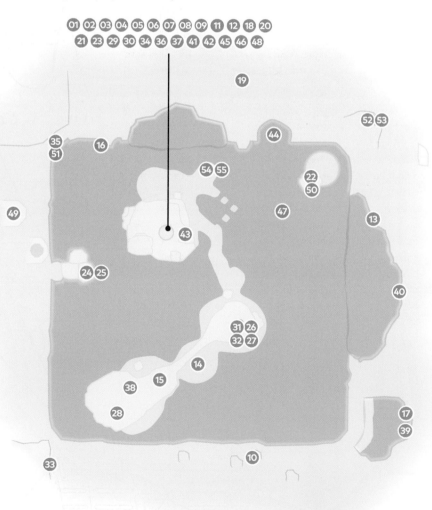

06 Entrance to Shiveria

This Power Moon is found in plain sight above boxes to the right of the pipe down into Shiveria Town. Climb the boxes by wall jumping or somersaulting then jump to the moon. If the boxes all get knocked away, just take the pipe back to the surface and return for another shot.

08 Shining in the Snow in Town

Up on the second-floor balcony of the main chamber in Shiveria Town, down in the ice well, a big pile of slushy snow can be found just past the hanging light fixtures. In a corner under all the snow, a suspicious glowing spot on the ground can be uncovered. Ground pound this spot to jar loose a Power Moon.

10 Caught Hopping in the Snow!

On the south bank of the kingdom, which is a mostly nondescript white expanse, you can find a rabbit cavorting around a double shelf in the bank. Chase the rabbit and it runs circles around these objects, away from Mario. Rabbits are quick, and can be frustrating to chase, but they can be tricked. Wait until the rabbit here stands still on the opposite side of one of the ledge obstacles, then run to one corner near it. The hare starts running in the other direction, but you already should be, too. Bait it then run around the other way too, catching up and stunning it with Cappy before it has time to readjust. Grab the rabbit for the Power Moon reward.

11 The Shiverian Treasure Chest

From the main chamber in Shiveria Town, climb the pole to the second floor then follow the path all the way around on the top—past the hanging light fixtures that can be used to cross the gap, and past the piles of snow heaped up on the other side. Climb the ramp up to the high bridge visible spanning above the souvenir shop. Crack open the treasure chest up here to get the Power Moon.

13 Snow Kingdom Timer Challenge 1

After giving the scarecrow a cap fitting, several circular ice platforms are temporarily revealed in the sea below. On the farthest platform lies a Power Moon. Take a breath to plan your path, then take a running long jump off the edge toward the platforms and begin leaping across. Take care not to plunge into the freezing drink below. Apart from that, if you keep moving forward and don't fall in, you'll probably make it in time.

14 Snow Kingdom Timer Challenge 2

The scarecrow here begins a tense timer challenge nearby. Two floating poles appear out over the water. Mario has to quickly climb the first one, jump to the second one, climb that, then jump from the top to the hovering Power Moon. Complete all that before the objects disappear to add the moon to your count.

The key here isn't to do anything fancy, it's to do everything as quickly as possible. Dive jump toward the first pole to avoid as much swimming as possible, shake the controller for fast climbing, and don't waste movements.

163

15 Moon Shards in the Snow

Once the weather clears up, five moon shards can be found outside spread about. Collect all of them and the assembled Power Moon appears near the Above the Ice Well warp flag. The moon shards are located as follows:

1. On a ledge on the southeast bank

2. On an ice platform just above the water, east of well

3. Underwater in the center of a ring of coins in the northwest sea

4. By the updraft spigot at the base of the Odyssey's platform

5. Atop an ice ledge watched by a Ty-Foo, next to the well

16 Taking Notes: Snow Path Dash

This timer challenge begins with a music note found on an unassuming ledge northwest of the ice well entrance, and ends on another unassuming ledge, northeast of the ice well. In between, Mario has to rush straight up the sloped hill, run over the length of the high bank collecting a curved swoop of notes, then rush down another hill, collecting notes along the way. Keeping a roll under control during the straight stretches helps speed collection up.

17 Fishing in the Glacier!

In the southeast corner of the kingdom, Lakitu can be found calmly fishing above a small glacial pond. Capture Lakitu to try Mario's hand at fishing. Fish shadows can be seen just below the surface. Tap a Cap Throw button to lower the lure into the water,

then wait for signs that one of the fish has noticed. Shadows move at first, but then they tug at the line, with motion control feedback to add some oomph to the cue. Use motion controls to tug upward, beginning the reel-in process. Catch the bigger shadow here to produce a Power Moon.

19 Captain Toad is Chilly!

To the extreme north, in a snow-clogged stone bivouac, you find Captain Toad holed up against the elements. Dig him free and say hello and he gives over a Power Moon for the consideration.

20 I'm Not Cold!

One of the Shiverians in town, right across the way from the souvenir shop, wants to see the ultimate in uncompromising and aerodynamic tundra racewear: underwear. Yes, it'd take a hearty individual indeed to brave the elements in skivvies here. Acquire the Boxers (in the store for a cool 1000 coins—they must be comfortable), change into them, and greet the Shiverian to inspire him into coughing up a Power Moon out of respect. Now change back into the Snow Hood and Suit before Mario catches a cold out there!

21 Shopping in Shiveria

Like in most regions, the souvenir shop here sells one unique Power Moon for 100 gold coins. Pick it up whenever it is convenient to add to the moon total for the kingdom.

22 Walking on Ice!

This is found in the room right by the Corner of the Freezing Sea warp flag. A chilly Koopa inside gives you a little footwork challenge:

walk in a triangle path of three straight lines, all along an icy floor. The Koopa scores your performance at the end, based on how well you trace the triangle. The target score is 80 points, and if you fail you can simply try again, correcting for error spots on prior attempts.

23 Snowline Circuit Class S

Return to Snowline Circuit later after conquering the first race to take on fiercer competition. It's the same course, a series of banked left turns, tricky straights with some curveballs strewn about, and seven other bouncing, roly-poly Shiverians looking to body check Mario off into the slush. Win this higher-octane race to score yet another Power Moon.

It's tricky, navigating the angled straightaways without bounding sideways off the course. It's OK to not bound if you're not sure about the exit angle.

Competitors are much more serious this time.

Ideal bounds take you right over tricky curves in the track.

24 Dashing Over Cold Water!

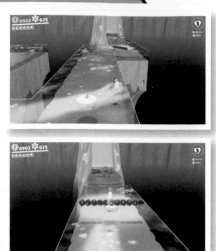

This challenge room is easily found just by swimming to the western island, inhabited by little blue penguins and drifts of snow. It won't be so easy once you're inside. The path ahead is a shallow, crystal-clear lake of chilly water with no platforms. Across the surface are Rocket Flowers and spinning Moonsnakes. Grab the first Rocket Flower to begin skating across the top of the water, rocket-powered. Move on down the path, jumping over Moonsnakes as needed and grabbing fresh Rocket Flowers on the go with cap throws. When barreling toward the sheer snow wall, make sure you snag a fresh Rocket Flower just beforehand, and plow straight upward to the Power Moon.

25 Dashing Above and Beyond!

Inside the Rocket Flower challenge room, as you rocket over the first sheer wall and toward the first Power Moon and exit pipe, don't veer at them. Jump past them, over a small ledge toward a slope that's almost totally vertical. Mario can keep zooming straight up it, as long as a Rocket Flower is still active. Running straight up the wall, watch out for one final trick—a brief gauntlet of obstacles that forces you to zig-zag to the center, the edge, then back to the center while running up a sheer surface. Make it past these blocks, though, and you're home free at the top, ready to grab the bonus Power Moon up here and greet an admiring Shiverian fan. If you still need the Power Moon below, fall down and grab it. If not, there's an extra exit pipe up top.

26 Jump 'n' Swim in the Freezing Water

At the base of the central pillar in the kingdom, supporting part of the second tier on which the Odyssey rests, you find a scarecrow door. It won't open unless you let the hay person here try out the fashionable Cappy, so Mario rolls solo inside. Inside, there's a unique platforming challenge: chunks of frigid water floating together in cubes, somehow. You'll have to swim through and jump between sections of moving water, all under the time limit of needing to get out before the cold starts digging into Mario's bones.

There are Goombas in here too, mostly as a nuisance and another way to scrounge up coins. Ascend the first wall, swimming up one passage of water high enough to be able to jump on top of the roof of other section. This "elevator roof" riding tactic comes in handy again in this room. Avoid the Goombas ahead and follow the coin rings into a long cavern, filled with water; dash through the water a couple times to get through the corridor faster, but don't dash right into the wall at the end. Swim up and into fresh air again, warming up a bit. One of the ? blocks here holds a Heart, if needed. The roving wall of water here can be ridden up the wall on the left, giving Mario enough height to move up the path. Another dual water-elevator section leads to more Goombas, some ? blocks underneath a hidden Heart block, and the final major water passage. This is a long vertical sea of water, with rows of coin rings in places, all the way down to a low exit. To plunge more quickly, use underwater ground pounds repeatedly. At the end, Mario pops out into the crisp air again, Power Moon nearby and ready to grab.

27 Freezing Water Near the Ceiling

Before plunging down the long vertical water channel that precedes the exit from this challenge room, jump on top of it, as though it were a giant elevator car. Ride the big water section upward, where extending poles from the background are evident. Swing to the left toward the hidden Power Moon!

28 Blowing and Sliding

Capture a Ty-Foo at a relatively low altitude near the ice well in the north, then fly to a low ledge to the south where a blowable block must be blocking something interesting. Puff it out of the way to reveal a door.

Inside, another Ty-Foo oversees a block puzzle. Two differently-shaped steps must be fitted into specific spots on the ground, but in order to do that, you have to blow them around the playing field in the correct order. You must consider the little divots found on the edges of the tracks, which prevent freely moving the two steps any way you want.

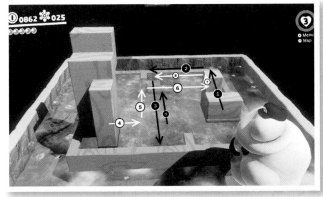

Follow this order for the two blocks to open the way to the locked Power Moon!

29 Moon Shards in the Cold Room

This room is accessed from the second-floor balcony overlooking the main chamber. Get up here with the pole nearby, then get the Shiverian attendant to let you in. He'll only budge if Mario is wearing the Snow Hood and Suit, though, so pick those up and change beforehand at Crazy Cap's local branch.

Inside, an 8-bit pipe leads to a wraparound room filled with Spinies and five collectible moon shards. Collecting some of the shards requires waiting for the right moment to duck in ahead of or behind the long string of Spinies patrolling together. Get all five shards to complete the Power Moon, but don't leave without also getting the moon hidden up high, too.

30 Slip Behind the Ice

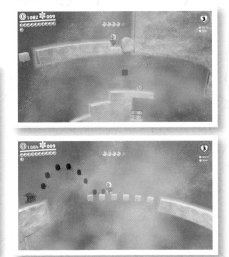

Inside the cold room, find a moon shard location on a relatively high ledge, right above the entrance pipe, near a Koopa Troopa marching. (Kicking this Koopa below is an excellent way to clear out all the Spinies.) Here, a floating brick can be seen before a strange-looking ceiling feature. Inspecting the area with jumps from the block will reveal that the area isn't solid, and Mario can pass up to another room in this chamber. Dash across the blocks without stopping to cross the small gaps, and jump to the Power Moon against the far wall.

㉛ Spinning Above the Clouds

Look for a seed above an ice ledge just by the ice well, the entrance to Shiveria Town. Carry this big seed across to where a wooden peg can be popped out, revealing a torrential updraft. Ride the updraft, seed in hands, to get it up to the planter spot above. Planting the seed grows a beanstalk that can be ridden up into the clouds, accessing this challenge area.

This is a linear path of hat trampolines, warm air updrafts, and coin rings. Keep drifting forward, and use the trampolines and updrafts to gain height. You find a Power Moon at the end, while descending through the final vertical coin ring clusters. You return to earth drifting down with these coin rings.

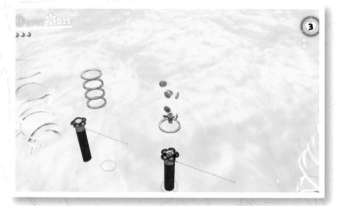

㉜ High-Altitude Spinning

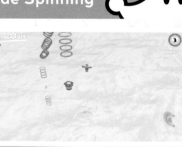

In the cloudy coin ring area accessed by climbing the beanstalk, a hidden Power Moon floats over the stage before the final stretch. Glide to the biggest updraft gust, then look backward over the path to here from the entrance. A lone hat trampoline floats just a bit back toward the entrance, a Power Moon floating above it. Fall down a bit on purpose, catch the big updraft again for some lift, and glide out toward that hat trampoline. With enough velocity you make it there, where you can easily bounce again to the Power Moon.

㉝ Secret Path to Shiveria!

A tempting ledge overlooking the Odyssey cannot be reached until much later in the adventure. After events in Metro Kingdom, Mario and Cappy must visit either Snow Kingdom or Seaside Kingdom first. It doesn't matter which is chosen, ultimately you visit both, but it affects where certain warp paintings go later. Between Snow and Seaside Kingdoms, whichever you opt to visit *second* will be tied to a warp painting in Bowser's Kingdom. Whichever you opt to visit *first* will have a warp painting from Mushroom Kingdom.

Either way, after stepping through the painting in a future area to arrive at the remote ledge here, be sure to touch the flag to acquire the Snow Kingdom Clifftop warp point. Then open the chest for the Power Moon.

㉞ Found with Snow Kingdom Art

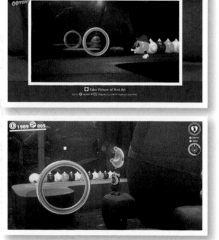

The Hint Art painting is found in Shiveria Town on the wall left of the entrance. From the colors, texture, and creatures pictured, the destination should be obvious. Head to Lost Kingdom and look along the low flank around one corner of the region, where Tropical Wigglers stretch just feet above the sludge, near a tree and its exposed roots. Pound one of the roots to sprout free the moon.

35 Snow Kingdom Regular Cup

Once the race starts, the contestants begin high above the ground in the northwest corner of the kingdom. The target is the ledge where the Odyssey sits. This means the route naturally leads over (or around) the ice well plateau, across the little land bridge over the water to the updraft spigot, up the updraft, then across the skinny path up past a Ty-Foo to the ship and goal line.

Lots of time can be made up against Koopas just by rolling as fast as possible from the Ty-Foo to the goal line, once the Ty-Foo takes a breather.

36 Hat-and-Seek in the Snow

When you've completed the adventure, many more people throughout the kingdoms are willing to visit different lands and try new things. One such person is a resident of Bonneton down here in Snowline Circuit checking out Shiverian racing. Look for a Shiverian with literal eyes on the back of its head, a Bonneter giveaway if ever there was one. Greet the Bonneter in hiding and receive a Power Moon for your powers of perception.

37 Peach in the Snow Kingdom

Complete the main adventure, and Peach wants to do some sightseeing of her own. Snow Kingdom is one of the places she can be easily found after that. Here, she's simply in the main chamber of Shiveria Town, taking in the teeth-chattering atmosphere. Pay her and Tiara a visit for a Power Moon.

Moons from the Moon Rock

38 Shining on High

Once the Moon Rock has released its energy, the easiest bonus Power Moon to grab is a pebble's toss from the Odyssey. Get on top of the Odyssey (somersault up there, or climb up the flagpole), spot the Power Moon in the air nearby, then take a running long jump toward it.

39 Above the Freezing Fish Pond

Look above Lakitu's fishing pond, in the southeast. On a high, precarious bank there, find a fresh Power Moon after releasing the energies of the Moon Rock.

40 Ice Floe Swimming

Go as far east as possible in Snow Kingdom, then look underwater there for a small cave. Inside, find coins and a new Power Moon. It's dangerous to go for this with Mario alone, so capture a Cheep Cheep nearby and wiggle safely through the chilly water to the moon.

41 Icy Jump Challenge

Inside Wind-Chill Cavern, where Ty-Foos wait to blow things cruelly into poison, there's a new Power Moon. It's located above the spot where two Ty-Foo clouds blow a wooden block back and forth. Climb atop the block while the cloud creatures toy with it, then somersault up from it toward the Power Moon while it's being blown underneath.

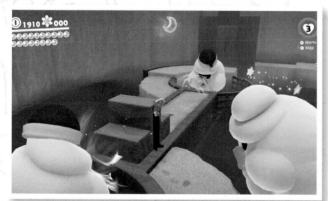

42 Forgotten in the Holding Room

When you return later, long after initially capturing a timid Shiverian in the waiting room and going on to win Mario's first ice race,

the waiting room is out of use. A bunch of boxes are in here as storage. Bash apart all the crates for some coins and, eventually, a Power Moon!

43 It Popped Out of the Ice

Travel to the ice well, then climb the biggest ice chunk here, to the very top. You're not up here for this chunk though, you're here for the second-highest ice ledge on this plateau. Take a running long jump or dive jump to the west from the tallest ice shard here, landing on an ice finger with a glowing, strange spot on top. Ground pound this spot after a safe landing up here to pop out the trapped Power Moon.

You can also capture the high-altitude Ty-Foo, fly it over the platform in question, then pop out with the Capture button and land on top.

44 Deep in the Cold, Cold Water

Check the center of what looks like an impact crater on the Travel Map in the northeast. There's nothing much of interest in the crevasse,

until you notice the glow in the center. Dive down as Mario (gritting teeth against the cold) and ground pound the center. This jogs a Power Moon loose from the grit at the bottom. Swim upward quickly to collect it and get Mario out of the frigid water.

45 Water Pooling in the Crevasse

Once the Moon Rock is opened, some new moons appear in the old "spoke" hallways which first allowed access to the racing circuit. In Hollow Crevasse, avoid the Bitefrost shadows and peer into the cold pools here for a glow on the floor. Ground pound into the water there.

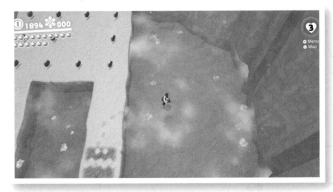

46 Squirming Under the Ice

Travel into the Snowy Mountain room from the main chamber and climb again to the top, where you once fought Rango on ice. A curious bump under the surface here is dragging around like the floor was merely a bedsheet. Stun it with cap throws to slow it down, then jump above it and ground pound, knocking loose a Power Moon stuck under the environment.

47 Snow Kingdom Timer Challenge 3

Mysteriously, a P-Switch now appears on the shallow seafloor of the northeast. Pushing the switch somehow (whether by brushing it swimming with Mario or a Cheep Cheep or by ground pounding into it) briefly reveals a Power Moon sitting on top of a platform to the west, past a

little sandbar. To get by this obstacle quickly with a captured Cheep Cheep, jump up out of the water at a narrow point for the land bridge, so you only have to flop across dry ground very briefly (flop around very long out of the water and the Cheep Cheep will perish, spitting Mario out).

48 Stacked-Up Ice Climb

Back in Icicle Cavern, there's a new puzzle to complete. A new button has appeared up on the second floor, across and above from the starting point. Triggering the button requires the precise weight of 10 Goombas! Capture a Goomba near the entrance, then keep the stack together and growing all the way up the icy cave to the top. Jump on the button with 10 Goombas to spawn the Power Moon, conveniently located at 10-Goombas-jumping altitude.

49 I Met a Snow Cheep Cheep!

The western banks of Snow Kingdom have small circular pools whose purpose is a mystery until a Bonneter

shows up here. The ghostly little fella is curious about the Cheep Cheep species indigenous to the region. Ah-ha, now the pools make sense. Go find a Cheep Cheep to capture, then swim back here and leap out of the lake and onto the bank, flopping as quickly as possible up to the first circle pool. From here, the fish can take its version of a breather, and then it's time to leap out again and struggle over land toward the top pool, where the Bonneter waits. Flop quickly enough, and the Cheep Cheep survives all the way to the Bonneter's inspection. Provide this specimen for the curious character to score a Power Moon.

⑤⓪ Even More Walking on Ice!

Return to the trace-walking Koopa in the cave by the warp flag in the northeast, and he has a new Power Moon to award. This time, he wants a score of 90 or more, trace-walking a triangle on the slippery cave floor. After this Power Moon, the only reason to keep trying out the event is to improve on your max score.

97 points!

⑤① Snow Kingdom Master Cup

This is the same cross-region free running course as before, but this time with the speedy golden Koopa added to the windy mix. At the beginning, running long jump off the high edge then dive jump to eat up a lot of lateral distance on the way down, without having to spend time jumping in and out of chilly

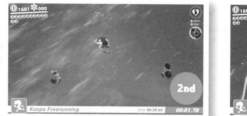
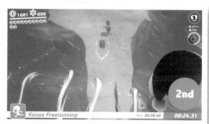

water heading for the ice well, like most Koopas do. The golden Koopa bends to the right just around the ice well's landmass rather than over it, saving lots of time. If you don't emulate the crafty turtle, you have to make the time by long jumping over the ice well quickly and by rolling up past the Ty-Foo on top with terrific timing.

⑤② Iceburn Circuit Class A

[1] Start/Finish: Brief, true straightaway.

Beyond the northeastern bank, in fact inside the gap where the Moon Rock once stood, look for a new opening in the rock. Inside, another Shiverian racing course! Capture the idle racer near the leader to participate.

While the other race course is basically just left turns, this one is much more technical. You have to place bounding bounces intelligently to maximize speed, and angle toward the next intended turn or bounce. Going off course badly at all is probably grounds for scrubbing a race attempt and selecting Retry from the Pause Menu.

[2] Angled step straight: Jagged slices of road face each other, aggressive bounding risks squirting off the sides of what's basically a straight. This is followed by a couple of short steps on a straight.

[3] Sharply banked S curves: the path snakes left—left—right—left. Bound hard from each jagged bank, ideally wasting no extra bounces on overcorrecting turns.

[4] Tunnel seam straight: Everyone is forced into close quarters on a straight path made of two angled shallow planes meeting in the middle. The angle on both sides complicates using bounding for forward speed boosts. It also just generally encourages racers in close quarters in here to dogpile each other.

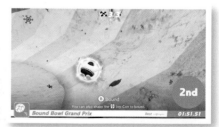

[5] Long sloping left: This lengthy turn is unlike most direction changes in Shiverian racetracks. It's not at a sharp angle nor across a relatively short distance so that one well-aimed bound is enough to take the turn at high speed. Instead, you'll have to bound several times along the length of the slope, being careful not to overcorrect into the slush.

⑤③ Iceburn Circuit Class S

Win **Iceburn Circuit Class A** and you'll get a chance to try the hottest race in chilly Shiveria. The main difference here is that the opposition is much stronger. You can't afford to make any bad mistakes here.

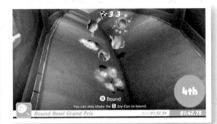

It's hard to separate from the pack here.

Don't give up—it doesn't matter what place you're in for any part of the race but the very end. A lot of ground can be made up in the tunnel and the long sloping left.

⑤④ Running the Flower Road

This ivy-laced challenge room is located down a moon pipe near the Above the Ice Well warp flag. Inside, an elaborate setup of spinning Moonsnakes, coin rings, and curiously few stable-looking platforms twists upward. Throwing Cappy onto the

scarecrow at the start reveals the secret: vine paths grow and curl around the obstacles leading upward, forcing Mario to keep moving and dodging. The first couple of segments just involve riding the vines past Moonsnakes, but the final stretch forces Mario to jump between dual vines crossing through an area peppered with Banzai Bills! During any vine-growing stretch, Cappy is unavailable, so dive jumps are off-limits, and Banzai Bills cannot be captured.

Thankfully, the distance between the vine paths is perfect for running long jumps.

⑤⑤ Looking Back on the Flower Road

Inside the ivy moon pipe, stay frosty during the final segment, running along growing vine paths while Banzai Bill cannons loom ahead. Jump to the right vine path to get past the first Banzai Bill cannon, then immediately look left, at the back of the mechanism. A hidden Power Moon sits here! Jump back across to the left vine path, then snuggle into the back of the cannon to pick up the Power Moon. If the vine growth is getting too far ahead at this point, just somersault onto the very top of the cannon and wait for the vine paths to pass through again.

Seaside Kingdom

Welcome to Bubblaine

REGION AT A GLANCE

Population	Middling
Size	Wide
Locals	Bubblainians
Currency	Shell-shaped
Industry	Bubbly Water, Tourism
Temperature	Average 88°F

INDIGENOUS FLORA & FAUNA

	Can Capture?			Can Capture?			Can Capture?
BINOCULARS	Yes		GOOMBA	Yes		MINI GOOMBA	No
MOONSNAKE	No		GUSHEN	Yes		CHEEP CHEEP	Yes
KOMBOO	No		MAW-RAY	No		GLYDON	Yes
						UPROOT	Yes

Nature's Fire Hoses

The unusual octopus creatures here collect seawater constantly. They use this water both to defend themselves and to propel themselves, sometimes straight up!

#9: Above Rolling Canyon
#10: Diving Platform
D
#1: The Odyssey
#2: Beach House
A
#7: Rolling Canyon
#8: Glass Palace
#3: Lighthouse
B
C
#4: Ocean Trench West
#6: Hot Sprint island
#5: Ocean Trench East

RAISE A GLASS

The spectacle known as Glass Tower isn't just majestic, it also fulfills the critical role of manufacturing the famous local product Sparkle Water.

It stands atop the Glass Palace, which has a uniquely beautiful architectural style. It's a treasure to be explored!

A MIRACULOUS MIXTURE

The four fountains in Bubblaine spray seawater toward the Glass Tower. The ocean here is carbonated but otherwise unremarkable. However, when blended in the Glass Tower, it takes on a deep, elegant flavor and becomes Sparkle Water!

This treasured beverage is said to bring good fortune, happiness, and even romance to those who drink it, which has led to it being featured in many wedding ceremonies.

THREE KEYS TO THE KINGDOM

1. Gasp at the sight of all four fountains spraying into the Glass Tower.

2. Refresh yourself with the fizzy delights of Bubblainian seawater.

3. Play in the action-packed Beach Volleyball tournaments.

A LOVE NEST FOR EELS

In addition to the fun resort spots found in Bubblaine, there are some notably dangerous locations as well. One of these is the underwater cave connected to the lighthouse where gigantic creatures called Maw-Rays make their nests and shoot out their long bodies in response to stimuli. A little caution can go a long way when exploring this place.

NATURE'S HOT TUB

A ways away from the beach sits an outdoor bath fed by a natural hot spring. Featuring full ocean views, it has become quite popular with tourists. This spring was formed by volcanic activity on the ocean floor, and it's said to have numerous medicinal effects. Take one dip, and we're sure you'll fall for its charms. It's also a lovely natural reprieve from the modern resort developments.

RELAXING COMPETITION

When in Bubblaine, be sure to enjoy a game of beach volleyball on the local court. The on-site coach gives strong guidance, even for beginners. As they say around here, "Let's play!"

The Glass is Half Empty!

On arrival, a snail-like Bubblainian near the Odyssey's landing spot fills Mario in on what's going on. This place used to be a gem of the seaside, until the mean-looking octopus clogging up the Glass Tower in the middle showed up. The baddie is drinking up all the Bubblainian's delicious Sparkle Water.

Follow nearby footprints—which seem suspiciously like Bowser's—to find that the fountains that are supposed to replenish the Sparkle Water flow are clogged up. As one step in the restoration of Sparkle Water, each of the fountains needs to be unclogged.

Ⓐ The Stone Pillar Seal

The nearest switch that can unclog a fountain is just slightly offshore, on a tall island. To mount the ledge here, capture a Gushen and use its waterjet to surge upward. Climb on top and grab Power Moon #01 to reveal the fountain's emergency flush button. Ground pound this button to send Bowser's cork hurtling at the obnoxious fiend at the Glass Tower.

Ⓑ The Lighthouse Seal

The top of the Lighthouse is where the next fountain switch is located, but you can't simply go up there (yet). An indirect path must be taken up there. Head to the northwesternmost landmass to find an unexpected well. The Bubblainians nearby claim that it leads

into the Lighthouse. Take a deep breath and ground pound downward into the murky depths.

Mario ends up in the Underground Tunnel to the Lighthouse. Capture a Cheep Cheep near the entrance to greatly boost Mario's swimming ability. This is a long waterlogged tunnel with one standout feature: hordes of Maw-Rays resting just inside the soft sand on the walls of this place. When the cavern starts shaking a little bit, watch out for a giant eel to erupt somewhere nearby, snapping for Mario. (They don't care whether Mario is in Cheep Cheep or Mario form; they are probably both equally tasty to a huge eel.)

Swim through the tunnel collecting purple coins and dodging Maw-Ray snaps. When some wooden crates blocking part of the corridor are visible up ahead, you're almost out. There's also one more series of Maw-Ray attacks coming, from all directions at once. Swim in the center, through the coin rings, to dodge everything.

Cross through the tunnel unscathed to emerge on the top of the Lighthouse. Touch the checkpoint flag here to enable warping at a moment's notice, then collect Power Moon #02. Ground pounding the switch here fires a second cork into the big octopus's dome.

© The Hot Spring Seal

The next clogged fountain is in the northeast, across a great expanse of ocean waters. Now is a good time to collect the warp flag checkpoints along the way in the northern trench. It's also a good time to pick up a couple of extra Power Moons along the way—you'll need them for the Odyssey even after the Bubblainian's Sparkle Water is restored.

Before arriving at Hot Spring Island, inspect the sandbar island in the northeast along the way. Underneath this place, on the seafloor underneath lots of hostile Komboo plants on the underside of the sandbar, ground pound a glowing lump to discover Power Moon #16.

While in the area, check the sea floor under the sandbar island to find a small tunnel underwater that leads beneath

the whole thing, from one end to the other. Power Moon #11 is found at the halfway point, which refills Mario's air and increases the Odyssey's moon reserves.

At the spring itself, what would normally be a paradise in miniature is instead overflowing with baking lava. The hot tub is too hot. Capture one of the nearby Gushens and begin flying back and forth over the lava-coated island with waterjet power. You'll notice the water washes away the hot coating!

Hot Spring Island is covered in some kind of molten goo. We have to clean it up!

One especially quick way to clear territory of hot stuff is to jet over an inundated area, fire water downward briefly to clear a landing spot, fall into the spot, then shake the controller for Gushen's 360-degree water spin.

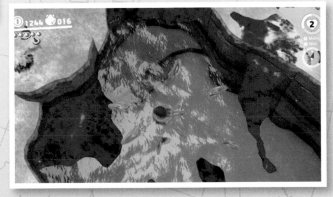

Once the hot spring is cooled down, register the warp flag on the island, then dunk into the main spring pool to get Power Moon #03. This reveals another red flush button, enabling a third good cork shot at the guzzling octopus.

© The Seal Above the Canyon

The fourth and final clogged Sparkle Water fountain is located above the southeastern crevasse known as Rolling Canyon. The warp flag at the foot of the gash in the mountain acts like a base camp, so be sure to touch it on the way. Before heading up, look around and notice the pirate-impersonating Goombas on the beach. Capture one of them and build a handsome Goomba stack before trudging up Rolling Canyon.

177

There's a forlorn Goombette in Rolling Canyon, perplexed why no suitors ever approach her. She perhaps hasn't considered that the clumsy Goombas all get squashed before they get even halfway up here. Luckily, a Mario-controlled Goomba stack

can fare much better. Begin the trek up Rolling Canyon, dodging shells to avoid damage. Rendezvous with the fairest Goomba to earn Power Moon #32.

After getting the Power Moon, ditch the Goombas and run up the canyon, dodging rolling shells along the way.

Near the top, a row of wooden crates is stacked in the gap leading forward. Break some of them with cap throws and pass through to find the Above Rolling Canyon warp flag, along with **Power Moon #04**. Grab the moon to reveal the final fountain-clearing button (assuming you followed the order here, on a clockwise path through the kingdom's map). When all four fountains are cleared, the octopus is finally forced down from his bubbly perch, and the boss fight commences, with the entire kingdom as the battlefield!

BOSS: BRIGADIER MOLLOSQUE-LANCEUR III, DAUPHIN OF BUBBLAINE

This bulbous fiend may consider itself Bubblaine's ruler, but it's mostly just the king of headaches. Now that the four fountains have knocked him off his water-guzzling perch, Mollosque-Lanceur is a formidable enemy, the heftiest seen so far. He's too big and mobile to take on on foot, so capture a Gushen to engage.

Initially, Mollosque-Lanceur is still covered in lava, remnants of his rage as you popped him with Bowser's corks, clearing the stopped-up fountains. What a hothead! You'll have to cool him down with Gushen water sprays.

There are three methods for getting good water shots in on Lanceur's face. One is to jet toward Lanceur, getting as close as possible, then jetting *away*. Gushens project water in the direction opposite their movement, so shooting forward at an enemy requires flying away from them. Another method is to fly over him, then just keep flying; when Gushen switches sides over Lanceur's head, the backward waterspout will now be hitting him square-on. The last method is to get above Lanceur to fire a continuous jet of water straight down onto him. Usually, he is too mobile to cooperate with getting pummeled by a straight-down waterspout for too long, but early in the fight he's sluggish. Jet above Lanceur and dump enough water on him to clear the protective lava coating, exposing his slick head, which makes a very big target.

Mollosque-Lanceur initially upchucks hefty shells, then hurls them at Mario. These are great weapons when Mario's on foot, but it's hard for Lanceur to hit Mario in Gushen form unless Lanceur throws a shell straight up right as Gushen flies over him.

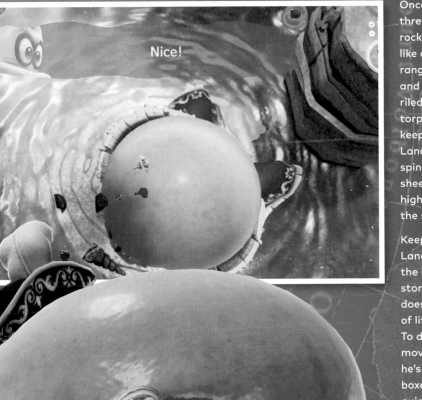

Nice!

Once it's apparent that Mario is a real threat, Lanceur gets serious, launching rocket-propelled red shells that look like drill bits. These have much more range than the shells he just tosses, and explode on impact. When fully riled up, Lanceur can fire red drill torpedoes repeatedly with no delay, so keep moving during these fusillades. Lanceur sometimes also startd spinning and moving rapidly, using sheer size as a weapon. Jet upward to higher altitude and move away until the spinning stops.

Keep getting in water shots on Lanceur's head to damage him. Once the lava is washed off, it's possible to stomp him with a ground pound, which does lots of damage all at once instead of little by little with little water spurts. To do this, wait until Lanceur isn't moving around too much (like when he's aiming drill projectiles, or when boxed in without somewhere to move quickly), then jet above him as Gushen, press the Crouch button to pop out as Mario, then ground pound straight down. Obvious, this runs a large risk if aim is poor!

Laying waste to the pompous water thief leaves behind **Power Moon #05**, a Multi-Moon! It also finally relieves the residents of the terror they've experienced by Lanceur's tentacles and Bowser's traps.

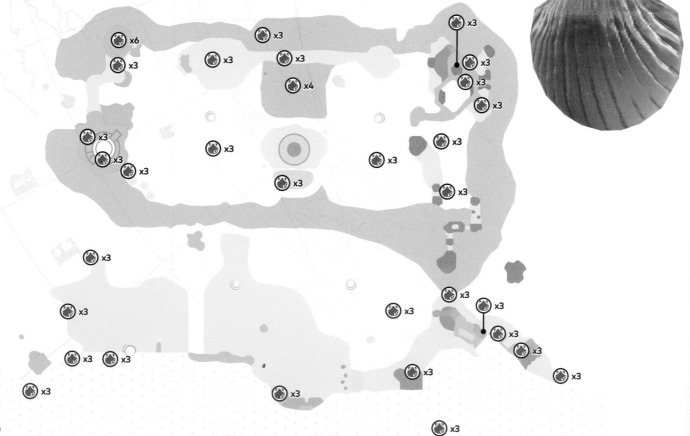

Extend Your Stay

Moving on from Seaside Kingdom requires 10 Power Moons, but that leaves many left to look for, and many underwater stones left unturned. Check out the Beach House and its accommodations, including an attire-appropriate dance, gardening using seeds from all over the kingdom, and a grueling game of volleyball.

Souvenir Shopping

Seaside Kingdom contains 100 coins in the form of purple Shells.

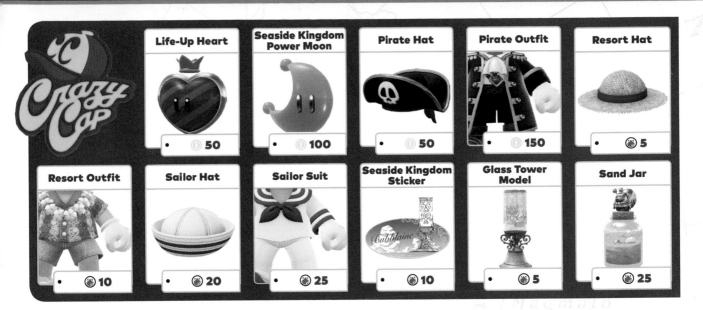

Life-Up Heart	Seaside Kingdom Power Moon	Pirate Hat	Pirate Outfit	Resort Hat
ⓘ 50	ⓘ 100	ⓘ 50	ⓘ 150	⊛ 5

Resort Outfit	Sailor Hat	Sailor Suit	Seaside Kingdom Sticker	Glass Tower Model	Sand Jar
⊛ 10	⊛ 20	⊛ 25	⊛ 10	⊛ 5	⊛ 25

Coins in High Places

The purple coins in Seaside Kingdom aren't hidden so much as they're simply spread out over a large area, many underwater.

Inside the 8-bit pipe maze on the seafloor in the center of the map are probably the most well-hidden Regional Coins. Enter from the top-right pipe, then kick the red Koopa Troopa's shell here so it bounces and breaks the waist-high block on the right. Run toward this hole and crouch at the last second to glide through it, arriving near a moving girder platform that allows access to the purple coins.

Power Moons

There are 71 Power Moons in Seaside Kingdom. Power Moons #01–05 are obtained automatically through the kingdom's objectives, which still requires three extra Power Moons for Odyssey refueling. In this guide those moons are #11, #16, and #32. Consult the prior pages for help.

06 On the Cliff Overlooking the Beach

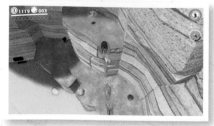

This Power Moon is found out in the open just south of the Odyssey, up the cliff's face on a high shelf. It's easy to jet up here thanks to the help of all the octopus-like Gushens in the region. Capture a Gushen and jet upward to the shelf underneath the Power Moon's ledge, then jet from there upward to the Power Moon.

07 Ride the Jetstream

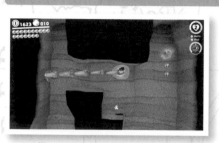

Along the southern rock wall, not far from the Hint Art painting, there's a small cave. Heading into this small cave while controlling a captured Gushen reveals that the entrance leads straight upward. Jet upward through a bunch of coin rings, then jet laterally where possible to discover another chamber, complete with a Tanooki Mario glyph on the wall like an ancient cave painting, and a Power Moon hovering above.

08 Ocean-Bottom Maze: Treasure

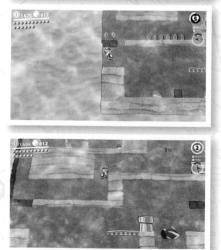

Between Lighthouse and Glass Palace on the seafloor to the west, four 8-bit pipes are arrayed in a square. They connect to different corners of a big 8-bit maze, beautifully clouded by the 3D ocean sitting above it. Figuring out how to get to the Power Moon at the middle is a bit of a puzzle. The first thing you have to do is enter via one of the bottom pipes, then head to the bottom-left corner of the 8-bit maze. Jump on the left here to reveal hidden blocks.

These blocks will later catch Mario when falling from the top half, where the green Koopa Troopas patrol. To get up there, enter from the top-right pipe.

09 Ocean-Bottom Maze: Hidden Room

An extra Power Moon is slyly hidden in the underwater 8-bit maze. Enter from the bottom-right pipe and look for a patrolling red Koopa Troopa. Knock him into his shell and kick him over the left edge and he'll break a brick block at crouch height below. Get a dashing start moving toward this waist-sized hole, then crouch right before getting to it. Properly done, Mario slides through the gap, ending up in a secret Power Moon vault.

10 Underwater Highway Tunnel

Just a bit northwest of the Lighthouse, under the waves, a square passage through the rock can be found. You'll know the right one because three Cheep Cheeps swim in formation at either entrance. Between the Cheep Cheep patrols, in the middle, are curious brick blocks on the floor. Swim down there and ground pound the brick blocks to reveal a Power Moon in the shaft below.

12 Gap in the Ocean Trench

The central feature of the north sea is a big trench that was perhaps carved out as an ancient impact crater or geological feature. Capture a Cheep Cheep and explore the northern rock face of the trench, looking for an entrance. There's a hallway-sized gap that leads to some coin rings up above, and a Power Moon down below. Bring a Cheep Cheep, because Mario doesn't have the lungs for these corridors.

13 Slip Through the Nesting Spot

The far northeastern corner of the ocean floor here is a notorious Maw-Ray nesting spot, with a cavernous den in the corner. Swim close enough, and a Maw-Ray can be baited out, giving some idea as to their snapping range here. Bait a Maw-Ray out, wait for it to retract, then follow it quickly into the passage. Trust us! There's a side passage inside, leading to a hoarded Power Moon.

14 Merci, Dorrie!

Dorrie is the huge purple top hat wearing creature supporting the purple Crazy Cap's shop. Climb aboard this friendly creature to do some regional souvenir shopping, but plunge into the water around it and look underneath where it swims to find a Power Moon.

15 Bonjour, Dorrie!

Dorrie is the giant yellow sea creature that one segment of Crazy Cap's has set up shop upon. Above its head, floating in midair, is a Power Moon. To get this, you'll need a Gushen, so you can jet up for altitude, then surge laterally to keep up with the gentle giant's surprisingly quick forward movement, which drags the Power Moon with it.

17 What the Waves Left Behind

On the eastern islands (which are more like rocky sandbars), there is a peculiar circular pool, perhaps attended by a Komboo or two. Clear the seaweed then ground pound the center of the pool to pop out a Power Moon.

18 The Back Canyon: Excavate!

Farther northwest along the cliff wall, beyond the path where spiky shells roll down a canyon, a network of small

ledges covered in Mini Goombas and Moonsnakes can be found. Somersault up the ledge side or use a Gushen to jet right to the top, then look around where the Moonsnakes spin for a glowing spot. Pound the spot from the air when the Moonsnake isn't immediately underneath to spring out a covered Power Moon.

19 Bubblaine Northern Reaches

At this location underwater, there are just three nondescript bumps surrounding a larger nondescript bump. However, look closer and notice that one of the bumps is glowing. Ground pound the underwater mound and you begin a flood of Komboos up from the muck of the ocean floor. A different mound then begins glowing. Ground pound each mound in turn while using Cappy to fend off Komboos. Eventually the largest mound glows. Spin throw the rest of the Komboos away from the big mound, then ground pound the center to release the Power Moon from the seaweed.

20 Wriggling on the Sandy Bottom

A bit northwest of the Lighthouse, there's a door to be found on the bottom of the sea. Open it with Cappy and swim inside to find a strange challenge indeed. Something's stuck under the floor in here, wriggling this way and that beneath the surface. Slow the fleeing bulge with hat tosses so you can ground pound it, stopping the scurrying and revealing a Power Moon.

21 Glass Palace Treasure Chest

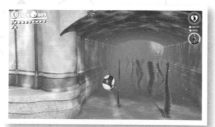

In the northern sea, capture a Cheep Cheep then look around underwater for the substructure of the Glass Palace. Approaching from the north, you find a passage underneath it, filled with Komboos. Swim inside, shaking the controller for the Cheep Cheep's Komboo-shredding spin attack, and look along the left wall down here. A gap can be found containing a treasure chest, with the Power Moon kept inside.

22 Treasure Trap Hidden in the Inlet

Look to the place where the sea channels in through the beach and under the stone walls in the southwest. Plunge underwater, dodging the Komboos creeping along the seafloor, and swim south in the inlet to discover that it leads to a

hidden cave! Inside are four treasure chests, but they must be opened in a certain order. If the order is botched, the treasure chests spit out Chincho enemies then disappear until the enemies are defeated.

23 Sea Gardening: Inlet Seed

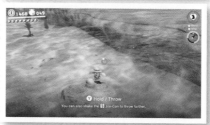

The resort roof is a perfect place for some horticulture, and there's a Bubblainian green thumb up here who wants some plants to look after. There are four prepared pots, and four unique seeds to find in the kingdom. The nearest seed is in the little inlet just slightly east, on the shallow seafloor. Retrieve it, plant it in one of the pots, then use a Gushen to generously water the plant until it blossoms.

24 Sea Gardening: Canyon Seed

This seed is on top of some ledges above the shore to the west, near the Rolling Canyon checkpoint flag. Climb the ledges to the seed, dodging Moonsnakes and Mini Goombas, and bring it to the resort in the northeast along the beach. Plant it in one of the four pots on the roof, then use a Gushen's downward water stream to water the plant, eventually causing a Power Moon to bloom.

25 Sea Gardening: Hot-Spring Seed

One of the seeds basically couldn't be any farther away. It's located around some Gushens at Hot Spring Island, in the northeast corner. You have to lug the seed from there all the way to here without losing it. Luckily, Mario can swim while holding items, so it's not really a big deal. As with other seeds, when this one is embedded in the soil and sprouted, it's time to dump a few Gushen water sacks into the plant to make sure it ripens.

26 Sea Gardening: Ocean Trench Seed

This seed is found near the riddling Sphynx statue, deep in the trench in the northern sea. Warp to Ocean Trench East or West then swim to the middle to get there directly. Locate the seed at the bottom on a pedestal, being mindful of Mario's oxygen. Grab the seed and swim all the way to the resort in the southwest to plant it in fertile, tended soil. Like with the other seeds, this one needs to be thoroughly watered once planted, but happily the octopus population here is thrilled to help with this.

27 Seaside Kingdom Timer Challenge 1

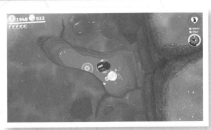

South of Hot Spring Island, a crack in the ocean floor can be seen from the right places. Find the right spot, and it's clear as day: a bright red button can be seen down in the gap. Swim down there to find an 8-bit pipe near the button. Ground pounding the underwater red button temporarily reveals several helpful blocks inside the 8-bit pipe's flat landscape. Quickly pop into the 8-bit pipe and run up and across the timed platforms, reaching for the Power Moon in the top-left part of the retro platforming challenge.

28 Seaside Kingdom Timer Challenge 2

Underwater in the northern sea, north of Glass Palace, a scarecrow can be found on the seafloor on the east side of a shallow trench. The area around it is fairly calm, just some Cheep Cheeps swimming about. Cap toss onto the scarecrow to trigger a Timer Challenge, which requires that Mario swim underwater to the west, over the trench to a temporary platform holding the Power Moon. No Cheep Cheep capture is possible with Cappy spinning the scarecrow to power the puzzle, so Mario has to swim alone. Use the water dash repeatedly for speed, and be sure to pass through bubbles along the way to refill Mario's lungs.

㉙ Found on the Beach! Good Dog!

There's an adorable dog enjoying a day on the beach, and it can be befriended with a little game of Cappy catch. Once the dog is heeling to Mario, lead it around and it sniffs out suspicious spots to ground pound. Usually this just reveals coins or Hearts, but here and there the dog sniffs out a Power Moon. Lead the dog to the west, in the direction of the resort, and see what it finds near the three rocks on the edge of the inlet. After a bit of pawing, the dog reveals the moon location.

㉚ Moon Shards in the Sea

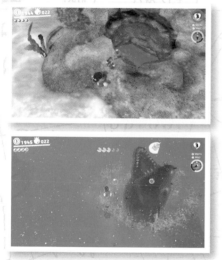

Far in the southwest, near the Rolling Canyon checkpoint flag, there's a giant challenge room waiting to be explored underwater. The access point requires Cappy sitting out on a scarecrow, which opens the hatch into the chamber.

Descend while grabbing air bubbles as necessary. Toward the bottom, you're sure to notice moon shards here and there. Four of them are located around the seafloor in the chamber, and a fifth is a bit higher up, on an underwater shelf. Beware erupting Maw-Rays when swimming near the bottom, collecting shards. When all five shards are gathered up, the Power Moon appears in the center of the area.

㉛ Taking Notes: Ocean Surface Dash

Near the Beach House checkpoint flag, a song note spins slowly just along the water. Grabbing this note places a lengthy row of music notes to collect extending out over the surface of the ocean. There's no way you'll get them in time just clumsily touching the note then splashing forward, jumping in and out of the water trying to grab notes. Instead, line Mario up with where the line of notes will appear, then grab a Rocket Flower and power into the first note.

Mario boosting along with rocket power can run across the surface of the water like it's glass, making quick pickup of all notes a cinch. The Power Moon that results pops up on a nearby island when Mario's done with the task.

㉝ Lighthouse Leaper

Once you have access to the top of the Lighthouse, you should also be able to warp up there using the checkpoint flag. When Bubblaine's local threat is cleared, a friendly Glydon takes in the panoramic view up here, wondering where the choice places to glide are. At least one choice place is Glass Palace, where a Bubblainian flight enthusiast desperately wants to see a glider land. Capture Glydon and leap for Glass Palace's base, a short flight to the east.

㉞ Good Job, Captain Toad!

Between the warp flags on the southeast part of Seaside Kingdom you can find Captain Toad camped out on a ledge, surveying the entire region. Loft up here using a Gushen, propelling upward with its water jet abilities. Once you jet above Captain Toad's platform on the Gushen, you may need to drop the capture and squad the octopus so Captain Toad won't be too frightened to give up the goods!

㉟ Ocean Quiz: Good!

The enigmas of the Sphynx have made it even to the bottom of the ocean. The stone riddler rests down upon a huge seafloor platform, awaiting curious adventurers. Today is the Sphynx's lucky day, because Mario is here, holding his breath, ready to answer questions.

The first correct answer here opens the way to Power Moon 40, The Sphynx's Underwater Vault. Continue playing Sphynx's question game until it coughs up another Power Moon in amazement at Mario's quiz finesse. Quiz answers in order:

1. **Bubblaine**
2. **Four**
3. **Attack**
4. **Resort Outfit**
5. **To ask questions**

36 Shopping in Bubblaine

Like most kingdoms, Bubblaine has its own branch of Crazy Cap's. Unlike other kingdoms, this branch is split up into multiple locations. The purple Regional Coin shop is open for business on the back of a blue Dorrie, and the gold coin shop is open on a yellow Dorrie. Here, a Power Moon can be purchased for the low, low cost of just 100 coins. Be sure to pick up the Pirate Outfit here too, yarrr!

37 Beach Volleyball: Champ

It wouldn't be a seaside resort without beach volleyball. Some Bubblainian athletes here at the beach house are always down to serve and return. Just step on the court to start up a game.

When the ball is headed for Mario's side of the court, watch its path and shadow to gauge where it'll end up. Either move Mario to that general area or be ready to throw Cappy precisely along that path. Balls can be returned either by hitting them with Mario directly or with a hat throw. Balls can even be returned by bopping them or tossing a cap into them for a split second after they've hit the ground, so there's a little grace period.

Return the ball successfully just 15 times to learn the novice volleyball ropes while scooping up a Power Moon along the way.

Beach Volleyball   Best 12

38 Beach Volleyball: Hero of the Beach!

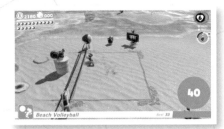

To score the second Power Moon available for bumping and spiking your heart out on the beach, you need 100 returns. That's

Beach Volleyball   Best 33

quite a step up from 15 for the first one. The most important thing to remember here is that it's a marathon, not a sprint, so take it easy and stay focused. It also may help to know that there is no limit to how early you can return the ball. The moment the Bubblainian beach bum launches the ball, it can be swatted back. This means you can jump by the net, throw Cappy upward, then hold him there, and he immediately returns almost anything coming his way. It's possible to chew away long stretches of returns just by jumping by the net and throwing Cappy upward like this. If you have an execution error and don't produce an upward throw, though, you'll have to be ready to dash toward wherever the ball is headed.

39 Looking Back in the Dark Waterway

The Underwater Tunnel to the Lighthouse (accessed from the landmass in the northwest) has secrets beyond the

access it provides to a valuable location. Just after entering, capture a Cheep Cheep for maneuverability then proceed forward through the little gap patrolled by more Cheep Cheeps. Just on the other side, turn left toward an inconspicuous corner to find a Power Moon! If Maw-Rays start bursting out of the cavern sands, you've gone too far.

40 The Sphynx's Underwater Vault

In the northern sea, deep in a trench, the mysterious Sphynx sits, awaiting anyone who'd like to play a guessing game.

Answer the first question correctly, concerning the name of the region (which is properly Bubblaine, of course), and the Sphynx grinds aside on its base, revealing a passage down into a room under the platform. Explore the vault for a Power Moon, and keep talking to the Sphynx even after it moves to try for Power Moon #35.

41 A Rumble on the Seaside Floor

Inside a pipe leading into the rock wall near the Odyssey, a Bubblainian can be found watching over a calm little inlet.

The local gives you a clue about what's going on in here: tread carefully over the sand, and subtle rumbles can be felt coming up from underground. (Now would be a good time to mention that you need to have force feedback enabled in Settings!) Walk slowly to zero in on where the rumbling is most intense, then ground pound that spot to reveal a Power Moon.

42 A Relaxing Dance

The beach house itself has a locked room that is only accessible, appropriately enough, for guests dressed in the correct leisurewear. Show up here with Mario decked out in Resort Outfit and Resort Hat, available from Crazy Cap's for purple coins. The attendant here is then happy to grant Mario entry.

Inside, enjoy the sense of good vibes imparted by the resort, and direct Mario into the middle for him to do a little easygoing dancing. At the end, he'll get a Power Moon reward.

To fully enjoy the pleasures of Bubblaine, you must wear clothes you can entirely relax in.

43 Wading in the Cloud Sea

The Mini Rocket on a high perch near the Beach House provides valuable lessons in mist-clearing. When a row of coins veers into the mist here, you can trust it: rolling down that platform will turn out fine. Farther, hat launchers and pulse beams work together with Cappy to blow aside big swaths of smoke. This reveals the platforms underneath clearly.

You don't have to wait for the mist to blow aside before these platforms are usable. It's just nice to have a clear view.

Farther still, the pulse beam mist clearing is complicated by a Burrbo infestation. They're unsafe to jump on, can at least be knocked out with cap tosses, and are a nuisance either way. Avoid them or consider the pulse beams anti-Burrbo as well as anti-mist.

After a stretch of platforms without pulse beams, where you have to rely on Cappy for defogging, a series of three pulse beams signals the end of the room, where there's a Mini Rocket to return to the surface, and a Power Moon to take as a souvenir.

44 Sunken Treasure in the Cloud Sea

In the cloudy challenge room, eventually there's a stretch without pulse beams and hat launchers to help clear the way. Where no pulse beams or hat launchers are present, Cappy himself continues to work just fine for smoke clearing, especially with spin throws. While pathfinding platforms ahead, watch for an unusually skinny platform across a small gap, pointed at a distant "pool" of mist. Leap to this little bridge and cross to the mist pool to find a treasure chest.

The southwest area of the region is a good place to get used to piloting Gushen captives, since there's a lot to do with many nooks and crannies. A crack in the rocks in this area has a hidden vertical channel, easily surmounted with a downward-aimed Gushen jetstream. When a special door is visible to the right, switch from downward to lateral jetting to fly over to it.

Inside, Mario gets more of a Gushen workout. This challenge room puts your Gushen flight skills to the test, forcing you to use every drop of water propellant jetting from one platform to another, with no safety nets in between. Water can only be replenished in the shallow pools on most platforms. After passing through square frames and bunches of coin rings, fully refill water at the larger platform before the next section.

This part requires threading through an area covered in poison liquid, instantly deadly to the touch. Hop out of the platform's pool ever so lightly, fall down until you're even with the poison hallway, then start jetting laterally through the first sets of columns and coin rings. You have to compensate left and right while jetting down this hall to dodge the columns. At the far end, there's a poison shaft upward. No side is safe, but you have to jet right to the center without touching anything, then begin jetting straight up the corridor. With enough height to jet laterally, blast forward over the lip. You just need at least enough water left to propel over this lip and fall into the wide chamber below, but if you've metered propellant really well, you should have enough to push over the gap and onto the treasure chest ledge beyond.

46 Treasure Chest in the Narrow Valley

In the Gushen challenge room, there's a reward for optimizing water use toward the end. As described in the previous entry, Mario in Gushen form just needs enough juice to clear all the poison surfaces and float out over free space. Gravity does the rest, taking him to the standard Power Moon and exit pipe below. But with sufficient water left when jetting out over the gap, you can just keep jetting, ending up on the treasure chest platform.

47 Hurry and Stretch

Swimming southwest of Hot Spring Island, you may notice a stone corridor underwater leading to a special door. Open the door to reveal a curious sight: a steep hill amid a sea of lava. Now we know why it's a hot spring up above, at least. Capture an Uproot at the bottom to begin a heated challenge: climb the hill using the Uproot's incredible leg-stems before the lava rises and engulfs it. Along the way, Moonsnakes roll back and forth on the hill's narrow ledges to make things spicier than they already are. The Uproot's

leg growth can be used as a little hop, by holding it only briefly before releasing, so use this to hop back and forth on ledges when Moonsnakes roll toward Uproot Mario. Climb all the way to the exit pipe to gain a Power Moon as well.

Remember that shaking the controller grows Uproot much faster than normal.

㊽ Stretch on the Side Path

In the Uproot room found underneath Hot Spring Island, there's a second Power Moon to find for Uproot pilots who hop quickly on the very thin walkways toward the end. When the route tapers to just two tiny slivers of land and two Moonsnakes

rolling around them, look to the right side to see a Power Moon hovering high above the floating catwalk. Hop over there using a quick Uproot leg stretch, dodging Moonsnakes when needed, and stretch up under the Power Moon to nab it. The lava's still coming afterward, so hightail it to the exit!

㊾ Secret Path to Bubblaine!

Seaside Kingdom and Snow Kingdom become accessible at the same time, and the first place visited is up to you. Warp paintings in Bowser's Kingdom and Mushroom Kingdom point toward these earlier kingdoms. Which future kingdom's warp painting points to which mid-adventure kingdom's secret ledge depends on the region you tackle earliest. Either way, hop through the warp painting to end up here. Grab the Diving Platform checkpoint flag and the Power Moon in the treasure chest, then somersault off the platform for fun.

㊿ Found with Seaside Kingdom Art

Like many odds and ends in Seaside Kingdom, this painting ended up on a low shelf overlooking the beach and resort. It seems to depict a Power Moon in relation to either the word "keep" or perhaps next to a keep or dungeon of some sort. The meaning may seem inscrutable for a time.

That is, except to New Donkers! Residents of the metropolis should recognize the text as being very similar to the iconography

used in street warnings and signs. Travel to Metro Kingdom and look around for anything distinctive that matches the painting. With an eye to the road below, you're sure to spot something!

51 Seaside Kingdom Regular Cup

This race's organizer can be found on a mostly barren island to the northeast. The Koopa sets up the free running

challenge to start on the ocean floor in the northern trench, before ending on a ledge above Rolling Canyon. Ambitious, with many possible routes to take.

The most direct is to swim upward furiously right from the start, seeking the surface. If it's

convenient to do so, you can capture a Cheep Cheep along the way. This provides a speed boost while underwater, but it's not the best idea to stay underwater for that long. The faster you get to the surface, the sooner you can start stacking Rocket Flowers on Mario's back. Rocket Flowers let him skate across the top of the water, crossing to shore much faster than merely swimming.

Once on shore in the canyon area, the typical way to ascend is to follow the herd into the Rolling Canyon channel. It's much faster to just scale the sheer wall leading to the goal by flicking upward on the fork-like Volbonans stuck in the wall, though.

52 Peach in the Seaside Kingdom

When the adventure is resolved and everything has calmed down, Peach and Tiara can be found in their beach ware on top of Glass Palace's Glass Tower, bathing in a Sparkle Water spritzing. Riding one of the Sparkle Water fountains is the fastest way to get up here. Greet Peach and Tiara for a Power Moon reward. There are other reasons you'll want to eventually visit Peach and Tiara everywhere they go, too.

Moons from the Moon Rock

53 Above the Parasol: Catch!

When the Moon Rock's power is unleashed, many Power Moons simply pop into existence throughout the kingdom. This one is located hovering high above a bouncy parasol at the Beach House. Warp to the Beach House and jump on top of the umbrella for an easy addition to the Odyssey's running moon tally.

54 What Shines Inside the Glass

Plunge into the fizzy waters contained in the tall Glass Tower to find a Power Moon down below. Don't worry about air, air bubbles rise from the bottom. Ride one of the unclogged carbonation fountains up to the top of Glass Tower, then dive in and ground pound to the bottom.

Note the warp painting while you're down here. If you flew to Seaside before Snow Kingdom, the warp painting leads to Cascade Kingdom. If you flew to Seaside Kingdom after Snow, the warp painting leads to Wooded Kingdom.

55 A Fine Detail on the Glass

Just on the other side of the glass from Power Moon #54 on the inside, this Power Moon is found on the outside. While Mario needed to dive in the interior of Glass Tower to find the other moon, this one requires falling down the exterior. For a slower, more controllable fall, rotate the stick twice quickly to start spinning right before jumping. Descent speed is slowed down during a spinning fall, making it easier to guide Mario toward the Power Moon on the way down.

56 Underwater Highway West: Explore!

In northwest Seaside Kingdom, look underwater in the shallows around the island where the secret Lighthouse passage begins. Down on a rock platform, find a stray Power Moon hovering.

57. Underwater Highway East: Explore!

Out in the eastern ocean here, search a nondescript seaweed grove. No, they're not Komboos, for a change, just regular nonviolent plants. Well hidden among them is a Power Moon. Spot it and swim into the plants to scoop it up.

58. Rapid Ascent on Hot Spring Island

A Power Moon floats high above the wading pool atop Hot Spring Island. Even after bouncing high off nearby parasols and then

dive jumping, Mario can't quite catch enough air here to pull down the treasure. Find a nearby Gushen and capture it and return to stack things more in Mario's favor, height-wise. Center the Gushen in the pool, then jet straight up. The Gushen ends up just a hair underneath the tantalizing Power Moon—drop the capture by tapping crouch for Mario to pop out, gaining enough extra high to grab the moon.

59. A Light Next to the Lighthouse

By now, lots of tourists and locals are atop the Lighthouse, enjoying the crisp air and the views. Stop by the Lighthouse observation deck to mingle and see what's new and you'll notice light coming from one of the poles next to the Lighthouse. Jump and toss Cappy onto the top and hold him there to generate another Power Moon.

60. The Tall Rock Shell in the Deep Ocean

Look at the top tip of a coral shelf overlooking the stoic Sphynx in the northern trench. One of them here gives of the unmistakable rainbow glow of an object hiding a Power Moon. Toss Cappy onto the stomp on top and hold him there to eke out the Power Moon.

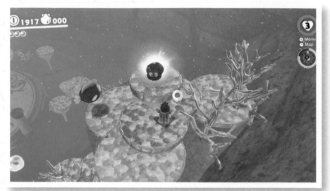

61. At the Base of the Lighthouse

Just northeast of the Lighthouse, a faint glow can be seen in the sand under the water, between some coral platforms. Nail this sandy

spot with an underwater ground pound and the Power Moon springs forth.

62. Bird Traveling Over the Ocean

It's hard to take your eyes off the water, but turn your gaze to the sky and you'll sometimes see a bird flying around the region, a familiar glow trailing it. It's usually high up in the sky, but there are points where it'll dip down and glide not high off the ground. To check to see if the bird has a Power Moon (it does), you'll have to get in striking distance. Get close enough where it dips down near the ground or passes close by a structure like the Lighthouse and either tap it with Cappy or Mario. Touching the bird merely reveals the Power Moon, it still needs to be picked up to get added to the Odyssey's tally.

If you'd rather go air-to-air, capture Glydon at the Lighthouse and chase down the bird like a hawk.

63 Caught Hopping at Glass Palace!

Look around the base of Glass Palace to find another pesky hare running circles around anyone trying to corral it. Chase the rabbit, using hat throws to slow it down if needed, and grab the bunny to score a Power Moon.

64 Seaside Kingdom Timer Challenge 3

A fresh scarecrow is set up on top of the Lighthouse. Stick Cappy onto it to start a Timer Challenge that leads all the way down into the water. A kind of diving board block will appear in front of the scarecrow, pointing the way toward the Power Moon on a temporary platform underwater. Immediately after the challenge begins, run off the diving board platform and running long jump at the edge, toward the Power Moon down below. (For even more reach, space a triple jump to launch just by the edge of the platform, then tackle from the apex of the triple jump.) Mario falls a bit short of the underwater moon platform, but there is time to swim quickly toward the Power Moon.

65 Taking Notes: Ocean-Bottom Maze

Once the Moon Rock has expended its energy, there is a new Power Moon to find inside the 8-bit maze on the ocean's floor in the middle of the kingdom. Enter from the top-right pipe of the group to find a 2D song note floating in here. Picking it up reveals more notes along three tiers of the maze, in an area patrolled by Koopa Troopas. There's no trick to getting all the notes quickly here, since 2D Mario can't throw Cappy or anything. You'll just have to dash and jump quickly to get all the pick-ups the old-fashioned way.

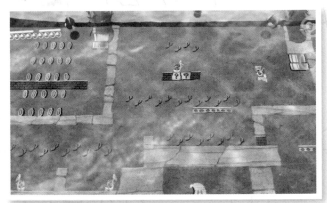

66 Taking Notes in the Sea

Underwater to the southeast of Glass Palace, a new song note can be found. Collecting it spawns three sets of nearby notes, big circular groupings. To collect these all before the challenge timer ends, you need the services of a Cheep Cheep. Either capture one first and start the challenge in Cheep Cheep form, or capture a nearby Cheep Cheep immediately after collecting the first note.

67 Seaside Kingdom Master Cup

This race adds the twist of the elite golden Koopa, who begins with a sneaky trick: he ground pounds right away, ground-pound jumps off the ocean floor, then begins swimming furiously upward. The ground pound jump off the seafloor gives an extra boost compared to racers who simply start swimming at the start.

Although the golden racer has tricks up his sleeve the others do not, if you race up the back wall of the goal, flicking upward from Volbonan to Volbonan, instead of taking the canyon like everyone else, you'll be hard to beat.

68 Aim! Poke!

This moon pipe is found among the islands in the east. Inside is a big, sandy half-pipe, which cannonball bombs are rolling across. Breakable cubes are spread about the area in places, along with a ramp at the far end, propped up by more breakable cubes.

This room may seem mysterious until you get a glimpse of the wildlife. The Burrbos in here are simply pests, and are run over by cannonballs more often than they pose any threat to Mario. But the Pokio here is the key. Capture the Pokio and its beak can be used to violently redirect cannonballs. This lets you target specific breakable cubes with the explosive balls. Peck cannonballs so they knock the breakable cubes out from under the ramp here, then launch a cannonball off the ramp and into the Power Moon cage, releasing it.

194

69 Poke! Roll!

The sandy cannonball room has a glowing, Moon Rock-like structure right by the entrance, easy to notice immediately. Right away, it should occur to you to try out the explosive cannonballs on the glowing box. But there's a bar grating in the way, so it's not that simple. Instead, try sending cannonballs up the left side, opposite the glowing cube. Ideally, the cannonballs skate along the circumference of the banked bowl, ending up in an explosion at the cube on the other side. When successful, the Power Moon within is blasted out by the entrance pipe, ready to be picked up.

70 The Spinning Maze: Search!

A moon pipe appears on a small mesa underwater in the western sea. Inside is a transparent maze made of fixed blue walls and movable yellow turnstiles. Inside the maze are undefeatable Spinies and five moon shards. The maze is encased in glass, and Mario can climb on top of it to take a look from any angle, but he can only enter from a door on the side. Inside the maze, twist turnstiles 90 degrees by hitting them with Cappy. Spinies can't be defeated head-on, unless pushed off a ledge by repeated cap throws.

Collect all five shards to generate a complete Power Moon near the entrance. Three shards are simply sitting in the maze, but two of them are on the right side (coming in from the entrance) near platforms hovering over empty space. This is not encased in glass and falling is very possible. Bash the Spinies around here off the edges then use Cappy to collect the shards while riding the platforms.

71 The Spinning Maze: Open!

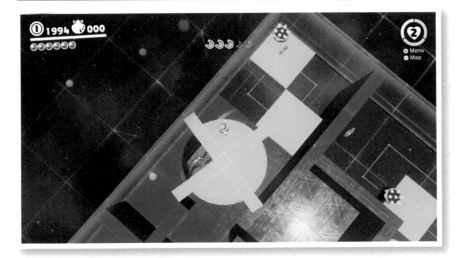

Inside the Spiny turnstile maze, there's more to find than moon shards and Spinies. Near the corner where two yellow platforms rotate around each other over an open drop, there's a turnstile with a cutout on a quarter of its floor. Rotate this turnstile around to see if there's any gap that lines up underneath and wouldn't you know it, there is! Find the turnstile position that reveals the hole filled with coins and jump in to discover a treasure chest.

Luncheon Kingdom

Welcome to Mount Volbono

REGION AT A GLANCE

Population	Plentiful
Size	Buffet
Locals	Volbonans
Currency	Tomato-shaped
Industry	Food, Minerals
Temperature	Average 93°F

INDIGENOUS FLORA & FAUNA

	BINOCULARS		GOOMBA		MAGMATO
	Can Capture?		Can Capture?		Can Capture?
	Yes		Yes		No

	LAVA BUBBLE		VOLBONAN		HAMMER BRO
	Can Capture?		Can Capture?		Can Capture?
	Yes		Yes		Yes

	FIRE BRO		SPINY		FIRE PIRANHA PLANT
	Can Capture?		Can Capture?		Can Capture?
	Yes		No		Yes

	MEAT
	Can Capture?
	Yes

#10: Floating Sky Island

#9: Remote Island in the Lava

#4: Meat Plateau

#3: Path to the Meat Plateau

#8: Salt-Pile Isle

#7: Top of the Peak Climb

#6: Start of the Peak Climb

#2: Peronza Plaza

#5: Volcano Cave Entrance

#1: The Odyssey

C E B A D

Cheese as Hard as a Rock

The cheese in Mount Volbono is quite hard, likely because it is left near the lava and dries out completely. The locals chisel it with hammers—you're welcome to join!

COOKING WITH A VOLCANO

Surrounded by strange pink lava, Mount Volbono is colorful and vibrant, a vision straight from a picture book. It is famous for its cuisine, with dishes simmered over the volcano, and chock-full of the local produce that grows to enormous size thanks to the volcanic climate.

COOKING CARNIVAL

The highlight of Mount Volbono's year is the Cooking Carnival, where visitors from all over the world come to sample the famous Stupendous Stew. While cooking on a volcano is of course a grand spectacle, the dish itself has a surprisingly delicate flavor, described most frequently in reviews as a "melty deliciousity."

THE HISTORIC "OLD TOWN"

On your way to Mount Volbono, you'll pass through the Old Town, ringed by the ruined walls that once enclosed the town. These sturdy, cut-stone walls even now suggest the prosperity of those times. Atop the walls are little mounds of salt, carried by the wind and piled up naturally. Visitors can walk along the tops of the walls—do so if you get a chance. The sights here are very different from the colorful scenery of Peronza Plaza, but equally breathtaking.

A RESTING PLACE FOR MEAT

The giant slab of meat used in the Stupendous Stew is crusted generously in salt and left to rest on a high perch near the volcano. Aging the meat high above the lava, cooled by the wind, is essential to creating the core flavor. If you arrived before the Cooking Carnival, be sure to take the opportunity to visit the platform and see the meat resting soundly before its long journey.

THREE KEYS TO THE KINGDOM

1. Sample the famous dish Stupendous Stew. It's what the locals eat.

2. Gape at exotic ingredients like gigantic vegetables and rock-hard cheeses.

3. Marvel at the preserved architecture, the best-kept secret in tourism.

PERONZA PLAZA

Be sure to visit the centrally located Peronza Plaza for a friendly welcome. Once among the colorful heaps of giant ingredients and succulent smells, you may find it hard to leave.

ⒶThe Broodals are After Some Cookin'!

With the Snow and Seaside Kingdoms tended to, the path narrows again. The hunt for Bowser brings Mario, Cappy, and the Odyssey to Luncheon Kingdom, a strange land of gigantic bright pastel foods and a friendly race of fork-like beings called Volbonans, who take to cooking like ducks to water.

After only moments in the kingdom, it's apparent that Bowser and the Broodals have already left a footprint. The Broodals' ship can be seen flying lazy circles ahead, above some flat expanse. It's time to go forth again expecting battle with the mercenary hares, while sniffing out any Power Moons that might be found along the way. Before moving on, you must confront whatever unfriendly visitors Luncheon Kingdom's attracted, and you'll need 18 total Power Moons to refuel the Odyssey.

CAUTION: HOT OIL

Whatever mixture bubbles all over Luncheon Kingdom—pink lava, melted frosting, warm oil, clarifying sugar, congealing cotton candy, the world's most appetizing-looking grease—is very unsafe to touch or land in. Awareness of the location of any nearby liquid must always be kept in mind. Lava Bubbles can safely swim through the sea around Luncheon Kingdom, so you'll be hitching a Lava Bubble ride often, using them like little fiery speedboats through the stew.

This area of Luncheon Kingdom is a ruin called Old Town. The durable ancient architecture has held up remarkably well considering the air here is like a kitchen mixed with a sauna mixed with a boiler room. While moving north, there are plenty of nooks and crannies to check out while familiarizing yourself with the new area.

Near the Odyssey, the only early threats are some clueless-looking Goombas convening, and a couple Magmatoes rolling about.

A forlorn Goombette can be seen across a gap. Perhaps the Goombas can be given purpose, and the Goombette some company. Capture a Goomba and assemble the local specimens into a stack, then head for the big piece of floating corn, dodging Magmatoes on the way.

Hop on top of the corn, carefully walk to the side you'd like it to travel toward, then walk slowly back toward the center of the corn. It's a cylinder in liquid, so this rolls the whole ear toward the Goomba stack's side. When you walk all the way to the middle, very carefully move back down the corn to get a lower foothold and start walking back upward to the center. In this way, the corn can be used as a rolling platform through the lava.

Reach the far side and hop off the corn, greeting the Goombette with the captured Goomba stack, to receive Power Moon #24.

Beyond the corn, there's a little acid-waterway between two ancient buildings, with Lava Bubbles in the channel. They're a path forward, so capture one and swim down the length, hopping out at the end onto a large flat arena.

BOSS: SPEWART

The Broodals swoop in to stop Mario in his tracks, bragging about how they've stolen copious amounts of the Volbonans' prized Stupendous Stew. Spewart is dispatched to take out the heroes.

Spewart can blanket the area in a coating of poison that would make a Poison Piranha Plant green(er) with envy. But his purple spewage is easily mopped up with cap throws, especially the spin throw. Safe room to maneuver and retaliate is never more than a spin throw or two away.

When Spewart gathers himself pointed in one direction, he's going to spew far and in a line. Simply getting out from in front of him is enough. When he gathers himself and starts spinning, he's going to cover everything in 360-degrees around him, forcing Mario to backpedal furiously.

Spewart himself doesn't have anything like Rango's blades or Hariet's bomb pigtails. His own hat is easily dislodged with a cap toss into Spewart's robust frame. Without his hat, Spewart is vulnerable to stomping. Jump and land on Spewart (ground pounding unnecessary) to deal him a point of damage.

He'll react in anger, bouncing around the arena for a while, leaving a trail of poison sludge behind him wherever he glides. Clean up his mess as needed with Cappy, and deflect him if he gets too close for comfort with a direct hit cap toss. When he rises back to his feet, continue to dodge poison and look for more changes to knock off his hat and stomp him again. Three stomps and Spewart is sanitized, revealing **Power Moon #01** and opening the way to Peronza Plaza.

Ⓑ Under the Cheese Rocks

Mario soon needs to go farther north and higher up the mountain, but for now a stop in town is in order. Peronza Plaza is the main settlement in the kingdom, populated with lively Volbonans who just want to entertain taste buds with their renown Cooking Festival. Unfortunately, Bowser has other plans. The path to the enormous stewpot above Mount Volbono is knocked out, rendering the cauldron inaccessible and sure to get way too hot. This will certainly ruin whatever Stupendous Stew the locals have left that the Broodals didn't already steal. Adding avian insult to hare injury, a giant bird named Cookatiel has designs on the Volbonan's salt-prepped meat.

I'd show you around but, uh...things are kinda on fire right now.

The meat is on that plateau, just sitting there!

The short alley between Crazy Cap's building and the one next door is crammed up with wooden supply crates, stacked almost to the roof. Tear apart these crates with hat throws or ground pounds from above and a stored Power Moon pops out, settling by the unlit lantern atop Crazy Cap's. Wall jump between the buildings to the roofs to pick up Power Moon #09.

The purple side of Crazy Cap's is selling a complete Chef's Outfit—Suit and Hat—for 15 Regional Coins. Even looking around in plain sight in Old Town and Peronza Plaza there are more than 15 purple coins to collect. It's worthwhile to do so, because the building right next door is a chef's academy that only admits people who look the part. Pick up the right attire once you have the local currency, change into it on the spot, then stop by next door to see what all the fuss is about.

While exploring the town, note the columns along the southern ledge, behind the stewmaster and around Talkatoo. These are spaced just about far enough apart for a running long jump to cross between each. Hop onto the first one by the giant pumpkin, then take three running long jumps across to the column at the very corner of the town's block of land. Ground pound here to pop free Power Moon #10 from the top of the pillar!

The Volbonan stewmaster handling duties at the big cookpot in the plaza wants golden ingredients to add real pizazz to the stew. There are three golden turnips hidden around Luncheon Kingdom, and adding any one of them to the pot here nets a Power Moon reward. The first golden turnip is sprouting very close, right next to Crazy Cap's souvenir shop. Throw the hat at the sprout to pull it out of the ground, then pick up the golden turnip and take a running leap to throw it into the pot. Power Moon #15 is served! Find the other two golden recipe solutions in the "Extend Your Stay" part of this chapter.

Inside, there are two cookpots bubbling away happily enough, but both would be better off with just a touch more heat. If only there was some way for Mario to accomplish this. Between the cookpots, there's a generous stream of lava from the exterior piped in to facilitate the cooking process. Lava Bubbles hop around in this heated stream, and on a ledge between the cookpots, lots of Magmatoes sit, presumably waiting to become super-spicy tomatoes in a gigantic pasta. It's easy to dump extra heat into the first pot by capturing a nearby Lava Bubble and then leaping into the pot, cooking up Power Moon #27.

As usual, the souvenir shop in Peronza Plaza's Volbonan town offers up a local Power Moon for the low, low cost of 100 coins. Hand over the coinage to proudly own Power Moon #25.

Getting a Lava Bubble into the other pot is trickier. You'll have to use squashed Magmatoes as little islands

for a Lava Bubble to jump between. As Mario on foot, you can prepare the central ledges by flattening Magmatoes with hat throws. Then capture a Lava Bubble from the entrance side and hop across the Magmato guts. Or, more aggressively, you can just start jumping into live Magmatoes as a Lava Bubble, crossing that way. If you land squarely on each Magmato, it'll pop instantly as Mario in bubble form begins to land on it, and it'll form a functional puddle for bubble-Mario to land in almost instantly. Either way, getting to the other side of the Magmato ledges as a Lava Bubble is the hard part. Once across, it's easy to hop in the other pot and earn Power Moon #28.

Once you feel familiar with Peronza Plaza, move on out of town to the east, off the pier-like outcropping to a captured Lava Bubble below. Swim through the pink muck toward the jetting geysers ahead. By jumping into the thick lava sprays, you can ride upward and leap out from higher up than normal, getting up to the taller lava shelf.

A tall, narrow crag sticks straight up to the east here, and a long flat platform patrolled by Hammer Bros is to the west. Hop out of the lava and run to the west, looking to mix it up with the Hammer Bros. Capture one of them and go brother-against-brother, taking out the other one along with the pesky Spinies afoot. The platform secure, keep heading west and start smashing the cheese blocks piled up here with a rain of pans. Hammer Bros can basically throw hammers or pans (whichever that particular Hammer Bro is packing) as fast as you can shake the controller! Bash up all the cheese on the west of this platform to clear large steps heading up to a second floor, where there are more cheese blocks (along with blue stone steps climbing back up into town via the souvenir shop's roof, if needed). Bashing apart the blocks up on the second floor reveals a hidden switch.

Pull the switch with Cappy to break the nearby Power Moon free of its cage. When heading back for it, watch out for the Hammer Bros and Spinies, who will have respawned by now. Snatch up Power Moon #02 and a new section of land rumbles up out of the depths, opening the way forward to Meat Plateau.

© Big Pot on the Volcano: Dive In!

Beyond the Path to the Meat Plateau checkpoint flag, there are now more Magmatoes and Fire Bros to contend with. Past the Fire Bros, take the ramped path upward. Follow a skinny bridge east over open air to a sheer wall upward with a Volbonan stuck into it. Capture this helpful local and flick upward, where you find a ledge and another Volbonan.

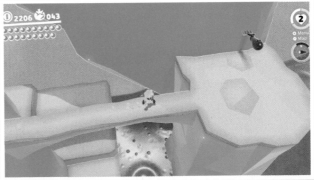

Another flick upward here places Mario at the Meat Plateau checkpoint flag, and right before a mammoth piece of spiced, capture-ready Meat!

This hunk of succulent meat is crusted in a salt preparation so thick it's almost frozen in place. Capture the Meat and perform the only action it's capable of—twitching—to slowly crack through the salt crust, freeing the Meat. Freed of the salt pack, the Meat finally attracts the attention of Cookatiel.

The big bird drops the Meat into the big pot atop Mount Volbono. Mario pops out onto a lip-smacking platforming challenge, with chunks of ingredients curling around toward **Power Moon #03**, a Multi-Moon worth three normal ones. There's a branch right before climbing to the Multi-Moon, with a choice between a few simpler jumps, or trying to balance on corn while grabbing coin rings (like moving on corn earlier with the Goomba stack). Arrive at the Multi-Moon and Cookatiel will be furious, flapping stubby wings and blowing Mario and Cappy clean out of the bowl and all the way back to the Odyssey. It's a good thing Mario doesn't take fall damage!

Ⓓ Climb Up the Cascading Magma

Opening up Meat Plateau, attracting Cookatiel's attention with the Meat, and getting Cookatiel riled up above the stew have all shaken the area up a bit more than is good for it. Mount Volbono is experiencing increased geological activity, and another section of previously-submerged land emerges to the west, providing a path around Mount Volbono's left flank. Meanwhile, parts of Old Town farther south have collapsed away, exposing new liquid pathways for Lava Bubbles.

The cave entrance is visible from the Volcano Cave Entrance flag, but there's a wide gap across bubbling lava. Enter the 8-bit pipe against a wall here to find a way across, picking up some Regional Coins and dodging a 2D Hammer Bro along the way.

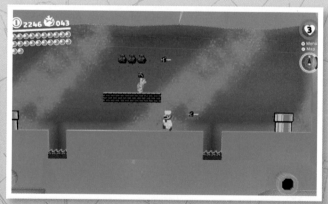

Walk west from Peronza Plaza or launch north from Old Town.

The new objective is to explore new pathways in the west. Getting there is as easy as wrapping around the rock wall from Peronza Plaza, where a new checkpoint flag can be registered as a future instant warp point.

After popping back out of the 8-bit pipe, you're just a corn-crossing away from the cave maw. While riding the corn through lava, jump to collect more Regional Coins. Inside the cave, the first section involves a steep liquid sluiceway. It looks like pegs are rolling down over a ramped waterfall of lava, perhaps aerating it. Capture a Lava Bubble at the entrance and swim up the ramp, leaping over wooden rollers when needed. There are three Regional Coins to collect on both the left and right sides of the ramp up.

At the top, there's a sheer drop-off overlooking some lava geysers below. Fall into the geysers then look behind them, back the way you came from, to see a cut-out room in the sheer wall, clearly sheltering Power Moon #29.

Hop into the alcove to grab it before continuing forward. On top of the lava on the far side is a platform with four lanterns on it, and three of them lit. Hop out of the lava with a Lava Bubble and land on the unlit lantern to spark it up, revealing Power Moon #04 for the taking!

Grabbing the moon opens the way out of the back end of this cavern, finally allowing access to the rear side of Mount Volbono, the only vector by which the mountain can be safely scaled (without tricking a bird into picking you up disguised as a tractor-sized piece of meat, that is).

One of these things is not like the others.

Ⓔ Cookatiel Showdown

From the back entrance of Volcano Cave, the path curves to the right, across several circular salt islands with Fire Piranha Plants embedded in some of them. At the end of this path of stepping stones over the lava, the Start of the Peak Climb warp flag clearly marks off the mountain summit path.

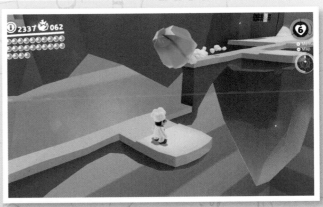

There are little ledges off to the side on the tiny walkway which give you a chance to step aside and let huge veggies roll past.

Look off the left edge before proceeding upward to find some hidden blocks leading to a ? block with a Life-Up Heart within.

Past the pepper-rolling tightrope and the bubble saucepans, a Volbonan stuck into the wall flicks Mario up one more level, to a grating that leads to the Top of the Peak Climb checkpoint flag (whew!), and an upward-sloped lava ramp. Capture a Lava Bubble and swim up the path to find a lava cannon at the top, primed to launch bubble-Mario high up, right into the stew under the patrolling bird boss.

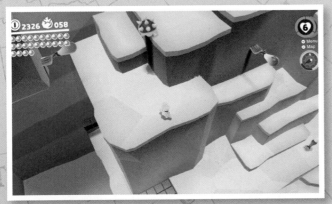

The way up features ascending ledges interspersed with Volbonans ready to flick Mario upward.

Rotating saucepans are safe on one side, scorching on the other. A woefully thin walkway along one flank has giant peppers rolling along its length.

Toward the top, a brief lava-strewn stretch allows Lava Bubble capture, so a Lava Bubble can be used to skip across through the hot sides of saucepans. Three Regional Coins are vertically spaced above one of those saucepans, practically waiting for a Lava Bubble to leap up from underneath.

BOSS: COOKATIEL

Cookatiel flaps about above the bowl, regurgitating spiky pods into the stew. Treat these like obstacles and avoid them, keeping track of the bird.

After some circling and spewing of seeds, Cookatiel spits a huge volume of viscous liquid into the broth. This goes on for a while, long enough for Lava Bubble Mario to swim up the stream! Cookatiel upchucks peppers and spike pods into the gushing ramp of liquid, so be ready to hop over them and continue moving up, toward the boss's head.

Get high enough and you can get a good shot at Cookatiel's head just by jumping into it. The bird stops barfing up liquid and veggies and knocks Mario back into the stew, and it redoubles its efforts next round. The more shots to the cranium Cookatiel has taken, the more frenzied its spewing of spike pods becomes. If health is low while dodging the rain of hard fruitseed, shake the controller while swimming for a speed burst that bashes apart any stew chunks in the way, potentially revealing Hearts.

When Cookatiel throws up the second time, it is in a zig-zag pattern, forcing Mario swimming and jumping up the stream to compensate for the sludge's changes of direction.

When Cookatiel throws up the third time, the stream is intermittent. This means you must jump up and forward through the air between blobs of liquid arcing down, all the while looking out for incoming projectiles!

But at least this is the home stretch! Persevere against the rain of bird gunk to hit the boss one more time.

204

Extend Your Stay

With the goose cooked and Luncheon Kingdom liberated from all these food thieves, the Cooking Carnival can finally be held! Peronza Plaza will surely be a hopping place, soon. There are many more Power Moons and secrets to find in Luncheon Kingdom beyond those explored in the itinerary. Now that the Cooking Carnival is coming, there will be far more visitors from other lands, too. The reshaping of the land also has fully exposed all potential pathways to purple coins, allowing a full stocking of food-oriented souvenirs.

Souvenir Shopping

Luncheon Kingdom contains 100 Regional Coins in the form of purple Tomato Disks.

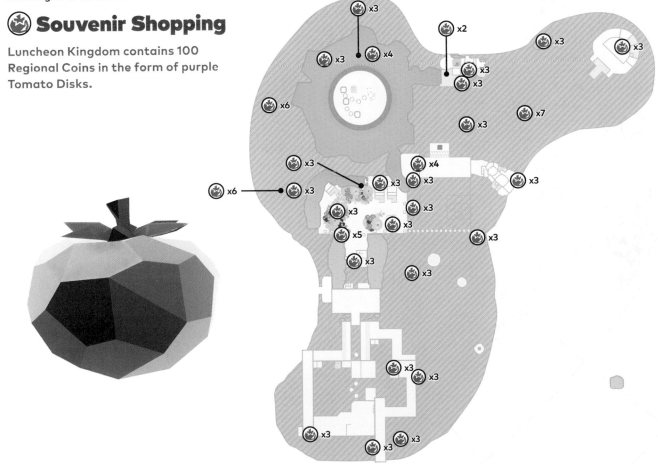

	Life-Up Heart	Luncheon Kingdom Power Moon	Clown Hat	Clown Suit	Chef Hat
	50	100	50	150	5

Chef Suit	Painter's Cap	Painter Outfit	Luncheon Kingdom Sticker	Souvenir Forks	Vegetable Plate
10	20	25	10	5	25

Coins in High Places

Hidden coins in Luncheon Kingdom are all low to the lava, usually tucked away in a narrow corridor that's out of the way and only accessible with a Lava Bubble. Once the kingdom is fully opened up after confronting Cookatiel, spend some time scouring bubbling corners in the soup.

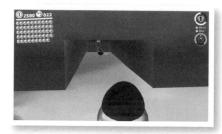

Power Moons

There are 68 Power Moons in Luncheon Kingdom. **Power Moons #01-05, 09, 10, 15, 24, 25, and 27-29** were obtained while ridding Luncheon Kingdom of Cookatiel and the Broodals. Consult the prior pages for help. This leaves the Odyssey one short of enough moons to continue onward, if no other moons were acquired. If this is the case, check the roofs of the old buildings in Old Town for several Power Moon opportunities, like **#06, Piled on the Salt.**

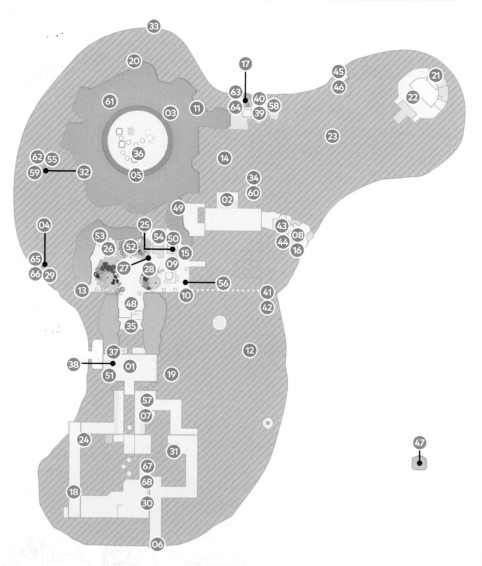

206

06 Piled on the Salt

From the flat arena in Old Town, hop on the ancient roof that stretches down the side opposite the Odyssey, on the eastern side of Old Town's landmass. Follow this roof all the way to its terminus overlooking the lava below to find a big pile of salt on the end. This Power Moon hovers above the salt, and at this point would go nicely with something sweet.

07 Lurking in the Pillar's Shadow

Right in the first plaza-like space in Old Town, a Power Moon hovers around a short, forgotten corner. Use an extra-long jump to cross to the platform on the opposite side from the corn, where a fissure on the ground coughs up eight coins if slammed. Stand on the platform and capture the Lava Bubble springing up nearby and swim just a bit north into the little acid-waterway to see the small platform and corner on the left, and leap out of the liquid behind the column to get the Power Moon. In the shadows no longer!

08 Atop the Jutting Crag

The forbidding, unsculpted rock in the east seems to have no way to scale its sheer surfaces, at least until you explore the lava north or south of the narrow mountain in Lava Bubble form.

Lava cannons throughout the region can place Lava Bubbles in distant or remote landing spots while offering scenic views along the way. A couple of these cannons launch bubble-Mario over the top of this big crag, where normal climbing won't reach. Of course, the soaring arc of the launched Lava Bubble carries it well over the little mountain. But it doesn't have to carry Mario with it. If you ditch the capture at the top of the arc by pressing the Crouch button, Mario begins falling. Guide him toward the top, throwing Cappy for a little pull then tackling to help making it over. After a safe landing on this precipice, look for the Power Moon in the center, noting the small grove of sprouting seeds on the far end.

11 Surrounded by Tall Mountains

Travel to the lower portion of Mount Volbono's back half, relative Peronza Plaza. You can either just hoof it here, past all the Fire/ Hammer Bros, or you can warp to Meat Plateau's checkpoint flag. The jagged rock surfaces here, which seem like rock candy, are more easily climbable than normal rock-like mountains. Climb the blue rock upcropping, looking ahead for a green counterpart. Look for the lowest platform-like footing on the back of the green mini-mountain. Jump across to that section and ground pound it to uncover the moon.

12 Island of Salt Floating in the Lava

This one is extremely difficult to puzzle out, but hopefully Talkatoo gives up the name as a helpful hint. For a lead, look for an island of salt floating in the lava. The one in question is near Salt-Pile Isle, where an eastern sea warp flag sits. An almost identical island nearby is only lacking a warp flag to be a twin. The glow also gives away that something else is going on. Ground pound the little platform for the Power Moon goods.

13 Overlooking a Bunch of Ingredients

High above Peronza Plaza, a rock wall curls around from the northwest to the west, shading from green to purple to blue. Although there are lots of steep angles trying to climb around on the candy walls around Peronza Plaza, they're more compliant with sheer climbing than similarly-sloped walls in other kingdoms. Climb up and curl around to the blue tip of the ledge, with all of town down below to the east, and ground pound the glowing spot here to knock free a Power Moon.

14 Light the Lantern on the Small Island

The area underneath Meat Plateau is a veritable hothouse, with simmering soup, molten Magmatoes, bouncing Lava Bubbles, and mean turtles who can throw fireballs. Despite all this, a green lantern centered on the small platform in the middle is somehow not on fire. To correct that, capture one of the Fire Bros and hurl fireballs at the center until catching the lantern square. With fire firmly seated in the pit, a Power Moon is quickly cooked up, ready for pickup on the platform.

16 Golden Turnip Recipe 2

One of the turnips needed for the master stewmaker is buried atop the tall eastern crag. Capture a Lava Bubble then look around the lava seas north or south of the crag for lava cannons. Hop in and launch the Lava Bubble over the crag, releasing Mario's control just over it. Drift toward the crag and land on top. The back end of the crag has a small group of sprouts, surely the location for the turnip. Pull the center one with Cappy's help, then heft it up and just off the crag heading back toward the west. Beware the Hammer Bros along the way, and run quickly past them before they can get clean tosses at the turnip.

At the cheese wall steps west of the checkpoint flag, where the Hammer Bros dwell, quickly set the golden turnip down off to the side someplace and capture a Hammer Bro. If you do this proactively while approaching, they shouldn't really have a chance to take a real shot at breaking the turnip. With one Hammer Bro, squash the other one and break the cheese up on the steps, opening a path to climb up carrying the turnip. With the golden turnip hoisted up the ledge here, jump up the blue steps inlaid into the mountain's arm here, landing on top of Crazy Cap's in the village. Toss the turnip into the pot to complete the errand, finding a Power Moon hidden within the shining veggie.

Or, take a running jump off the left side and throw the turnip toward the pot, tackling after it to land in town and avoid a plunge into the magma. Unnecessary, but stylish!

⑰ Golden Turnip Recipe 3

It's hammer time for this golden turnip recipe. Capture one of the Hammer Bros around the Path to the Meat Plateau warp flag, then head north to the little collection of cheese blocks tucked around behind the pillar leading up to Meat Plateau. Use the Hammer Bros pots to crack up all the cheese, uncovering promising sprouts underneath. End the Hammer Bro capture and pluck up the golden turnip, then prepare for a harrowing journey of ingredient life. This turnip has to make it to the cookpot in town, but there are a lot of enemies and jumps over lava between here and there. You must also note that Fire Bro fireballs and Hammer Bro pots *can* destroy the golden turnips, so always keep moving and give them a wide berth when rushing past with golden cargo.

You'll have to deal with the cheese steps near the Hammer Bros and the Path to the Meat Plateau checkpoint, just like when carrying the tall crag turnip for Power Moon #16. It makes sense to do them back to back, since the same homework clearing off the steps for turnip passage benefits both trips.

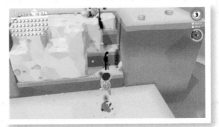

⑱ Luncheon Kingdom Timer Challenge 1

From Old Town's shaved-flat arena, either of the old main buildings of Old Town can have its roof mounted, allowing access to a bigger stretch of the opening area. Run up the roof that passes by the Odyssey's balloon to find a scarecrow standing sentinel up here over the lava. When Cappy's on its brow, a wall jump challenge appears hovering here over the goop below. Before time runs out, wall jump back and forth between the hovering platforms to reach the Power Moon floating right above the scarecrow.

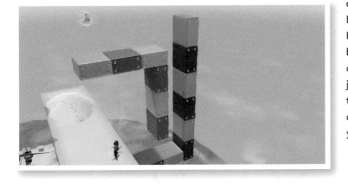

⑲ Luncheon Kingdom Timer Challenge 2

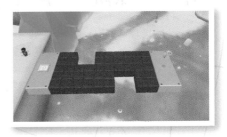

Once the local threat is cleared, a scarecrow appears on the Old Town arena platform. Let the scarecrow borrow Cappy for a bit to undertake this challenge overhanging the lake of delicious-smelling lava. A Lock appears near the Scarecrow, on solid ground, but the Key appears on a platform out over the bubbling liquid. In between float darker blocks, which begin disappearing if you don't skedaddle. Rush across the blocks, with a running long jump over the small gap in the platform in the middle. On the way back from grabbing the Key, be prepared to jump over sudden gaps in the vanishing platform. But as long as you don't dillydally, this Power Moon will be in hand soon.

⑳ Luncheon Kingdom Timer Challenge 3

Look for this Timer Challenge Scarecrow on one of the many islands in the swamp behind Mount Volbono. Once it's activated with Cappy, it generated two green cylinder platforms in the lava. A Key hovers above the larger far platform, out of reach of standard jumps.

To reach the Key, you need one of Mario's best hops. The green platforms are situated obligingly for this purpose, giving you a good runway to time a triple jump to peak heading into the floating Key. You can also acquire the key by crouching in its shadow then back somersaulting, or by running across its shadow then doubling back with a side somersault. Whichever method you use, rush back to the scarecrow to claim the Power Moon popped from the Lock before time expires.

21 Beneath the Rolling Vegetables

An 8-bit pipe on top of the remote island in the northeast leads to a flat challenge hidden just under the surface. Mario begins in one half of the chamber, attacked by 2D Hammer Bros. Take them out then enter the pipe beyond them to flip to the other half of the 2D chamber, riding a hovering girder above deadly lava.

Step out of the way of fireballs that leap up and down from the lava below, and don't worry about the peppers rolling around overhead—they're in 3D land! At the far end of the hallway, pick up the Power Moon before passing through a small gap past it, re-emerging into 3D space.

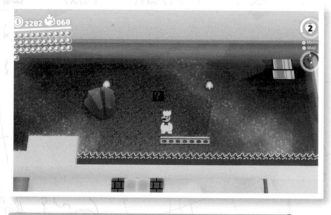

22 All the Cracks Are Fixed

The distant island in the northeast has a few secrets making it worthy of investigation. A Volbonan is already here, hoping to fix up the many cracks across the island's unattended and eroding surface, but that fork body isn't good for quickly dodging the roasted peppers being spat out of the geyser here. If Mario's willing to do the Volbonan's job, there might be something in it for fuel tanks of the Odyssey.

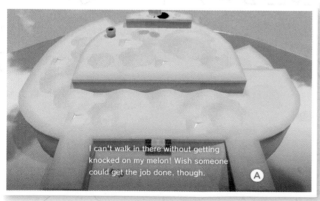

Scour the small island, ground pounding flat any of the fissures you find. When they're all smoothed out, the Volbonan has the moon for Mario's taking near the checkpoint flag.

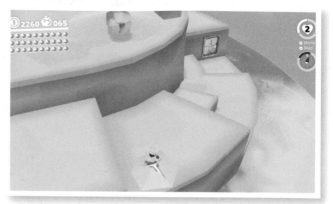

23 Taking Notes: Swimming in Magma

The northeastern lava sea is out of the way, and only navigated by the most inquisitive travelers. Moving about here at all requires a Lava Bubble capture. In the middle of the lake, a song note floats just above the scorching waves. Collecting this note begins a snaking music collection route, which ends at the semi-secret island tucked away at an outskirt of the kingdom. Pilot the Lava Bubble through all the notes, leaping onto land to collect the last few and spawn the Power Moon. Don't forget to register the warp flag here on the island, too, or to investigate its shallow summit.

26 Luncheon Kingdom Slots

The Tostarena business-skeleton who's set up shop here can be found in the building covered in a pyramid of food cans. Inside,

the friendly Sand Kingdom ghoul has a game of slots going. Once you enter, Cappy throws at the spinning slots lock them in place. Once all five are locked in, your reward is tallied. For a Power Moon from the game, you have to lock in Power Moon symbols in every slot. When timing a cap throw to overlap with Power Moons, remember that Hearts show up just before Power Moons in the slots.

30 Treasure Beneath the Cheese Rocks

Digging up these spoils takes a fair bit of Luncheon Kingdom hiking. Begin around the Path to the Meat Plateau flag, where the wannabe-chef Hammer Bros roam. Capture one of them and use a pots-and-pans flurry to blast through the first cheese blockade on the steps heading west toward Peronza Plaza.

Hop up the steps and then up the blue stone steps beyond to enter the city, and enjoy the terror inflicted on the locals as a Hammer Bro on the loose hops through their midst.

Back in Old Town, go brother-against-brother taking out the Fire Bro with Hammer Bro-form Mario, and hop back to the field on which the Odyssey rests. The cheese blocks to the left here have crusted over something on the ground here. Hurl pans to knock apart the cheese, clearing out this edge of the field. Where the cheese once stood, you find a glowing spot on the ground, which naturally gives up a Power Moon when nailed with a ground pound.

31 Light the Two Flames

Once Fire Bros are in evidence in Old Town, near the Odyssey, this Power Moon can be acquired. Capture the Fire Bro near the big floating piece of corn, then carefully hop across the yellow grated platforms to the twin lanterns.

32 Light the Far-Off Lanterns

At Volcano Cave's back entrance, facing the uninhabited side of Mount Volbono, there are two lanterns on either side of the door. They're not lit, though, which can be easily corrected considering the local flora. Fire Piranha Plants can be found rooted on salt pile islands near the door here. Get the attention of the nearest one, then jump around the lanterns while it shoots fireballs at you, trying to get it to do Mario's work for him. Or to take the more direct approach, pick up a stone and chuck it into the Fire Piranha Plant's mouth, then toss Cappy onto the plant while it's choking, capturing it. Now, launch all the fireballs you like at both lanterns. When they're both lit, a Power Moon is revealed.

33 Bon Appétit, Captain Toad!

The always-adventurous Captain Toad has gotten himself into a bit of a pickle, pathfinding to a lonely island far behind Mount Volbono, seemingly without a way to return to solid ground. Well, he'll probably figure it out. That's why they made him Captain, after all. There are two ways to get back here: one is to swim here

in a Lava Bubble, and the other is just to bounce here in extreme pain, relying on Mario's reserve Hearts to hold out until arriving on Toad's platform. If using the "ouch, ouch, OUCH!" method, grab a Life-Up Heart first. There's one hidden in a ? block nearby at the base of the mountain climb, beyond a hidden block bridge to the left.

Once Captain Toad hands over the Power Moon, capture a Lava Bubble nearby and vault away using the lava cannon nearby, or make your own path away in the liquid.

34 The Treasure Chest in the Veggies

This is as straightforward as Power Moon rooms come. Check a little bit northeast of the Path to the Meat Plateau checkpoint to find a normal door standing facing the lava sea, standing out with its inconspicuousness. Enter to find a treasure chest placed with big piles of vegetables. Open the treasure chest to get the Power Moon within and leave. That's it, it's a vegetable storage room with a treasure chest in it. Move along. Nothing to see here.

35 Caught Hopping at the Volcano!

This region's pesky bunny can be found cavorting up and down the steps leading from Old Town to Peronza Plaza. It's easy to catch up with the rabbit as it tries to get away just by using gravity against it. Start at the top and leap down at the rabbit, aiming at a ledge past where it is. Mario cuts it off at the pass, essentially, landing on the floor it's fleeing to. Catch up with the rabbit to earn a Power Moon for the trouble.

36 Taking Notes: Big Pot Swim

Warp to the Top of the Peak Climb flag, capture a Lava Bubble, and launch with the lava cannon up into the main pot. Once the coast is clear of gigantic meat-stealing birds, look again in the huge cookpot bubbling over the volcano to find a music note floating inside. Swim into the note to kick off another note collecting musical challenge. This time, you must swim through lines of notes in the broth, leaping precisely out of the lava to snag notes places at arcing intervals.

There are three progressively harder lines of notes to scoop up, with one hop required in the first line, two hops in the second, and three hops in the third. It helps to center the camera directly behind Lava Bubble Mario while swimming and leaping through these note sequences.

37 Magma Swamp: Floating and Sinking

Just above the lava between Old Town's flat arena and Peronza Plaza, a challenge room is tucked at the bottom of some stair-like ledges. Inside, an intense bubbling expanse is revealed, with blocks throughout rising in and out to simmer. The tops of the blocks taper like inverted stove ranges, so sometimes the platforms are above liquid, so the top is square and comfortably-sized, and sometimes they sink below and become barely bigger than Mario himself.

Five moon shards are found in the hot room, among a few Fire Piranha Plants turning up the heat. Dodge the plants' fireballs and take care not to touch any liquid on the changing platforms, or Mario's fire panic without room to maneuver will probably quickly doom him. Choke up Fire Piranha Plants with Cappy, if desired, preventing them from firing. This also allows Mario to bounce off them, smashing them flat.

212

38 Corner of the Magma Swamp

Inside the cooking swamp found just above lava level, a hidden moon is kept just behind the entrance pillar. Who'd think to look back there, after all? Curl around behind the pillar thanks to the rising and falling platforms in the stew here, carefully grabbing the moon above one tapering platform without taking damage from the pink-hot mix cooking underneath. After scooping this up, return to collecting any moon shards left in the room for Power Moon #37.

39 Magma Narrow Path

This challenge room is found under Meat Plateau, just around one corner from the cheese blocks blocking a golden sprout, and around another corner from Fire Bros hopping around causing havoc. Inside is calmer. If it wasn't for most surfaces being covered in burning liquid, it would be downright calm in here. This is a platforming climb using a Lava Bubble, crossing lava-covered beams and jumping on floating liquid platforms.

When jumping with a Lava Bubble, it's best to always keep the Cap Throw button held down, which maximizes Lava Bubble momentum. Otherwise, drift controls right after launching from the liquid, and while controlling movement in midair can seem sluggish, you'll often fall short of targets. Push forward confidently and surge from the liquid hard when going for jumps.

The trickiest section is a narrow square of lava beams, with a lone lava girder in the center. Be sure to collect the purple coins off to one side here before moving on. The main Power Moon in here can be found by progressing to the end. But, like with most challenge rooms, a second Power Moon can be had in here for the most observant collectors.

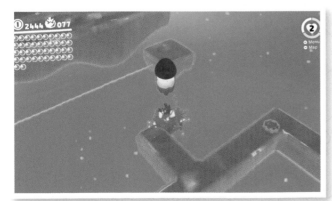

40 Crossing to the Magma

The molten platforming of this stage has a little puzzle contained within it. After the first stretch of traveling across liquid beams as a Lava Bubble, there's a normal platform with a lava channel up its left side. On the right edge of the platform, away from that lava channel, is a rocky structure slick with more unsafe molten covering. Normally, you leap from the liquid beam into the lava channel, swimming across it to rejoin the lava beam and continue on the other side. But there's a secret to find if you make it across to the rocks covered in lava.

Note the Magmatoes here: they'd just be an annoyance for Mario, something else to jump over and run past, but to a Lava Bubble they're a potential stepping stone. A defeated Magmato bursts into a pool of lava, which remains there until you leave the area. Bursting the Magmatoes close to the lava channel provides another "foothold" for a Lava Bubble to jump from. Use the Magmato remains to cross open ground, bridging the lava channel and lava rocks for the Lava Bubble. At the top, hovering at a bubble's jump distance, is a hidden Power Moon, and a great view of the area.

41 Fork Flickin' to the Summit

This out-of-the-way gauntlet is found at the very northeastern edge of the southern half of the kingdom. Draw a straight line east of Talkatoo's perch and you'll find it. Travel to the platform surrounding the door with a Lava Bubble. Within, there's a unique climbing sequence involving lots of Volbonan captures and hat launcher assists. Volbonans are used in here to flick Mario around, like with Metro Kingdom Poles. Hat launchers merely take a hat throw and amplify it along a specific path, but they're sometimes arrayed in sequences so that a hat entering one hat launcher ends up several throw's distance away. The combination of the two sometimes allows Mario to capture Volbonans out of sight around corners, enabling flings to unexpected landing spots.

Carefully fling and hat launch up the pillar to make it to the Power Moon at the exit. The most difficult thing to pull off, during a jump or Volbonan flick, is to throw Cappy accurately at an intended capture target or hat launcher. This is needed in a couple of places here to keep a fling sequence going after being flicked high up by a Volbonan.

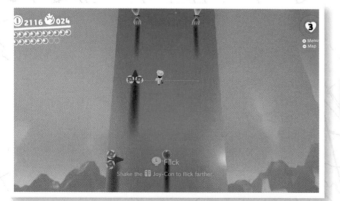

42 Fork Flickin' Detour

In the Volbonan fork-flicking challenge room, there's the pillar you're climbing to access the exit and the standard Power Moon, and another nearby. The nearby pillar can only be accessed from near the top of the first pillar, in striking distance of the standard Power Moon. From the final Volbonan pair, where Mario would flick upward to mount the exit platform, flick to the right instead, adjusting to catch enough air to make it to the second pillar. Here, you have to pull off a deft midair capture of another Volbonan fork-person, stopping Mario's descent and giving time for an aimed flick up to the cubby inside this second pillar. Inside the little cubby, of course, is a Power Moon!

43 Excavate 'n' Search the Cheese Rocks

The entrance to this cheesy room is at the base of the big eastern crag, but it's blocked by a crust of rigid cheese blocks. Capture a Hammer Bro from around the Path to the Meat Plateau checkpoint then hop to the challenge room entrance to break apart the cheese blockage with a pot barrage. The cheese knocked aside, ditch the Hammer Bro and enter.

Inside, capture a fresh Hammer Bro and look around. This is a cheese wonderland, seemingly an entire area made of breakable cheese. It's not quite that dense, but almost.

One moon shard can be seen above one of the cheese blocks, but only one. Experience has shown that one moon shard means many, so where must they be? While watching out for the Spinies, start dismantling the cheese with a barrage of Hammer Bro throws. By digging through all of the cheese, you naturally pick up the buried moon shards as they're uncovered, because thrown Hammer Bro hammers/pots work like Cappy tosses, so they'll pick up small items like coins and moon shards.

When all four buried moon shards are dug up in addition to the one found on the surface, the Power Moon appears for the taking.

The hardest moon shard to find is hidden in a little compartment under the cheese.

44 Climb the Cheese Rocks

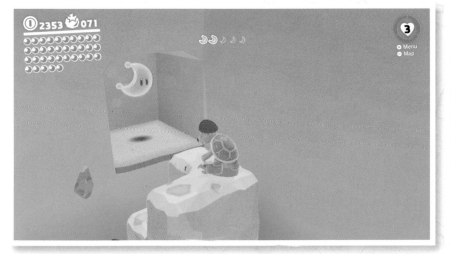

While laying waste to the hardened cheese room assembling moon shards for Power Moon #43, you'll probably stumble upon this moon incidentally. It's hidden in the wall beyond the tallest cheese pile. Break enough of the cheese with Hammer Bro pots to get inside and retrieve the Power Moon.

45 Spinning Athletics End Goal

The popping pepper island isn't the only place in the northeast lava sea. There's a much smaller island here which is little more than a scarecrow and a door. The door won't open without a hat on the scarecrow, so offer up Cappy then head inside.

This dreamy floating platform challenge spaces out lots of spinning blocks along the path to the exit. The blocks don't spin continuously, but rather change position every few seconds, rotating 90-degrees. Standing on the floor might suddenly become sliding down a wall if you're not careful. Keep moving forward, timing forward jumps onto new blocks to occur just as the blocks rotate. Get a rhythm of this going and Mario may even be able to triple jump across multiple blocks at once.

There are spinning disc platforms at a couple of spots along the way, almost as interludes to the rotating platforming challenge. On these discs, Mario won't be at risk of falling off, just getting dizzy, or getting stabbed by a Spiny. With no hat, there's no way to fend off Spinies, so vacate the area fast when the mean little things realize Mario is nearby.

㊻ Taking Notes: Spinning Athletics

Inside the room of rotating blocks, one of the spinning yellow discs hosts a music note on top. Touching this note spawns a bunch more notes around the rim of the spinning disc, as well as off one edge. The edge the notes lead off has firm footing underneath, so the best way to begin the challenge is to grab the main note, then hop off while grabbing the notes along the way to the platform below.

There, turn around and hop back at the song note disc so Mario clings to the ledge, but don't press Up on the analog stick or the Jump button—you don't want Mario to climb back up. Ride the rim of the spinning disc all the way around as it rotates and all the music notes get picked up in time, creating another Power Moon!

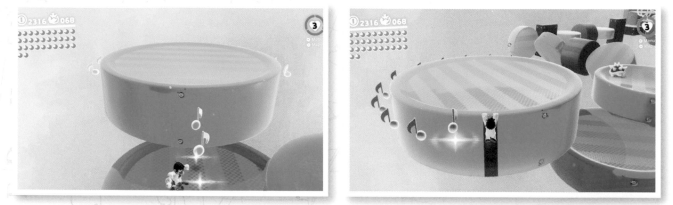

㊼ Secret Path to Mount Volbono!

Depending on which kingdom you chose to visit first, either Wooded or Lake Kingdom will contain a warp painting that pulls Mario through and dumps him out on Floating Sky Island. Be sure to register the warp flag, along with picking up the Power Moon isolated up here.

㊽ A Tourist in the Luncheon Kingdom!

This task can't be tackled for a while. Once the pressing threats in each kingdom are taken care of, and once the chase for Bowser is seen through to its conclusion, then Mario can look after the exploits of the Tostarena tourist. Initially encountered in Sand Kingdom, this skeleton wants to see the world. The tourist and a hired cabbie are seen next in Metro Kingdom and then in Cascade Kingdom before they can be found in Peronza Plaza, about to take in the Cooking Festival. Greeting the tourist on the rounds around the world will score a Power Moon in each new location.

Desert Wanderer

No way, no way! We've already met in the Sand Kingdom, Metro Kingdom, and Cascade Kingdom.

㊾ Found with Luncheon Kingdom Art

This Hint Art painting is located at the base of Mount Volbono facing the Path to Meat Plateau flag, near the blue stone steps leading back to town from Hammer Bros land. In the painting, Poochy is in some sort of aquatic territory, inspecting a piece of coral.

To find the place in question, travel to Seaside Kingdom and explore the northwest reaches underwater. In a coral patch just like in the painting, ground pounding the top pad springs forth the treasure Poochy buried.

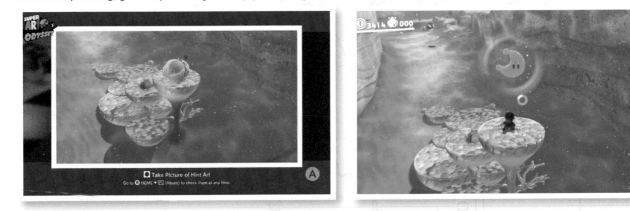

㊿ The Rooftop Lantern

Cooking up this Power Moon asks for some Hammer Bros. juggling. The target is an unlit lantern on the roof of the building next to Crazy Cap's. Warp to the Meat Plateau checkpoint flag to find Fire Bros on the ledges underneath. Capture one of them and head south, jumping carefully over the platforms over the lava while avoiding Magmatoes and Lava Bubbles. At the large platform where Hammer Bros patrol in chef hats, drop your capture of the Fire Bro and quickly capture a Hammer Bro. Ultimately, you want to take the Fire Bro up the western steps into town, but you need to cut some cheese to get there.

Throw some pots at the cheese clogging the way to break it up. Once there's clearance for a Fire Bro to jump through, drop capture again and go retrieve the Fire Bro you left a moment ago, who should still be dazed. Jump up the steps through the gap in the cheese, then jump farther up the blue rock steps ahead.

From the perch up here (on the same ledge where the Hint Art is located, to the right), it's easy to jump on top of Crazy Cap's. Then, jump from the very edge of the roof of Crazy Cap's to mount the building next door, putting the captured Fire Bro in perfect position to light the lantern with a fireball toss.

51 Jammin' in the Luncheon Kingdom

This audiophile Toad doesn't visit Luncheon Kingdom until Bowser is beaten. Once he does, he hangs out on the platform where Spewart once confronted Mario. As in other appearances, he's got a particular vibe he's going for, so if Mario can strike that nerve, he'll offer up a Power Moon in the spirit of music appreciation. His requests are a clue, like Power Moon names. Here, the theme he's after is "I've become a monster!"

DJ, play Toad Honeylune Ridge: Escape.

52 Mechanic: Repairs Complete!

When the Cooking Carnival is in full swing and visitors from all over inundate the town to try out the amazing Volbonan food, even the robots of Wooded Kingdom stop by. They must have some taste circuits installed. This unit is having some problems though, and has its settings stuck in "harsh-critic" mode! The robot just wants to have a good time, so a mechanic is needed for a quick mechanical check-up. Change into the Mechanic Outfit and Cap (available long before, in Wooded Kingdom) and talk to the rusty robot for a Power Moon.

53 Diving from the Big Pot!

Early on, the Tostarena entrepreneur running slots here won't have a pot simmering on the roof; just a pyramid stack of cans, very satisfying (if rude) to kick over. But later on in the adventure he has stew up there bubbling away for the Cooking Carnival. (That seems like it would be hard for a Tostarenan to check on.) At this point, the name becomes a big clue. What's the biggest pot here? Warp to the Top of the Peak Climb flag, capture a Lava Bubble, and launch up into the stewpot on top of Mount Volbono. Now swim to the southern rim of the pot and use the camera to peer over the edge. Spot the town below and the bowl on the roof, then jump from the big bowl to the smaller one below. If you miss, no big deal. Just instant warp back to the flag atop the mountain and try again.

54 Hat-and-Seek: Among the Food

A visiting Bonneter wants to try out life like Mario and Cappy do it, and is hiding on a resident's head somewhere in the region. This is a needle in a haystack type challenge, if the needle were a pair of telltale Bonneter eyes and the hay was people.

Look for someone with a suspicious pair of eyes in the back of their head and interrogate them to reveal the missing resident of Bonneton.

Look for a Volbonan and Bonneter pair behind the shops.

55 Luncheon Kingdom: Regular Cup

This interesting freerunning course begins near the Volcano Cave exit and concludes near the mountaintop, on the platform holding the Top of the Peak Climb warp flag. The Koopa Troopa racers jump along with the floating salt pile islands, curving forward and right toward the beginning of the peak climb. The peak climb gives racers many angles to cut the path short through acrobatic jumping tricks. There are also Volbonans stuck in the walls here and there who can be used to flick forward over gaps or upward to high ledges.

Running up to the top along the straightforward route, the most challenging segments are the narrow walkway with huge peppers rolling over it, and the spinning saucepans where one side is solid, usable as a platform, and one side is bubbling liquid, the opposite of safe. With the narrow walkway and pepper, just take it easy, moving forward carefully but smoothly, and just jump straight up over the pepper without jerking or altering Mario's path. Stay along the track of the path and he'll be fine. As for the saucepans, the easiest solution uses segments with lots of poles to swing between.

Get the longest jump possible lined up and dive jump at the top of that, bypassing saucepan platforming entirely with enough distance.

At the narrow walkway with the rolling pepper, one confident jump forward clears the obstacle. Don't panic!

56 Peach in the Luncheon Kingdom

After everything has settled down with the main adventure and citizens are free to travel the world and visit where they please without fear of Broodal or Bowser assault, Peach arrives in Luncheon Kingdom in time to enjoy the region's famous and festive Cooking Carnival. She's well-prepared for the heat in her boots and overalls, and she and Tiara survey the scene near the main cookpot in town. Stop by and chat about Luncheon Kingdom's unique, delicious-smelling charm. Peach and Tiara on tour must be visiting most places in the world (and off it) before they return home.

🌙 Moons from the Moon Rock

57 From Inside a Bright Stone

Between Old Town and Old Town's arena, a pink channel flows between the old hard buildings, with blue blocks floating in the stream below, safe to stand on. Hop down on the right side (coming from the Odyssey) after opening up the Moon Rock to find a glowing spot on one of the floating blue blocks. Ground pound it for a hidden Power Moon.

58 Under the Meat Plateau

This new Power Moon is hidden under an arch in the northern part of Luncheon Kingdom, near the blocks of cheese covering a seed. Getting it requires a little jumping ingenuity, and may require getting a little burnt. Just a little bit! Warp to Meat Plateau, then head down from the warp flag and capture a Fire Bro. Approaching the edge by the Power Moon, preferably with a bouncing start, bounce off the edge then jump at the top of the little bounce (Hammer/Fire Bro bounces and jumps not being the same thing). At the top of the forward jump of the Fire Bro, tap the Crouch button to drop the capture and spring Mario forward, gaining a bit more height. For good measure, throw Cappy at the moon at the apex of this "drop jump"—throwing Cappy moves Mario forward slightly. This combo is enough to put Mario's outstretched hand on the Power Moon, pulling it in. Immediately afterward, you have to worry about hightailing it back to land that isn't burning hot, but it's a small price to pay!

59 On Top of a Tall, Tall Roof

This Power Moon is found above the arch supporting the exit of Volcano Cave. This is on the back end of Mount Volbono, relative to Peronza Plaza and the Odyssey. Take the Top of the Peak Climb instant warp to get here quickly. Why the top warp and not the entrance-level warp at the bottom? You're going to need the height from the side of the mountain for enough airtime to jump over to the moon! From a running start, running long jump off the edge of the warp flag's platform, aiming toward the distant Power Moon above the Volcano Cave exit. After drifting a bit with the long jump, throw Cappy across the gap then tackle toward him, holding the Cap Throw button.

This makes Mario bounce off Cappy. Continue drifting forward during the cap bounce jump, and tackle one more time as Mario starts falling, which makes his arc of descent a bit shallower and longer-reaching. Done correctly, Mario lands right on this narrow arch's roof, gaining access to the fresh Power Moon.

60 From a Crack in the Hard Ground

The extreme temperatures and temperate variance in this place play havoc with surfaces, which moisten, dry, crack, and buckle above the soup. Cracks on the ground sometimes reveal coins or even enemies when stomped with a ground pound. One of the cracks even kicks out a Power Moon. Find it on the top of a ledge on the northeastern platforms near where Fire and Hammer Bros dominate.

61 By the Cannon Pointed at the Big Pot

Instant warp to the Top of the Peak Climb flag. From up here, capture a Lava Bubble for the lava swim up to the lava cannon above. Don't jump in, though. Look around the rocky orange rim holding the lava in here to see a glow coming from the ground on one portion. Hop out of the lava to this spot with the Lava Bubble, which ends the capture and pops out Mario. Ground pound the spot here to discover another Power Moon. Getting down from here can be a bit dodgy. You can run down the orange rim back to the warp flag, or take a leap of faith to a target below, or just pull up the Travel Map and warp to one of the checkpoint flags.

62 Luncheon Kingdom: Master Cup

A tougher group of freerunning opponents has lined up by the back of Volcano Cave. Participants who have cleared the Regular Cup can take a crack at this one, which features the legendary golden Koopa Troopa among the racers. The course is the same, curving around the bubbling stew then up and around the twists of the mountain climb, and the competition is fiercer.

Happily, this stretch provides many opportunities to shave distance and time. With good jumping tricks, Mario can forego most of the beginning stretch and get a leg up on the climb. Instead of curving widely right with the rest of the pack, turn sharply right immediately at the beginning and use running long jumps into dive jumps to cross the wider gap to a couple of smaller circular salt pile islands, then a couple of square islands, then the base of the climb.

Higher up, the entire final stretch of the climb can also be skipped, by taking a subtle back route. Between the sets of spinning saucepan platforms near the top of the climb, look for a stepped ledge upward that seems at first like a dead end. Look above and behind Mario though and you see a Volbonan placed midway up the way, fairly high up from Mario's vantage. With one of Mario's high jumps (a somersault or ground pound jump works with the amount of launch space available here, which is basically none), he can get enough altitude to stick a cap onto the Volbonan. From here, flick upward and Mario's right at the race's goal!

63 Stepping Over the Gears

Accessed from the top of Meat Plateau, this challenge room contains a peanut-butter-and-ketchup style mash-up. Right away, notice the Fire Bro and Bitefrost working together to pin Mario in. The room involves crossing a series of spinning gear-like platforms, while avoiding Bitefrost bites from underneath and Fire Bros fireballs from the sides and above. You can capture a Fire Bro for fun or to also tackle the objectives for Power Moon #64, but it's not required. Once you arrive on the final platform, the Power Moon for surviving the room is alongside the exit pipe.

Fire Bros can use snapping Bitefrosts as platforms too!

64 Lanterns on the Gear Steps

Inside the gears challenge room, you have to traverse the whole thing, not only surviving but also lighting all the lanterns. Mario can't throw fire, so you need someone who can. Capture the first Fire Bro, light the first green lantern here, and proceed onward onto the spinning gear platforms. Use a Bitefrost as a stepping stone to get to the second level of gears, which allows access to a staircase platform with another green lantern to light. A platform full of Bitefrosts up ahead vie for the privilege of trying to bite Mario, but they really just create temporary tall jumping platforms. Use them to get atop the columns here where you find a hostile Fire Bro and another flammable lantern.

Up ahead, again use a Bitefrost to reach the second level of gears, lighting another lantern on the left. Another platform for a lone Bitefrost up ahead is a way to get higher still—jump to the small platform and be ready for the guaranteed Bitefrost lift and snap. Use the height to get to the third gear level.

On the last platform, find one side that has a tab platform sticking out just a bit. A lantern can be seen a stone's—or fireball's—throw away. Hurl Fire Bros fireballs toward the lantern until catching it with a solid throw, lighting it aflame. Lighting all the lanterns makes an extra Power Moon appear for pick-up next to where the regular moon appears.

65 Volcano Cave Cruisin'

The entrance to this cavern is found just outside the maw of the Volcano Cave, to the northwest. Extreme caution must be used in this drenched cavern. The blue grated platform that pushes through is a safe haven, along with cap clouds when they're activated. But anywhere else here is treacherous. Mario begins bouncing around, smoking from the heat, on any contact, and defeat comes quickly if you can't regroup back onto the blue grating.

The platform travels to the right through a channel with some ? blocks along the side. Mario must stay away from sections of lava-drenched level that pass through the platform. The blue grating then heads up a vertical path, and Mario must step out from under molten ledges along the way. At the top, a vertical diversion to Power Moon #66 is possible. The platform itself heads left for a bit before dropping away, leaving Mario to scale the rest of the way to the exit pipe (and Power Moon!) by leaping from cap cloud to cap cloud.

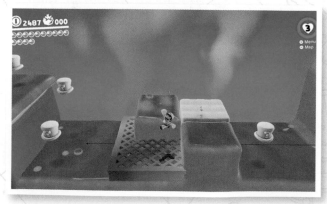

⑥⑥ Volcano Cave and Mysterious Clouds

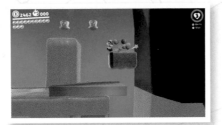

This Power Moon is hidden in a high corner inside a moon pipe near the entrance to the Volcano Cave. At the top of a vertical channel, the blue platform begins moving left. It continues ferrying Mario safely most of the way to the exit, but there's also a secret right above this bend in the path. Look to the deflated cap clouds above, the cloud-shaped blocks with a question mark on the side. Before the grated platform gets out from under Mario, jump up and throw the hat to active the first cap cloud. Jump aboard and continue activating cap clouds heading upward, where you find the Power Moon above.

For jumps that give enough height to consistently leap aboard the next cloud, use somersaults and ground pound jumps. Once the Power Moon up top is secured, you have to make a leap back down to the moving blue platform before it gets too far away. Depending on its distance, you might even need to dive jump from the cloud platforms above the shaft! Even if you fall in, it's ok, as long as you get the moon beforehand. You'll just lose some coins.

⑥⑦ Treasure of the Lava Islands

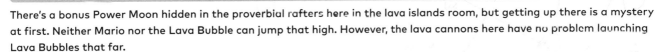

The moon pipe here leads to a gorgeous-looking land of platforms made of what looks like melted bubblegum. None of that is safe for Mario to touch. Capture a resident Lava Bubble for a safe way around. Lava Bubbles can pass through the blue grated platforms drifting around in here, but fizzle out when touching solid ground. On the other hand, it's safe to end a bubble capture over a grated platform, where Mario can safely land.

Make your way across the platforms, capturing Lava Bubbles to traverse liquid and hopping out as Mario to ride grated platforms. At the far end from the entrance, a lava cannon overlooks a wide chasm. Hop into the lava cannon and launch across the gap. Be ready to drop the Lava Bubble capture just before passing through the grating along the landing path, so you can land safely on Mario's own two feet, ready to grab the Power Moon and exit the room.

⑥⑧ Flying Over the Lava Islands

There's a bonus Power Moon hidden in the proverbial rafters here in the lava islands room, but getting up there is a mystery at first. Neither Mario nor the Lava Bubble can jump that high. However, the lava cannons here have no problem launching Lava Bubbles that far.

Find the cannon perched alone on a platform and jump to it, fitting inside in a captured Lava Bubble. The cannon shows the arc before launching, indicating the path over the platform where the Power Moon perches. Launch from the cannon and be ready to press the Crouch button just over it, ditching the Lava Bubble in order to fall on the moon as Mario.

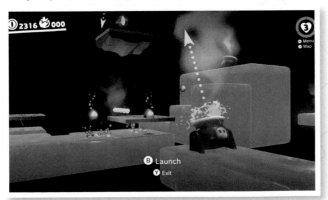
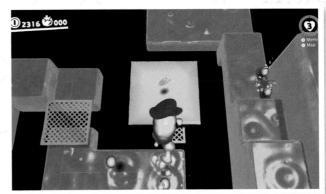

Welcome to Crumbleden

REGION AT A GLANCE	
Population	Unknown
Size	Unknown
Locals	Unknown
Currency	Unknown
Industry	Unknown
Temperature	Average 68°F

Buried Treasures

You'll see glowing spots scattered around on the ground. Engage in some amateur archeology by giving them a hearty stomp!

THREE KEYS TO THE KINGDOM

1. Visit the vast, crumbling tower still standing watch over the area.

2. Investigate the deep, clawlike marks in the stone.

3. Admire the durable construction techniques of a once proud kingdom.

Ⓐ

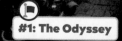
🚩 #1: The Odyssey

REACHING FOR THE HEAVENS

This tower once collected energy from lightning in the thunderclouds that constantly swirl here. Some say that it was destroyed by repeated lightning strikes, but others note the unnatural shapes into which the tower crumbled and wonder if it fell into ruin for different reasons entirely.

RUINED DREAMS

It's only because of the people of Crumbleden's skill in construction that there are ruins left here to see. Their building style was reliable and straightforward, but whatever they'd hoped to accomplish by harnessing the fearsome power of lightning remains unclear. Some have theorized that the circular plaza atop the tower was built for a standoff of some kind.

THE GREAT ALTAR

It's thought this altar was built so this former kingdom could communicate with (or perhaps confront) something. This is the only altar built here, and scholars have been keen to discover its intent. It's also said to be shaped like something in particular. The idea that it was meant to charge lightning has been disproven. The new theory is that it was built to call something down and then restrain the lightning.

HIGH STAKES

Amid the ruins, these swords surely stand out. They're thought to be left over from a large battle here in Crumbleden. One certainly feels a sense of intentionality in the way they're stuck straight down, as if fallen from the sky.

Some see them not as swords, but rather nails or stakes. Perhaps the eyelets at the top allowed ropes or chains through to anchor something, but it's impossible to say what.

ARE THOSE...CLAW MARKS?

The stone here has numerous large slashes cut through it, often in parallel tracks suggesting giant claws. But that can't be right—what could claw through stone?

Ambushed Again

When the crew shoves off from Luncheon Kingdom, it seems it's finally time to take the battle to Bowser's homecourt. But Bowser has other plans. Yet again, the fiend intercepts the Odyssey while it's in transit between kingdoms. For the vile Koopa king, it seems all's fair in love, war, and forced matrimony. It's a drag, but Mario will once again have to gauge unexpected surroundings and find a way to get the Odyssey back into sky-faring shape. But these are foreboding surroundings indeed.

The "Bowser" in Bowser's Kingdom is THAT 👑 Bowser?!
I've...got a bad feeling about this.

Ⓐ

Ⓐ Battle with the Lord of Lightning!

This kingdom is barely holding together. Ancient cobbling makes up the decrepit tower upon which the smoldering Odyssey now rests. A survey of the surrounding area reveals strange swords embedded in the ground. Use Cappy to pull them up, revealing coins and, at the end of the path, a Spark Pylon.

There's nowhere else to go, so ride the Spark Pylon to wherever it leads. It turns out that this pylon zips Mario to a second, much taller tower, the largest one looming in the background. Naturally, it's guarded by the very weapon Bowser just used to take out the Odyssey.

This place is cheerful.

BOSS: RUINED DRAGON

This towering beast must be deeply puzzled at the strange sight of the colorful plumber and his living hat showing up suddenly in the dragon's blighted realm. The Ruined Dragon shakes off its puzzlement soon enough and commences breathing lightning at the platform. Rolling rings of electricity spark into existence where the dragon zaps the platform. Run out of the way as these roll past. Often, the easiest way to dodge them is to keep your distance as the dragon sparks up some rings, but then immediately run toward their point of origin as they start rolling. As the fight goes on, the dragon makes more lightning rings when he zaps the arena, and the rings roll toward Mario more aggressively, even doubling back if you attempt to run inside their expanding paths as suggested.

After a round of electric rings, the Ruined Dragon slams its head on the ground, sending waves of electricity roiling across the arena's floor. Jump over the waves on the ground while also carefully approaching the dragon's sparking head. Depending on how lightning waves coming in from different angles criss-cross, there may be very challenging patterns of electricity to jump over. Any jump rope practice garnered in Metro Kingdom might pay off now! When the sparking ends, be ready to climb up the dragon's resting face.

Note the swords standing in the dragon's head, just like those on the dreary path up here. Use Cappy throws to pull these free. You're not doing the dragon any favors—you just need to be able to get at the top of its dome! The swords act as stakes securing a heavy protective crown above the vulnerable top of his head.

When all the swords are removed, the protective crown atop the dragon's head breaks apart, leaving the beast vulnerable to a ground pound attack. As the fight progresses, Burrbos begin appearing on top of the dragon's head while you're de-swording it, but move quickly enough and they won't have any time to swarm Mario. Plus, because you must move quickly anyway, a few extra pests don't really add much urgency. After the dragon slams its head down and sends out lightning waves, you only have a limited time to pull swords and smash its brain before it rises again.

When the dragon rises, whether because enough time went by or because Mario smashed the top of its head, it progresses back to the lightning ring attack. Each time Mario smashes its head, its attacks become more ferocious, the rings and electric waves more difficult to dodge, and the swords more numerous that pin the cap to its head.

If health is needed during the fight, look for glowing spots on the ground in the arena. Ground pound these to reveal Hearts.

Ground pound the dragon's head three times to dethrone the beast, earning the **Battle with the Lord of Lightning** Multi-Moon in the process. Three Power Moons just happens to be enough to repair the Odyssey, too. There are no more detours... it's straight to Bowser's turf this time. Or, to other places first, if you *want* a detour.

Extend Your Stay

The collapsed land of Crumbleden lacks Regional Coins or a souvenir shop. Only Power Moon #02 can be collected before facing the boss, and #03 and #04 after, but the rest must wait until Mario is much further along in the plot.

Power Moons

There are 10 Power Moons in Ruined Kingdom. Power Moon #01 was obtained while defeating the area's boss.

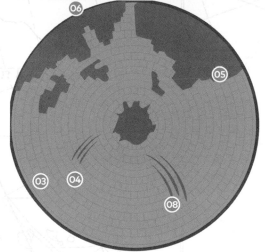

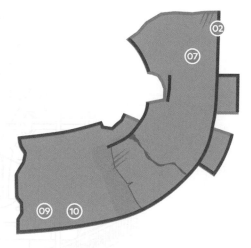

02 In the Ancient Treasure Chest

Climb the stairs up from where the Odyssey is moored and keep an eye on the left. One flight of stairs has given way on the left side, revealing a hidden path. Getting across requires ledge shimmying, so jump against the wall and Mario grips the handhold. Travel hand over hand to the left and open the treasure chest to reveal the Power Moon.

03 Roulette Tower: Climbed

After defeating the dragon, return to the arena and ride the Mini Rocket to this challenge tower. The Power Moon is earned by climbing to the top. The climb takes place mostly inside 8-bit pipes, but you'll also have to use P-Switches outside the pipes to freeze 2D blocks in the right place so they work as platforms. If you err in hitting a P-Switch at the best time, a nearby ground pound switch resets the rotating 2D blocks.

04 Roulette Tower: Stopped

Along the way to the top of the Mini Rocket challenge room, keep your eyes peeled for a chamber filled with 8-bit Koopa Troopas. Some are on the ground, and some are roaming on floating bricks. You want to kick the one on the top-left—the red-shelled turtle—to the left, and follow it. The shell curves around the bend and breaks apart lots of bricks, revealing a hidden side of the 8-bit tower. Exit the pipe here, use the P-Switches to freeze the rotating sections as usable steps to the Power Moon, then climb back into the 8-bit pipe, hop up on the P-Switch blocks, and collect the Power Moon.

05 Peach in the Ruined Kingdom

This Power Moon isn't available until after the main adventure is completed and the princess can be found visiting various kingdoms. Look here to find her noting the quality of the local décor, and offering up a Power Moon she found along the way.

🌙 Moons from the Moon Rock

06 Caught in a Big Horn

Return to the arena where the dragon lies, exhausted, and climb its head once again. Look toward one of its massive horns, the one on the dragon's right side. There's a glimmer coming from the very tip. Carefully climb the horn, then throw Cappy onto the very tip and hold him to slowly pull out the Power Moon.

07 Upon the Broken Arch

Once the Moon Rock opens, exposing extra Power Moons, this one is easy to find. Heading up the stairs from the Odyssey, look for a broken pillar and arch extending up on the right side. Climb up on top of what's left of the arch to find a telltale glow wafting up from the floor. Ground pound here to reveal the Power Moon.

08 Rolling Rock on the Battlefield

There was always debris up here, but after the Moon Rock opens up, one of the rocks partially embedded in the floor contains a surprise. Check rocks in the arena until you uncover one that gives off a rainbow shimmer. This rock is exceptionally durable, and you may need to give it a stronger-than-usual impact. If only there was some way to get extra height on a rock toss here...

Jump atop the dragon's head with the glowing rock in hand for more height on a jumping rock throw.

09 Charging Through an Army

Open the Moon Rock and a strange pipe emerges right next to the Odyssey. Duck into it to find a strange world populated with infinite Chinchos, and a Chargin' Chuck. Watch out for Chincho swarms—spin throws work wonders here—and acquire a Chargin' Chuck of your very own with Cappy capture. Pilot the Chargin' Chuck up the ramp to the top deck, where a Power Moon is trapped in a cage. Charge up Chargin' Chuck's special sprint and bash the cage apart.

10 The Mummy's Army Curse

When exploring the Chincho challenge pipe tucked away behind the Odyssey, either commandeer Chargin' Chuck or lead him across the playing field to the row of breakable blocks under the entrance. Smash the blocks apart with football-derived strength

to reveal a huge bounty of coins. More importantly, after scoring these coins, it's time to double-check the deck directly above, with the entrance pipe. A glowing Chincho resides (or hangs around undead-style) up here. Use the pole to quickly return to the second floor, find the glowing Chincho, and tear it apart with cap throws or jump attacks. Don't leave without scooping up the moon it leaves behind (plus giving Chargin' Chuck a high-five).

Welcome to Bowser's Castle

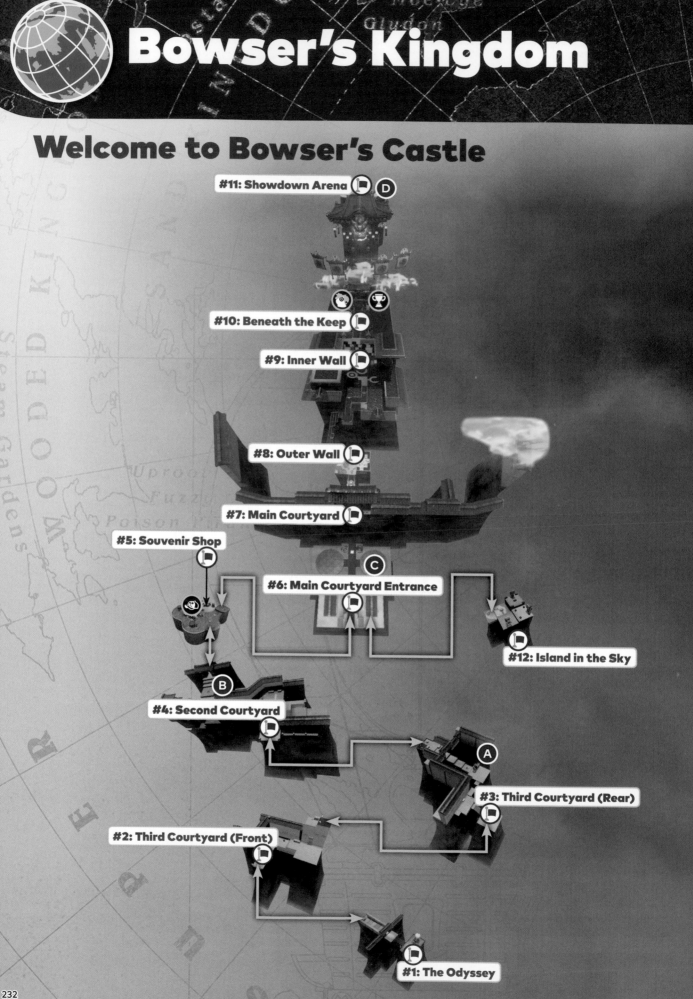

#11: Showdown Arena **D**

#10: Beneath the Keep

#9: Inner Wall

#8: Outer Wall

#7: Main Courtyard

#5: Souvenir Shop

#6: Main Courtyard Entrance **C**

#12: Island in the Sky

B

#4: Second Courtyard

A

#3: Third Courtyard (Rear)

#2: Third Courtyard (Front)

#1: The Odyssey

INDIGENOUS FLORA & FAUNA

Creature	Can Capture?
BINOCULARS	No
POKIO	Yes
JIZO	Yes
YOO-FOE	No
GOOMBA	Yes
MINI GOOMBA	No
LAKITU	Yes
BURRBO	No
SPINY	No
STAIRFACE OGRE	No

REGION AT A GLANCE

Population	Middling
Size	Sprawling
Locals	Stairface Ogres
Currency	Oblong
Industry	Hanafuda cards
Temperature	Average 79°F

The Hole Thing

All along the walls, small holes were meant to allow defenders to shoot at invaders, but nowadays you're more likely to find a demon or a snake coming out than an arrow.

TERRIFYING GATEKEEPERS

Don't run afoul of the Stairface Ogres that guard this kingdom. When they spot an intruder, they bring their huge mallets down, no questions asked. On the other hand, you have to admire their tenacity and work ethic. The scars on their faces show that they don't give up easily.

BEAUTIFUL TILE WORK

This kingdom's architecture is unique. Roofs are made of heavy, layered tiles that do not budge, even if walked upon. They also create a uniformity in the overall design, enhancing the beauty of the palace.

Though you can move along the roofs, this palace rests quite high in the sky, and if you fall off, you will most definitely die. It's not the surest footing either, so be careful.

THREE KEYS TO THE KINGDOM

1. Dart past the silent and lethal Stairface Ogres.

2. Avoid being distracted by the ominous (yet brightly glowing) clouds.

3. Survive the various traps designed to end your trip early.

STATUES GUARD THE COURT

The palace tower highlights the inner citadel, and the gate leading to it is guarded by fearsome statues.

The statues are fashioned after gods of wind and thunder, the perfect motif for a sky palace, and since they are modeled on Bowser, the ruler of this kingdom, they serve as a warning to foes here and abroad.

IMPRESSIVE FORTIFICATIONS

Surrounding the inner citadel are the second and third courts. The second court is especially fortified, with many cannons to repel invaders. Cannonballs often roll along the ground, and many tourists fall trying to evade them. Legends speak of invaders repelling the cannonballs with spears, but no mere mortal could hope to do this, so try not to get too close!

AN OASIS OF CALM

This elegant garden is a balm for the brutality of this kingdom and will help you forget all the hardships you faced to reach it.

You can even buy souvenirs, so be sure you stop by!

Ⓐ Infiltrate Bowser's Castle!

It's finally time! Mario has tailed Bowser back to his home turf. Bowser's Castle isn't just one place. It's a series of fortifications floating separately in the sky, connected by Spark Pylons. Bowser's Keep is far too fortified to bring a balloon anywhere nearby, so the Odyssey lands on the farthest structure from the target. Mario will have to do some scouting to get closer to the action.

Out here, past the advance gate, there's just an early troop of Goomba guards, far from the Koopa king's elite forces. Capture a Goomba and build a big stack with all the guards, then head to the end of the right side of the corridor and look for a way around. The path curls to a special button that can only be activated by a stack of 10 Goombas. Hop onto it with a huge Goomba stack to reveal Power Moon #19 on top of the wall. Normally this would be too high to jump toward, but from a huge Goomba stack you can just release the capture right next to the wall and pop up to the top level in Mario form from the highest Goomba. Up here, scoop up the four purple coins and the gold coin piles before triggering the Spark Pylon below.

The Third Courtyard (Front) platform is one of several floating structures that serve as an extended foyer into Bowser's domain. Register the checkpoint flag here to enable instant warps in the future. Bowser's guards here get more serious, as Pokios advance upon Mario. Capture a Pokio and flick onto the roof, collecting the Regional Coins up here and peering over to the other side to spy a Power Moon on the ledge. Fall down and collect Power Moon #05, then flick back onto the roof.

Put a Bird on It

Don't underestimate this diminutive, flightless bird. Pokio more than makes up for any shortcomings with a versatile beak. Its peck is one of the most potent attacks to be found in *Super Mario Odyssey*. Pecks are powerful and can be used rapidly, quickly beating down anything that isn't invulnerable, whether that's a multi-coin block or a boss's weak spot.

Pokio's jumping power is weak, but there are two ways to compensate for this. One is by shaking the controller for a shake spin while jumping. This works like a little double jump for the bird, and is immensely helpful for cleaning up its jumping weakness. (The shake spin only boosts airtime once per falling period. Shake spin and peck together with good timing for a special spinning peck!)

The more important solution is that Pokio's beak allows it to flick itself! Permeable walls allow Pokio to stick into them with a beak strike. From here, either pull Pokio back with the analog stick then release to flick Pokio, Pole or Volbonan style. Better yet though, aim quickly by pulling the stick back opposite the intended launch direction (think of a slingshot), then shake the controller (rather than building flick tension, then releasing like normal). Pokio flicks farther and faster than normal.

At first, Pokio might seem sluggish. But on the contrary, Pokio becomes one of the most mobile capturable creatures once you learn to put its special movement options together. Before long you can be shake-flicking into spinning double jumps into wall pokes for new beak holds, launching rapidly up or around vertical surfaces faster than just about anything. Meanwhile, if anything bothers you, just peck it to pieces.

The Spark Pylon found on top of Third Courtyard (Front) leads to Third Courtyard (Rear). Ditch the Pokio (don't worry, there will be many more) and ride the Spark Pylon to the next floating battlement. Snag the warp flag here too and head up the steps, avoiding the Spinies in their pen.

To the right, past the Spinies, is a flat platform with a fierce-looking new enemy, the Stairface Ogre. These huge Thwomp-like

enemies clomp about and try to flatten Mario with a huge stamp. An indicator on the ground shows when they're about to bring the hammer down, so get out of the way! For a moment while they recover from the effort of the attack, the stamp becomes a jumpable staircase allowing access to the top of the Stairface Ogre's head.

Quickly hop up to the top and ground pound the Ogre to break it apart in one shot. Defeat the Ogre here to reveal Power Moon #01. Collect the moon to open the gate and extend the drawbridge ahead.

Follow the broad steps to the Spark Pylon platform. Before moving on, turn around and jump to the rooftop on the right, easily mounted with a triple jump or dive jump. Several groups of Regional Coins are on the winding roof atop Third Courtyard (Rear), along with a ledge on the back end only accessible by falling from the roof. Fall down there to find a Pokio. With this Pokio under control, it's now possible to flick around the entire Third Courtyard (Rear) structure, making sure all the purple coins are pocketed, including some floating over a sheer drop on the side.

A Hero's Purpose

So close they're breathing down Bowser's neck, his Keep beckoning, Mario and Cappy feel a renewed urgency. Bowser's Kingdom has many hidden moons, like all kingdoms. And you'll have plenty of time to explore them. But aside from the very early Power Moons already covered, from here on out Mario's Itinerary will only detail Power Moons received for completing objectives. All other Power Moons are covered under Extending Your Stay.

Mario and Cappy might as well push forward and see what unfolds anyway—once you arrive in Bowser's Kingdom, you can't leave without seeing it through.

Ⓑ Smart Bombing

In the Second Courtyard, Bowser's defenses are ramped up. Turrets unleash cannonball bombs, while armored (or at least hat-wearing) Pokios relentlessly approach. The important thing to know about Pokios in the presence of cannonball bombs is that Pokio beak strikes can redirect the bombs with amazing force. With the right angle or object to ramp a bomb off of, Pokios can easily become mad bombers around turret ports; accidentally, for hostile Pokios, and intentionally, for captured Pokio-form Mario!

Under the first turret, notice the moon shard. The Second Courtyard's under lockdown, and the Power Moon to release it is broken up and spread out, minimizing the risk of an intruder putting it together.

1. Under the first turret

2. Over the fire pit on the lowest level

3. Within flicking distance hovering in front of the large wall

4. Hidden in a bomb-weak box resting between two turrets

5. Tucked up on a ledge on the backside of the structure

Collecting all the moon shards reveals Power Moon #02. The gate revealing the next Spark Pylon is opened by picking up this moon. A treat is coming up, the souvenir shop island!

© Big Broodal Battle

Use the time at the souvenir shop island as a brief respite. Buy some new outfits, especially the new Samurai Outfit, since wearing it lets Mario access a special room right here on this island, on the opposite side from Crazy Cap's entrance. Don't miss the Regional Coins hidden right inside Crazy Cap's outside roof.

Whenever you're done with the souvenir break, use the Spark Pylon past the stone garden to move on toward the first floating structure that's actually attached to Bowser's Keep: the Main Courtyard Entrance.

The Heart of a Jizo

Main Courtyard Entrance is a mostly empty area, though the building on the right (relative the checkpoint flag) has a lone Jizo statue installed facing out over the clouds. Capture this Jizo and move it over the glowing spots around the building on the opposite side to reveal a Life-Up Heart.

BOSS: HARIET

Beyond the long buildings on either side of the path, the Main Courtyard Entrance has two ornate golden Bowser statues in the way ahead, with large round platforms on either side. Hop onto the left platform and Hariet leaps from the Broodals' patrolling ship above, eager for a rematch. Hariet again attacks with her assortment of spiked bombs and rigged pigtails. She skips about tossing pairs of time bombs around the arena, which leave behind unsafe pits of fire in their wakes.

The bombs can be deflected with a cap toss, getting them out of Mario's vicinity. With a little skill and luck, a tossed Hariet bomb can be smacked right back in her face! If not, after a few pairs of bombs, Hariet spins to wind up tension, then whips her pigtails (with bombs threaded into them) toward Mario, creating an explosive mace swing. Run around Hariet while putting distance between her and Mario to make this brutal attack miss, then toss Cappy into the embedded bombs while Hariet struggles to get her hair unstuck from the ground.

Her pigtail-bombs snap around and detonate, knocking off her steel helmet and briefly exposing Hariet to a stomp attack! Hariet is quite slippery while she wails looking for her hat, so slow her down with a hat throw to make it easier to jump onto her head before she recovers.

Hariet goes through a phase of dropping bombs to regroup, then sets about attacking with her hair-bombs again. Continue to dodge bombs and fire while sending ordinance back at Hariet when possible and this Broodal bomber's blastathon will soon be over.

BOSS: TOPPER

Step onto the right circular platform in the Main Courtyard Entrance and Topper drops in, his stack of top hats in tow. He'll begin trotting toward the heroes, hoping to get close enough to begin his top hat spin.

This attack gives a brief warning of where it's going to hit, but it's not enough time to dodge purely on reaction. Always be ready to move away from Topper.

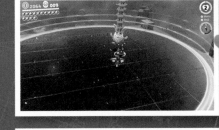

Whenever there's a safe distance to do so, throw Cappy repeatedly at Topper, preferably from the tip of Cappy's range. This briefly waylays Topper, and knocks hats from his tall stack. The fewer hats in his stack, the shorter the reach on his spinning attack. Hats knocked away from his stack become independent projectiles bouncing around the platform, though, and they'll have to be dealt with or avoided.

Knock the full stack of hats off of Topper's head to leave him susceptible to stomping. Get a solid shot in on his cranium and he practically blankets the arena in rebounding top hats, but these can be jumped over, flattened with stomps, and knocked aside with Cappy. If Hearts are low during this fight, look for replacement power-ups to show up periodically when smashing Topper's surplus top hats.

Defeat Hariet and Topper to destroy the two Bowser statues, unsealing **Power Moon #03**. Gather this moon to open the way forward to the Main Courtyard.

Ⓓ Showdown at Bowser's Castle

Be sure to touch the checkpoint flag here, since it will be a future hub for lots of moon-hunting activities. Now that Mario is beyond the great gate, looking ahead and up, Bowser's Keep is visible towering above, beyond a long vertical wall full of obstacles.

Ahead, a pair of Binoculars offers a scouting opportunity at the foot of the climb, and a pair of Pokios present both a threat and a capture opportunity. Control one of the Pokios and jump to the right (coming from the checkpoint flag) over small platforms floating in the southeast moat. A pokable wall extends upward at the end of the platforms, providing a place for Pokio to show off its climbing chops.

Dig your beak in and begin flicking up the wall, poking the wall again while falling to re-plant and flick again, if necessary.

On top, a skinny bridge leads across to yet another structure. A turret array here spews several cannonballs at once across the walkway. Use Pokio's beak to safely bat incoming cannonballs away.

Follow the path turning inward toward the huge vertical wall ahead to find the Outer Wall checkpoint flag. Look just over the railing before the stairs to the flag to see three Regional Coins hovering down low, at the end of a section of beak-friendly wall.

The stretch ahead is a real marvel. One of Bowser's final lines of defense is this immense, two-stage climbing wall leading up the front of his biggest fortification. The base of the climb is guarded by a Stairface Ogre and a poison moat. The wall behind the Stairface Ogre is covered in rotating dials, which can be ridden by inspired Pokios and used to move upward. Lots of Regional Coins are floating around the rotating, pokable dials, too.

Atop the three dials is a safe, standard-issue ledge, with the Inner Wall checkpoint flag planted here before the second wall. For this climb, alternating conveyor belts of wall move left or right, and only the lighter sections of wall can be pierced by the Pokio beak. Unmoving spiked strips serve as impediments in places here, and three more purple coins can be found by moving behind the spike strip on the left.

Atop the second run of wall obstacles, you'll mount the roof, discovering the checkpoint flag Beneath the Keep. This is the last checkpoint before a major encounter, so if you want to explore earlier in Bowser's Kingdom on foot or through the use of instant warps, now's the time. (You can't leave the kingdom until you clear the threat here.) Whenever you're ready, cross the path between poison moats to the raised Spark Pylon platform, and ride the Spark Pylon wire up, finally, to the roof of Bowser's Keep.

Proceed forward to confront the Koopa king. Finally, Mario catches up to Bowser on his own terms, but the vile lizard retreats yet again, leaving minions to do the work.

Again?!

BOSS: ROBOBROOD

The Broodals assemble for a chance to redeem themselves, joining forces inside a huge mech called RoboBrood. This big bipedal combat platform can stomp small prey underfoot (naturally), can eject explosive cannonballs, and spawn swarms of spinning snake-like ground obstacles.

RoboBrood sometimes dispatches Pokio helpers, which provide Mario a little extra punching power. However, the legs are still a bit too heavily armed to take on with the beak, and staying this close with the tiny bird is risky at best against the heavy legs. Back off as Pokio and let RoboBrood launch some cannonballs your way, then poke them right back at the big mech's legs. One cannonball blast severely cracks a leg's armor, and another blast knocks the protective layer off entirely!

Poke the cannonballs at the legs' armor plating.

The RoboBrood can't support itself without the armor on its legs, so it'll collapse in the direction of the damaged appendage. Watch out if it's falling in your direction. While the mech lays on its side, helpless, approach it and jump up to the top, using whichever combination of jumps, pokes, and flicks make sense. Some sides of the RoboBrood body have large wood sections, enabling poke-flicking quickly up to the top, while the sections with collapsed legs sticking out create lots of ledges for jumping. Whichever route you take, get to the top ASAP and peck the top globe apart, taking whichever Broodal was inside out of the fight. Taking out the RoboBrood requires shattering all four globes, so it'll have to be knocked off its feet at least four times.

RoboBrood gets more aggressive as the fight goes on, stomping after Mario/Pokio quicker, firing more cannonballs, and unleashing fields of snake-like spinning drones. The drones can be cleared out with Pokio pecks or Mario hat tosses, or they can simply be avoided. The RoboBrood itself will probably step on many of them.

If RoboBrood's legs begin glowing, watch out; this is a signal that it's going to charge back and forth across the stage trying to ram into Mario. Pokio simply won't be fast enough to dodge RoboBrood in this state, so end the capture and roll back and forth out of the mech's way until it calms down and returns to its normal patterns.

Use spin throws to clear out spinning snake drones, don't get squished, and capture another Pokio to use to bounce cannonballs right back at RoboBrood's legs.

When all four globes are busted, the Broodals' best weapon is toast. RoboBrood's destruction leaves behind **Power Moon #04**, a Multi-Moon. Since Bowser himself ran off to the moon, taking Peach, Tiara, and all the stuff the Broodals stole for him, that means Bowser's Kingdom is secure!

Extend Your Stay

Most of Bowser's Kingdom wasn't in full swing yet before clearing out the Broodal bosses. There are more enemies roaming and many more Power Moons available to collect. Hint Toad and Uncle amiibo set up shop on the Odyssey's platform, and a pipe now leads from the very beginning all the way to just beneath the Keep!

Souvenir Shopping

Bowser's Kingdom contains 100 coins in the form of purple Oblong currency.

x3
x3
x3
x3
x3
x3
x3
x3
x3
x4
x3
x3
x3
x3
x3
x3
x3

x3

x3
x4
x3
x4
x3
x3
x3

x4
x4

x4

x4

Life-Up Heart	Bowser's Kingdom Power Moon	Samurai Helmet	Samurai Outfit	Happi Headband
① 50	① 100	◎ 5	◎ 10	◎ 20

Happi Outfit	Bowser's Kingdom Sticker	Paper Lantern	Jizo Statue
◎ 25	◎ 10	◎ 5	◎ 25

Crazy Cap

Coins in High Places

Many Regional Coins here are hovering along beak-friendly walls above sheer drops, asking you to do some clever rappelling and flicking with Pokio to pocket them all. Be sure to look around the edges of each structure for purple coins along the sides.

Don't miss the purple coins above the doorway near the Stairface Ogre halfway up Bowser's great wall. The Ogre itself can help you get up here by making a temporary step nearby with a missed smash. The nearby beanstalk also provides a way up, if planted.

The cleverest coin hiding place is just to the left of Bowser's nose on the enormous statue of his face mounted on the front of the Keep. Fall from the roof above to Bowser's face, then carefully jump and climb to the purple coins.

🌙 Power Moons

There are 62 Power Moons in Bowser's Kingdom. **Power Moons #01-05 and #19** were obtained while ridding Bowser's Kingdom of its Broodal threat. Consult the prior pages for help.

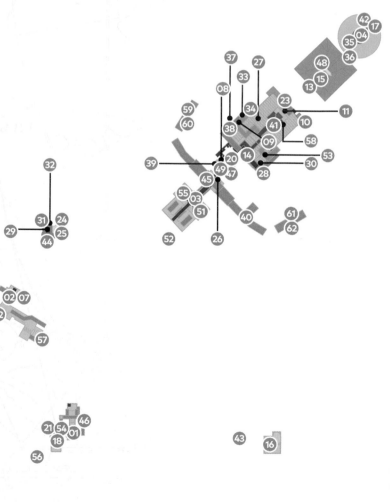

06 Treasure Inside the Turret

On the Second Courtyard structure, there are a couple of routes into a secret passage along the side. One is to keep an eye out off the left edge for beak-friendly material, which a Pokio could stick to after taking a step of faith off the side.

The other way is to climb to the back of the two-turret tower here, then look off the back edge, where a compartment can be seen below. Fall down toward the opening then either (as Pokio) shake the controller to spin-jump into the room, or (as Mario) throw Cappy into the room, then tackle in after him. After collecting the Power Moon, a pipe here can be taken back to the surface.

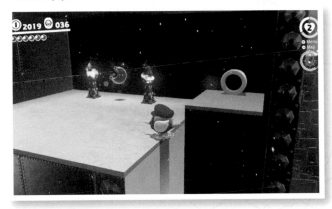

07 From the Side above the Castle Gate

Slide as high as possible on the wall on the moon's side.

Wall jump. Be ready to act again at the top of the wall jump's arc.

The fastest way to get to this Power Moon location is to instant warp to the souvenir shop, then take the Spark Pylon here back to Second Courtyard. At this far back end of Second Courtyard, a Power Moon can be seen just out of reach on the roof here. To get up there, try out a little trick jump.

Nail the jump to have the run of the roof. Grab the Power Moon, then explore the roof tier of Second Courtyard for good measure.

The wall jump gained a lot of height, so a tackle from that position can land Mario atop the wall! At the wall jump's apex, throw the cap first to make this more consistent.

08 Sunken Treasure in the Moat

Travel to the Main Courtyard, where there's a small moat guarded by Pokios, and look for the northwest surface of the water. This is next to the Binoculars on the ledge. Dive in and descend, observing three Regional Coins for the taking on the way down. Of course, also very noticeable is the glowing Power Moon down here, hidden in the moat under the platform. Swim to it quickly and collect it to replenish Mario's air, giving him enough lung power to swim back up and out.

09 Past the Moving Wall

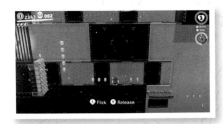

From the northwest corner of the top of Inner Wall, just beneath the Keep, descend a couple tiers, past the Stairface Ogre to the Spinies' ledge, and peer over the side. A series of conveyors on the wall could only be navigated with the beak of a Pokio. Conveniently, a ledge with a lone Pokio is below around the western corner. Fall down to this ledge and capture the Pokio, then tackle the horizontal wall challenge. You'll have to successfully flick Pokio from a stationary section of wall to a moving one, then off again before running into a spike strip. Make this movement series, and the Power Moon is just a bit farther to the left, hovering above another Pokio behind bars. Flick in from the side to collect it.

10 Above the Poison Swamp

The poison pond adds a strange relaxing character to the roof of the Inner Wall, in the shadow of the looming Keep just above. That's as long as you don't fall in. Capture Lakitu and then head to the northwest platform around the pond, to follow a route described in Power Moon #11. Grab that moon by breaking the nice frame, if you haven't, then look at the east edge of the arch. There's a clear runway to jump to a platform that overlooks the northeastern edge of the pond. Jump and dive toward that platform and you find this Power Moon here ready for collection.

11 Knocking Down the Nice Frame

Head to the Beneath the Keep checkpoint flag. Look around the poison pond here for Lakitu, who is a peaceful fisher turtle here despite the setting. Capture Lakitu and float over the swamp to the northwest corner, where a ledge with a Slingshot can be found. Trigger the Slingshot to launch Mario on top of the big arch ahead, where some Regional Coins can be scooped up from the back. In the front, there's an ornate decorative frame hanging here that the Power Moon's title issues a pretty clear clue about. Peg the frame hanging up here with a hat throw to knock it off the arch and into the poison, creating a Power Moon for pickup atop the arch!

12 Caught on the Iron Fence

The iron fence caps in much of Bowser's territory are hideous impressions of the Koopa king's face. Tossing Cappy onto the vast majority of these merely produces a coin or three, if anything. But one of the fence caps behind the Odyssey is different. Find one that spews fire when Cappy is held on top of the post. That's a bit unusual. Toss Cappy onto this fence cap and hold him until the Power Moon emerges!

13 On the Giant Bowser Statue's Nose

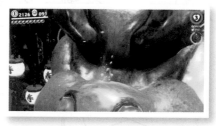

This kind of gives itself away, if you get it as a clue from Talkatoo. One side of the Keep itself sports a huge statue of Bowser, and you can leap from the roof and land here and move around on it. There's a Spark Pylon to get back, so it's fine as long as you don't miss when falling. Hang off the ledge above then just fall, or start a spin near the edge, then spin jump off for a slower descent. Once safely on the statue, just find the glowing spot on Bowser's nose and smash it with a ground pound. If only it were that easy the rest of the time.

14 Inside a Block in the Castle

From the Outer Wall checkpoint flag, heading just a bit to the right finds a Stairface Ogre overseeing a path to the climb beyond. The path is cluttered a bit with metal Bowser boxes, the kind Mario can't break, not even with ground pounds. They can be broken, though, with turret cannonballs or Stairface Ogre smashes. Lure the Ogre to the edge here, where one of the boxes can be seen emitting a rainbow glow, and coax it to bash open the box (preferably getting out of the way while it does so). Metal box or not, there's no match for the Ogre's crushing power. The boxes are destroyed but the Power Moon survives.

15 Caught Hopping at Bowser's Castle!

Once the coast is cleared of major baddies, as usual, the mischievous hares emerge. This one scampers along the perimeter of the Keep's roof itself, taunting Mario as it flees. Head it off at passes by cutting corners, toss Cappy to slow it down when close enough, and use rolling (while shaking the controller) to move much faster if the rabbit flees over a straight, open stretch of roof.

16 Exterminate the Ogres!

From the Main Courtyard Entrance, mount the roof of the building on the right, above the lone Jizo statue. Here, find another Spark Pylon. Hop aboard to see where the line leads and you'll end up on a secret structure way off to the side of Bowser's normal emplacements. This seems to be a Stairface Ogre training ground. Bait these brutes into smashing down their stamps, then climb aboard and ground pound their heads to defeat them. You can simply run back and forth in front of them to bait a missed blow, or you can even run directly at them and cross under between their legs as they attack!

This platform is under (way, way under) the secret platform holding the Island in the Sky checkpoint flag. You can't go upward from here to there, but you can skydive down from the island to here. The warp painting leading to the secret island above the secret island is found in Cascade Kingdom, but only after finishing the main adventure.

17 Bowser's Kingdom Timer Challenge 1

The Showdown Arena is where the RoboBrood boss battle goes down, but now it's much more relaxing. Register the checkpoint flag for this platform, then flip Cappy onto the scarecrow to start up a Timer Challenge. A Power Moon is held above a series of spinning platforms. Their varied sizes and shapes create a morphing platform challenge to the top as the structure spins. Get a lot of extra height at the start with a triple jump or dive jump to start as far along the platforms as possible, then just keep jumping and climbing as quick as you can.

18 Taking Notes: Between Spinies

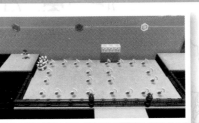

Spinies roam around in a little pen near the checkpoint flag on Third Courtyard (Rear). A song note floats near them, activating a timed note collection challenge if touched. The notes are among the Spinies, who can't be killed, since there's no ledge to knock them off of. While watching out for the Spinies, touch the note and hop into the middle of all the timed notes. Spin throw, which hands a lot of coin-collecting/Spiny-deflecting work to Cappy, then run around to collect straggler notes.

20 Hidden Corridor Under the Floor

The Pokio climb begins just beyond the Main Courtyard gate, heading up sheer walls easily navigated thanks to the small bird's beak. The first sheer wall to climb has a secret just around the back side of the platform. After climbing up the first wall from the moat, fall off the back side of the Spiny ledge here and stick into the wall with Pokio's beak. Here you can see a Power Moon behind bars. There's an opening to get behind the bars but it's blocked by four breakable crates. Fall past the crates, stick them with Pokio's beak to shatter them, then immediately stick Pokio's beak into the wall under the gap to keep from plunging into the abyss. Now, flick up into the opening left by the broken crates and get the Power Moon. The pipe here spits Mario out up top, by the turret.

21 Poking Your Nose in the Plaster Wall

Third Courtyard (Rear) has a ledge on its backside that can only be accessed by dropping down from the roof. There's a Pokio to capture here, and some coins to collect. Conspicuously, there's an opening in one of the fort's archer ports. Almost all of them are plugged up, but not this one. Poke Pokio's beak in there to force out a hidden Power Moon.

22 Poking the Turret Wall

Take the instant warp to the Second Courtyard checkpoint flag, then grab a Pokio friend and head over to the main cannonball corridor, where two turrets sit side by side. Poke their cannonballs past the left turret, at the boxes just before the edge of the platform. Blow these away, then look behind them to find another opened archer port, which is a perfect match for Pokio's beak, good for one Power Moon.

23 Poking Your Nose by the Great Gate

More open archer ports can be found on the backside of the Spark Pylon platform leading on to Bowser's Keep. Instant warp to the Inner Wall checkpoint flag, capture a Pokio, then flick up the conveyor belt wall. You can't just warp to the Beneath the Keep flag for a quick trip, because you need to be able to beak-poke with a captured Pokio. Saunter behind the platform to find the two opened ports, plus a couple of Spinies. Poke the Spinies, inspect the left port with the beak for some coins, then inspect the right port with the beak for a Power Moon.

24 Jizo All in a Row

There are interesting capturable statues found on the souvenir shop island, which can be quickly accessed with Souvenir Shop checkpoint flag warp. These Jizo statues are heavy and inflexible stone, so they can't really do anything besides bounce around heavily, which is how they get around. Capture a Jizo near the shop, then look to see if there's anywhere else here it might be comfortable. In the little stone garden adjacent the shop here, find a gap in a long row of Jizo statues and park there for a Power Moon.

25 Underground Jizo

Capture one of the souvenir shop Jizo statues, then clomp heavily into the stone garden. If you look around for anything odd, you're likely to literally stumble

into it, in the form of a suspicious section of sandy ground that clearly can't support the weight of a Jizo statue. Hop onto the sandy depressed square to push down into a hidden underground chamber where even more Jizo statues are lined up. Hop over to the gap in this line and hop in with this statue for another Power Moon.

26 Found Behind Bars!

Warp to the Main Courtyard and jump up onto the long roof running northwest to southeast. Run along the roof to the southeast, looking for an outcropping extending off the left side. On the end of this is a Spark Pylon. The line from this Pylon tucks back down along the side of the great wall toward a fortified room hidden just above the Main Courtyard main gate.

The Power Moon is stashed in this room, and the Spark Pylon provides a way in through the tight bars. After collecting the moon, use the Spark Pylon in here to move back out of the room and along the wall back down the southeast wing.

27 Fishing(?) in Bowser's Castle

Instant warp to the Beneath the Keep checkpoint flag then head east to find a fishing Lakitu. Capture him and float to the northwest corner of the poison pond, being sure to fly through the Regional Coins that hover under the bridge on the way. At the northwest corner, lower the reel and carefully cast about for the biggest shadow under the toxic waves. When you get a nibble, shake upward quickly or press the Cap Throw button to attempt to start reeling in the bite. If successful, you'll have to close the deal by tugging on the analog stick. Succeed here, and you'll get a Power Moon, but not from a fish, exactly...

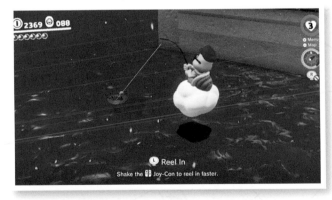

28 Good to See You, Captain Toad!

Instant warp to the Outer Wall checkpoint, then head along the edge of the roof to the southeast, sticking to the green tiles. At the southeast edge of this roof tier, a gap can be found that leads down to a small ledge finished with roof tiles that wraps around the corner a bit. Captain Toad has made it all the way out here, on this remote ledge. Greet him (not while controlling Pokio, or he'll just be frightened!) for a Power Moon.

29 Shopping at Bowser's Castle

Crazy Cap's has its own island here among Bowser's sky forts. For 100 coins, a unique Power Moon can be purchased here. Look over the outfits, too.

30 Bowser's Castle Treasure Vault

Several tiers of roof on Bowser's biggest structure aren't really fully accessible until the local bosses are chased off. Starting from  the pipe exit from the Odyssey to just beneath the Keep, descend a couple levels along the northwest side of the multi-tier building, down to the roof level with a swarm of Spinies and a beanstalk planter. Run all the way around the edge of this ledge to find a Slingshot installed on the end, pointed toward the opposite wing of this level. Hat toss onto the Slingshot to launch across the gap, then capture a Pokio here and wrap around to the southeast along the green tiles. On the wall, you'll find a more challenging rendition of the circular dial climb, with skinny portions of beak-friendly material spinning around a wall of steel. Ascend the wall with the help of a Pokio and venture inside the room found at the top. Inside, piles of coins, and a Power Moon inside a treasure chest.

31 Scene of Crossing the Poison Swamp

With the Samurai Armor and Helmet on, the New Donker wearing his own Samurai Helmet behind the souvenir shop lets Mario into a very special challenge room. Hop into the pipe in this room to be transported into a folding screen that closes itself then reopens into a new stage design each time you successfully cross from left to right. Make it to the last folding screen stage to find a 2D Power Moon.

32 Taking Notes: In the Folding Screen

Inside the New Donker's whimsical 2D folding screen, one of the folding stages has a music note hovering by itself under a platform, so the only way to get at it is to ride a platform underneath. Do so, then jump up and touch the note while passing by. Several more notes now appear all over the little stage, but all along the path of the platform you had to ride to get at the song note to begin with. Quickly scoop up music notes along the way and stick with the platform for sure footing and the bonus 2D Power Moon is yours.

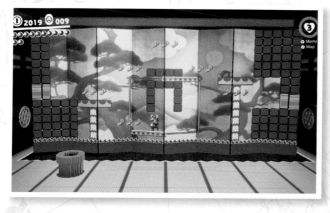

33 On Top of the Spinning Tower

The big ceremonial door to this challenge area is opened by defeating the Stairface Ogre just outside, who patrols along a thin strip of land around a poison moat. Inside, a dizzying tower reaches upward, with sections spinning in opposite directions. Portions of the walls are beak-friendly for Pokio climbing, so you have to poke walls for a firm starting point, then flick upward to higher terrain, poking again to stop yourself from losing height. At the top section, use a controller-shake flick for extra speed and height when threading the needle through the moving vertical shafts. At the top, collect the Power Moon before exiting.

34 Down and Up the Spinning Tower

The spinning Pokio-friendly tower has a secret near the bottom. Carefully move downward along poke-friendly sections of wall on the backside to see a compartment. Fall toward this compartment and shake-spin to guide the Pokio into the little room, probably squashing the Pokio who's already in here upon entry. Grab the Key hovering in the back of this secret room to make a bonus Power Moon pop out of the Lock on the top of the tower. Carefully exit the little room, getting a beak-hold on the wall outside, before flicking up the tower as normal to collect the moons.

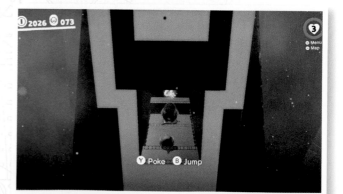

35 Jizo's Big Adventure

You'll find the pipe into this room on Showdown Arena after knocking out the Broodals. Dive in to find spike tiles that alternate between being safe and unsafe to stand on, P-Switches that only register when weight stays upon them, and several Jizo status to maneuver.

The first Jizo is poised upon some spikes. Capture it and hop forward onto the left or right P-Switch ahead. These activate bridges to platforms off to the side where more Jizo statues can be acquired. More statues equal more switch-pushing power. To the left, capture the Jizo statue on this platform and then hop onto the cracked spot on the ground. The weight buckles several platforms under the statue, until it hits the bottom. A P-Switch here lowers the elevator that returns to the surface, and that allows this Jizo statue to cross the bridge and join the first Jizo statue in the center.

Park this Jizo statue on the right P-Switch in the middle and cross the on/off spikes to the next statue. Control it and hop carefully back over the moving spike platforms.

With three Jizo statues in the center, you have enough stone weight power to solve the room. Moving the new Jizo statue onto the forward P-Switch reveals a bridge ahead to two more P-Switches next to a blank wall. Drive the left and right Jizos off their P-Switches and onto these new buttons. Two vertical shafts are revealed, the perfect channel to wall jump back and forth to the top, where the Power Moon awaits.

36 Jizo and the Hidden Room

Complete all the steps for Power Moon #35, creating a wall jump channel up to the last platform. (You'll still have to do it all over again even if you already got that moon on a prior visit.) Now, move the Jizo statue enabling the bridge to the final two P-Switches back to near the entry pipe. Here, there's a lone P-Switch, which opens a special compartment most of the way up the final vertical wall. Park the Jizo statue on this switch, then head back to the vertical channel.

You'll have to jump across without the Jizo statue creating the bridge to the end now, but the distance is no problem with a triple jump or dive jump. Wall jump up the vertical channel to find an extra Power Moon hidden in the new compartment.

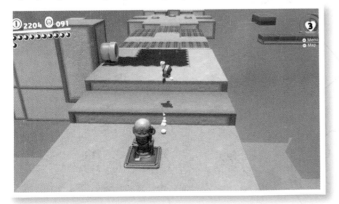

37 Dashing Above the Clouds

Plant the beanstalk seed on the Spiny-covered rooftop (on the northwest side of the Inner Wall) and ride it up into the sky to tackle this challenge area.

In the clouds, hat throw forward to collect three Rocket Flowers immediately, then hold onto your socks. This is a rocket rollercoaster in the sky, where you've got to stay on the track and collect more Rocket Flowers along the way to keep up speed. Any coins or coin rings you collect are a bonus. Make it all the way to the end, nailing the final long jump onto the Power Moon platform, to collect the moon, just before plunging back down through the clouds.

38 Dashing Through the Clouds

During the Rocket Flower-fueled sprint in the sky, an extra Power Moon is tucked on the left side of the path, just after a big jump. It's easy to see where—the piece of land leading to the Power Moon is conspicuously skinny. Think of this like trying to veer into a pitstop at full speed. Land off the previous jump and immediately angle left on the course, toward the little offshoot and Power Moon. Of course, be ready to veer to the right, back onto the course proper.

39 Sphynx Over Bowser's Castle

Just beyond the Main Courtyard checkpoint flag, inside the gate, a pair of Binoculars can be found on a stone ledge on the left, out of the reach of the Pokio guards here. These Binoculars are in prime position to see a rare sight: the Sphynx traveling between kingdoms with a balloon of its own! Scan the skies carefully from this Binocular position, zooming in and fixing your gaze on the Sphynx once it's spotted. Keep your view focused on it long enough to produce a Power Moon as reward. Good eye!

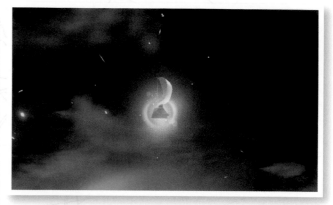

40 I Met a Pokio!

Once the main adventure is resolved and citizens are freer to travel as they please between kingdoms, a curious Bonneter is found on the southern stretch of the Main Courtyard's lengthy wall. The little ghost is curious about the local Pokios. Capture one and bring it here to satisfy the Bonneter's scientific curiosity, earning Mario a moon in the process.

41 Bowser's Kingdom Regular Cup

Entry into Koopa freerunning in Bowser's Kingdom is made near the Beneath the Keep checkpoint flag. From the starting point beneath the Keep, the finish is all the way over by the Odyssey. Basically, the course is the whole kingdom! And, since the race begins at the top of Bowser's great wall, the first thing that happens after the start is a heart-stopping drop all the way down to the courtyard. Roll while shaking the controller for speed boosts when the situation allows for it, like when crossing the Main Courtyard's central path. Complete the race in first to take home the Power Moon prize.

Koopa Freerunning   Best --:--.-- 1st   00:08.25

42 A Rumble Under the Arena Floor

In the flat expanse of Showdown Arena, there's a peculiar spot that can be found with HD Rumble. Move slowly with Mario to detect the source of maximum shaking. When on the correct spot, a ground pound stomp knocks free the rumbling Power Moon. Toe around the northern part of the circular arena to find it.

43 Secret Path to Bowser's Castle

The secret platform is skydiving distance above the Stairface Ogre fortification!

After completing the main adventure, a warp painting frame in Cascade Kingdom fills in with the image of Bowser's Kingdom. Visit Cascade Kingdom again and look for the painting in a cave hidden underwater to access the secret floating island high above the rest of Bowser's floating forts. Don't miss the checkpoint flag up here while picking up the Power Moon.

44 Peach in Bowser's Kingdom

When the adventure's main drama is over and Peach and Tiara are doing some sightseeing of their own, they can be found outside Crazy Cap's on the souvenir shop island. Stop by and greet the princess to receive a Power Moon, and to get credit for checking in with her here. You'll eventually want to make sure to see Peach everywhere she travels!

45 Found with Bowser's Kingdom Art

Once the Broodals are cleaned out of Bowser's Kingdom, the Hint Art painting is viewable alongside the main gate in the Main Courtyard. In it, you can see Poochy digging about in some sand near a cactus. Well, that doesn't leave very many possible locations. Pack up the Odyssey and set sail for Sand Kingdom, then head to the western edge of the territory, near a poison lake inhabited by gentle Moe-Eye creatures. Find a cactus along the edge here and a backdrop that matches the one in the Poochy picture and you're in the right place.

Take Picture of Hint Art   − / + Fullscreen   B Back   A Editing and Posting

🌙 Moons from the Moon Rock

46 Behind the Tall Wall: Poke, Poke!

Get to Third Courtyard (Rear), capture a Pokio, and head to the eastern rooftops. Peering down over the eastern wall, which is normally blank, you'll now find one opened archer's port. With caution, step out over the edge and fall alongside the wall, poking to plant Pokio before falling all the way off the stage. Now carefully flick Pokio into position to spear the open port, revealing the Power Moon inside. It'll appear on the rooftop for collection, so flick back to the top.

47 From Crates in the Moat

Originally, the larger section of the Main Courtyard's water moat has nothing noteworthy in it. After the Moon Rock is accessed, a stack of wooden crates rests down on the watery floor of this section of the moat. Swim down here and break the crates open with underwater cap tosses and ground pounds to reveal the stored Power Moon.

48 Caught on the Giant Horn

The rooftop above the Keep itself has ornate decorative horns at the peaks. The northernmost of the horns can be seen giving off the telltale Power Moon glow. Holding Cappy over the giant horn quickly draws out the hidden prize.

49 Inside a Block at the Gate

One of the metal Bowser boxes by the Main Courtyard gate clearly has something special inside of it, but Mario can't destroy these crates on his own. Capture a Pokio and climb up far enough so the turret above begins rolling out cannonballs. A Pokio can redirect these rolling explosives just about anywhere, if you have the right poking angle. Line up Pokio's beak with the block below and redirect cannonballs toward it until it's blown open, coughing up the Power Moon within.

50 Small Bird in Bowser's Castle

After the Moon Rock is opened, a small flock of birds congregate on an outcropping that's nondescript otherwise. The birds give off a suspicious glow, warranting further investigation. Tiptoe out to the ledge where the birds dwell, getting as close as possible without scaring them off. At the last moment, toss Cappy toward the brightest bird to release a Power Moon.

51 Invader in Bowser's Castle

The right stage-style platform in Main Courtyard Entrance hosts a rare enemy indeed: the Yoo-Foe, a flying saucer that attacks by dropping Goomba troopers. Its own weapons prove its downfall though, since you can capture a Goomba and build a stack of them, reaching high enough to release the capture next to Yoo-Foe and stomp the top of it.

Two stomps brings down the Yoo-Foe, revealing a Power Moon in the wreckage. After one stomp, you have to rebuild the Goomba stack for another shot, and the saucer sprouts an extra row of anti-stack blades, so step lively within the space allowed.

52 Jumping from Flag to Flag

At Main Courtyard Entrance, a mysterious Lock appears near the Spark Pylon landing point. The Key is so well hidden you may not even realize it's around, though. The dancing Bowser flags waving just off the structure's edge might look like just background window dressing, but they're actually functioning flagpoles, so they can be climbed.

Leap from one to the next all the way to the end to find the Key for the Lock. Take your time on the climb to snag the Key and unlock the Power Moon.

53 Bowser's Kingdom Timer Challenge 2

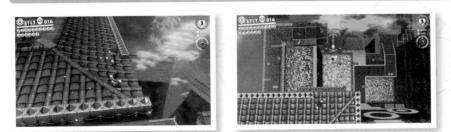

Near the top of the kingdom, around the Beneath the Keep checkpoint flag and Lakitu fishing, another scarecrow can be found next to a steep drop-off positioned right down the barrel of the Outer/Inner Wall climb.

Letting the scarecrow borrow Cappy for a bit generates a green cylindrical platform in the poison moat of the Outer Wall, far away but very distinctive from this height. Jump right off and plunge toward the green cylinder, aiming to land right on top. A Key is on the platform, and the Lock for it is on the roof right in front of the cylinder. To avoid a hard landing, saving both Mario's poor knees and some precious time, ground pound or do a midair cap throw just before falling onto the key floating just over the platform. This lets Mario start moving right away after landing, instead of shivering with the harsh impact for a few seconds. Those seconds might matter, you still have to leap off the green platform and onto the roof, grabbing the Power Moon to complete the challenge.

54 Taking Notes: On the Wall

At Third Courtyard (Rear), on the back ledge that just had an open archer's port before, there is now a music note hovering here. Make sure you're already in Pokio form or have a Pokio ready to capture nearby and touch the note to reveal several duos of notes spread out along the nearby wall. Use Pokio beak-planting and flicking to quickly loft between each group of notes before the timer expires.

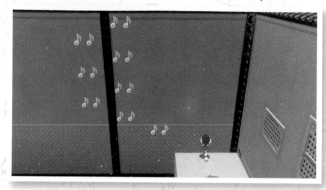

55 Taking Notes with a Spinning Throw

The Main Courtyard Entrance has two stage-like circular platforms just before its big bridge. The left platform eventually has a music note hovering on it. Collecting this begins a challenging timed note-taking challenge. The key here is not to be shy about using spin throws. Spin throw anytime you have a moment to do so then keep running through music notes. Cappy keeps tracking with Mario during a spin throw, making this superbly effective for picking up lots of minor power-ups at once, like here.

56 Third Courtyard Outskirts

A new key-type symbol made of coins appears hovering in the air between Third Courtyard (Front) and Third Courtyard (Rear).

While crossing between them using the Spark Pylon, be ready to shake the controller to make electric Mario divert from the normal path, collecting all the coins and the Power Moon they point toward in one fell swoop.

57 Stone Wall Circuit

On the lowest level of Second Courtyard, where Spinies roam around a small fire pit, there's now a Lock in the floor, and a Spark Pylon along one edge. Traveling along the Spark Pylon reveals a square electrical circuit around the end of the landmass. Hanging in the middle of the square is the Key.

Traveling along the top leg of the square circuit, right above the key, press the Crouch button to end the capture and drop down as Mario. Carefully slide down the wall to the Key, which pops open the Lock! Now, as soon as control returns to Mario, throw Cappy at a nearby pylon within the circuit to return Mario to the electric wire in spark form, before he plunges off the stage. If successful, ride the Spark Pylon wire back to the ledge, then collect the Power Moon revealed by the opened Lock.

58 Bowser's Kingdom Master Cup

Complete the Regular Cup with a championship finish and then open the Moon Rock to reveal the Master Cup. The golden Koopa racer here is much faster than any of the competition in the Regular Cup, making this much more challenging to take first place in. Roll whenever possible, and cut corners on long jumps by using dive jumping and other techniques for max horizontal distance. In places like the Second Courtyard, if you can quickly get onto the rooftop on the right with a little bit of trick wall jumping, it saves time.

Koopa Freerunning — Best 01:46.92 — 00:35.34 — 1st

59 Searching Hexagon Tower

A Slingshot is needed to get to the rooftop containing this Moon Pipe, on the northern section of the Main Courtyard's long wall. The room contains a tall hexagonal tower, with sides colored in alternating orange and green. A Power Moon in here is shattered into five moon shards, but can be reassembled. Capture a Parabones near the top, then use it to fly around the full height and circumference of the tower, collecting coins and moon shards and avoiding other enemies and the poison swamp at the bottom.

Three moon shards are found in orange sections and are just out in the open. Two moon shards are found in green sections, hidden in opaque rooms. To find the shards, fly into the rooms from the correct direction. With all the shards in hand, the Power Moon appears on top of the tower.

60 Center of Hexagon Tower

Atop the hexagonal tower is a Lock. The Key is hidden somewhere in the tower. To find it, fly around the very bottom

of the area, just above the fatal purple muck. One of the green-colored sections has an opening at very low altitude that leads to a Key at the tower's center. Flap in there with Parabones (carefully!) and collect the Key to crack open the Lock back up top. Flap back to the roof of the tower to collect the hidden Power Moon.

61 Climb the Wooden Tower

It's a Pokio endurance climb in here, with long, thin branches of beak-permeable material, ready for athletic Pokios to travel along the length gracefully flicking and spin-jumping. Although there are other creatures along the expanse in places, they shouldn't be an issue to a Pokio.

Advance up the structure, using the beak to climb. When planted by Pokio's beak,

shaking the controller for instant extra-springy flicks is much faster than repeatedly stretching the Pokio's beak down for tension, then releasing.

Some of the pillars spin, so all you need to do is plant the Pokio's beak and then wait for the pillar to spin you around in whichever direction you'd like to let go.

62 Poke the Wooden Tower

As is often the case in Pokio territory, there's a secret here just off the edge near the beginning. Capture a Pokio and look over the side behind the first pillar upward. The Pokio-friendly wall extends downward. Fall down the back side (relative the entrance pipe) to find a stretch of the wall blocked with crates. Fall or flick past the crates and poke to shatter them, making sure to poke again to snag the wall before falling away from the stage. Flick into the gap left by the broken crates to find a stray Power Moon, and a pipe that leads back up to the platform above.

Y Poke   B Jump

Moon Kingdom

Welcome to Honeylune Ridge

REGION AT A GLANCE

Population	Unknown
Size	Lunar
Locals	Rabbitish?
Currency	Star Bit-shaped
Industry	Tourism, Weddings
Temperature	Unknown

INDIGENOUS FLORA & FAUNA

BINOCULARS Can Capture? Yes	**MOONSNAKE** Can Capture? No	**FUZZY** Can Capture? No
ASTRO-LANCEUR Can Capture? No	**PARABONES** Can Capture? Yes	**SHERM** Can Capture? Yes
HAMMER BRO Can Capture? Yes	**TROPICAL WIGGLER** Can Capture? Yes	**BANZAI BILL** Can Capture? Yes
BULLET BILL Can Capture? Yes	**MOE-EYE** Can Capture? Yes	**CHARGIN' CHUCK** Can Capture? Yes
FROG Can Capture? Yes		

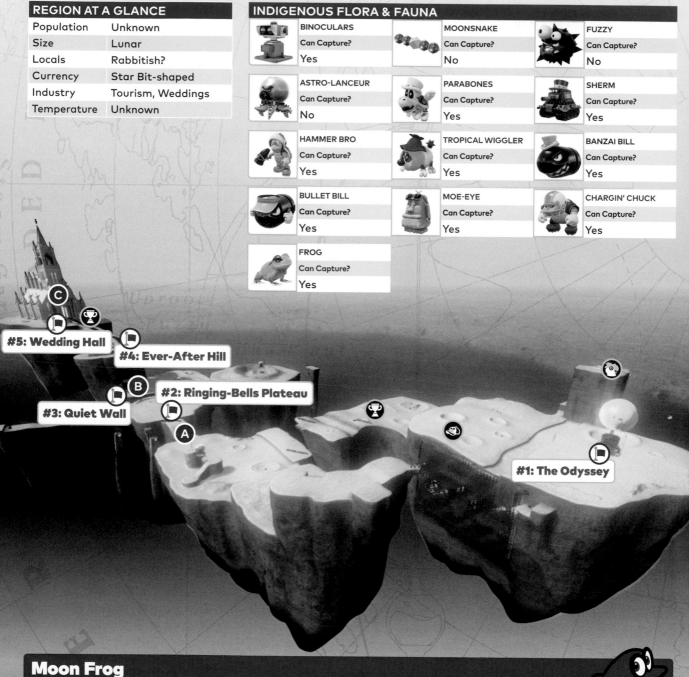

- C
- #5: Wedding Hall
- #4: Ever-After Hill
- #3: Quiet Wall
- B
- #2: Ringing-Bells Plateau
- A
- #1: The Odyssey

Moon Frog

This frog now lives in Honeylune Ridge. Brought to the moon by the first pioneers, it's now considered a good omen for visitors. See one and you'll have a hoppy day

WEDDING HALL

Legends tell of a moon goddess, and this wedding hall is said to have been created in her honor, though no one knows for sure. The stunning exterior contrasts beautifully with the black sky, a symbol of Honeylune Ridge. Weddings here are often open, so lucky travelers can join the party.

LUNAR LIFE FORMS

The surface of the moon is harsh, but a few creatures do live there. Take heed if tempted to study their unique shape and movement up close, as they have sharp spikes. It's probably best to observe them from a safe vantage point.

Interestingly, similar creatures can be found in the Seaside Kingdom. Did life on our planet (which began in the seas) actually originate on the moon?

THREE KEYS TO THE KINGDOM

1. Experience the floaty feeling of lighter gravity.

2. Listen to the glorious bells of the Wedding Hall.

3. See the mysterious Moon Rocks, supposedly energy made solid.

CUBES OF MYSTERY

Possessing unique metallic properties, it's hard to imagine how these cubic Moon Rocks formed naturally, but they can be found in great abundance up here. Similar rocks have also been found in various areas on the planet, and the method of their formation remains shrouded in mystery. We recommend seeking one out and pondering its mysteries up close!

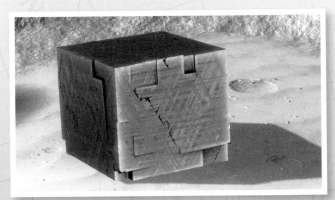

LUNAR INTERIOR: SECRETS

We've heard stories about extensive caverns beneath the lunar interior. There's an entrance directly into the moon rock that's easily accessed, but it sounds quite dangerous inside.

On the other hand, tales abound of thrills and mysteries waiting within, so it may be worth investigating. Be sure to take the necessary precautions before you go, though!

A VIEW TO REMEMBER

Our world as seen from the Wedding Hall is something everyone needs to experience at least once in their life. With the planet as your witness, it's no wonder weddings are held here.

Bowser's Moon Wedding

How many times can the Koopa king run? Is he finally cornered? Are Mario and Cappy going to have to put the saying "to the moon and back" to the test? No comment yet on the first two, but for that last one: absolutely.

The Odyssey touches down on a wide, peaceful plain, sporting unbelievable views of the world dominating the moon's southern sky. In the distance in the other direction you can see the sun, looking oddly cold without hazy air to make the luminosity bloom. To the north, the Wedding Hall can be seen clearly in the distance through the vacuum, and is obviously the destination here. Mario and Cappy are decked out appropriately for the occasion, and the fancy Tux has been added to your wardrobe.

An even more welcome checkpoint is found just over the gap. The Quiet Wall flag is an appropriate name, standing solemnly before a foreboding cavern. There's no way up the high ledge above right now, so you'll have to plunge inside to move on.

Ⓑ Underground Moon Caverns

There's a real capture parade about to take place in the depths of the moon. Deep underground is closer to the core, so gravity feels normal here and jumps are back to normal. Move forward and drop down to the platform visible over the lava below to encounter Parabones, undead flying Koopas. Capture one to gain passage forward over the lakes of lava.

Ⓐ Lunar Crossing

From the Odyssey, the land leads naturally northwest, with diversions along the way available if desired, like stopping by the moon's souvenir store (Crazy Cap's is very forward-thinking in their franchise placement) and hunting for hidden Power Moons and Regional Coins. We advise against using this chapter's "Extend Your Itinerary" section before completing story events in this kingdom, though! No spoilers!

The moon is a much smaller planetary body, so the gravity is lessened here. High jumps are that much higher, and running long jumps and cap jumps cover ground for days. Watch out for spinning Moonsnakes along the way, leaping over them easily thanks to the floatiness of low-G. Astro-Lanceurs are the strongest foes on the moon's surface. These lunar cousins to Brigadier Mollusque-Lanceur III, Dauphin of Bubblaine are just as susceptible to ground pounds from above as their earthbound relative. If avoiding them, also dodge their explosive drill projectiles, which they'll launch at Mario whether he engages them or not.

North across a narrow land bridge from an Astro-Lanceur, the Ringing-Bells Plateau checkpoint is a welcome landmark. High-five the flag and note the focket flowers surviving in the harsh environment. Use one to soar gleefully over the gaps leading to the next northern plateau.

This is a large area, ripe for aerial Parabones exploration.

Aggressive Parabones continue to be pests throughout this area. Platforms farther in are guarded by Sherm tanks. Commandeer a tank or fly around them and dodge their anti-air fire.

Cages in here guard a Life-Up Heart and a Spark Pylon. Opening the cages is straightforward: capture a Sherm and blast the cages apart. The Life-Up Heart cage is optional, but recommended. The Spark Pylon cage must be busted open to progress.

Ride the Spark Pylon upward and slap the big red button found on the next floor with a ground pound. This gets the Bowser platform moving slowly forward. Board the platform and get ready to battle Hammer Bros ahead. Capture one of them, smash the other, then be ready to clear the path ahead. As the platform lurches forward, there are breakable stone walls you'll need to destroy with a rain of hammers.

Beyond the Hammer Bros, another big red button starts a platform that tracks slowly past a series of grates and Tropical Wigglers. Ground pound the button again and start riding the second platform. Capture a Tropical Wiggler to navigate this section, twisting around blockades as the platform moves under them. Stretch out to the left of the platform during a calm section to collect three Regional Coins floating in space there. At the end of the platform's path, you'll need to ditch the Tropical Wiggler and jump onward.

Crossing a bridge ahead, Mario's in for a large surprise—Banzai Bill demolishing the wall ahead and barreling down the bridge toward our heroes.

Naturally, for passage forward capture Banzai Bill with a double cap throw (one throw to knock off Banzai Bill's own hat, another to capture him). Steer the giant bullet over the lava stretches ahead, using the coin rings hovering in midair as a guide. Fly faster (covering more ground before the bullet inevitably explodes after a fleeting time) by shaking the controller. Incoming Bullet Bills won't phase Banzai Bill, and he can shoulder through breakable stones, but don't run head-on into any solid surface. Lose a bullet near a platform here, and you can capture another one as they continue to swarm. Lose a bullet over open lava, however, and it's curtains!

Ditch the current Bill (whether Banzai or Bullet) at the platform with a lone Moe-Eye atop it. Who knows why this poor guy is stuck down here, but his shades provide a way to see the upcoming path. Slap the red button here with another ground pound to create a temporary bridge ahead. It'll be visible for just a second upon creation, but quickly fades into full transparency. Only with a Moe-Eye's shades can you see the bridge then. The Moe-Eye isn't required to get across the gap here—hit the switch, and the bridge exists for a few seconds, whether you can see it or not—but the Moe-Eye can make things easier. Try to get the Regional Coins found on one arm of the invisible bridge along the way, whether with a hat toss as Mario or by flipping up the Moe-Eye shades to scamper across to the coins in time.

Beyond the Moe-Eye's hidden bridge, a Spark Pylon climbs even farther upward. Here you find your first encounter with a classic *Super Mario World* villain: Chargin' Chuck! Capture Chuck and use his charge-up sprint to plow through the onslaught of moon rocks rolling down the path ahead. Chuck has to be left behind to jump up some steps beyond the first bridge of boulders, but another opportunity to recruit a football player is available ahead.

An even narrower bridge is inundated with rolling rocks, with a Chargin' Chuck guarding a small platform at the end of the moving rocks' path. Run along with the flow of the rocks to arrive at Chuck, then capture him. Before moving on, be sure to use his charge sprint to dash effortlessly over the tiny steps and small gaps behind his platform, leading to some Regional Coins. It's just like dashing over small gaps in 8-bit pipes—just don't stop. After collecting the coins and sprinting back across, again lower Chuck's shoulder and plow through a full bridge of oncoming rocks. Another Spark Pylon ahead takes Mario upward a final time, all the way to the cavern's exit... well, almost all the way.

BOSS: MADAME BROODE

It's been a long time since you faced Madame Broode way back in Cascade Kingdom, and in the meantime Mario has thoroughly stomped on all four of her Broodals. She's taken it a little bit personally.

Like before, she tries to squash Mario with the help of her trusty custom gold Chain Chomp. Prioritize dodging the Chain Chomp (and Madame Broode herself) above all other actions. It's faster than it looks! Immediately after dodging Chain Chomp lunges, take the time to hit it once or twice with Cappy, knocking off hats. Once the Chain Chomp has no protection for its perfectly round, shiny head, Cappy can capture it. Madame Broode takes exception to this and swipes at the captured Chain Chomp, so pull heavily left or right to dodge her punches. When she's exhausted, you can pull away and release to trigger the Chain Chomp's special rushing attack, right into her face. Lather, rinse, repeat to silence the Broodals' leader and escape back to the lunar surface.

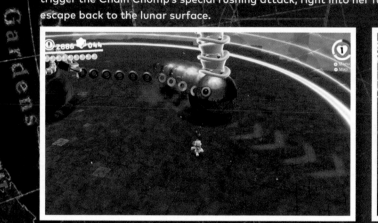

Ⓒ Crashing the Wedding

Take a whiff of fresh vacuum outside and head up and around the path to the Ever-After Hill checkpoint flag. Although you can revisit the Underground Moon Caverns if you want, you can now quickly get back up here with the warp flag. Head across the bridge upward toward the Wedding Hall. Feel the tension building? Before entering the Wedding Hall through the main entrance, detour slightly to the right and check out a little crater with a rock in the center. Crack this rock open for a Life-Up Heart, surely helpful against whatever might be ahead.

Enter the Wedding Hall, pass through the entry foyer, and barge in through the forbidden double doors ahead.

Mario and Cappy's best wedding-crashing faces.

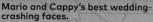

BOSS: BOWSER

Although Bowser gets the literal drop on Mario, it's still finally happening: a climactic straight-up fight, with Mario and Cappy versus Bowser and his bag of tricks and brute strength. Like during the Cloud Kingdom fight, Bowser has a special hat much like the Broodals' or Mario's, and he sends it spinning out at Mario as one of his attacks. Later in the fight, he sends out his white hat along with a slew of purple decoys, just there to get in the way.

Dodge or destroy purple hats, and stop Bowser's white hat cold with a cap throw. While it's upended, run into it to put it on! Bowser loathes this, and leaps away immediately to take defensive measures. He sends out flaming waves along the ground, so jump over these while advancing.

After Bowser stops sending out flaming ribbons on the ground, depending on how far away Mario is, he rolls huge cannonballs into the way. He alternates directions while doing this, so Mario has to zigzag to dodge incoming boulders. Stone boulders can safely be punched apart with Mario's jumping tackle, which ends in a jumping punch thanks to Bowser's hat! Don't try this if Bowser throws out flaming cannonballs, though.

When Mario's finally in boxing range of the lizard, close in and start swinging! Keep an eye on Bowser's posture while unloading with punches from his hat. Eventually, he gets his bearings, starts blocking, and builds up power, unleashing it as a 360-degree flaming tail whip. After feeding him a banquet of knuckle sandwiches, you've got to see this tail swipe coming, and jump over it. After Bowser's used up his energy on this countermeasure, return to punching him. Two full rounds of punches back-to-back sends Bowser spinning off the arena into the spiky background.

Immediately upon recovering from the chin music, Bowser angrily takes to the middle of the battlefield then spews a huge gout of flame back and forth across the whole place. Watch the flame spout carefully and jump over it when Bowser sweeps it past Mario. While it's scary looking, it's not hard to jump over without any tricks, just careful timing.

During the first round of punches to Bowser's chin, he just tail swipes once before he dizzies again and you can feed him more punches. The second round, he tail whips twice, back to back.

For a chance at Hearts, stomp or cap throw purple hats.

In the third and final up-close quarrel, he retaliates to a punching flurry with three tail whips in a row, followed by one more as a last gasp! Be patient, and let him wear himself out before committing to another round of speedbag on Bowser's mug.

The Escape

Cleanly winning three waves against Bowser sees Mario win by TKO, but it's not quite that simple. Mario might have won a temporary battle, but the whole cavern is starting to collapse around them. If an escape route isn't found in a hurry, it won't matter who the victor was!

Brief convening among allies makes it clear: there's only one path out.

Falling debris and boulders present a constant hazard from above from here on out. And, at this point, even the floor becomes an enemy: standing on a section of ground causes it to light up, which signals it'll fall slowly away into the abyss soon. Moon platforms falling away beneath and the roof falling in from above forces the issue: it's time to move forward ASAP.

Where a breakable stone wall appears in the way, slash it apart up close or, far away, shake the controller to destroy it with a fireball. You may encounter some larger pillars, which must be attacked repeatedly to knock them down. Keep watching out for falling boulders when hacking away at a breakable pillar!

Keep pushing forward, and eventually the escape path opens into a wider chamber, with four large pillars set at points around a big blocky central hub. Rush around the circumference of the room, avoiding falling pieces of floor and roof while methodically dismantling each of the four pillars.

Take out all four of the spoke pillars and Cappy announces that the central block now seems vulnerable. Rush to the center and focus attacks on the strange locus here.

Extend Your Stay

Post-Victory: Tourist Season

Once Bowser and the Broodals are no longer roughing up and stealing from residents of kingdoms the world over, people are much more willing to travel and sightsee and explore. You'll find things changed in every kingdom, with eager tourists pouring in and relaxed locals relieved to go about their errands again happy and carefree.

Souvenir Shopping

Moon Kingdom contains 50 Regional Coins in the form of purple Star-bits.

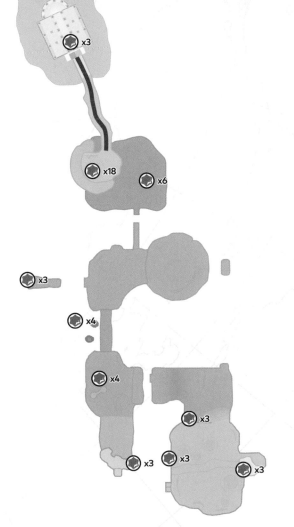

263

Post-Victory: Moons from the Mysterious Moon Rocks

After diving into battle with Bowser in the bowels of the moon and emerging victorious, peace restored, an amazing revelation occurs: there are many more Power Moons locked away in the strange cubes found in each kingdom. Revisit a kingdom and find the Moon Rock within to unleash many new secrets throughout the region. Better yet, the location of all these Power Moons is marked on the Travel Map! Finding their locations usually won't be the hard part, but figuring them out might be.

The Moon Rock here is also ready to be opened, springing eleven new Power Moons into existence throughout the Moon Kingdom.

Crazy Cap

Life-Up Heart	Moon Kingdom Power Moon	Football Helmet	Football Uniform
50	100	50	150

Space Helmet	Space Suit	Moon Kingdom Sticker	Moon Rock Fragment	Moon Lamp
5	10	5	5	25

Coins in High Places

Regional Coins are squirreled away in several places within the Underground Moon Cavern. Controlling Parabones, look for places under shallow bridges where the bone bird can flap to score purple coins.

During the Banzai Bill spring, veer wide to the right around a platform that serves as a Banzai and Bullet Bill cannon to find several hidden purple coins.

The moon's low gravity, the tall reaches of the Wedding Hall's spires, and the springy legs of a captured Frog all combine for some serious lift.

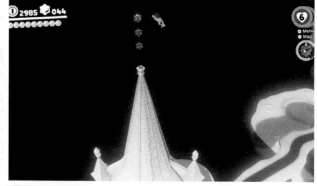

Power Moons

There are 38 Power Moons in Moon Kingdom. It's possible to clear the story portion of Moon Kingdom without collecting any Power Moons at all here. Many Power Moons here aren't available until after Bowser is defeated or after the Moon Rock is opened.

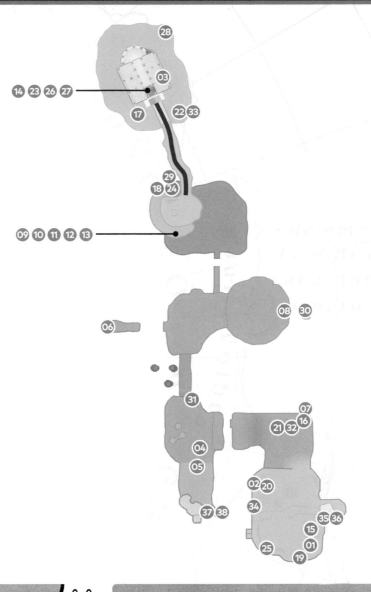

01 Shining Above the Moon

Look around in the airless sky around the Odyssey's balloon and you see a Power Moon floating seemingly high out of reach. It's hovering directly over a small crater just behind the Odyssey. Jumping in the center of this little crater, far under the Power Moon, reveals a hidden block. Jumping on top of this block, then jumping straight up again, reveals another hidden block! See a pattern? After revealing three hidden blocks straight up above the crater, Mario can reach the Power Moon.

02 Along the Cliff Face

An 8-bit pipe can be found straight to the west from where the Odyssey is parked, just a short distance down from the drop-off. The flat landscape it shows access to can be seen stretching along the side of the sheer moon wall here. Enter the pipe and go retro, running sideways along the moon wall in 2D. The Power Moon is found all the way to the left here, beyond some pits to jump over and Fuzzies to avoid.

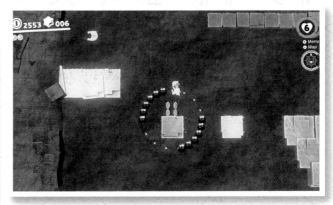

265

03 The Tip of a White Spire

Once you've progressed to Ever-After Hill and gained access to the Wedding Hall exterior, this is one of the easiest Power Moons to find. Observe the spires on the east side of the beautiful building and you notice one spire's tip that's giving off a familiar rainbow twinkle. Use the moon's low gravity (and/or the Frog found behind the building) to climb high enough to get to the spire, then toss Cappy upon it and hold him to draw out the Power Moon.

04 Rolling Rock on the Moon

Locate the concentric double-crater on the large landmass facing the one the Odyssey is planted upon, beyond a series of Moonsnakes and over a pit. The area is guarded by a powerful Astro-Lanceur, so watch out. Check the center of the crater for a curious rock that glows once it's dislodged. Kick and toss the rock around until it breaks, freeing a Power Moon stuck inside.

05 Caught Hopping on the Moon!

South of **Rolling Rock on the Moon** and the Astro-Lanceur, a hare can be found scampering timidly away on the moon's dunes. Slow the rascally rabbit down by smacking it with a rock or Cappy, then grab it before it recovers to shake loose a Power Moon.

06 Cliffside Treasure Chest

West of the Ringing-Bells Plateau warp point is evidence of a bridge that once stood across a gap but is now broken. A short platform trails off into space, and a treasure chest is visible on a finger of land over the gap.

Around the warp point and this gap, Rocket Flowers are sprouting on the moon. Pick one up with Cappy and jump across the gap with rocket power. After cracking open the chest and collecting the Power Moon, check the back end of this rock for three well-hidden Regional Coins. Rocket Flowers are available here for leaping back over the abyss. More lazily, Mario could simply warp back to the nearby checkpoint flag.

A running long jump into a dive jump also grants enough distance to cross the gap.

07 Moon Kingdom Timer Challenge 1

Heading directly north from the Odyssey until there's nowhere else to go, look for a little shelf down off the edge of the moon, in the northeast corner of the first general area. You find a lone scarecrow down here. Affix Cappy to its brow to reveal a series of checkered blocks along the side of the plateau here, leading to a distant Power Moon. In the low gravity of the moon, Mario's lengthier jumps travel quite far indeed. To make it to the moon on time, run confidently to the edge and perform a running long jump at the last moment, launching toward the next platform. Repeat this all the way to the Power Moon, long jumping off the edge of a platform three times in a row.

⑧ Taking Notes: On the Moon's Surface

East of the Ringing-Bells Plateau checkpoint, look for a subtle crater nestled up to the edge, with a featureless platform about a moon-gravity long jump's distance out from the drop-off. Hovering in this crater is a glowing music note, which triggers a note-collecting challenge when Mario picks it up. Notes appear out over the gap to the blank platform in two lines. Both conform to the arc of a running long jump, so the solution is natural: line up one row of notes, running long jump over the gap through the whole mess of them. Then line Mario up and do it on the way back too, over the other line, back to the Moon Kingdom's main landmass. Grab all the notes quickly before the timer runs out to unlock the Power Moon hidden in the crater.

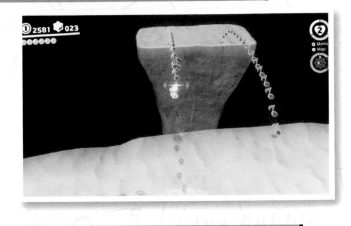

⑨ Under the Bowser Statue

This is one of several moons hidden inside the cave near the Quiet Wall warp flag. Enter from here (the lower entrance, not the one above at Ever-After Hill) and don't drop down to the Parabones platform below. Instead, stay up here and inspect the robust statues here. One of them looks like it can be fitted with a cap... Jump and toss Cappy onto the statue to capture it, allowing it to be nudged slowly forward, exposing a Power Moon underneath.

⑩ In a Hole in the Magma

When passing through the Underground Moon Caverns leading from the Quiet Wall checkpoint flag all the way up to the Ever-After Hill flag, there are a few secret moons to uncover. In the first section, with Parabones flying aggressively and Sherm tanks ready to fire, capture a Parabones and flap over nearby where the caged Spark Pylon leads out of this lava bowl. Flap curiously around the lava surrounding the Spark Pylon platform, looking for an odd, deep, cylindrical gap in the lava's flow. It's safe to carefully drift down this hole if the Parabones doesn't touch the

edges. Deep in the hole in the magma, the Parabones collects a Key, which automatically pops the Lock tucked away behind the Spark Pylon. Flap furiously back up out of the gap, and fly back to the Spark Pylon platform to collect the Power Moon held in the Lock.

⑪ Around the Barrier Wall

In the Underground Moon Caverns, progress to the section where a Banzai Bill plows through a wall of breakable bricks and blazes across a bridge at Mario. Throw Cappy twice quickly to knock off Banzai Bill's protective hat then capture him, and begin flying along the normal path, following the coin rings and batting aside Bullet Bills with Banzai Bill's bulk. While flying forward, watch out to the left. Behind one of the walls along the way here, on a lower ledge, a Power Moon rests. Go ahead and smack Banzai Bill right up into this ledge to pop Mario out, allowing you to collect the hidden moon. To get back on track, wait for Bullet Bills to sniff out Mario's location here and come swarming, then capture one and fly onward.

⑫ On Top of the Cannon

There's almost no hint that this moon exists, except for the title, obtained from Talkatoo! Down in the depths of the caverns, there are several Power Moons to snag with the help of the Bills (Bullet and Banzai). One of these is right on top of one of the main Banzai Bill canon emplacements. Not the first one, which takes Mario by surprise as he crosses the bridge heading into the Bullet Bill segment, but the next canon, which floats freely in space. Ride a bullet to this platform, slam right into it to pop Mario out and onto the top, then ground pound the center to dig up the Power Moon.

⑬ Fly to the Treasure Chest and Back

While taking a breather somewhere in the bullet-dominated section, high above the lava, look around and locate the lower entrance, where Mario comes in from the Quiet Wall flag. Spy where the dual Bowser statues are, then look high above that. Look for a square-shaped cutout in the rock above the entrance. That's the target. Hijack a Banzai Bill and make a beeline for that square cutout, shaking the controller for speed bursts. Pilot the bullet into the gap and pop out, ready to open the hidden Power Moon treasure chest up here.

⑭ Up in the Rafters

Climb up the exterior of the Wedding Hall all the way to the golden ringing bell and look underneath it. Surprisingly, there's a circular hole here leading into the Wedding Hall. Drop down and Mario ends up standing on narrow rafters above a room inside. Carefully tip-toe around up here to grab the Power Moon, then drop down. If you haven't yet entered the church proper, don't progress farther inside yet unless you're ready to set off irreversible events. If you're not done exploring, walk back outside after dropping down.

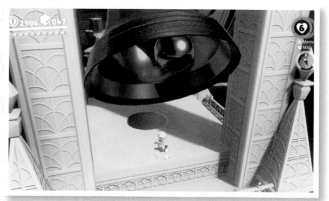

15. Sneaking Around in the Crater

On return trips to the moon, inspect the large crater near where the Odyssey touches down. Looking carefully, you might see a strange stretched spot in the terrain, like something moving just under the surface. Slow this spot down like chasing a rabbit, by pegging it with Cappy. Then jump above the dazed spot and ground pound it, revealing the Power Moon sneaking around just under the ground.

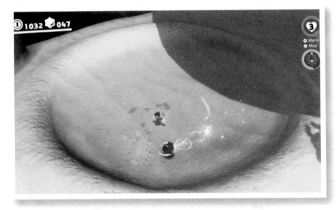

16. Found on the Moon, Good Dog!

Befriend the dog idling near the souvenir shop, then head down the ramps slightly north to the open plain where the trace-walking Koopa and Moonsnakes are found. There are lots of spots where the friendly pooch will sniff and dig, revealing a glowing spot you can stomp for coins, but guide the dog to the northeast corner of this area to reveal a buried Power Moon.

17. Moon Shards on the Moon

Once Bowser no longer occupies the Wedding Hall, moon shards can be found floating around its exterior. To assemble a full Power Moon from the pieces, track down all five. The Frog found behind the hall can help Mario climb more easily.

1. In a crater near the Wedding Hall warp flag
2. On the rear roof in the center
3. On the left-side roof (looking at the main entrance)
4. On the back of the top spire, above the bell
5. In front of the stained glass window on the right side of the tower (looking at the main entrance)

Collect all the shards to produce a Power Moon above the main entrance.

18. Moon Quiz: Amazing!

Surprisingly, the Sphynx is up here too, around a back corner at the foot of the Quiet Wall. He won't have time to entertain Mario's riddle itch while Bowser's still up to no good, but he'll indulge when things have calmed down. Complete Power Moon #24 first, revealing Sphynx's vault. Continue talking to Sphynx after he's moved aside and he keeps asking questions, realizing Mario isn't done yet. Answer all of Sphynx's questions correctly for another Power Moon! The answers to his riddles here are:

1. Sheep
2. Moon
3. Below the bell
4. Floated by airship sail

⑲ Thanks, Captain Toad!

Look for Captain Toad enjoying the spectacular view near the edge south of the Odyssey's landing spot. Talk to him to receive a Power Moon. He won't show up here until Bowser's scourge is ended. He'll be here later, once it's safer for folks to look around and explore.

⑳ Shopping in Honeylune Ridge

Like other Crazy Cap's stores, the souvenir shop here offers a unique local Power Moon for 100 coins. Take note also of new outfits available here in space. Pick up the Football Suit with gold coins, and the Space Suit with purple coins.

㉑ Walking on the Moon!

On return trips to the moon, look for a Koopa wearing a space helmet to start up the trace walking challenge. This Koopa is found around the Moonsnakes, north of Odyssey's base of operations, or Crazy Cap's. He wants you to walk in a big, precise circle for him, but the guidelines disappear quickly after you get started.

㉒ Moon Kingdom Regular Cup

The freerunning challenge here is one of the longer ones, stretching from one end of the kingdom to the other. The starting point is by the Wedding Hall, and the finish is on the crag overlooking the southwest corner.

The route takes Mario across the gaps and bridges leading south. Veer hard left when jumping from Ever-After Hill to the bottom, to make the skinny bridge below. In open areas, keep rolling and/or long jumping to move forward quicker, but be careful not to smack into anything or career off an edge. The final mesa can be mounted by wall jumping up the facing walls there.

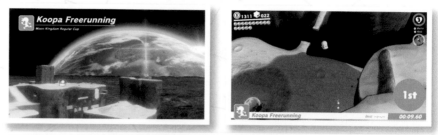

㉓ Doctor in the House

What with cake and stew, I have overeaten and my stomach hurts. Is there a doctor nearby?

After the wedding is successfully crashed, some reception attendees remain behind, enjoying the ambiance of the hall, or maybe just cabbaging some leftovers. One such guest is a shivering Shiverian found on the right side of the main chamber inside. The poor thing ate too much food and needs medical attention! How can Mario help here?

Show up decked out in Dr. Mario's coat and cap to help alleviate the Shiverian's tummy ache. These costume pieces become available in shops once the Odyssey is powered up with 220-240 Power Moons.

24 Sphynx's Hidden Vault

After completing the main adventure, visit the Sphynx tucked around in the kingdom's quietest corner, contemplating whatever things Sphynx contemplates. Talk to him and he is enticed to ask a question for an attentive observer of *Super Mario Odyssey's* ending. Answer correctly ("Rocket Flower") and Sphynx rumbles aside, uncovering the entrance to his vault. Step inside to pick up piles of coins, and to pop open a treasure chest holding a Power Moon.

25 A Tourist in the Moon Kingdom!

The moon is eventually paid a visit by the Tostarenan tourist who can be set on his way from Sand Kingdom after Bowser is defeated. After finishing the story and clearing any outstanding emergencies in each kingdom, visit the tourist and cabbie in the order Sand, Metro, Cascade, Luncheon, Moon, Mushroom, and Sand again to receive Power Moons along the way.

26 Peach in the Moon Kingdom

Mario and Cappy might be ready to relax after their adventure is over, but Peach and Tiara aren't. They go exploring all the kingdoms themselves, and finding them in each region is good for a Power Moon and a choice photo opportunity. After you visit Peach and Tiara at every terrestrial location, they check out the moon, on purpose this time. Find them at a dizzying height, enjoying the view from just under the Wedding Hall's resounding bell.

27 Found with Moon Kingdom Art

Hint Art in the Moon Kingdom is found in the Wedding Hall, after defeating Bowser. The art depicts a red industrial area partially overgrown with lush vegetation, a scarecrow on one side and adorable Poochy burying something on the other. If this looks an awful lot like Wooded Kingdom, that's because it's Wooded Kingdom. Find a similar cubby containing a scarecrow on one end and nothing on the other, and ground pound the empty side to garner a hidden Power Moon.

🌙 Moons from the Moon Rock

28 Mysterious Flying Object

Inspect behind the Wedding Hall by the sheer edge, around where the lone Frog hangs out, in the northeast corner. A rainbow glitter can be seen, and the source can be traced to a tiny little UFO that lands skittishly on the edge. No matter how quickly you advance upon the UFO, it flits away before Mario can get his hands (or cap) on it. But move carefully to the UFO's landing spot, then look around in first-person view, panning Mario's gaze back and forth around the area. The curious UFO reappears nearby, almost like a Boo ghost sneaking up on Mario facing the other way. Position Mario properly while looking around, and he scores a Power Moon from the UFO!

29 Hidden on the Side of the Cliff

This Power Moon is hidden directly above the sneaky Sphynx, directly below the upper exit from the Underground Moon Cavern. Warp to Ever-After Hill and run to the cavern's mouth here and look over the side to find it. Hop off the side and drift down into the floating Power Moon to collect it.

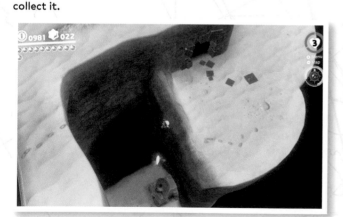

30 Jumping High as a Frog

This Power Moon is located high above the platform involved with Power Moon #08. This is east of the trace-walking Koopa and the Moonsnakes on the surface, and the Power Moon is far too high for Mario to reach on his own.

The solution is to capture the Frog hanging out behind the Wedding Hall. Hop back over here using the Frog's tremendous jumps, then jump straight up from the center of the platform here to pull in the Power Moon.

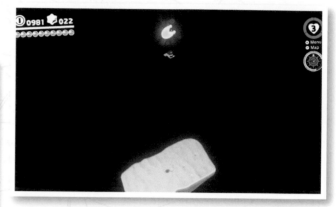

31 Moon Kingdom Timer Challenge 2

A scarecrow can initiate a Timer Challenge just south of the land bridge leading to the Ringing-Bells Plateau warp flag. Fit Cappy onto the Scarecrow to reveal the Power Moon on a small platform to the left of the land bridge. Take a running long jump forward over the Moonsnake here to arrive near the platform quickly. Take a careful jump across from the bridge to the platform, then another up onto the Power Moon blocks.

32 Walking on the Moon: Again!

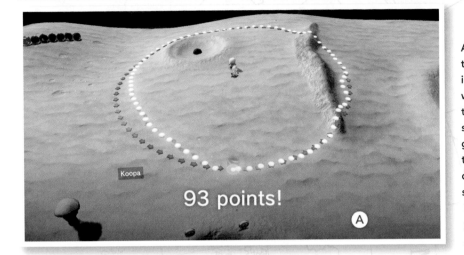

93 points!

Koopa

(A)

After Power Moon #21 is acquired and the Moon Rock is opened, this contest is available. Talk to the Koopa trace-walking fan in the Moonsnake plains to try it out. Again, you have to walk the same circle that's displayed, and the guide arrows fade out before you have time to complete the path. This time, the arrows fade out much faster. The target score to gain the moon is 90 points.

33 Moon Kingdom Master Cup

Unlock the Moon Rock and complete the first freerunning challenge to unlock this one. The same Koopa by the Wedding Hall in the north gets Mario set up against the usual Koopa racers, plus a notorious gold racer.

As before, roll and long jump when the coast is clear, and stay steady elsewhere. Cross the first major gap on the left, across the skinny bridge.

From the rabbit hill below to the high plain holding the finish, it's possible to jump all the way up without using back and forth wall jumps. This requires a max-height triple jump off the top of the hill, topped with a dive jump for even more height, drifting toward the ledge all the while. Wall slide near the top, wall jump away from the wall, then cap toss and tackle in the direction of the goal. Gain enough height at each stage and you'll make it all the way up from the bottom, shaving off a huge amount of time.

Koopa Freerunning
Moon Kingdom Master Cup

Koopa Freerunning   Best 01:04.86   00:30.40   1st

34 Taking Notes: In Low Gravity

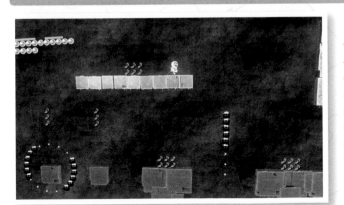

Walk west of the Odyssey, drop down to the 8-bit pipe off the edge, and hop in to explore the large 8-bit chamber on the side of the wall. At the very top of the chamber, where some hidden Regional Coins are located, a song note can now be found. Pick it up to begin a note-collecting Timer Challenge. Fall from up here and run and jump quickly around the Fuzzies, collecting all the notes before time is up to reveal another Power Moon in here.

(35) Center of the Galaxy

Enter the Moon Pipe that appears on Talkatoo's tall bluff. Inside, a huge 8-bit vista spreads vertically before Mario.

Enter the 8-bit pipe here to warp inside of the 2D landscape. Circular globes in this 8-bit pipe act as little celestial bodies when Mario moves close enough, pulling him in with their gravity. Controlling Mario depends on his current orientation, which takes some getting used to while running circles around tiny planets.

From the first area, head to the small moving planet in the top-right. Ride it to the top of its path, then dash and jump upward toward the coins above. Get high enough and Mario's center of gravity flips and he falls upward to the next portion. From here, use more moving planets to navigate up and to the right, counter-clockwise over the lava, homing in on the Power Moon and exit pipe at the center.

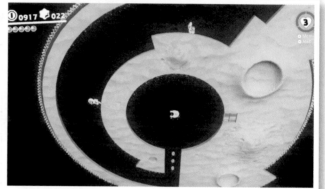

(36) Edge of the Galaxy

When going for Center of the Galaxy, divert near the top and jump toward a little ledge standing before a sea of lava. Just above, the hint of another planet can be seen. From the highest ground, jump upward to get pulled in to an orbiting pair of planets tucked away up here, spinning around a Power Moon at their barycenter. Collect the Power Moon by leaping between the planets, before jumping back downward toward the exit.

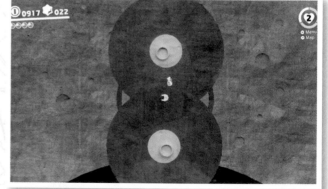

(37) Navigating Giant Swings

Head to the tall crag with the shaved-off top in the southwest, and start climbing. The summit can be achieved by wall jumping between facing walls on the way up. At the top, a Moon Pipe leads to an especially tricky challenge room.

Huge blue pegs swing back and forth in here, in between small permanent platforms and some Astro-Lanceur enemies (who can also be used as bounce platforms thanks to ground pounding off their octopus domes). A Power Moon along with the exit pipe are located at the far side. A blue peg swinging up from under Mario while he falls can catch him and carry him up to the top of the peg's path. A blue peg swinging down and away from Mario drops him to his doom unless you take evasive maneuvers, jumping off the peg to another foothold, or quickly running up to the top of the peg, where Mario can still find a foothold while it swings the other way. Blue pegs mounted high in the air over platforms Mario needs to jump past can be nuisances to avoid, but also a means to gain higher ground.

The most challenging platforming stretch is at the end. Three blue pegs swing over space before an Astro-Lanceur serving as bouncer for the exit pipe! You have just enough time on each blue peg in the horizontal position to jump to the next one. Bounce right off the top of the floating octopus and collect the Power Moon behind it before exiting.

(38) A Swing on Top of a Swing

In the swing challenge room found from a Moon Pipe, look upward to see where a swinging blue peg is located above another one. This presents an interesting upward platforming challenge. Get underneath the lower blue platform, then jump straight up into it as it swings back down, picking Mario up along the way. Run up its length to the hinge, and be ready to repeat the process on the fly as the blue peg above swings down in turn. After successfully transitioning to the upper blue peg on its upswing, it's just a short hike to collect the Power Moon up here.

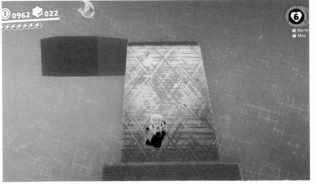

Welcome to Peach's Castle

REGION AT A GLANCE

Population	Middling
Size	Wide-ish
Locals	Toads
Currency	64-esque
Industry	Pipes, Tourism
Temperature	Average 81°F

INDIGENOUS FLORA & FAUNA

	BINOCULARS		GOOMBA		MINI GOOMBA
	Can Capture?		Can Capture?		Can Capture?
	Yes		Yes		No

	MAW-RAY		CHINCHO		BURRBO
	Can Capture?		Can Capture?		Can Capture?
	No		No		No

	BULLET BILL (2D)		FUZZY
	Can Capture?		Can Capture?
	No		No

#3: Goomba Woods

#2: Peach's Castle Main Entrance

A

#4: Mushroom Pond

#5: Yoshi's House

#1: The Odyssey

Not Mushrooms

These Fruits thrive in the warm climate here and are a favorite of many creatures that reside in the Mushroom Kingdom.

A LOVELY PORTRAIT IN GLASS

Because Princess Peach is so often absent from her kingdom, her citizens took it upon themselves to create a stained-glass portrait of her on the castle balcony. While a pale reflection of the genuine article, the portrait brings comfort to the citizenry when their princess can't be with them.

TOWERING MYSTERIES

In older times, the towers dotting the landscape here were watchtowers. Now they hold and preserve a series of mysterious paintings. These incredibly detailed works are so real that admirers speak of being pulled into another world by the paintings.

However, it's extremely rare for tourists to be permitted to see them, due to some undescribed danger, and casual visits are discouraged.

THREE KEYS TO THE KINGDOM

1. Visit Peach's Castle, the face and heart of the kingdom.

2. Relax in the various soothing spots scattered about.

3. Stroll through the rolling hills and dales of the castle grounds.

PLACES TO RELAX

The Toads of the Mushroom Kingdom value their relaxation and have created several lovely spots on the castle grounds for that purpose. Neither too small nor too large, and with just the right amount of ornamentation, these plazas and courtyards exemplify the best traits of this kingdom.

SLIGHTLY SCARY WOODS

Even the serene Mushroom Kingdom has its more dangerous locales. This forest was originally planted for mushroom cultivation, but while the mushrooms have flourished, a large number of wild Goombas have also moved in. While it's come to be known as Goomba Woods, it's still a pleasant place for a stroll, so if you're not afraid of these fearsome beasts, why not treat yourself to a walk?

A CASTLE'S WATER FEATURE

The only lake on the castle grounds features a small but lovely waterfall and is a popular spot to visit. The lake formed naturally, but some claim that its shape is familiar. Hmm...

Talk to the Toad at the Castle!

The most pressing concerns of Mario and Cappy's strange odyssey are dealt with, but that doesn't mean everything is done. Far from it! Immediate danger dispensed with, the heroes are only now returning to Mario's home, the Mushroom Kingdom. In this cheerful green realm, there's more to see and do, and surprises still to come.

The first order of business is to visit the castle and see how Princess Peach is doing!

...except you'll quickly discover that Peach and Tiara have already packed up and left. They're going on a trip of their own, on purpose this time! Perhaps you'll see them around as you revisit previous kingdoms.

While Peach may not be here, one of her trustiest attendants is. Greet Archivist Toadette by the empty throne inside the castle. The archivist can award bonus Power Moons for many different feats, some obvious, some not. For example, just by showing up here, you'll be ready to receive the award for rescuing Princess Peach, so that'll get Mario started on really amassing Power Moons for fun. For a full list of achievement Power Moons available from Archivist Toadette, see the end of this chapter, beyond Power Moon #43.

Aside from the fun of it, there are material reasons to keep exploring and collecting Power Moons. More Power Moons means more outfits unlocked for purchase in Crazy Cap's. And there are still whole new locations to uncover, for garnering 250 and 500 Power Moons...

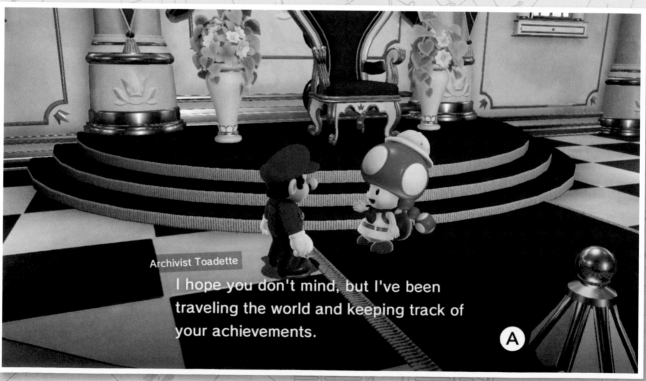

Archivist Toadette

I hope you don't mind, but I've been traveling the world and keeping track of your achievements.

Extend Your Stay

Home is Where the Hearts Are

The Mushroom Kingdom is ripe for exploration right from the get-go. There's no immediate threat to deal with, nor Moon Rock to pry open.

⭐ Souvenir Shopping

Mushroom Kingdom contains 100 pieces of souvenir currency in the form of star-branded Regional Coins.

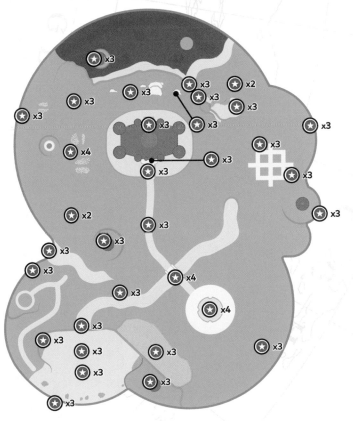

279

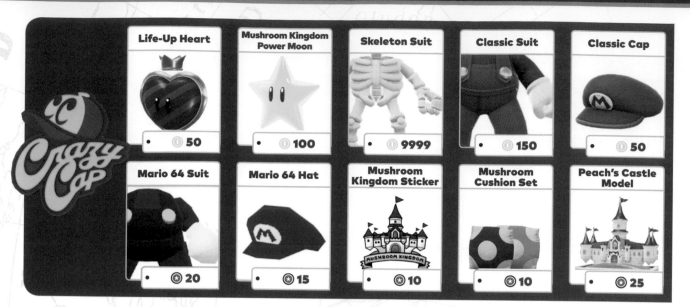

Life-Up Heart	Mushroom Kingdom Power Moon	Skeleton Suit	Classic Suit	Classic Cap
• ⓘ 50	• ⓘ 100	• ⓘ 9999	• ⓘ 150	• ⓘ 50

Mario 64 Suit	Mario 64 Hat	Mushroom Kingdom Sticker	Mushroom Cushion Set	Peach's Castle Model
• ✪ 20	• ✪ 15	• ✪ 10	• ✪ 10	• ✪ 25

Coins In High Places

Plenty of Regional Coins are found along edges of tall tower roofs, or hovering above the flagpoles and spires atop the towers. Look to the skyline to spy many glimpses of purple.

On the west side of the area, look for a small tunnel cutting under the terrain. Four coins are tucked away inside.

The sneakiest coins in the realm are just the edge. Look past the waterfall pouring out from Mushroom Pond to see Regional Coins hovering above the sheer drop-off. Downward hat throws from the edge can safely recover the purple coins below.

★ Power Moons

There are 43 unique Power Moons at Mushroom Kingdom, and an additional 61 attainable by fulfilling achievement criteria for Archivist Toadette.

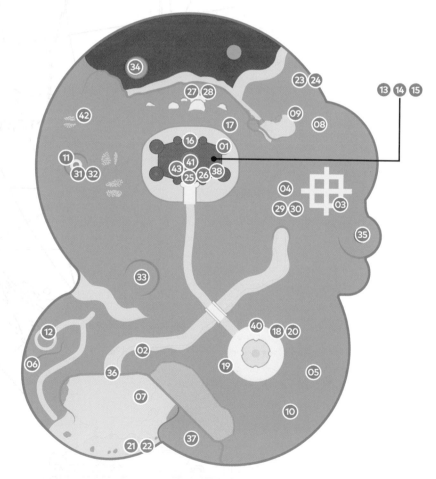

01 Perched on the Castle Roof

Peach's Castle's roof can be accessed from the west side of the castle. Find the scarecrow here and cap throw toward it to briefly reveal a big staircase leading all the way up to the top. Jump up quickly and head toward the northeastern-most spire. Climb to the top of the flagpole and handstand jump off to collect the Power Moon.

There are several reasons to want to access the castle's roof.

02 Pops Out of the Tail

Standing along the stream west of Talkatoo is a tree with a leafless, tail-like branch. It almost looks fluffy. Toss Cappy upon it and hold him for several seconds to coax a hidden Power Moon out of the tree.

03 Caught Hopping at Peach's Castle!

The garden found in northeast Mushroom Kingdom is well-tended, but nevertheless has a mild hare problem. The rabbit here quickly runs away among the garden paths. Slow it down with cap throws to make it predictable enough to catch up to.

04 Gardening for Toad: Garden Seed

A Toad fascinated by artful horticulture maintains a little hedge garden in northeast Mushroom Kingdom. Seeds can be found throughout the kingdom that help Toad populate four empty flowerpots in a little square in the middle of the garden. The closest seed is located just a short distance away, in the small valley to the immediate west. Grab it and toss it in one of the pots and forget about it for a while—you don't need to water these seeds, Toad takes care of that, but it will still take some time for the plant to grow.

05 Gardening for Toad: Field Seed

A seed can be found in a pleasant grove of flowers, trees, and chipmunks south of the garden, near the Odyssey itself. Retrieve the seed and get it planted in a pot to begin the growing process. Check back occasionally and eventually the plant will have a glowing golden bulb at the top, ready to burst open and reveal a Power Moon as the fruit.

06 Gardening for Toad: Pasture Seed

Explore the western edge of the land just south of the sheep herder's pen, just north of the path to Mushroom Pond. Tucked away behind a solitary tree and some sprouting mushrooms is another seed. Haul this one over to the garden and plant it, then check back sometimes to see if it's ready to cough up the Power Moon spoils.

07 Gardening for Toad: Lake Seed

Under Dorrie splashing about in Mushroom Pond, a seed can be found resting on the seafloor. Ground Pound down to the bottom to grab it, then return to the surface and carry it back to Toad's garden to get it planted properly. Like the other seeds, this one takes some time before it's ready to blossom, revealing the Power Moon instead.

08 Grow a Flower Garden

At the northeast corner of the land, a dense double-circle of plant sprouts are found clustered together. Stand in the center and spin throw to make them all blossom as hat flowers, brightly uncovering a secret Power Moon.

09 Mushroom Kingdom Timer Challenge

At the northeast edge of the shaded Goomba Woods, a scarecrow can be found. Fitting Cappy onto it triggers a local Timer Challenge, where a Power Moon at the other end of the Goomba Woods (to the northwest) must be snatched up before it disappears. It's difficult, but possible, to pull off this challenge by gracefully rolling down the hill away from the scarecrow into the woods, bouncing toward the Power Moon at Mario's top speed.

He's not wrong.

If doing it under Mario's own power proves difficult, it's possible to game the contest in his favor. Before giving up Cappy  to the scarecrow and starting off the event, look around nearby and find a Toad admiring a Motor Scooter. A Motor Scooter that can be parked close to the scarecrow before starting this challenge. With a motor vehicle purring under Mario's command, getting down the hill and through the woods in time should be no problem.

10 Found at Peach's Castle! Good Dog!

The friendly and fashionable pooch seen previously in Seaside Kingdom is here too, man's best friend to Toads and plumbers alike. Befriend the dog with a brief game of Cappy catch, then lead it around the kingdom to see if the dog will reveal treasure just under the grass anywhere. To uncover a buried Power Moon, lead the dog to the southeastern part of the map, on a little hill overlooking the Odyssey and the nearby fountain.

⑪ Taking Notes: Around the Well

Toward the west side of the region, near the scarecrow who enables castle roof access, you find a wide well. Around the base of the well is an 8-bit pipe that begins a music note challenge. Enter the pipe and run to the right, wrapping around the cylinder of the well's wide, earthen base. You can keep running right behind the 3D environment, sliding through in a 2D secret. Grab the music note on the far end of this path and be ready to dash back to the pipe entrance. Grab all the notes along the way, which spawns another ring of music notes outside of the 8-bit pipe. Exit and spin throw in the middle of all the notes to collect them all at once, completing the challenge and scoring a Power Moon for Mario.

⑫ Herding Sheep at Peach's Castle

A Toad shepherd has lost his sheep flock. His pen is on the west side of Mushroom Kingdom, just north of Mushroom Pond. He's lost a half-dozen sheep, all spread throughout the area. To drive a sheep home, locate it, then just coax it naturally—

they're naturally skittish and run from Mario. Chase them all back toward the pen, speeding the process with cap throws to flick them forward if you like. Assemble Toad's sheep and he'll gratefully hand over a Power Moon. The sheep are located as follows:

By Mushroom Pond

North of the shepherd's pen, by the 2D well

East side of Goomba Woods

West side of Goomba Woods

East side of Mushroom Kingdom

South of the Odyssey by the warp painting on the ground

Herding multiple sheep at once is possible, if a handful.

⑬ Gobbling Fruit with Yoshi

Yoshi's egg can be found atop Peach's Castle. Scarecrow stairs on the west side of the castle lead to the top, allowing the dinosaur friend to be captured and controlled. Yoshi has a floaty flutter jump that is more controllable than Mario's non-Cappy jumps. The speedy dino also runs faster than Mario, and can stick his tongue out in an attack that doubles as an item collecting move and a movement option. While getting used to controlling Yoshi, gobble up fruits found in pairs and trios throughout the kingdom. Eating ten reveals a Power Moon.

This is Yoshi's favorite food!

14 Yoshi's Second Helping!

After the first Power Moon received from chowing on Fruits, there are still more to find. A couple of Fruits are wedged in pipes, blocking access to challenge rooms. Some Fruits are simply hovering in the open, like those in a few spots around the castle's moat. Plenty of Fruits are found under or above tree canopies. Gather 20 total to gain a second Power Moon from seeking fruit.

15 Yoshi's All Filled Up!

To get the third and final gustatory Power Moon, you need to coax Yoshi to wolf down all 30 of the Mushroom Kingdom's Fruits. Use Yoshi's tongue to pull in Fruits hovering over drop-offs or high above tall trees, near a ledge or hill that allows a running start into a full-height flutter jump. Yoshi can also mount the tip-top of tall trees, standing gingerly on the spire, by jumping next to the tree then sticking the very top with his tongue. Yoshi flips up onto the top like a ledge, allowing him to jump straight up to collect Fruits that seem impossible to reach.

16 Love at Peach's Castle

Finding love for this Goombette is a little more involved than matchmaking Goombas elsewhere. The nearby Goomba Woods to the north provides plenty of Goomba suitors, but the Goombette waits across the castle's moat on a little ledge, and Goombas are not water faring creatures. The water must be drained somehow.

Plunge into the moat and check out the wooden pegs stuck in the floor here. There are four pegs stuck around the circumference of the moat. Pop them all out with some help from Cappy, which allows the water to drain out of the moat. At this point, you're free to build a healthy Goomba stack in the woods, then bring them all over. Hop into the dried-out moat and approach the Goombette for a well-earned meet cute, and a Power Moon.

17 Toad Defender

At the little encampment of friendly Toads between Peach's Castle and Goomba Woods, a stoic Toad can be found guarding a small opening containing a Power Moon. He vows to keep the Power Moon inside safe against all the icky Goombas found close by in the forest. His fortitude, shamefully, doesn't stand up to a real stress test. Gather up a stack of captured Goombas in the woods, then hike up here with the baddies to scare Toad off his post. Then, drop the Goomba capture and step inside the gap, scooping up the Power Moon.

Sorry, buddy!

⑱ Forever Onward, Captain Toad!

All this traveling can wear out even the hardiest, most intrepid explorer. No one is happier to be home in the Mushroom Kingdom than Captain Toad, found relaxing in the sun atop Crazy Cap's

mushroom-shaped souvenir store. Toad may be temporarily semi-retired, but he still has one last Power Moon to hand over to Mario for visiting him in another kingdom.

⑲ Jammin' in the Mushroom Kingdom

I'm traveling all over in search of all different kinds of music.

Ⓐ

A Toad near the fountain is clearly rocking out, with music notes drifting pleasantly out of his headphones. He's listening for tunes in particular, and if you play them for him you might get a pleasant surprise. He'll show you how to open the music list and put on your favorite tracks at will. Here, he asks for a "Flat-N-Blocky classic," a clue pointing toward 8-bit stages. Pick a retro tune from the music list and Toad offers up a Power Moon as a sign of mutual music appreciation.

Jammin' Toad can be found in some other kingdoms, where he'll request other tunes, too! Visit more unique areas to uncover more tracks in the music list.

⑳ Shopping Near Peach's Castle

Stop by the Mushroom Kingdom's mushroom souvenir stand to find a local Power Moon for sale for 100 coins, as usual. Gather it up, then peruse other goods to see what's new.

I'll Take Ten, Please!

After journeying to the moon and back and ridding the Bowser scourge from the kingdoms, the Power Moon inventory of shops has changed a little bit. There's still the unique Power Moon to purchase in each kingdom that actually shows up on the regional Power Moon lists. But, post-finale, packs of ten Power Moons can also be purchased. The point of this is to inflate Power Moon count for Odyssey fuel power. Sure there, are 880 unique Power Moons to collect throughout the world, but you can add upon this count with bulk purchases in shops, if you like.

㉑ Mushroom Kingdom Regular Cup

Talk to the hotfooted Koopa near Mushroom Pond in the south to begin this event. Mario must race several other speedy turtles all the way up to the foot of Peach's Castle. Since the path leads across gentle dunes and hills, and is lined with Rocket Flowers eager to be plucked, this is actually one of the breeziest race challenges. Either roll quickly to the castle, or pluck Rocket Flowers and jet toward it, picking fresh flowers along the way with Cappy tosses to replenish rocket propellant.

Koopa Freerunning
Mushroom Kingdom Regular Cup

22 Mushroom Kingdom Master Cup

This course is available after completing Mushroom Kingdom Regular Cup. The difference here is the addition of the golden Koopa. Apart from that, it's the same race, with the same easygoing, roll-friendly terrain, blooming with Rocket Flowers. Blaze across the Mushroom Kingdom again to claim a second Power Moon prize.

23 Picture Match: Basically Mario

The Mini Rocket leading to Mushroom Kingdom's Picture Match event is at the north edge of the territory. Like with the Goomba Picture Match event in Cloud Kingdom, Mario is tasked with rebuilding a face from scratch, maneuvering captured facial features into the right place after the face fades away. Here, it happens to be Mario's own mug. For a perfect reference, use the built-in ability of the Nintendo Switch to take a screenshot of Mario's face before it fades away. During this first challenge, Mario's eyebrows, eyes, nose, mustache, and mouth disappear, but the outlines of his head and hat remain. A reconstructed Mario face worth 60 points or more is required to get the first Power Moon out of Toad here.

Gazing into the mouth of (mushroom) madness.

...Really, Toad?

24 Picture Match: A Stellar Mario!

Complete the previous Picture Match event, rebuilding Mario's face for 60 points or more, and you'll gain access to this follow-up. Two differences this time: 80 points are needed for a Power Moon, and the outlines of Mario's hat, hair, and head disappear also! The loss of these guidelines makes this challenging indeed. Use a system screenshot for reference, or (ahem) this very guide. This challenge is much more exacting, so take your time placing Mario's facial features.

25 Light from the Ceiling

This clue is quite the tip-off. What's to do with light inside the Princess's main chambers? There's a bright, domed ceiling, and an insignia of the sun on the center of the first floor. Stand on the sun symbol and look upward at the middle of the dome above in first-person view and a hidden Power Moon might just reveal itself.

26 Loose-Tile Trackdown

Within Peach's Castle, Archivist Toadette is ready to hand out surplus Power Moons for any achievements achieved since the last time Mario stopped by, and there are also a couple of others to uncover. Poke around the checkered floor on the first floor, left of the main staircase, and you'll notice a slightly raised section. Ground pound this to reveal, surprisingly, a number. It appears there's a sequence of raised tiles to find and slap down in here.

1. First floor, left of central stairs

2. First floor, left of central stairs

3. Upstairs, right from throne

4. First floor, right of central stairs

5. First floor, left of central stairs

6. Upstairs, left from throne

7. First floor, right of central stairs

8. Near throne

Complete the sequence to knock a moon free from under the tiles.

27 Totally Classic

A Toad can be found guarding a locked room just north of Peach's Castle. He won't allow anyone modern-looking in. You'll need to have a decidedly, oh, 1996 look about you. Collect at least 35 Regional Coins, then stop by Crazy Cap's to purchase the Mario 64 cap and suit. Change to the blocky new outfit, then return to Toad to gain entry. Inside, notice a telltale glow from the top tip of the star fountain. Toss Cappy onto the point and hold him until a Power Moon emerges.

28 Courtyard Chest Trap

Inside the room Toad won't open without the Mario 64 look, there's another Power Moon to dig up. Check out the many treasure chests spread throughout here—they must be cracked open in the correct order for treasure to be revealed. In the wrong order, they all pop open to reveal undead Chinchos, who need to be defeated before the treasure sequence can be retried.

Luckily, a quick tip shows up from an eagle's eye view to show the correct treasure chest opening order. Pro tip: be ready to tap the Screen Capture button just as the order of all eight chests is onscreen, so a reference map is available right from the console's photo gallery.

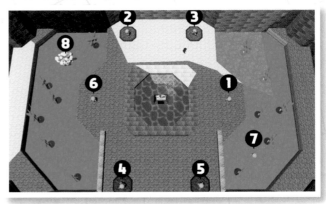

29 Yoshi's Feast in the Sea of Clouds

Head a bit southwest from Toad's garden and look for a drainage cutout in the hill. A pipe is tucked away in here, but is clogged with a Fruit. Come down here with Yoshi and eat the Fruit to allow access to the challenge room inside.

Inside is a room of colorful platforms floating over a dense fog. The clouds can obscure the view of platforms on the lowest level, and the dense mist coating also conceals a vast drop-off and some snapping Maw-Rays.

The goal in here is to collect all the Fruits. Yoshi's flutter jump is very useful for getting around in here, allowing the dinosaur to easily transfer between platforms gracefully, where Mario would require some kind of dive jumping aerobatics with Cappy. And his tongue lets him pull in Fruits from afar, off the edges of platforms or at tongue's reach from the top of a jump.

On seesaw block platforms, stand on the edge of one side for a bit to get it to dip lower, the run up the other side while it's still ramped upward, adding crucial height to the starting point of a flutter jump.

Watch for Maw-rays erupting up from the murk as you pass over jumps here!

287

㉚ Sunken Star in the Sea of Clouds

Just under the cloak of mist in the cloud challenge room, a hidden Power Moon can be found not far from the entrance. From the starting platform, simply step off into space from the two-Fruit dropoff. A platform is just underneath the cloudtop. Continue forward to find the Power Moon. This hidden platform can also be found by heading off the edge of the most remote seesaw platform.

㉛ Secret 2D Treasure

Fall into the wall found near Power Moon #11 on the west side of Mushroom Kingdom and you end up in a strange and dangerous 8-bit environment. Enter the 8-bit pipe before Mario, jump on the far left to pop a hidden block containing a Heart, then proceed to the right to discover something new: Mario can only proceed forward in front of a dark strip of 2D background with 8-bit clouds floating on it. Go outside of the dark square moving patch, and Mario snaps back into 3D form, falling away from the flat 2D plane. Near the entrance, there's a kind of gutter for Mario to fall into to save him, but later, it'll just be a sheer drop to doom. Don't advance more quickly than the 2D stretches of background.

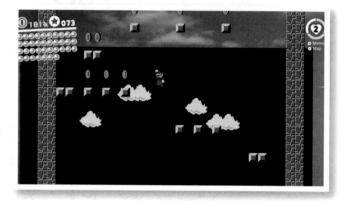

Head right, sticking to the flat background, and navigate a horizontal and vertical stretch of Bullet Bill cannons. Beyond this bullet dodging festival, you find a vertical section filled with steel block platforms with small gaps between them. These stretches can be crossed by dashing with no stops, so run across them holding the Cap Throw button the whole time. Jump to the top of this section along the rising black background.

At the top, Mario is flipped upside down onto a small globe like a tiny planet. *Super Mario Galaxy* in 2D anyone? Mario runs along the circumference of each of these, with controls adjusting depending on where he's located. For example, crouching will always be pushing the stick in the direction of the current globe (if this is confusing, the Crouch button still works just fine). Travel between globes is only possible when their flat backgrounds overlap. Time jumps to arrive into the overlapping 2D space and Mario flips from one globe to another. Run around the globes in time with the rotating backgrounds to avoid being booted off the flat plane this far in. Proceed to the right carefully jumping between globes and dodging Fuzzies. The globe farthest right has a pipe on the underside. Navigate to this pipe, ducking under the Fuzzies here as needed, and crouch to find the last secret 2D room containing the Power Moon.

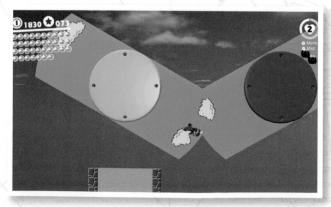

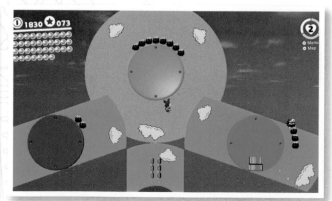

32 2D Boost from Bullet Bill

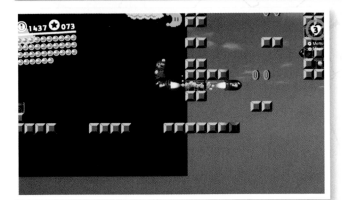

The well's elaborate 8-bit setup has a Power Moon resting in plain sight fairly early on, in the middle of the Bullet Bill section. The Power Moon is high above anyplace Mario can reach by normal jumping, but is easily grabbed by jumping on top of a nearby Bullet Bill, bouncing high off the stomped bullet to touch the moon.

BOSS GAUNTLET

33 Tussle in Tostarena: Rematch

The most centrally-located of the secret painting towers contains a portal leading back to Knucklotec, the fist-fighting stone deity of the desert. He's not at all interested in a fair fight this time, though. Hordes of Chinchos rise from the ground from all directions throughout the battle, forcing extra attention on where Mario is running toward. Nothing's stopping undead cloth wraiths from appearing suddenly in his path. Just avoid them or use spin throws as needed to economically clear out lots at once.

As Chinchos swarm, Knucklotec attacks with punches from above. Keep moving to make them miss, then capture a stunned fist as it recuperates on the ground from a missed hit. Steer Knucklotec's Fist into Knucklotec's face to damage it, then run wide to get out of the way of its double-fisted attack as it returns to the arena.

The boss can also slap the ground firmly with both hands, shaking the room and breaking ice stalactites free from the ceiling. These are a danger to anyone in the path of the shadow below. Move fast to get out from under shadows during this phase, continuing to be mindful of Chinchos. If Knucklotec holds his hands apart, palms up, he's going to slap them together, so move toward or away from his face to get out of the space between them.

Continue looking out for a ground-punching phase that allows you to capture a stunned fist to feed to the face. Knucklotec gets craftier defending itself here, using its remaining hand to swap sides of its face shooting ice as Mario rockets forward in fist form. To avoid the ice and continue closing in on that punchable face, tack back and forth in midair to confuse Knucklotec's defensive hand.

34 Struggle in Steam Gardens: Rematch

This tower is placed high up a tall dirt column, and takes some doing to access. Search around the base and you find a spot ripe for planting. Look around to the east in Goomba Woods to find a large, plump seed. Toss it into the pot at the base of the column to sprout a big beanstalk, which Mario can climb up to the tower. Enjoy the view, check the backside of the tower for some Regional Coins, then head inside.

Torkdrift attacks in a replica of Cascade Kingom's secret flower garden! Mario needs to do battle with him with the help of a captured Uproot. Torkdrift tethers itself to energy cores protected by clusters of brick blocks. Stretch up from below with Uproot to bash through the blocks and destroy each core from underneath. Knock out each core tethered to Torkdrift for a chance to give the saucer itself an Uproot uppercut right from underneath.

Be ready for taller pulse beam waves to hop over.

Deliver a full hit from Uproot and Torkdrift reels and rises, blanketing the battlefield in pulse beam waves while it recuperates. Stretch and release over the pulse waves with Uproot's spindly legs to avoid damage, and just wait out the laser storm.

(35) Dust-Up in New Donk City: Rematch

We certainly hope you loved fighting Mechawiggler, because inside the eastern Mushroom Kingdom tower, you get to fight two at once! This ultimate tank battle pits Mario in a Sherm against dual Mechawigglers in a rain-soaked New Donk City arena.

Avoid the converging paths of the dual bosses when they're emerging from portals to charge across the arena floor. When they emerge to crawl all over the nearby building, blast each glowing segment with tank shots, while also shooting the floating purple projectiles the Mechawigglers output. Allow these projectiles to fully ripen, and they pop into triple mortars that fall toward the Sherm. If the Mechawigglers launch many projectiles and you fail to shoot them down, you'll have many falling projectiles to dodge at once very soon. On the other hand, shooting these flaming yellow projectiles down can reveal Hearts.

(36) Battle in Bubblaine: Rematch

Check out the pipe underwater beneath Dorrie in the Mushroom Pond to find the painting that allows a rematch with Seaside Kingdom's head octopus. Capture the Gushen near the entrance pipe and proceed to jet upward to Lanceur's altitude. This battle occurs during a rainstorm, which results in a much improved Gushen—you won't need to land in water to replenish propellant as the bubble diminishes, so jet around freely.

If Lanceur spins around rapidly at Gushen's altitude, dodge it with horizonal jetting. While Lanceur spins about at a lower altitude, jet above and then jet upward in place to spray a high-pressure stream of water straight down onto Lanceur's head. Keep up the waterspray onslaught for several seconds to build up enough pressure to qualify as a hit, damaging the king. Dodge its spinning and its drill projectile shots and continue spraying it when possible, either flying up close to it then jetting directly away for lateral shots, or flying above and jetting upward to shoot down.

37 Blowup at Mount Volbono: Rematch

The reprise of the Cookatiel recipe atop Mount Volbona adds a few twists. Three Moonsnakes now spin in the stew, adding extra obstacles to dodge while swimming through the hot liquid as a Lava Bubble. Meanwhile, Cookatiel hovers above and tosses out spike pods, which are not a good addition to this broth at all. Dodge them falling and avoid them while swimming, these unpleasant seeds sink eventually. Cookatiel eventually tires of spitting out spiky seeds, and starts barfing out a nasty stew of its own—which is actually your ticket up to its vulnerable forehead! Swim up the muck with the Lava Bubble, waggling motion control repeatedly to speed burst upward, and run right into Cookatiel's head to register a bubble stomp.

The second time Cookatiel commences to spitting up at Mario, the descending liquid wobbles back and forth in midair, forcing corrections left and right up the stream. The third time, Cookatiel wises up a bit and breaks up the chunks, spitting out only a glob of liquid at a time. This doesn't account for jumping, though. Leap from glob to glob on a path up to a final hit on Cookatiel's cranium.

If health gets low, swim around in the stew and break up chunks of food, which potentially uncover Hearts.

38 Rumble in Crumbleden: Rematch

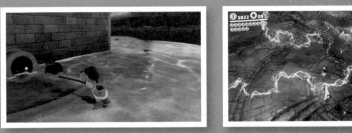

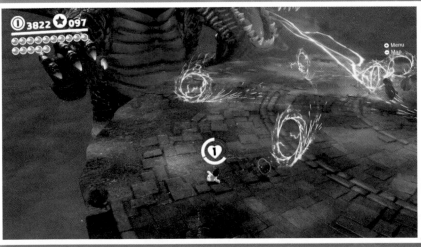

It takes a little uncovering to reveal the path to this fight. First, drain the castle's moat by popping out all the wooden pegs at the bottom. Next, climb to the castle roof (via the staircase produced by the scarecrow to the west) and capture Yoshi. Return to the drained moat and find a pipe clogged with a Fruit. A certain dinosaur adores Fruits, so scarf it down (which counts toward Power Moons #13-15) then climb inside.

Inside, Yoshi will be gone, unfortunately. Hop into the painting here to revisit the Ancient Dragon. Early on, the huge beast is much the same as before, in the Ruined Kingdom. After it slaps its head on the ground, you find more intricate electric wave patterns along the ground. These have gaps that can be run underneath, rather than jumped over. Instead of having to dodge waves on the ground, you'll have to gauge whether it's better to run underneath tall gaps in the waves, or to jump over toe-level waves. Once the dragon has taken a couple of hits, the homing electric rings it shoots out are also more numerous and aggressive.

39 Secret Path to Peach's Castle!

A taste of Mushroom Kingdom can be had much earlier in the game, thanks to a secluded part of Luncheon

Kingdom. Capture a Lava Bubble in the vast eastern lava ocean around Mount Volbono, then swim northeast to find an island containing a warp painting. Jump into this image to end up here, on a floating cottage island with a terrific view of Mario's home region.

Touch the flag checkpoint here to make it easy to return (well, once you can access Mushroom Kingdom at will). Use Cappy to extinguish the fire burning in the fireplace, then step inside and wall jump all the way up the chimney to find a Power Moon perched on the top of the small smokestack.

40 A Tourist in the Mushroom Kingdom!

There's a Tostarenan tourist who takes off on his own world tour the instant the taxi ice is melted enough for movement. This chap sets out on his vacation once you visit him in Sand Kingdom after the main adventure is complete and the immediate threats in each kingdom are fully quelled. He'll visit several kingdoms each in turn, with his visit to Mushroom Kingdom taking place after he and the cabbie somehow end up on the moon!

Once the tourist gets around to the Mushroom Kingdom, he is found near the store.

41 Found with Mushroom Kingdom Art

The Mushroom Kingdom's Hint Art is mounted handsomely inside Peach's Castle, to the right of the central stairs. Examine the painting to get an idea of where it might be. Keep this clue in mind while exploring the world. This clue is illuminating. Where does something look like the image? Cap Kingdom, perhaps? Find the place in Cap Kingdom where the looming moon and the cap tower can be positioned just like the Hint Art, and you find the place where a Power Moon can be sprung from the ground with a firm ground pound stomp.

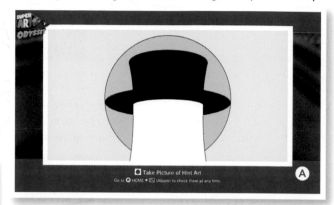

42 Hat-and-Seek: Mushroom Kingdom

Speak to the concerned Bonneter found left of the entrance to the castle, and he shows concern for a friend he hasn't seen in an uncomfortably long time. He thinks this missing Bonneter is probably just spending some time as the hat of a local, but isn't sure. As with Cappy, a sure sign that someone is wearing a Bonneter are the eyes that pop out.

Take a little stroll around Mushroom Kingdom, keeping a keen eye out for any strange-looking headwear. The missing Bonneter can finally be found atop a Toad in northwest Mushroom Kingdom.

(43) Princess Peach, Home Again!

Completing the adventure and restoring peace and order to the kingdoms doesn't satisfy Peach's own curiosity to see the world. She sets off with Tiara and a suitcase full of region-appropriate outfits to explore all the kingdoms. Not until Mario has visited Peach and Tiara in each kingdom does Peach return home to her castle, the travel itch scratched. Once she's back, she and Tiara can be found on the balcony outside, just in front of the gorgeous stained glass portrait window of Peach. Pay them a visit to reflect on what a long, amazing trip it's been, and to snag a final Power Moon from tourist Peach!

Archivist Toadette's Achievements

Congratulations, Mario! You've survived your journey to the Moon Kingdom and have returned home to the Mushroom Kingdom. But this is no time to relax. Archivist Toadette awaits your presence in Peach's Castle—there are urgent matters to discuss! Among them are the following 61 achievements. Report to Archivist Toadette whenever you complete one of these tasks to receive another Power Moon.

Mushroom Moons

Archivist Toadette updates the Power Moon list for Mushroom Kingdom once you speak to her. The achievements listed in this section are tracked as Power Moons for Mushroom Kingdom, extending the in-game list from 43 to 104.

Well-Played, Mario

The first Power Moon from Archivist Toadette is automatic—you wouldn't be here without rescuing Princess Peach. But you've probably already earned many more. Continue speaking to Archivist Toadette until she has no more Power Moons to award then check back with her whenever you've completed one of the following tasks.

Many of the achievements are self-explanatory, and are awarded as a way of celebrating the Power Moons you collect elsewhere. You complete the overwhelming majority of the achievements listed here by scouring each of the kingdoms in the world for their hidden Power Moons.

By methodically completing each kingdom's list of Power Moons (including those obtained by opening the Moon Rock), you earn all of the following bonus Power Moons. Of course, you'll also have to capture a whole lot of enemies, buy every souvenir, and sprint, leap, and throw many, many times too. But don't worry, Mario! You can do it!

ACHIEVEMENT POWER MOONS

No.	Title	Description (Qty)
44	Rescue Princess Peach	Rescue Princes Peach from Bowser.
45	Achieve World Peace	Bring peace to all kingdoms in the world (14).
46	Power Moon Knight	Collect Power Moons (100).
47	Power Moon Wizard	Collect Power Moons (300).
48	Power Moon Ruler	Collect Power Moons (600).
49	Regional Coin Shopper	Buy things using Regional Coins (13).
50	Flat Moon Finder	Collect 8-Bit Power Moons (10).
51	Flat Moon Fanatic	Collect 8-Bit Power Moons (20).
52	Treasure Chest Hunter	Collect Power Moons from treasure chests (15).
53	Super Treasure Chest Hunter	Collect Power Moons from treasure chests (25).

ACHIEVEMENT POWER MOONS

No.	Title	Description (Qty)
54	Note-Collecting World Tour	Collect Power Moons from taking Notes (5).
55	Note-Collecting Space Tour	Collect Power Moons from taking Notes (20).
56	Timer Challenge Amateur	Collect Power Moons from Timer Challenges (10).
57	Timer Challenge Professional	Collect Power Moons from Timer Challenges (25).
58	Captain Toad Meeter	Meet up with Captain Toad (5).
59	Captain Toad Greeter	Meet up with Captain Toad (10).
60	Touring with Princess Peach	Meet up with Princess Peach as she travels the world (5).
61	Globe-Trotting with Princess Peach	Meet up with Princess Peach as she travels the world (10).
62	Master Sheep Herder	Herd sheep to collect a Power Moon (4).
63	Gaga for Goombette	Collect Power Moons from Goombette (5).
64	Lakitu Fishing Trip	Fish for Power Moons as Lakitu (3).
65	Flower-Growing Guru	Grow seeds to collect Power Moons (5).
66	Flower-Growing Sage	Grow seeds to collect Power Moons (10).
67	Running with Rabbits	Catch rabbits to collect Power Moons (5).
68	Racing with Rabbits	Catch rabbits to collect Power Moons (10).
69	Ground Pound Instructor	Dig up Power Moons by Ground Pounding (15).
70	Ground Pound Professor	Dig up Power Moons by Ground Pounding (40).
71	Rad Hatter	Collect Power Moons by throwing your hat on things (3).
72	Super Rad Hatter	Collect Power Moons by throwing your hat on things (10).
73	Traveling-Bird Herder	Collect Power Moons from migrating birds (5).
74	Wearing it Well!	Collect Power Moons by wearing certain outfits (3).
75	Wearing it Great!	Collect Power Moons by wearing certain outfits (8).
76	Wearing it Perfect!	Collect Power Moons by wearing certain outfits (15).
77	Hat-Seeking Missile	Find Bonneters hidden on people's heads (5).
78	Music Maestro	Play the music that Toad wants to hear (5).
79	Art Enthusiast	Collect Power Moons using Hint Art (5).
80	Art Investigator	Collect Power Moons using Hint Art (15).
81	Slots Machine	Collect Power Moons playing Slots (3).
82	Koopa Freerunning MVP	Win Koopa Freerunning races (5).
83	Koopa Freerunning Hall of Famer	Win Koopa Freerunning races (12).
84	Supernaturally Sure-Footed	Receive passing scores in Koopa Trace-Walking (5).
85	Quizmaster	Answer all of the Sphynx's questions correctly (3).
86	Souvenir Sampler	Collect souvenirs and stickers (10).
87	Souvenir Sleuth	Collect souvenirs and stickers (20).
88	Souvenir Savant	Collect souvenirs and stickers (40).
89	Capturing Novice	Capture targets (20).
90	Capturing Apprentice	Capture targets (35).
91	Capturing Master	Capture targets (45).
92	Hat Maven	Collect hats (15).
93	Hat Icon	Collect hats (35).
94	Fashion Maven	Collect outfits (15).
95	Fashion Icon	Collect outfits (35).
96	Moon Rock Liberator	Open Moon Rocks (14).
97	World Warper	Travel through warp holes (10).
98	Checkpoint Flagger	Activate Checkpoint Flags (40).
99	Checkpoint Flag Enthusiast	Activate Checkpoint Flags (80).
100	Loaded with Coins	Collect coins (1,000).
101	Rolling in Coins	Collect coins (7,000).
102	Swimming in Coins	Collect coins (10,000).
103	Jump! Jump! Jump!	Jump (10,000).
104	Fly, Cappy, Fly!	Throw Cappy (5,000).

Welcome to Rabbit Ridge

REGION AT A GLANCE

Population	Unknown
Size	Unknown
Locals	Rabbitish?
Currency	Unknown
Industry	Wedding Planning
Temperature	Unknown

INDIGENOUS FLORA & FAUNA

	HAMMER BRO		BULLET BILL		BANZAI BILL
	Can Capture?		Can Capture?		Can Capture?
	Yes		No*		No*

	POISON PIRANHA PLANT		BIG POISON PIRANHA PLANT		SHERM
	Can Capture?		Can Capture?		Can Capture?
	No*		No		Yes

	MOONSNAKE
	Can Capture?
	No

*No Cappy? No capture.

One Last Door

For those travelers who survive the "hospitality" of the Broodals, a new challenge may await...

Well-Hidden Rabbit Home

The way to this secluded region of space is opened only after visiting Moon Kingdom and collecting at least 250 Power Moons. This small and remote area hides a few surprises, not least of which is the home of the rabbits, and a shot at redemption for the rejected and dejected Broodal clan.

The obstacles found here on the Dark Side of the Moon will test even the most hardened globe-jumping plumber. Try them out on your own before seeking answers in this chapter for the hardest tests.

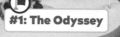

#1: The Odyssey

A

A TASTY-LOOKING TOWER

This ostentatious stone tower was carved at the direction of the vegetable-loving Madame Broode, who lords over Rabbit Ridge.

Her underlings, the Broodals, live within and always have a warm "welcome" for visitors.

TOPPER, CLIENT RELATIONS

Responsible for client relations on behalf of the Broodals' wedding-planning firm, Topper is usually found on-site, troubleshooting.

You can tell how serious he is about a battle by the number of hats he has stacked up on his head; he doesn't tap into his full hat reserves except for the most dangerous opponents. So if you square off with him and he seems to be mostly hat, you should feel honored...and afraid.

THREE KEYS TO THE KINGDOM

1. Watch out for the moon's light gravity; you can still die falling off a cliff.

2. Investigate behind all those stone-carved vegetables.

3. Greet all FOUR of the keys to this kingdom. You know who they are.

RANGO, THE BOUNCER

He's not the most focused, but Rango is a valuable player on the Broodals team, always coming through in the end. A master of his boomeranging trampoline hat, he can throw it both straight and curved with almost unnatural control over the way it flies. On the other hand, he sometimes zones out a bit and looks confused. That's your chance to counterattack!

HARIET, PYROTECHNICS

The least predictable of the Broodals, Hariet is most often found throwing bombs with her hair. When her homemade bombs explode, they leave a pool of fire on the ground, so try knocking them away before they explode. While it may seem reckless to have filled her hat with bombs, Hariet is devious and keeps a lot of spare explosives with her, so watch out!

SPEWART, THE ENTERTAINER

Spinning around while spitting poison in a wide area, Spewart is the least subtle of the Broodals. But he also has an unexpectedly artistic side, as his poisonous ground-paintings show.

Mario's Itinerary

Well, this is unexpected. Amassing a grand enough collection of Power Moons reveals the way to the Broodals' lair itself. It's time to teach these rude mercenary wedding planners a lesson. What is it up here that makes some of these rabbits go bad? Is it something in the water? But isn't the moon a desert? Anyway, marvel at the site of Madame Broode's enormous carrot tower, and explore the rabbit's small village of odd stone vegetables below.

Ⓐ Arrival at Rabbit Ridge

The Broodals aren't going to take kindly to Mario and Cappy bursting in on their home. That's really adding insult to the injury of thwarting their plans with Bowser. It's their home turf, so the Broodals are naturally more aggressive here. The other big variable is moon gravity. This isn't deep enough to the moon's core to increase the gravity to earth levels, like in some moon challenge rooms. Jumps here are as floaty as on the surface. You have to account for that in your hat-avoidance strategies against the Broodal quartet.

Inevitably, you must capture the Spark Pylon and zip across the wire leading to the giant carrot, base of the Broodals.

BOSS GAUNTLET

Rabbit Ridge Tower, First Floor

Topper attacks right away upon Mario's entrance. When Topper's hats begin bouncing around in large numbers, if several hats are incoming at once, jump straight up and let the loftiness of the jump take care of things—the hats bounce around underneath Mario and spin off to other parts of the arena by the time he descends.

When Topper approaches, stack of top hats on his head, hat toss early when Topper's still out of range, then hold Cappy. Topper advances into Cappy, sometimes taking multiple hits and losing multiple top hats at once. This helps deplete top hats without getting close enough for Topper to perform his hat spin attack.

Rabbit Ridge Tower, Second Floor

Hariet returns with her pigtail bombs and armored saucer hat. When she's tossing bomb pairs, run wide circles around her to dodge them, then step around any lava pools left behind.

In her saucer form, the main danger she poses is dropping bombs directly down on top of Mario. Stay out from under Hariet's saucer form wherever she is, and divert around the lava trails she leaves behind. They'll dissipate before too long.

When Hariet finally strikes with mace-like attachments, hit her lodged spiked balls to send them swinging back in at her. The impact dislodges her helmet, granting a few precious seconds for Mario to sail into her head with his feet. Without her protective hat on, Hariet panics more than any other Broodal, making her the hardest to stomp on in the moon's low gravity. To make things easier, stun hatless Hariet with a cap toss right before jumping at her.

Rabbit Ridge Tower, Third Floor

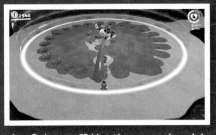

Spewart continues doing his best impression of a Poison Piranha Plant, saturating the battlefield in dangerous purple glop. What does

he think he's doing, playing *Splatoon 2*? Hat throws soak up ink underneath, clearing patches Mario can safely stand on. A spin throw de-inks lots of real estate at once.

Sliding around under his hat, Spewart glides on a cloud of poison liquid, leaving a trail behind him. If he approaches Mario, knock him away with Cappy and just wait the phase out. He's no threat when he's gliding around on the other side of the arena. When Spewart is walking around upright, he's probably about to eject poison barf in a 360-degree fan, so back up to the wall. After he soaks the room, mop up a path to Spewart, knock his hat off, and stomp on him.

Rabbit Ridge Tower, Fourth Floor

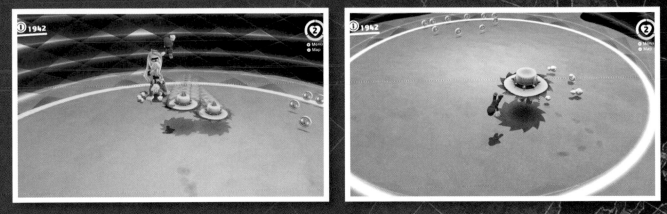

Rango has the deadliest direct weapons of the Broodals, and can be the hardest, if you make things complicated. Keep things simple though and this wedding planner will be out of a job. In standard rabbit-to-plumber combat, Rango winds up briefly and throws several sharply-bladed hats at Mario. Throwing his hat as a weapon means Rango isn't wearing head protection. Jump right at him as he readies a hat throw so Mario is already soaring in when Rango releases his buzzsaw headwear. With good timing, Mario bounces right off his forehead just after he throws the hats.

Now it gets tricky, but is really not so bad. Rango shelters inside an oversized version of his bladed hats, bouncing relentlessly at Mario. Rango can bounce straight in any direction much faster than Mario can run. He can only adjust his angle when he lands, though. Keep running around Rango in one direction, changing direction abruptly whenever necessary to make sure Rango's buzzsaw bounce keeps missing.

Rabbit Ridge Tower, Roof

The Broodals collective reprise their Bowser's Kingdom ace up the sleeve, the enormous RoboBrood machine. The irony here is that, although moon gravity is in effect, and this is a fiercer version of Robobrood, the fight is probably easier than before, as you get to capture a Hammer Bro instead of a Pokio. A Hammer Bro can stand far back from the RoboBrood and hop up and down unloading hammers at a hilarious rate, shattering the armor around RoboBrood's legs much faster than Pokio could manage. With a Hammer Bro, you can also choose to shatter the control globes of Broodals who aren't on the upward-facing portion. You can nail the globe of whoever's in reach of the ground and the Hammer Bro's huge hammer arc.

Captain Toad

After vanquishing Rango, Mario exits the boss arena for another tower-circling interlude. Here, there's a small recharge in the form of a Heart halfway along the path. For a bigger health boost, one-time-only, stop at the pipe exit and don't enter. Keep pushing right, past the wall. This reveals the endlessly inquisitive Captain Toad, who coughs up the Power Moon he's found in the carrot tower. Getting the Power Moon fully replenishes Mario's health, so make it count going forward.

You can't get this Power Moon health boost from Toad more than once, since there won't be a dotted outline of the moon he gives Mario.

Still, the Hammer Bro has its weaknesses. Once the RoboBrood is sufficiently enraged to begin charging back and forth across the arena at Mario, it's time to cease the current Hammer Bro capture. You can tell it's time to step up movement speed when the RoboBrood's legs are glowing. Mario's ability to roll, tackle, or running long jump to get out of the way quickly helps avoid damage here, where a Hammer Bro is too slow. Once the RoboBrood settles down again, track down another Hammer Bro to capture. RoboBrood begins launching swarms of swirling, captivating, candy-like firework explosives, but keep moving and tossing tons of hammers and they shouldn't be a real issue.

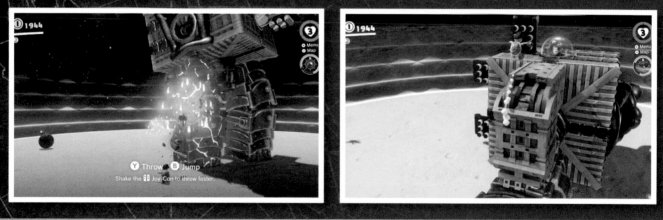

Finally, these annoying Bowser underlings are dealt with, and the rabbits of the moon are free to hop about in low moon gravity in peace. After knocking out all the Broodals back to back, Mario wins the **King's Crown** and **King's Outfit!** Several new moons are available to find here on the Dark Side of the Moon. Just as Dark Side was discovered with 250 Power Moons in hand, even more remote reaches might be uncovered with yet more moon power.

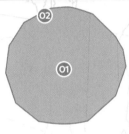

Extend Your Stay

Rabbit Ridge doesn't have a souvenir shop or local currency, though someone should see about finding a way to ship normal vegetables here to sell to the rabbit residents.

🌙 Power Moons

There are 24 Power Moons on the Dark Side of the Moon. **Power Moons #01** and **#02** were obtained while ridding Dark Side of those hares gone wrong, the Broodals. The rest of these moons are available once their threat is removed.

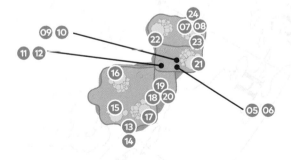

This scarecrow challenge room is found on a shelf just behind where the Odyssey is parked overlooking Rabbit Ridge. Mario must turn in Cappy to access the room, so Mario won't have captures, hat attacks, or hat jumps. He's regular old Mario for this one.

There's a Lock near the entrance, a Key across a large gap, and a second-floor-height network of fragile blocks between them. This amounts to a rickety bridge, basically, as there are still gaps that must be crossed with jumps.

Many gaps just happen to be perfectly spaced for running long jumps.

It's not quite that simple though. On both sides, rows of cannons are locked and loaded, ready to launch Bullet Bills at anyone foolishly trying to cross the middle to grab the Key.

Mario must get across without falling, grab the Key, then return without falling to grab the moon. On the way back, there is even less of a bridge as on the way out, since Bullet Bills have blasted apart segments of it on the first pass. If that wasn't enough, grabbing the key coaxes a Banzai Bill out of hiding from the far side. One way or another, a return trip posthaste is strongly incentivized!

The Bullet Bill room has a lower floor, but it's even dicier than the top. Just as a Banzai Bill plows across the proceedings on the top deck when Mario finally reaches to the Key, the same is true on the lower deck. Mario must coax a Banzai Bill out of hiding on the lower deck, then lead it all the way back along the bottom. The platform on the entrance side has a fragile wall of blocks visible, and it's these the Banzai Bill must demolish to reveal the Power Moon.

On the bottom level, just above the cloudy pit, there are a series of evenly spaced, small platforms connecting the entrance and Power Moon side with the Banzai Bill and Key side. They're spaced out just right for running long jumps between every block, with no room for error on the leaps. If you're going for both moons at once, you can cross on top, grab the Key, then fall to the lower level to antagonize the lower Banzai Bill launcher, then jump back, requiring just eight perfect running long jumps on the way back; if you've already cleared the Key Power Moon before, you can cross both ways on the bottom and avoid the Bullet Bill nuisance up top, requiring 16 flawless running long jumps in a row.

Either way, on the way back, don't worry at all about the speed of the Banzai Bill behind Mario—Mario is way faster than a bullet while running and long jumping! Just focus on timing each running long jump to be from the edge of the current platform, aimed straight forward. On each landing, don't jump right away, let Mario take a running step across the current platform before pressing Crouch and Jump together at the edge for the next running long jump.

05 Invisible Road: Rush!

You can choke up plants with rocks, but it's best to just keep moving.

This scarecrow challenge room is found on a precarious shelf hanging down the east slope of Rabbit Ridge, just above the abyss. Beyond the door must be among the scarier sights in the game, at least at first glance: invisible platforms, Poison Piranha Plants, and no Cappy to help.

The first part involves a passage that cuts across the poison below with right angle turns. Past the first plant, turn right, then left, then left. At the halfway point is a spinning cross-shaped platform, with another plant on one of the points.

The purple poison given off by the plants at least provides some guideline for movement, and the rocks provide some form of defense. But it's probably better to just forego trying to improvise offense with the rocks, and instead focus on crossing the stage. If there's a rounded purple splotch (indicating it's not the very edge of a platform) or a Poison Piranha Plant, it's a safe area to stand, probably. If there's a straight-edged purple splotch, it's a ledge edge—watch out!

Toward the end, beyond the lazy Susan platform, are three Big Poison Piranha Plants. The section around and in between the three big plants is all safe to stand on, aside from near the snapping, spitting plants or upon their poison spit, of course. Solid, blessedly visible ground is also right beside the big plants, a bit raised like a stage. Here, a Power Moon is locked down in a cage. To release it, squash all three Big Poison Piranha Plants.

The one closest to the stage is easy to stomp on with a jump from the stage, but the other two are not. The easiest way to get enough height on a jump near them to stomp their noggins is to run slightly past them on one side, then turn 180 and jump to side somersault up next to them. Steer the side somersault onto the beast's leafy head. Getting all three down reveals the Power Moon, and the Moon Pipe here leads back out.

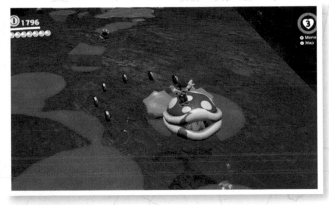

06 Invisible Road: Secret!

Look out from the spinning invisible platform halfway across the Poison Piranha Plant room to see a curious cutout in the wall across seemingly empty space. That's the trick: it's not empty. There's a platform running from the spinning cross platform to the hole in the wall. Charge bravely across this space and enter the secret room in the wall to find a treasure chest containing a bonus Power Moon.

07 Vanishing Road Rush

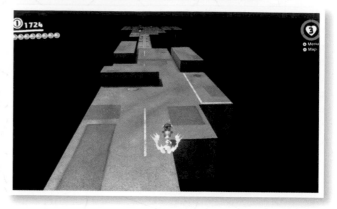

Tucked away in a crevasse on the back side of the northeast corner of Rabbit Ridge is another scarecrow challenge room.

This stretch is some nightmare vision of Metro Kingdom, where Mario must cross punishing urban environments with a harsh time limit. Hit the P-Switch at the start to begin the first section. Tuck into a roll and bounce across the whole path, curving around the rise in the road ahead on the left. Don't slow down over the collapsible bridge, just keep trucking. Rolling is much faster with rapid motion shakes than it is with repeated Cap button presses, so keep that in mind.

The next section starts with another switch press. A stair-like section of roads snaps into existence. The steps up are just wide enough apart so Mario can't fully jump from one to another, but they're too close together for rolling in between jumps to make sense. The time limit here is very harsh, so Mario must gain some extra speed somehow. The keys are continuous jumps, triple jumps, and tackling forward to reach the next step early when possible. While moving forward at full speed, launching off the ground with a continuous/triple jump gives a little speed boost, as does tackle, as does landing from a high-speed tackle. Keep up the little speed boosts and don't slow down (don't hit a wall with a tackle, don't miss a jump, etc.) and Mario makes it across the roadway staircase to the next P-Switch before the ground gives way.

The closing section is a lot less hard to navigate than the previous two, which required precise and rapid rolling and jumping. This section is just complicated by the presence of, oh, a dozen Sherm tanks! There are so many tanks on this narrow stretch of road that half of them probably shoot each other apart in a crossfire trying to get at Mario. It's a good thing, because that provides the opening needed to sprint to the finish, beyond a long beam extending out beyond the tanks. Dive for the moon below to finish the challenging sprint.

08 Vanishing Road Challenge

After the timed staircase road, when the tank rooftop portion of this challenge room begins, spy the right side of the roof to see a series of collapsible platforms stretching off the main path and above it. This is a bit like the stair sequence you just completed, if that sequence was also falling apart while you crossed it, and if tanks were also shooting at you! Luckily, the tanks aren't really a problem if you keep moving forward, which you have to anyway, because any piece of floor falls away after Mario touches it. Race to the top in a series of well-timed continuous jumps, triple

jumps, and tackles, then dive for the Power Moon hovering beyond the fragile platforms. Don't worry, after grabbing the moon, you should have room to maneuver and land amid all the tanks below!

09 Yoshi Under Siege

The horizontal Moon Pipe found on the hanging shelf down the side of Rabbit Ridge leads to a rain-swept alley under assault by a battalion of Sherm tanks. Yoshi's resting here in egg form, ready to be busted out and captured. You have to use a combination of Sherm captures and Yoshi to explore the area, feeding Yoshi all the Fruits. Several block sections are rusted out and warped, ready to be blown up from Sherm fire. Usually, this collapses sections that can then be used as bridges. Collect 10 Fruits for a Power Moon.

Jumping or falling while extending Yoshi's tongue is key to getting some airborne Fruits.

10 Fruit Feast Under Siege

Collecting all the Fruits while under Sherm siege is a little more challenging. While plenty of the Fruits are out in the open, a couple are hovering in midair underneath high platforms. Grabbing them requires falling from above, using Yoshi's tongue to snag them as he falls past. A few Fruit groups also hover over space along catwalks above, forcing tongue swipes or jumps out into free air to gobble them down. The final two Fruits might be the most deviously placed of all—just keep going farther into the area, away from the entrance, and you'll find them tucked just under stairs on the far side.

11 Yoshi on the Sinking Island

This Moon Pipe puts Mario into contact with old dino friend Yoshi, whose skills are needed to survive this scorching challenge. Take a quick look around, then break the egg and capture Yoshi to begin. The island starts sinking into the lava, forcing a rapid upward climb.

Yoshi's unique movement tricks aid the climb greatly. There's the flutter jump, which is like Yoshi's giving himself a double jump out of sheer effort, flapping his feet. And there's his tongue extension, which lets him cling just under the edges of cliffs and flip to the top. Use flutter jumps and tongue clings to advance up the hill as it's overcome by rising lava. Dodge Moonsnakes to avoid taking needless damage.

Along the way, be sure to scarf up the Fruits that are Yoshi's favorite food. Eat them either by running over them with Yoshi, or pulling them in with his tongue. Collect 10 Fruits during the climb and Yoshi produces a Power Moon.

12 Fruit Feast on the Sinking Island

The magma island room in which Mario captures Yoshi has 20 Fruits total, starting with two at entry level where Yoshi's egg is found, and concluding with two right before the Moon Pipe exit. Along the way, 16 other Fruits can be found in pairs, usually every two or three jumps up the sinking island. They're all in plain sight, and they can be scooped up easily with Yoshi's tongue if they're too far to grab up close. They don't have to be collected all at once—acquired Fruits show up on return visits as ghostly outlines, like Regional Coins or Power Moons you've already picked up. 10 Fruits in this room scores you the first Power Moon, but for the second Power Moon you need Yoshi to eat all 20.

Take it easy and don't rush. Just kidding, you gotta rush.

⑬ Yoshi's Magma Swamp

The Moon Pipe in plain sight to the south in Rabbit Ridge leads to this colorful cauldron. Break the egg and capture Yoshi to begin. Like some other rooms in Dark Side of the Moon, you accumulate Power Moons by getting Yoshi fed. Touching the hot liquid ends a Yoshi capture and hurts Mario, sending him smoking, almost out of control. The platforms here slowly rise and fall, so safe footing grows and shrinks. Keep these notes in mind while flutter jumping around, chewing up Fruits. Eat 10 Fruits to score a Power Moon here.

⑭ Fruit Feast in the Magma Swamp!

In the magma swamp, the most-hidden Fruits are right behind and above the entrance pillar. Be careful of the devious hidden blocks just to the right of the entrance door, which can bounce you into falling into the lava.

Trigger them carefully, then flutter jump straight up from the hidden blocks then tongue cling to the edge to get on top of the entrance pillar, scoring three Fruits up here. From here, it's an easy downward hop to the small platform behind the pillar, above which hover two more Fruits. Eat all 20 Fruits in the room to gain the second Power Moon.

⑮ Found with Dark Side Art 1

In the south of town, on what looks like a pile of stone tomatoes, you'll find the first of several new pieces of Hint Art, which take you back all over the world. The image here pictures Poochy burying something in a lush area overlooking waterfalls. Where could that be?

The waterfalls are the giveaway. This is in Cascade Kingdom, high up on the top shelf near the large triple step. Get near an edge with floating platforms visible to the north and ground pound the terrain to find the buried treasure.

16 Found with Dark Side Art 2

This piece of art is on ground level on a giant stone pumpkin. It's some kind of diagram with a big letter H. The roadway iconography should be a big clue.

Travel to Metro Kingdom and climb or warp to the Heliport. Slam the ground to dot the "i" on the warning stripes to turn up the hidden moon.

17 Found with Dark Side Art 3

Another ground-level stone pumpkin painting in the first part of Rabbit Ridge displays a grid with what seems to be either a pattern or map on it, a light path threaded through green blocks. At least the pattern looks artificial, not natural, so this points to something potentially man-made. Or Toad-made...

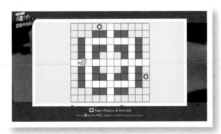

If you've explored Mushroom Kingdom much by now, you should recognize the garden found in the northeast corner. The Hint Art indicates which of the entrances to check out. Ground pound the east entrance to the hedge garden to solve the puzzle.

18 Found with Dark Side Art 4

Found hung at ground level on a stone wall before a shelf up to another section of town, this painting depicts the moon phases. The Power Moon icon on the image is placed over the last quarter moon.

Cloud Kingdom's main arena is basically a big, bright moon phase calendar. Head to the westernmost of the circular platforms to find a large last quarter moon. Stomp along the margin between night and day on the moon symbol to extract a Power Moon.

19 Found with Dark Side Art 5

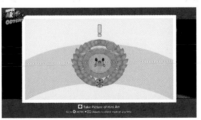

The fifth new piece of Hint Art is tucked away on a small shelf off the eastern edge of Rabbit Ridge. Fall carefully down from above to drift to it and have a look. The face and wreath should tip you off quickly. This is a Shiverian, and it has something to do with racing.

Sail to Snow Kingdom and head down the well into Shiveria Town. From here, go down farther still, to the gem of Shiverian culture, the Snowline Circuit. The arch you step under to watch or enter races looks suspiciously like the Hint Art. Use a high jump like a ground pound jump or dive jump up from one side of the arch to climb atop it. Ground pound the center of the arch above the Shiverian face design to pop free the Power Moon inside.

⑳ Found with Dark Side Art 6

A small stone silo has this Hint Art image mounted on it for viewing. The Hint Art depicts Talkatoo, Binoculars, parasols, and columns. With the arrows between them, perhaps it's directing you to follow one to another?

The solution is found in Seaside Kingdom. You don't have to visit most of the tips in the Hint Art, they're just there to lure intrepid treasure seekers to the wateriest realm. The Power Moon can be found by slamming the ground between the two columns on the beach toward the eastern shore of the kingdom.

㉑ Found with Dark Side Art 7

Tip-toe around precarious walkways on the edge to find extra Hint Art paintings. This painting is mounted on a big stone pumpkin just before a small ledge. The clue is shockingly nondescript, the most spartan of all the Hint Art—it's basically just a shadow. However, luckily, the texture and a tiny swatch of foliage point the way to the right region.

The right spot will be found in Lost Kingdom. The Hint Art has another helpful clue: the Travel Map coordinate. It's found very near to Hint Toad and Uncle amiibo. Toe around the area looking for a spot of ground that's just right compared to the tip graphic.

㉒ Found with Dark Side Art 8

Right out in the open in Rabbit Ridge you find this Hint Art, which presents a fun challenge—spot the single miniscule thing that's different in the Luncheon Kingdom Cooking Carnival picture. It's a safe bet that if you can find something off between the two carnival pictures, you'll probably find something of interest in that actual spot.

Spot it yet? Look around the main stewpot in the square. The columns behind it are missing a Volbonan cook in one image. Find this spot in Luncheon Kingdom and ground pound for some Power Moon cooking.

㉓ Found with Dark Side Art 9

This Hint Art is tucked around a corner on a low wall. A row of columns is shown, with the Power Moon supposedly near a column broken off at the base. Not many kingdoms are bristling with lots of columns of this style, so this should narrow down the search.

Check out Lake Kingdom, within the town in the aerated dome underwater. Look for the chamber with a row of columns, a couple broken right underneath a ledge holding piles of coins. The Power Moon can be found in the tile just below where the coins are piled up.

㉔ Found with Dark Side Art 10

Another painting inconsiderately placed on a precipice near a drop-off, on a giant pumpkin. These rabbits must have some conception of smaller footpaths. What if Mario had New Donkian proportions? Anyway, all that's shown is desolate rubble, and Poochy keeping himself busy with some sort of errand. There's no clue here besides the decrepitude of the location.

Ruin and rubble describe one place more than any other: Crumbleden. Set out for Ruined Kingdom. The Power Moon's resting place is actually very close to the Odyssey, in an area eroded free of any evidence of human cobbling. Ground pound the raw stone while wondering how Poochy got out here to bury treats.

Welcome to Culmina Crater

REGION AT A GLANCE

Population	Unknown
Size	Unknown
Locals	Rabbitish?
Currency	Unknown
Industry	Unknown
Temperature	Unknown

Capstone for an Odyssey

Only after collecting at least **500 Power Moons** will the Odyssey be powerful enough to land here, deep in vast Culmina Crater. This region is a devious treat, and contains the pinnacle of many kinds of challenges from throughout the game. Retain some surprise and try not to read this chapter before you need a helping hand!

Moon Mysteries

When you look up inside the caverns you may see deposits that look like the cubic Moon Rocks. Were the rocks that fell planetside originally formed here?

INDIGENOUS FLORA & FAUNA

BINOCULARS Can Capture? Yes	**FROG** Can Capture? Yes	**GOOMBA** Can Capture? Yes	
YOO-FOE Can Capture? No	**LAVA BUBBLE** Can Capture? Yes	**MOONSNAKE** Can Capture? No	
MAGMATO Can Capture? No	**UPROOT** Can Capture? Yes	**BURRBO** Can Capture? No	
FUZZY Can Capture? No	**GLYDON** Can Capture? Yes	**URBAN STINGBY** Can Capture? No	
VOLBONAN Can Capture? Yes	**POKIO** Can Capture? Yes	**DONKEY KONG** Can Capture? No	

(A)

#1: The Odyssey

ONE SERIOUS CRATER

This giant crater was formed by a huge meteor collision long ago. The impact destroyed the civilization that flourished on the moon, which is how Culmina Crater came to be. The crater itself is so massive, you cannot see the bottom.

SEEING THE BRIGHT SIDE

From her you can observe galaxies shining in ways you never could from home. Culmina Crater features vistas entirely unique from those you can find on the Dark Side of the Moon and Honeylune Ridge. If you're feeling down or disheartened, just take a look up at the Milky Way from here. You can see each star twinkle as they nestle close to one another.

It will all be OK—you are not alone.

THREE KEYS TO THE KINGDOM

1. See the mysterious building that so closely resembles New Donk City Hall.

2. Reach the far recesses of the giant cavern where none dare tread.

3. Test your skills as a hardened tourist one last time.

A BEWILDERING BUILDING

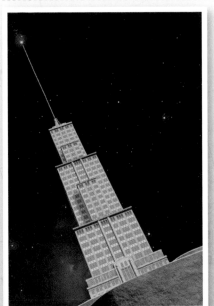

This colossal building stands in Culmina Crater. If you look closely, it seems to resemble the city hall in New Donk City. According to researchers, it might be one of the last remnants of the civilization that once flourished on the moon. But with little evidence, this theory lacks credibility.

A LONE PIPE IN A CRATER

This is the only pipe that connects to the lunar interior. If you find it, we don't recommend jumping right in. What awaits is a trial so harsh, it lives up to the name Culmina Crater.

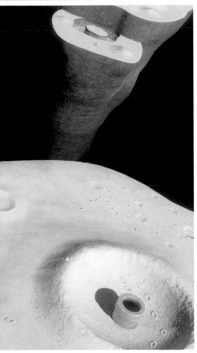

Of course, if you have the confidence of a traveler who has done everything else the world has to offer, give it a shot! Overcome this, and adventurers the world over will sing your praises.

INSIDE THE MOON

A lava zone spreads throughout this giant cavern. What waits ahead? How far does it go? These answers await

those brave enough to enter this unknown, unexplored world.

Confused on Arrival

It took 500 Power Moons to get here, and the reward seems austere indeed: The Odyssey touches down on a skinny island of land in a sea of nothing. Binoculars near the landing zone allow some surveillance of the surroundings. Mario fans from every kingdom have already arrived, all set to cheer him on. High on a rise nearby, there's a solitary green pipe. Capture one of the Frogs found near Mayor Pauline and use it to leapfrog up to the top. Enter the pipe and brace yourself.

Ⓐ Culmina Caverns

Deep in the moon, gravity is like earth's. Mario won't float around like he does on the surface. The way here is winding and long, and a fatal fall or loss of health makes Mario start all over at the beginning. Although there are no explicit checkpoints, this cavern can be described by distinct segments.

Goombas

The first section is a little steppe covered in Goombas. The Goombas have air support in the form of a Yoo-foe. The Yoo-foe drops bombs and, when

the bombs sometimes occasionally kill a Goomba or two, replacement Goombas.

It's not actually necessary to engage any of the Goombas, or the Yoo-foe, but destroying the Yoo-foe rewards a Life-Up Heart, and health is precious here indeed. This is a marathon, not a sprint, and every Heart matters.

To take down the Yoo-foe, build a Goomba tower tall enough to allow jumping onto the Yoo-foe from above. Watch out for the saucer's spinning blades while maneuvering a stack of Goombas. After dealing with the saucer (or not), jump up the big stone steps and move on to the big wall ahead.

Pole Crossing

This section tracks along a huge sheer wall, far too tall to consider mounting. Mario has to go around, complying with the path of sinking poles and grates. The trick here is that it's not as complicated as it looks. When transitioning between poles, just rotate around each pole and jump off quickly. Don't worry about climbing poles to maintain height, ascending quickly is easy whenever encountering a grate that bars Mario's way. Here, wall jump quickly from the grate to the nearest pole and back, all the way up to the closest gap.

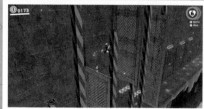

After the sinking pole section, another section follows of swinging poles that rise and lower along tracks that enter bubbling magma. It's only safe to vault forward toward the swinging poles just as they're rising from the lava. Quickly swing forward from pole to pole using Mario's momentum, jumping while his feet are aimed at the next pole, without waiting for a backswing between forward jumps. Take a breath at the fixed poles. With a dive jump after leaping off one of the poles here, you can cut a lot of distance off this tricky section, but then you also risk plunging into hot lava, too. You might be able to hotfoot-bounce toward one of the poles as it rises from the lava, and Mario happily clings on if he's close enough, but it's chancy.

Hill Crossing

Beyond the poles, a row of solid hills spins through the lava without corroding, like the teeth of some enormous gear. The hills roll right past Mario, with grates here and there as obstacles along the way and another platform farther down, along the rolling path.

Look at the positions of the grates along the rolling path, then take a running long jump right off the side, toward the hills. Keep the Crouch button held down during this entire sequence so that whenever Mario touches solid ground, he immediately rolls forward. When Mario's airborne, steer him generally away from upcoming grates. When rolling forward, be ready to go right from rolling right back into another running long jump at the top of each hill. At the far end, be ready to jump off the right side of the rolling hills and onto the platform leading onward.

Pause briefly and hit the triple ? block for some coins and a Heart.

Bubbling Up

This section is like a platforming challenge for Lava Bubbles over solid moon. Capture one of the nearby Lava Bubbles and swim up the lava flow to find circular pits of lava in between sections of cold, hard stone. What's worse is that Moonsnakes slowly spin nearby, each muddying up the entry path to each pit. To proceed, a Lava Bubble must travel all the way across, so touching down on regular ground extinguishes the current capture, forcing Mario to go recruit another Lava Bubble and start over.

Hold a cap throw button throughout this sequence to keep the Lava Bubble swimming as quick as possible, adding a little extra reach to jumps. As a timing trick, jump for the next lava pit just before the nearest Moonsnake in the way swipes over the current lava pit. This usually grants a relatively clear shot falling into the next pit. When jumping, commit hard, and don't be sheepish about jump momentum; you can keep going if you take a hit from a Moonsnake while falling into the next lava pool, but you can't keep going if you hit solid ground and pop the Lava Bubble.

Hop across the lava pits and jump up to the shelf ahead to find a lava canon, all ready to launch the Lava Bubble across a huge chasm.

313

Uprooted

After splashdown from canon launch, swim around the right side of this curious structure to find a Heart hovering above the smoking murk. The Lava Bubble can easily leap high enough from the lava to get the Heart.

Swim back to the platform near the arrival zone to find a lone Uproot. This Uproot is the ticket upward here, since it's all vertical, with some coverings along the way that Mario can't bypass under his own power. The Uproot has to do it with its incredible on-the-spot growing power. Duos of moving cog-like platforms line the way up this tower. At several points along the route upward, you have to extend an Uproot's legs to quickly land on the higher of two moving platforms. This needs to be handled while Burrbo hordes appear on motionless platforms along the way. You can drop out of the Uproot capture and slay the Burrbos with cap tosses, quickly re-capturing the dazed Uproot, but more Burrbos reappear. It's better to navigate around the Burrbos, using their predictable movement to stay ahead of where they'll be clumsily pouncing. Just avoiding the Burrbos in a small space rather than engaging them is good practice for later in this very kingdom, too.

Keep an eye out for movable covers above the lifts and platforms along the way, and quickly move underneath them and raise them quickly by shaking motion control for a rapid, extra-tall Uproot extension. Atop the last vertical lift, right before the final platform that must be pushed down, stand atop it and fully extend by shaking the controller to reveal a ? block containing another Heart. This may be a diabolical marathon, but there's proverbial hydration along the way.

At the top, a coin ring gives away a semi-hidden vertical chamber that can be ascended either by wall jumping or using Uproot. The final corridor in here requires bypassing some Fuzzies in a tight space that strangely fills and empties of icy water from the *ceiling*. Time short stints in the water to take you over short climbs and around the string of Fuzzies in the way, before finally popping out on a normal ledge beyond the ice water hallway.

Conveyors Licked

An old friend is here to help with the next bit. Break the egg and throw Cappy onto Yoshi, avoiding the Fuzzies who are in the way. Yoshi's unique ability to stick to walls by licking is the key to traveling up the beams ahead, which have conveyor surfaces. Jump between them, then stick to one side by jumping and sticking Yoshi's tongue to it.

From here to the top, you need only hold the Cap Throw button as necessary to make Yoshi swap sides, whether to collect coin groups or to dodge Fuzzies. At the top, stick to the left side, ride it comfortably higher than the right side, then jump off. From here, you can either travel forward, or turn and look back down at the top of the rock you just climbed past—the crag topping the Uproot tower and icy hallway swim. There's a big pile of coins atop it, which you can easily collect by jumping down from here, but you'll need to take the conveyors up again using Yoshi's tongue clings. You can keep Yoshi for the next section too, but he isn't required for it.

Ivy League

The P-Switch ahead heralds a tricky time-limited segment. The switch triggers a rapid growth of vines, forming a moving path ahead. Ahead on the vine road, a pulse beam floats a little to the right of the path, near a bunch of breakable blocks. You can easily just jump over them and pick them up on the other side, but striking the pulse beam (either with a cap toss or Yoshi's tongue) causes an energy wave that destroys the blocks, netting a few coins.

This path is just for the fun of it, and requires a bracing drop back down to the moving vines.

Farther along the weaving path, blocks hover to the right, leading on a precipitous gapped stairway upward toward a Heart. This is a fun path to take for the challenge of the climb, but is a little misleading, since a better health situation is up ahead on the vine road to the left.

Before that, though, three sheer walls of breakable blocks lie in the path of the vine road. Either use deft, accurate jumping to clear the three increasingly tall block walls, or activate a nearby pulse beam, dodge the energy waves it emits, and run along the vine road underneath the block walls when the path is clear.

Ahead on the left a large flat platform hosts yet another appearance of the mysterious Sphynx, who has just one question: where hasn't he visited? The correct answer reveals a Life-Up Heart in the chamber underneath him! If you fail somewhere farther along and restart at the beginning, this chamber is open already on future attempts, so you don't have to keep answering the Sphynx's final riddle.

This Life-Up Heart is a great boon and a nice recharge, the first one you find since the Yoo-foe at the very start. It's also the last one, so guard the extra Hearts well. A fresh P-Switch on the Sphynx's platform creates a vine bridge that leads to the next portion, which is where the previous vine path leads, if you don't detour to the Sphynx plateau.

Sphynx

What is the only kingdom that I, the great Sphynx, have not visited?

- Wooded Kingdom
- Mushroom Kingdom
- Sand Kingdom
- Seaside Kingdom

Block Party

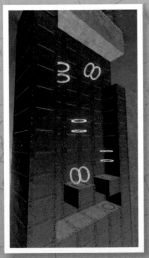

This is another tower climb like the one cleared with Uproot's help, but with a twist. A sheer metal wall stands under a narrow platform, with a scarecrow dangling upside down from its own platform near the base. Standing on the narrow platform and throwing Cappy onto the scarecrow activates a dangerous sequence on the tall wall, where individual blocks thrust across the walkway and lock in place. If Mario's in the way, they push him off and into the lava. If he's to the left or right of the section pushing out, it becomes a new platform or wall jump surface. Sections of the wall shake in the background briefly before jutting out, giving Mario just a second (literally a second, it's not long) to get out of the way. There's no Cappy for cap/dive jumps here, since the Bonneter is riding the upside-down Scarecrow's platform up next to the tower, powering the puzzle in the first place. He rejoins Mario at the top.

The first half of the climb is mostly just an exercise in learning not to get pushed off. On the first floor, go right as far as is safe, and be ready to wall jump up when jutting wall segments make that a possibility. Up one level, move as far to the left as is possible, and wait again for a new way upward to appear. Up on this third tier, move quickly back to the far right, wall jumping up through some coin rings. Up a fourth layer, quickly move under the next coin rings leading upward, then stop—this is the first time you don't want to go as far as possible. Wait for walls to compress around the rings above, then wall jump up through them. Survive until this jutting of the wall makes a chimney snaking upward and you're most of the way there—the rest is mostly just wall jumping back and forth all the way up as quickly as possible.

The coin rings don't steer Mario wrong.

Soaring Underground

Before, Yoshi waited to help before a crucial area. Now, Glydon does the honors. The gliding lizard sees Mario across the next gap, which is saturated with clouds of Urban Stingbys. Hey, it doesn't look very urban down here.

Capture Glydon and leap off the edge, immediately gliding and keeping an eye out for flies directly in Glydon's flightpath. Steer left or right to avoid taking head-on hits, but not too much, since any effort besides neutral gliding loses a little lift. To make it across, you have to catch the spiraling updrafts along the way. Shake the controller for extra height when passing through the vortexes. At the far end, with a mix of skill and luck, Glydon lands unscathed on a solid platform before a large stretch of inhospitable lava.

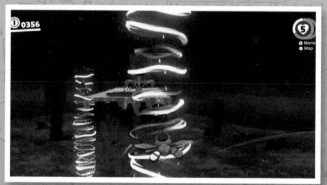

Trick Homing Throw

Delightfully, it's possible to skip this section and uncover a secret Heart with some creative hat throwing. Instead of standing on the narrow platform just under the huge wall, stand on top of the platform with the scarecrow underneath, with Mario's toes just at the edge. Do a downward throw, then use motion controls to drag Cappy at the full extension of the downward throw. It may take a few tries, but by throwing Cappy straight down along the platform then dragging him under it, you are able to ride the scarecrow's platform to the roof!

Forkfuls of Lava

The stretch beyond the Glydon landing pad would be solutionless, if not for some trusty Volbonans who've trekked a tad ahead of Mario. Whether they're here to help or just researching experimental cooking methods is no matter. Handholds are handholds.

Mario must be flicked from one Volbonan to another in midair—capture a Volbonan fork, torque it back to build up power while aiming, then launch Mario toward the next Volbonan. On the way, just even with the fork and right above the lava, throw Cappy toward the next Volbonan head. Remember that throwing Cappy in midair briefly stops Mario's vertical momentum, so make sure to wait and throw the cap at the right moment on the downward fall, rather than tossing Cappy too early, overeagerly.

At each successive Volbonan, take a breath and aim carefully again. Miss the flick or the cap toss capture of any given step here and it's probably curtains, since neither side will likely be within reach as Mario bounces across a sheer lava field, along the Volbonans but unable to throw his cap while burning. Make it all the way across and hop down the pipe here to continue onward.

Clouds of Burrbos

The moon gets ever more mysterious the farther inward an intrepid explorer plunges. Here, a sea of clouds blankets a vast pit, across which a single platform travels. Powering the platform is a pulse beam, located at its center. Along its route are numerous other pulse beams, which can resonate with energy emissions from the platform's pulse beam, depending on the distance. And above the platform's route are several platforms that mysteriously spawn frightening numbers of idiotic Burrbos. The colorful Burrbos hop and stumble down from these platforms and onto the moving platform. A bunch of Burrbos hopping around toward Mario on a small platform is naturally not an ideal situation. Using the Burrbo perches as platforms along the way might seem appealing, but is dangerous considering spiky Burrbos can suddenly appear anywhere on them. Riding the platform without triggering pulse beams can be done, but requires attentive stepping around the perimeter of the platform, baiting Burrbos into pouncing at Mario, then rotating around the edge or jumping over all of them to the other side.

Of course, triggering the pulse beams and reveling in mass destruction of Burrbos in all directions works too, but you have to keep your attention on the platform instead of the Burrbo fireworks, because this sets up a variable platforming challenge for Mario along the way. Nearing the end, don't be afraid to jump well off the platform and dive jump off Cappy toward solid ground to end the Burrbo and pulse beam chaos as early as possible. Ahead is a more sedate but exacting challenge.

Pokio's Starring Role

After crossing the misty sea down here, now it's time to climb back toward the greater crater. A lone Pokio guards this climb, which is noble, but a single bird is no match for Mario by this point. Capture Pokio and observe the wooden pendulums swooping back and forth overhead.

Facing the abyss at the edge, jump straight up as the lowest cog swings down, poking it with the beak as it passes. Make sure to do this smoothly, without also inadvertently shaking the controller or tilting analog sticks.

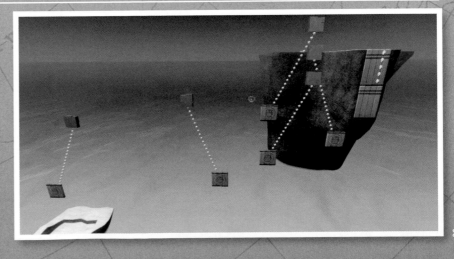

With true aim, Pokio will now be stuck to the pendulum, swooping back and forth. At the edge of each pendulum's swooping path, flick upward to the next level, deftly stabbing the next beakhold on the way up. You can drag back on the stick and release to flick upward, like aiming on a Pole or Volbonan, but you can also just shake the control (with no input on the analog stick) for a perfect upward launch. When stabbing at the next platform in midair, aim using the analog stick while poking with the beak, but release the analog stick immediately after aiming, to avoid accidentally pulling back for a flick right after sticking with the beak.

Midway up, a Heart can be had by riding one pendulum all the way to the left. Detour for this if you only have a Heart or two of health left. If at some point on this climb you *miss* a Pokio beak and begin falling, your first saving grace is the motion-shake Pokio spin, which works as a double jump once per airborne period. Your second saving grace is ditching Pokio in midair and tackling back toward the platform down below where you originally captured Pokio to begin with. Bailing out and redoing the section is a lot better than redoing the entire flaming cavern!

Donkey Kong at the Center of the Moon

At the top, Pokio's considerable talents aren't needed anymore, and a curious 8-bit challenge ensues. Enter the 8-bit pipe here to begin a mind-bending platforming battle against Donkey Kong. The barrel-tosser resides in the center of the field here, and Mario must travel inward in a curving path around Donkey Kong. Wherever Mario is, it can be briefly confusing to reorient control after running all the way around part of the circle. Controls reset anytime you release the directions, so just remember to push in the direction you want Mario to go. If he's facing up and you want him to run up you can just press up on the stick, you don't need to worry about whether he's facing up on his left or his right side or what have you.

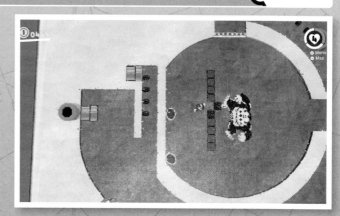

Circle inward toward the classic nemesis and jump to trigger the four ? blocks located directly under him. Defeating Donkey Kong opens the way to the pipe leading back up out of this area to the larger chamber.

Escape, Redux

Now for something completely different. Ascending back to the cave proper, Mario finds a framed painting of a familiar enemy, but something about it is different...

Jump into the Bowser painting to take on a new challenge path with the king baddie! Lumber forward, shattering walls with Cap button claw swipes and motion-flick fireballs, to reveal a long stretch of narrow rock bridges over the abyss, guarded by cannons at almost every step along the way. Cannonballs come lumbering one after another for long stretches ahead. Luckily, Bowser's attacks destroy incoming boulders, and he has a surprisingly mobile vertical jump. Move forward through the maze of rolling threats, either weaving through them, jumping over them, bashing them apart, or a mix of all three as needed.

The toughest stretch probably occurs in a lengthy sideways corridor with boulder after boulder rolling in from behind, and a long stretch of hall ahead clogged with breakable sand. Bowser can advance, but only without getting greedy. Take one swipe to clear a block ahead, then turn and swipe at an incoming boulder, repeat. Don't get anxious and think you can speed it up trying to squeeze in an extra swipe to bash another section of wall before attending to the cannonballs rolling in from behind. You can't.

Culmina Town Hall

Emerge from the Bowser nightmare and you find some more ground to cover before escaping the cavern, but the threat is over. Enter the pipe at the end after crossing some congratulatory pylons to return to the moon's surface, finally! Here are more Binoculars and Frogs, as well as the strange replica of New Donk City's Town Hall.

Capture a Frog again to get a leg up ascending the tower, which is quite tall. Use motion-flick jumps to get extra high while frog jumping. After climbing high enough to access the main antenna, it's time to drop the Frog capture and drift to the spire as Mario. Mario hugs the antenna like a flagpole. Climb all the way to the top to reach the only Power Moon in this kingdom, but the single hardest Power Moon to acquire in the odyssey: **Long Journey's End!**

Earning this Multi-Moon also unlocks the **Invisibility Hat!** Wearing this hat makes Mario almost totally invisible, with only his shadow and Cappy's eyes as indications that he's there at all.

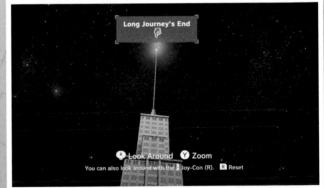

Explore around the tower for a couple of fun finds.

Extend Your Stay

It's Not *Really* Long Journey's End

Let's say you really persevered to complete Darker Side of the Moon as soon as you could access it, with 500 Power Moons in Mario's accomplished hands during the antenna climb. That means you now have 503 Power Moons. Our hats are off to you! But, there are still literally hundreds of moons left to find. Your odyssey probably isn't over by a long shot. Explore all of the kingdoms more thoroughly to your heart's content: gather clues from Hint Toad, Talkatoo, and amiibo; tackle Archivist Toadette's achievements list; keep up with an adventurous Tostarenan tourist or wandering royalty; collect missing souvenirs and build up your wardrobe with cool fashions as a growing moon count unlocks bonus stuff.

Mario's Suitcase

Mario couldn't have known the journey that awaited him when he set off to stop Bowser. But with no chance to pack a bag, the plucky plumber soon found himself on his biggest adventure without a Tanooki or Frog Suit in sight. Poor Mario didn't even have time to pack extra underwear!

Fortunately for Mario, the Crazy Cap brand of fashionable clothing is never far away. With stores popping up around the world—often in the least likely of locations—the latest in cultural, professional, and formal attire is never far away. Crazy Cap stores carry a variety of hats and suits

guaranteed to fit every mood. Though most of the outfits can only be purchased with the region's local currency, others can be bought with standard gold coins, though many of these items are reserved for V.I.P. customers.

Every Crazy Cap store contains a wardrobe closet identical to the one aboard the Odyssey. Through powers best left unquestioned, both wardrobes can be used to change Mario's clothing whenever you wish. And yes, he can even find a fresh pair of Boxer Shorts.

Random Threads

Don't know what to wear? Give the Random option a try. Each time Mario runs out of Hearts, he'll reemerge with a different hat and suit combination. It's a great way to experiment with all the different outfits you've bought him.

Matching Outfits

The following outfits come as two-piece outfits with matching hat and suit.

Mario Odyssey Costume

Mario Cap

· **N/A**

A red hat that has seen its fair share of adventures.

Availability: Starting hat.

Mario Suit

· **N/A**

This tried-and-true outfit has weathered many adventures.

Availability: Starting suit.

Bonneton Tuxedo

Black Top Hat

· 🎩 5

This classy number is the best seller at Bonneton's Crazy Cap shop.

Black Tuxedo

· 🎩 10

Bonneton's Crazy Cap shop is famous for these impeccably tailored outfits.

Availability: After returning to Cap Kingdom.

Crazy Cap

Employee Cap

· 🪙 50

A Crazy Cap original!

Availability: After completing Cascade Kingdom.

Employee Uniform

· 🪙 150

Show your Crazy Cap brand loyalty with this striking outfit!

Caveman

Caveman Headwear

· (●) 5

Primitive plumbers fashioned these from the skulls of Parabones.

Caveman Outfit

· (●) 10

Early adventurers wore these outfits for maximum freedom of movement, if not maximum warmth.

Availability: After returning to Cascade Kingdom.

Tostarenan Outfit

Sombrero

· (◆) 5

Traditional Tostarenan hat. Keeps the sun out of your eyes and is just plain fun to wear.

Poncho

· (◆) 10

Traditional folk dress of the Tostarena region. Keeps the sun off and the breezes on.

Availability: After reaching Sand Kingdom.

Cowboy

Cowboy Hat

· (◆) 20

A classic hat, perfectly suited for wearing as you ride into sunsets.

Cowboy Outfit

· (◆) 25

Old-fashioned duds with a frontier feel. Gunslinging and cow-punching optional.

Availability: After reaching Sand Kingdom.

Swimming

Swim Goggles

· (◉) 5

So fashionable you'll want to wear them on land.

Swimwear

· (◉) 10

The floaty ring does not actually float—it's just an accent on the outfit.

Availability: After reaching Lake Kingdom.

Fashion

Fashionable Cap

· (○) 50

An upscale upgrade to an upstanding hero's upper half.

Fashionable Outfit

· (○) 150

I'm not clashing. YOU'RE clashing!

Availability: After reaching Lake Kingdom.

Explorer

Explorer Hat

· (●) 5

Just because the territory is uncharted doesn't mean your head should be uncovered.

Explorer Outfit

· (●) 10

Clothes that keep you comfortable even in the deepest heart of the wilderness.

Availability: After reaching Wooded Kingdom.

Scientist

Scientist Visor

● ◎ 20

A strange piece of headwear that gives off a science-y vibe.

Scientist Outfit

● ◎ 25

It's a scientific fact that nothing says "scientist" like a lab coat.

Availability: After reaching Wooded Kingdom.

Mechanic

Mechanic Cap

● ◎ 50

A good hat to wear when it's time to get down to work.

Mechanic Outfit

● ○ 150

An outfit seemingly doomed to get stained in motor oil.

Availability: After reaching Wooded Kingdom.

Aviator

Aviator Cap

● ◎ 5

Gotta keep those ears warm at 33,000 feet.

Aviator Outfit

● ◎ 10

This jacket is how you let people know you're a pilot when you're not in a cockpit.

Availability: After reaching Lost Kingdom.

Construction

Builder Helmet

● ◎ 5

Whether you're building or inspecting, you gotta keep your head safe.

Builder Outfit

● ◎ 10

The perfect outfit whether you're constructing or inspecting the construction work of others.

Availability: After reaching Metro Kingdom.

Golfer

Golf Cap

● ◎ 20

You're not playing golf unless everyone is staring at your hat.

Golf Outfit

● ◎ 25

"What?! Wait, let me turn down my outfit so I can hear you!"

Availability: After reaching Metro Kingdom.

City Suit

Black Fedora

● ○ 50

Perfect for business, business casual, casual, or casual business!

Black Suit

● ○ 150

You can wear this outfit just about anywhere—it always looks good.

Availability: After reaching Metro Kingdom.

Snow

Snow Hood

· ❄ 5

A down hood that keeps the cold from making you bitter.

Availability: After reaching Snow Kingdom.

Snow Suit

· ❄ 10

After decades of ice levels, FINALLY a good, warm jacket.

Resort Wear

Resort Hat

· ❀ 5

This hat is made for breathability, aiding in relaxation.

Availability: After reaching Seaside Kingdom.

Resort Outfit

· ❀ 10

This outfit lets everyone know you take your relaxing seriously.

Sailor

Sailor Hat

· ❀ 20

A hat respected the world over, especially the parts near water.

Availability: After reaching Seaside Kingdom.

Sailor Suit

· ❀ 25

Of all uniforms, the one that is most likely to get really, really wet.

Pirate

Pirate Hat

· ⬤ 50

YARRRR!

Pirate Outfit

· ⬤ 150

Whether plundering cargo or burying treasure, you're gonna need an extremely fancy coat.

Availability: After reaching Seaside Kingdom.

Chef

Chef Hat

· ⬤ 5

Anyone wearing one of these makes many friends on Mount Volbono.

Chef Suit

· ⬤ 10

Red scarves are a staple of fashion on Mount Volbono.

Availability: After reaching Luncheon Kingdom.

Artist

Painter's Cap

· ⬤ 20

Is it even really painting if you're not wearing one of these?

Painter's Outfit

· ⬤ 25

Just the outfit you would expect to see on a painter. Pre-stained for your convenience.

Availability: After reaching Luncheon Kingdom.

Clown

Clown Hat

🪙 50

The perfect hat for pratfalls, teeny cars, and wasting good pie.

Availability: After reaching Luncheon Kingdom.

Clown Suit

🪙 150

Roomy enough for all your tumbling needs, colorful enough to be seen from space.

Samurai

Samurai Helmet

🪙 5

The samurai wore helmets that were functional AND fancy.

Availability: After reaching Bowser's Kingdom.

Samurai Armor

🪙 10

The samurai basically walked around wearing works of art.

Happi

Happi Headband

🪙 20

This coiled headband is perfect when you want to cover just a BIT of your head.

Availability: After reaching Bowser's Kingdom.

Happi Outfit

🪙 25

Traditional clothing designed to be easy to move around in at a festival.

Mario's Wedding Tux

Mario's Top Hat

🪙 N/A

A white silk hat, perfect for the biggest day of one's life.

Mario's Tuxedo

🪙 N/A

An exquisite coat with tails. WARNING: Do not engage in plumbing while wearing.

Availability: After reaching Moon Kingdom.

Astronaut

Space Helmet

🪙 5

When you need to avoid the void.

Space Suit

🪙 10

The preferred outfit for steps and leaps of any size.

Availability: After reaching Moon Kingdom.

Football Player

Football Helmet

🪙 50

A colorful helmet to help keep one's head safe from the sporting life.

Football Uniform

🪙 150

Bright colors and big shoulder pads never go out of fashion.

Availability: After reaching Moon Kingdom.

Mario 64

Mario 64 Cap

· ⭐ 15

A charmingly blocky version of a classic.

Mario 64 Suit

· ⭐ 20

When you just want to wrap yourself in nostalgia.

Availability: After reaching Mushroom Kingdom.

Classic

Classic Cap

· 🪙 50

For the truly nostalgic, it doesn't get any more classic than this.

Classic Suit

· 🪙 150

This outfit is still loved by longtime fans. DK has never been a fan, though.

Availability: After reaching Mushroom Kingdom.

Luigi

Luigi Cap

· 🪙 100

The standard cap in a vivid green. The L stands for "winner."

Luigi Suit

· 🪙 200

A bright green version of an established classic. Green means "let's-a go"!

Availability: 180/160 Power Moons.

Dr. Mario

Doctor Headwear
· 🪙 100

Headwear worn by a doctor famous for extremely colorful prescriptions.

Doctor Outfit

· 🪙 200

White coat worn by a doctor famous for fighting our most colorful viruses.

Availability: 240/220 Power Moons

Waluigi

Waluigi Cap
· 🪙 100

A cap with an upside-down L on it. It's barely used!

Waluigi Suit

· 🪙 200

This outfit makes you want to lurk in the shadows, waiting for a turn in the spotlight.

Availability: 280/260 Power Moons.

Diddy Kong

Diddy Kong Hat

· 🪙 100

A red cap with a strikingly long brim. Smells unusual.

Diddy Kong Suit
· 🪙 200

A popular outfit among tail enthusiasts.

Availability: 320/300 Power Moons.

325

Wario

Wario Cap

• 340

A cap bearing a distinctive W. It doesn't fit well and kind of chafes.

Wario Suit
• 200

The kind of outfit that you want to wash at least once before you wear it.

Availability: 360/340 Power Moons.

Bowser's Wedding Tux

Bowser's Top Hat

• 1000

A replica of the unique hat Bowser had made for the big day.

Bowser's Tuxedo

• 2000

For a terrifying, fire-breathing monster covered in spikes, Bowser sure cleans up nice.

Availability: 440/420 Power Moons.

Peach's Bridal Dress

Bridal Veil

• 1000

A perfect replica of Princess Peach's veil.

Bridal Gown
• 2000

A replica of Peach's wedding dress (though it did have to be altered a bit for Mario's measurements).

Availability: 480/460 Power Moons.

Gold Mario

Gold Mario Cap

• 1000

A seriously shiny hat.

Gold Mario Suit

• 2000

This outfit just goes all the way with the gold thing.

Availability: 520/500 Power Moons.

Metal Mario

Metal Mario Cap

• 1000

A metal cap that seems somehow familiar...

Metal Mario Suit

• 2000

When you want to wrap yourself in nostalgia, and then in aluminum foil.

Availability: 560/540 Power Moons.

King

King's Crown
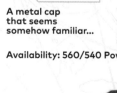
• N/A

An impressive crown acquired in Rabbit Ridge.

King's Outfit

• N/A

This majestic outfit was obtained in Rabbit Ridge

Availability: After completing Dark Side.

Extra Hats

Captain's Hat

Hat for the captain of the Odyssey, brimming with authority.

Availability: After completing Cascade Kingdom.

- **N/A**

Invisibility Hat

A very rare hat acquired at Culmina Crater. Easy to lose in the closet.

Availability: After completing Darker Side.

- **N/A**

Extra Clothes

Boxer Shorts

Comfortable, breezy boxers in a vibrant mushroom-like pattern.

Availability: After completing Cascade Kingdom.

-  **1000**

Skeleton Suit

This skeleton costume uses cutting-edge, er, something to, um... Look, we're not sure how this works. But it's cool, right?

Availability: After reaching Mushroom Kingdom.

- **9999**

Hakama

This traditional outfit has a nontraditional M monogram.

Availability: 380 Power Moons.

- **500**

Souvenirs and Stickers

There will come a time when the memories of Mario's adventure aboard the Odyssey fade; when the aches and pains from his struggle against Bowser and the Broodals heal; and when life returns to normal. It happens faster than expected.

But when it does, Mario need only glance at the shelves of the Odyssey to be reminded of all he's seen, the friends he made, and the wonders he experienced. From the Rubber Dorrie commemorating his swim with the gentle giant, to the Pauline Statue that will forever remind Mario of the New Donk Festival, his collection of souvenirs will be there, helping him relive the memories of his incredible journey.

Whether in the form of stickers slapped on the side of the Odyssey or a Butterfly Mobile hanging from the ceiling, souvenirs aren't to let the world know where we've been. They're to remind the traveler of all they've accomplished.

There are forty-three souvenirs and stickers for Mario to purchase. Help him—and you—preserve the memories of this amazing journey by collecting them all.

Souvenirs for the Odyssey

Plush Frog

These little froggies wear tiny top hats for self-defense, which looks so darn cute they made a toy version.

🎩 5

Bonneton Tower Model

This model of a tower in the Cap Kingdom is popular with tourists thanks to its faithful re-creation and detailed craftsmanship.

🎩 25

T-Rex Model

This dino's pose is so impressively lifelike, you can almost hear it roar!

◉ 5

Triceratops Trophy

A replica of a real dinosaur fossil from the Cascade Kingdom. Hang this on a wall, and it'll completely transform a room.

◉ 25

Inverted Pyramid Model

A famous location in the Tostarena ruins. Even the tiniest details are faithfully re-created, like the reliefs etched onto the walls.

◈ 25

Jaxi Statue

In the Tostarena region, the Jaxi has lived alongside the people since ancient times. This statue is made from the stones of the ruins!

◈ 5

Underwater Dome

This snow globe featuring the Water Plaza in Lake Lamode uses water from the Lake Kingdom.

⬡ 25

Rubber Dorrie

Fans of the universally loved Dorrie have been clamoring for a quality reproduction like this. It's designed to feel just like the real thing!

⬡ 5

Flowers from Steam Gardens

This popular arrangement of flowers from Steam Gardens is often given as a gift.

◎ 5

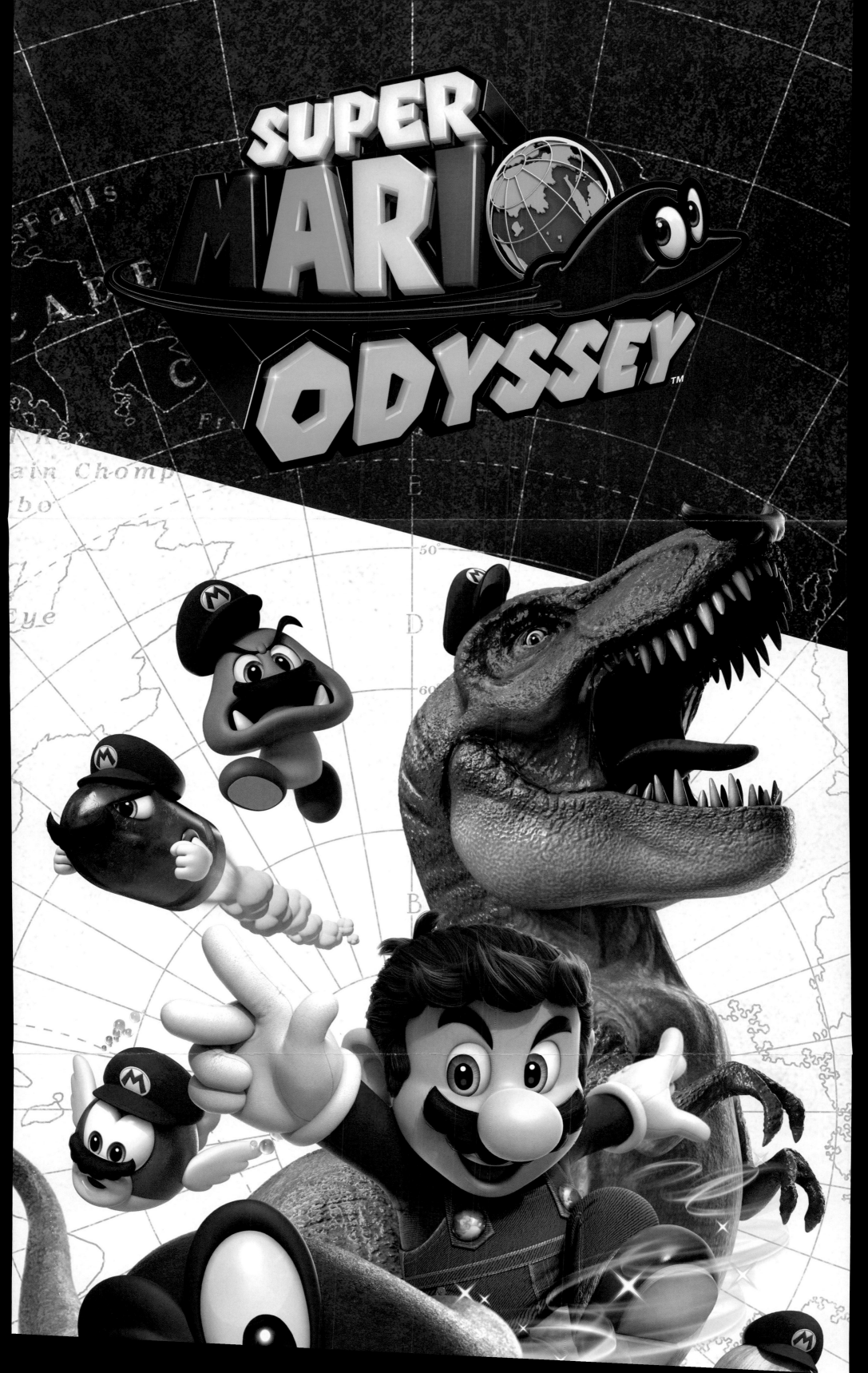

Steam Gardener Watering Can

This robot-shaped watering can is deigned to look like the people of the Wooded Kingdom. A nice souvenir, it's also great for gardening!

• ⦿ 25

Potted Palm Tree

This plant grows all over Forgotten Isle. Hardy enough to thrive even in a poisonous swamp, it has become quite popular with gardeners.

• ⦿ 5

Butterfly Mobile

Inspired by the butterflies that live on Forgotten Isle, don't be surprised if you find yourself mysteriously losing track of time as you gaze at this beauty.

• ⦿ 25

Pauline Statue

This statue of New Donk City's mayor, Pauline, was made as a testament to her enduring popularity.

• ⦿ 25

New Donk City Hall Model

This miniature model of New Donk City Hall (with working lights!) has been a big hit with fans of the Metro Kingdom.

• ⦿ 5

Shiverian Rug

Featuring the same patterns as those found on Shiverian clothing, this rug is great for keeping warm from the toes on up!

• ⦿ 5

Shiverian Nesting Dolls

Open one of these folk-art dolls and another Shiverian pops out! It's hard to tell them apart, but they're based on winners of past races.

• ⦿ 25

Sand Jar

Each glance at this jar filled with sand from the Bubblaine coast evokes sunny scenes of carefree days at the beach.

• ⦿ 25

Glass Tower Model

A replica of the Glass Tower that rises in the center of Bubblaine!

• ⦿ 5

Souvenir Forks

Inspired by the people of Mount Volbono, this cute pair of tall and short forks looks a bit like a parent and child.

• ⦿ 5

Vegetable Plate

This toy food lets you pretend you're cooking with real ingredients from Mount Volbono. They can also be stacked up like blocks!

• ⦿ 25

Paper Lantern

These lanterns are found in Bowser's Castle. In the old days, people used to walk around with them like flashlights.

• ⦿ 5

Jizo Statue

Found placed all over, these guardian deities watch over travelers in silent protection.

• ⦿ 25

Moon Rock Fragment

This strange rock fragment was found on Honeylune Ridge. Its effects are... unknown.

• ⦿ 5

Moon Lamp

This spinning moon is a fashionable way to brighten up any room. It's also quite well-made and sturdier than it looks!

• ⦿ 25

Mushroom Cushion Set

The mushroom pattern on these cushions has certainly withstood the test of time. A tablecloth is also included in the set!

• ⦿ 10

Peach's Castle Model

Who wouldn't want a scale model of this famous castle! Even the beautiful stained glass window in the center has been faithfully re-created.

• ⦿ 25

Stickers

Cap Kingdom Sticker

A sticker inspired by Top-Hat Tower.

• ⬤ 5

Cascade Kingdom Sticker

A sticker inspired by T-Rex.

• ⬤ 5

Sand Kingdom Sticker

A sticker inspired by the Inverted Pyramid.

• ⬤ 5

Lake Kingdom Sticker

A sticker inspired by the Lochlady Dress.

• ⬤ 5

Wooded Kingdom Sticker

A sticker inspired by the Soirée Bouquet.

• ⬤ 10

Lost Kingdom Sticker

A sticker inspired by Forgotten Isle.

• ⬤ 5

Metro Kingdom Sticker

A sticker inspired by Mayor Pauline.

• ⬤ 10

Snow Kingdom Sticker

A sticker inspired by Bound Bowl Grand Prix.

• ⬤ 5

Seaside Kingdom Sticker

A sticker inspired by the Glass Tower.

• ⬤ 10

Luncheon Kingdom Sticker

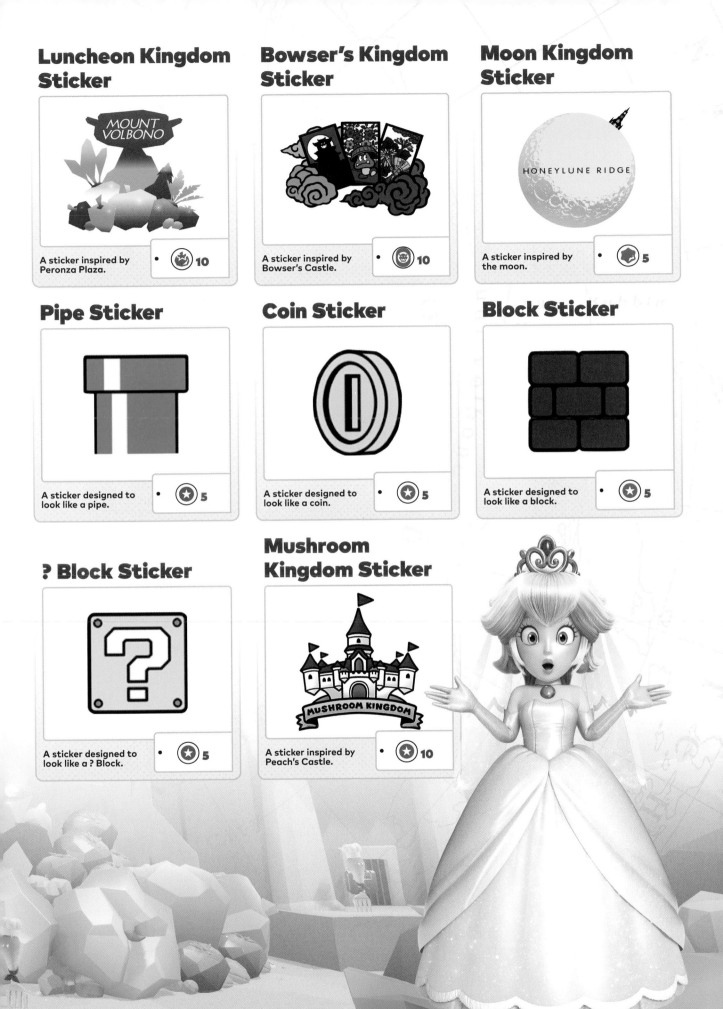

A sticker inspired by Peronza Plaza. • 10

Bowser's Kingdom Sticker

A sticker inspired by Bowser's Castle. • 10

Moon Kingdom Sticker

A sticker inspired by the moon. • 5

Pipe Sticker

A sticker designed to look like a pipe. • 5

Coin Sticker

A sticker designed to look like a coin. • 5

Block Sticker

A sticker designed to look like a block. • 5

? Block Sticker

A sticker designed to look like a ? Block. • 5

Mushroom Kingdom Sticker

A sticker inspired by Peach's Castle. • 10

Odyssey Ecology

It's a wide world out there, and Mario and Cappy encounter all manner of regional flora and fauna throughout their long journey. These listings were compiled from the notes of many brave explorer Toads, and first detail harmless things that are also candidates for Cappy capture. The second group includes dangerous, perhaps even hostile, wildlife and creatures who can at least hurt Mario, if they don't outright come after him. These can also be captured. Then, there are those hostile creatures who simply attack and cannot be captured. The boss listing follows the enemy group. *Super Mario Odyssey* is packed with surprises, so tread lightly exploring these pages before exploring a fair bit on your own!

Friendly Capture Targets

These objects, plants, and animals are not hostile, and won't hurt Mario if he bumps into them. Capture them with a cap toss. Most of these capture targets give Mario extra movement options, unlock new areas, or help solve Power Moon puzzles.

Binoculars

Get an eagle's-eye view of the surrounding kingdom with Binoculars. Mario launches up into a hovering position, able to scope in any direction. Use the zoom function to focus on items of interest. Pop back out of the Binoculars (or any captured creature or object) with the Crouch button.

Boulder

The Boulder is one of a few captures where Mario uses Cappy's spectral capturing magic to move an inanimate object. Mario in Boulder form can...well, he can scoot around a little bit.

Bowser Statue

Like capturing a Boulder, but more regal and evil.

Cactus

Like capturing a Bowser Status, if a Bowser Statue were a Cactus.

Coin Coffer

This strange little creature won't be visible at first, but may be revealed when you stumble upon it resting in the forest. It stumbles off, trying to cloak and hide again. Coin Coffer can be stomped repeatedly for many coins, or captured and used as a rapid (and expensive) coin dispenser.

Glydon

This ambitious lizard doesn't fly, exactly, but gracefully glides. He can't gain more altitude while gliding unless he passes through a spiraling gust of rising air. Shake the controller to gain extra lift when passing through an updraft.

Frog

This is the first capture Mario experiences, early on in Bonneton. Frogs are one of the few animals capable of jumps even springier than Mario's, and they can drift in midair even slower than during Mario's spin jump. Shake the controller for an even taller Frog jump.

Jizo

This heavy stone statue isn't the most mobile vehicle in the world, but it's at least heavy enough to clomp the items out of any glowing spots on the ground. Shake the controller to make Jizo statues bounce around more quickly.

Lakitu

The worst day fishing is better than the best day working, that's what Lakitu says. Take over Lakitu with Cappy to try it out. Cast the reel, wait patiently for shadows of fish underwater to tug at the bait, then lift up with motion control to try reeling them in.

Meat

Like a Boulder, but much more appetizing. Once it's properly salted and cooked, anyway.

Letter

Some large novelty letters can be controlled, like with the Boulder and Cactus.

Mini Rocket

Mini Rockets lead to special challenge stages nearby, either launching up through the clouds, or even plunging into deep valleys for Mini Rockets located right alongside cliffs.

Manhole Cover

That's one way to get past a locked or secured door; become the door and move out of the way.

Moe-Eye

These skittish Moe-Eye statues just want to relax somewhere warm with their sunglasses. Snap on the sunglasses to reveal hidden platforms, snap off the sunglasses to move more quickly. If you've exposed hidden platforms temporarily by triggering a P-Switch then snapping on Moe-Eye shades, you might have to take the shades off to lumber across quickly before the P-Switch activation wears off. Pop the shades back on briefly whenever you need to get another look at the (invisible) lay of the land.

Picture Match Part (Mario)

This is just like the Goomba Picture Match puzzle, but a little harder because of Mario's more complex face. Like with kingdom hint art, you can use the Nintendo Switch console's built-in snapshot feature to save a perfect reference, which helps with lining up Picture Match Parts.

Picture Match Part (Goomba)

A couple of Power Moon puzzles involve trying to reconstruct a Goomba's face as accurately as possible, taking control of facial features to rebuild the baddie.

Pole

Once a Pole is captured, aim by moving the stick away from the intended target, then release to launch Mario. Shake the controller to launch farther. Volbonans and Pokios work similarly.

Puzzle Part (Lake Kingdom)

The Puzzle Part puzzles involve rolling a square block around a small grid, trying to get one side affixed to the correct spot on the ground. In Lake Kingdom, it's a stone pillar with the base broken off in a specific shape.

RC Car

The RC Car controls delightfully like classic remote-controlled toy cars, so sort of like a speedy and weightless tank.

Puzzle Part (Metro Kingdom)

The Puzzle Part in Metro Kingdom is huge (but standard!) three-prong power outlet, which must be lined up and plugged in correctly.

Shiverian Racer

The bouncy Shiverians make ideal snowbound vehicles themselves, just rolled up and bouncing. There are multiple races to undertake in Snow Kingdom as a Shiverian Racer. The key to winning races in Shiveria is to "bound" consistently whenever the Shiverian Racer bounces on the ground. Shake the controller or press the Jump button with good timing every time a Shiverian Racer bounces to surge forward and maintain high speed.

Spark Pylon

These electric ziplines are first found in Bonneton, leading to Cascade Kingdom. Mario temporarily transfers into the line, sparking along in lightning form. Ziplines can quickly cross long distances and otherwise-impassable gulfs. If coins or other pick-ups of interest are near the line in transit, shake the controller to divert briefly to the pick-ups before continuing along the line.

Volbonan

The fork-like inhabitants of Mount Volbono can be captured and used as Poles, flicking Mario over gaps or up sheer walls. Some challenging sequences involve flinging from one captured Volbonan to another.

Taxi

It's too bad it's only one Taxi, but keep an eye out for the car that looks like it can be fitted with a cap. This Taxi can take Mario and Cappy somewhere special.

Zipper

One of modern life's conveniences, in over-sized, cap-friendly form. Zipper creases in walls reveal spots where Cappy can unzip new paths in the environment.

Tree

Like Cactus or Boulder, a straightforward capture, but much more pine-scented.

Unfriendly Capture Targets

These critters include hungry wildlife, aggressive varmints, and servants of Bowser and the Broodals. One way or another, they can harm Mario. They can be captured, too. Capturing one of these baddies changes Mario's controls in the new form. Usually, these creatures are more capable or agile than Mario in specialized ways. Tap the Crouch button anytime to drop out of captured form as Mario and Cappy. The captured enemy is dazed for a while before disappearing.

Bullet Bill

This classic bullet adversary launches from a cannon nearby then seeks out Mario. It can turn left or right, but can't pitch up or down to change altitude. In 8-bit pipes, standing right next to a Bullet Bill cannon prevents it from firing, but this isn't true in regular environments like Sand Kingdom. After capturing Bullet Bill, pilot him to otherwise unreachable platforms before he flashes red and explodes. Shake the controller for a speed boost while flying.

Banzai Bill

An enormous Bullet Bill, basically. Banzai Bill plows through breakable bricks, unlike a Bullet Bill who is destroyed by the impact. Banzai Bill also has a much longer max flying range, so he can access even more remote platforms. When flying a captured Banzai Bill, shake the controller for an extra speed burst.

Chain Chomp

Gnashing Chain Chomps hop around and snap on their chain-link tethers, watchful for anything within their reach. They telegraph their paths briefly before sliding forward, snapping all the while. A captured Chain Chomp can be stretched and primed to launch in the other direction, destroying other enemies or shattering breakable surfaces.

Big Chain Chomp

A much bigger momma to the regular Chain Chomps. Big Chain Chomps hop around and stretch on their chains in the same way.

Chargin' Chuck

This heavily-padded football line-Koopa lowers a shoulder and plows at targets, smashing anything in the way. Capture Chargin' Chuck and you can barrel through anything breakable too.

Cheep Cheep

Normally, Cheep Cheeps are typical fishbrains, drifting languidly. A captured Cheep Cheep is a surprisingly agile underwater swimmer, able to wriggle quickly along while producing a headlamp-like effect with the glow of its huge eyes. Produce a spinning attack by shaking the controller.

Cheep Cheep (Snow Kingdom)

These Cheep Cheeps are just very much like their relatives in warmer kingdoms. These can survive the extreme temperatures found in the waters around Shiveria, which damages other creatures (Mario included) after just a few seconds of exposure. They can even survive a few errant bounces on freezing ground, outside of the water, before expiring and returning Mario to his own skin.

Fire Piranha Plant

Like Fire Bros, Fire Piranha Plants can set Mario on fire with their fireballs. Like Poison Piranha Plants, these toothy predators must be choked with a throwable item before they're vulnerable to Cappy capture. If flammable objects are nearby, captured Fire Piranha Plants can burn them down, Fire Bro-style.

Fire Bro

The classic *Super Mario Bros.* enemy returns, switching between flurries of fireballs and big hops to new vantage points. If Mario gets tagged by a Fire Bro fireball he'll be briefly scorched, forced to run around cooling off for several seconds. After capturing a Fire Bro, mash Cap Throw or shake the controller quickly for rapid fireball fire. Fireballs are obviously strong attacks, and will also light flammable objects.

Goomba

These small mushroom-like creatures clomp around in groups, aggressively ganging up on Mario. They can be squashed by jumping on them, or captured with a cap toss. When controlling a Goomba, start stacking his friends by jumping on other Goombas. Dash while using Goombas by holding the Cap Throw button, and shake the controller for an extra-high jump. Running around as a captured Goomba and building up Goomba stacks ends up being more useful than you might expect!

Gushen

These angry little octopuses can jet around aquatic environments with a reserve of water contained in a bubble around their bodies. Capture a Gushen to pilot it around, keeping an eye on the size of the water bubble to tell when the Gushen needs to touchdown on a body of water to recharge. Shake the controller for a spray of water in all directions. The water jets Gushen ejects are a forceful weapon, on top of being great propellant.

Lava Bubble

While most things don't want to be immersed in bubbling liquid, Lava Bubbles are right at home. Normally, they just leap up and down in place somewhere in a scalding pool, usually above somewhere Mario would want to jump. They're not expressly hostile though. A captured Lava Bubble becomes like driving a speedboat through hot soup. Shake the controller to leap forward in a spinning leap above the stew. Lava Bubbles can pass through chain-link grates, but landing on a solid surface extinguishes the bubble and returns Mario to normal form. Slain Magmatos collapse into lava puddles that work as "platforms" for Lava Bubbles across regular terrain.

Hammer Bro

Hammer Bros hop around like Fire Bros, but throw heavy objects in arcs instead of hurling fireballs. Hammer Bros don't only throw hammers. Some Hammer Bros who are aspiring cooks on top of their Koopa duties sling heavy pots. The heavy hammers or pots thrown by Hammer Bros can shatter some objects like crates, bricks, breakable rocks, and huge hunks of brittle cheese.

Parabones

These undead bags of Koopa bones have little wings, granting them the ability to hover over any gap. Stomping a striking Parabones only causes them to briefly collapse into bones, but they'll reanimate and renew their pursuit of Mario soon enough. Capture a Parabones to experience the joy of undead flight. Shake the controller for faster flapping and airspeed.

Paragoomba

Flying Goombas aren't naturally as aggressive as their earthbound relatives. Paragoombas usually just flap around a little path. Capture a Paragoomba to take advantage of its flight ability. Flap faster for quicker flight with motion controls.

Pokio

This little woodpecker packs an unexpected punch, stabbing targets with a long, sharp beak. Captured Pokios can climb certain walls by planting with the beak, then launching from it like off a Pole or Volbonan. Shake the controller while planted for a stronger launch than a regular flick. Shake the controller while jumping for a spinning little double-jump. Shake the controller while poking with the beak for a special spinning slice!

Poison Piranha Plant

These Piranha Plants spit poison around them. They're not safe to stomp on unless they're choking on something like a seed, rock, or hat. To capture a Poison Piranha Plant, throw a seed or rock into its gullet first, then toss Cappy onto it.

Sherm

Dodge tank shots and ground pound them to destroy Sherms. If captured, a Mario tank is a dominating offensive force, with a turret that can be motion-controlled for greater accuracy while launching rapid-fire tank shells.

T-Rex

The apex predator of all time is no match for a magical cap and a perseverant plumber. Naturally, no one wants to go toe-to-claw with a T-Rex, but get a little height with a nearby ledge or platform to get a clear cap throw at the dinosaur's cranium.

Ty-foo

These voluminous cloud beings blow forceful gusts that push anything movable out of the way. As enemies, they'll be dangerous for the threat of blowing Mario off the stage. In captured Mario cloud form, Ty-foos can float across huge gaps and blow platforms and enemies away effortlessly.

Tropical Wiggler

These spiky, stretching inchworms aren't hostile, but they still aren't safe for Mario to touch without getting hurt. Captured Wigglers allow unique and fun movement, extending to seek new footholds over gaps and around corners with the front segment of the worm.

Uproot

Uproots are round seed creatures who can sprout straight up at will on rapidly-growing legs. Blocks and seeds above are smashed apart by the Uproot rocketing upward. Releasing the grown legs to drift back down works like a makeshift jump. Shake the controller to sprout higher and quicker than normal.

Anything listed here is purely an adversary to Mario and Cappy, can't be captured, and actively works to harm our heroes. Dodge these creatures or subdue them. Often, a capturable foe nearby is the best means to take out all its uncapturable allies!

Big Poison Piranha Plant

This overgrown specimen spews purple poison like its normal-sized cousins. Throw Cappy over poison purple splotches to mop them up. Clog this big plant's gullet with an object like Cappy or a rock to leave it vulnerable to stomping.

Bitefrost

Found only in frigid environments, these strange creatures exist as shadow faces traveling just under the ice. They pounce on prey above them, rising from the ice as living platforms with snapping maws. Ride rising Bitefrost monsters all the way up, then leap to avoid the snapping jaws. As they rise up to snap at our hero, Bitefrost pillars can become unwitting allies by serving as temporary raised platforms.

Burrbo

Burrbos may seem adorably clueless, but these spiky and colorful critters can still overwhelm Mario in colorful packs. Take them out with Cappy attacks.

Chincho

These gossamer undead apparitions are little more than rags, easily knocked apart with cap tosses or by jumping on them. But where one Chincho rises, there are usually many, and they'll keep coming. Watch out for Chinchos rising from the earth right in front of Mario's running path.

Donkey Kong

The original *Super Mario* franchise antagonist, dating back to 1981's *Donkey Kong*! Donkey Kong long ago made a turn toward good guy status, but for old time's sake his original form shows up to roll barrels at Mario once more.

Fuzzy

These clusters of pests follow preset paths mindlessly. Fuzzies are obstacles to be dodged whether in full 3D or in 8-bit pipes.

Klepto

This thieving tropical bird has a particular affection for unique hats. This may test Mario's dependence on Cappy in a dire situation.

Komboo

These aggressive reeds drift together underwater, waiting for tasty-looking plumbers to swim nearby. They attack in fragile crowds. Knock their plant bodies apart with underwater cap tosses or a captured Cheep Cheep's motion control spin attacks.

Koopa Troopa

The classic turtle foe in 2D glory. Jump on top of it once to make it withdraw into the shell. Then run or jump into the shell to kick it, sending it spinning across the stage.

Magmato

These scalding balls of lava burst if they take a hit, spilling lava into a small pool that becomes off-limits to most creatures, but a kind of improvised platform for a captured Lava Bubble.

Maw-Ray

In the depths of the ocean, creatures can grow to incredible size. These enormous eels surge forward opportunistically to snap at movement in the murk in front of their dens.

Mini Goomba

Mini Goombas are smaller than Goombas, and cannot be captured. They're just as crushable, and since they can't be captured and aren't armored, cap throws will defeat them too.

Moonsnake

These curious, dangerous structures spin around a main segment, like living blades. They might spin in one place, or travel back and forth along a certain route.

Spiny

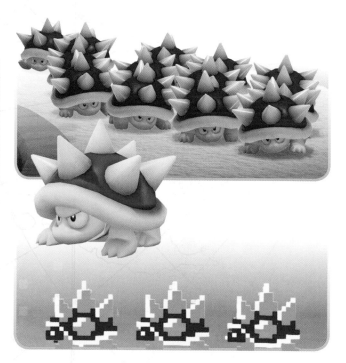

Of the smaller enemies who often swarm Mario, like Goombas and Chinchos, perhaps the most dangerous are Spinies. Their armored spiky shells mean they're guarded from jumps or cap tosses. They must be dodged, or defeated with some other weapon.

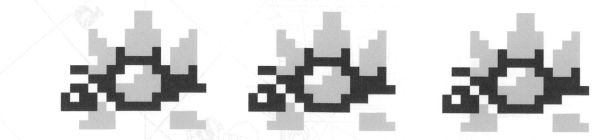

Stairface Ogre

These enormous Thwomp-like creatures carry a stamp-like club. They'll telegraph where they're going to attack, so vacate the space then climb the stamp and ground pound the crown of their noggins on the impact symbol.

Trapeetle

These slow but insistent beetles advance after Mario slowly. Throw Cappy at a Trapeetle, and it'll catch the hat and then hurtle toward Mario rapidly, exploding when the Trapeetle hits anything! Dodge out of the way with a jump, roll, or tackle before Trapeetle detonates on Mario, then think twice about throwing Cappy at more Trapeetles without a plan for where the exploding beetle will go.

Urban Stingby and Larva

Larva thrive in the heat and moisture of the city's garbage-strewn streets. They'll pop from their old skins into buzzing, charging Urban Stingby flies when heroes approach.

Yoofoe

This miniboss is a small flying saucer, flying just out of reach above Mario while dropping Goombas as minions. The Yoofoe saucer is vulnerable to jumping attacks from above, but when you consider its spinning protective blades and high hovering altitude, it's a puzzle to figure out how to get up there.

Bosses

Torkdrift

This strange organism floats about like an otherworldly saucer, coveting the most beautiful flowers the kingdoms offer.

Mechawiggler

Bowser's electrical pet loose in the storming Metro Kingdom is sure to cause problems for the power grid. Hardware like this needs to be confronted with equally powerful hardware.

Knucklotec

An ancient, and surprisingly expressive, evil force that attacks with huge stone fists.

Knucklotec's Fist

Unfortunately for Knocklotec, its fists can be controlled by Cappy!

Brigadier Mollusque-Lanceur III, Dauphin of Bubblaine

The pompous self-proclaimed king of Seaside Kingdom is clogging local access to their prized water sources. The hot-headed octopus can be cooled off with Gushen waterjets.

Cookatiel

This hulking bird flaps lazily above Luncheon Kingdom, staying watchful for the choicest-looking hunks of salted meat.

Ruined Dragon

The fallen lord of lightning rules ruefully over the collapsed and dismal land of Crumbleden.

Madame Broode

This matron to the fiendish Broodals comes armed with her heft and a huge, personalized Chain Chomp.

Astro-Lanceur

A cousin of the Dauphin of Bubblaine, with a little less pretense about it.

Broode's Chain Chomp

Broode's Chain Chomp might be gilded, but it's not more guarded against Cappy than a regular Chain Chomp.

Topper

The classiest Broodal goes into combat with only the tallest of hats.

349

Rango

Rango's southern-inflected style is bolstered by razor blades.

Hariet

Hariet gleefully peppers the battlefield with explosives.

Spewart

The most uncouth of the Broodals doesn't hesitate to barf up poison sludge in self-defense.

RoboBrood

With their strengths combined, the Broodals form RoboBrood! Or they drive it together, at least.

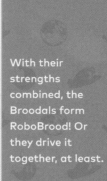

Bowser

The one and only, the Koopa king who's the perennial villain and thorn in the side of Peach, Mario, and the Mushroom Kingdom since back when *every* videogame was inside an 8-bit pipe.

Written by Doug Walsh and Joe Epstein

Maps by Loren Gilliland

DK/Prima Games, a division of Penguin Random House LLC
6081 East 82nd Street, Suite #400
Indianapolis, IN 46250

ISBN: 9780744018875

Printing Code: The rightmost double-digit number is the year of the book's printing; the rightmost single-digit number is the number of the book's printing. For example, 17-1 shows that the first printing of the book occurred in 2017.

20 19 18 17   4 3 2 1

001-310008-October/2017

Printed in the USA.

Credits

Title Manager
Jennifer Sims

Book Designer
Brent Gann

Production Designer
Wil Cruz

Production
Beth Guzman

Prima Games Staff

VP & Publisher
Mike Degler

Editorial Manager
Tim Fitzpatrick

Design and Layout Manager
Tracy Wehmeyer

Licensing
Paul Giacomotto

Marketing
Jeff Barton

Digital Publishing
Julie Asbury
Shaida Boroumand

Operations Manager
Stacey Ginther

Acknowledgments

Prima Games would like to thank Jeremy Krueger-Pack, Melena Jankanish, Emiko Ohmori, Kevin Williams, Corey Beedle, Mairo Small, Eric Spornitz, Samantha Robertson, Gatlin Brown, Melody Marselle, and the rest of the Nintendo team for all their help and support on this project.

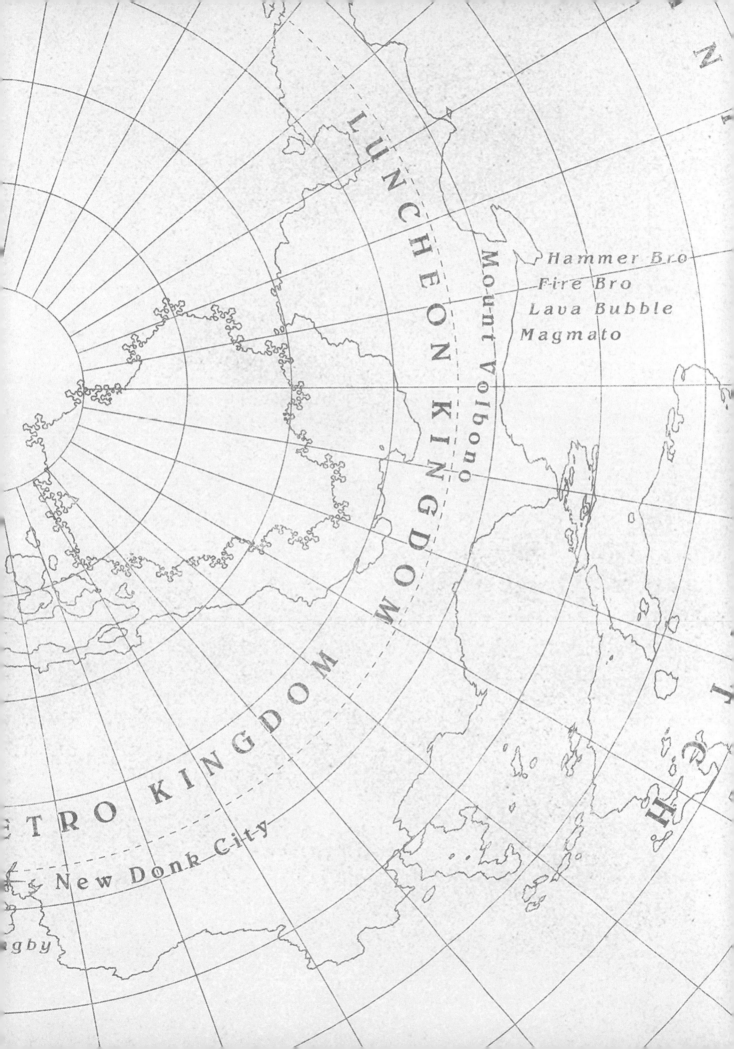

LUNCHEON KINGDOM

Mount Volbono

Hammer Bro
Fire Bro
Lava Bubble
Magmato

ETRO KINGDOM

New Donk City

gby